Church and people in interregnum Britain

Church and people in interregnum Britain

Edited by
Fiona McCall

LONDON
ROYAL HISTORICAL SOCIETY
INSTITUTE OF HISTORICAL RESEARCH
UNIVERSITY OF LONDON PRESS

Published in 2021 by

UNIVERSITY OF LONDON PRESS
SCHOOL OF ADVANCED STUDY
INSTITUTE OF HISTORICAL RESEARCH
Senate House, Malet Street, London WC1E 7HU

Available to download free or to purchase the hard-copy edition at https://www.sas.ac.uk/publications.

ISBNs
978-1-912702-64-0 (hardback edition)
978-1-912702-65-7 (paperback edition)
978-1-912702-66-4 (.pdf edition)
978-1-912702-68-8 (.epub edition)
978-1-912702-67-1 (.mobi edition)

DOI 10.14296/2106.9781912702664

New Historical
PERSPECTIVES

Cover image: Frontispiece to: Sparrow, Anthony, 1843, A rationale upon the Book of common prayer of the Church of England Oxford: John Henry, 1801–1890.

Contents

Contents

List of figures

List of tables

List of contributors

Bernard Capp is emeritus professor at the University of Warwick and a Fellow of the British Academy. He has published extensively on the British Civil Wars and interregnum and on many aspects of seventeenth-century history. His most recent books are *England's Culture Wars: Puritan Reformation and its Enemies in the Interregnum, 1649–1660* (Oxford, 2012) and *The Ties that Bind: Siblings, Family and Society in Early Modern England* (Oxford, 2018).

Alex Craven is an associate fellow of the Institute of Historical Research and currently employed by the Victoria County History of Gloucestershire, having previously worked for VCH Wiltshire. His PhD thesis, 'Coercion and compromise: Lancashire provincial politics and the creation of the English Republic, 1648–53' (University of Manchester, 2005), looked at the relationship between central and local government during the 1640s and 1650s. He has published four articles drawing upon his research into the politics and society of the 1650s, two of which dealt with the reform of the Church.

Trixie Gadd completed her PhD at the Centre for English Local History, University of Leicester in October 2019, with a thesis entitled '"Tis my lot by faith to be sustained": clerical prosperity in seventeenth-century Dorset'. She is an honorary visiting fellow at Leicester, contributing to the AHRC-funded project 'Conflict, welfare and memory during and after the English Civil Wars, 1642–1710' led by Professor Andrew Hopper.

Andrew Foster is an honorary research fellow at the University of Kent, and a visiting researcher with 'Lincoln Unlocked' at Lincoln College, Oxford. Andrew has written chiefly about the early modern Church of England, its bishops and clergy, its cathedrals, parishes and churchwardens. He is currently working on a history of the dioceses of England and Wales between 1540 and 1700, and an edition of the papers of Archbishop Richard Neile for the Church of England Record Society.

Maureen Harris was awarded a PhD in 2015 by the University of Leicester for a thesis on conflict between clergy and laity in Warwickshire, 1660–1720. She contributed to the 'Battle-scarred' exhibition at Newark National Civil War Centre and is leading a National Lottery Heritage Fund volunteer project to explore the human cost of the English Civil Wars through the transcription of all the Warwickshire 'Loss Accounts' of 1646/7, to be published by the Dugdale Society.

Alfred Johnson gained his PhD from the University of Sydney in 2018 with a thesis entitled 'Civility and Godly society: Scotland 1550–1672'.

Rosalind Johnson is a visiting research fellow at the University of Winchester, where she was awarded her PhD in 2013 for her thesis on Protestant dissenters in Hampshire from 1640 to 1740. She has taught at the universities of Winchester and Chichester, and is currently a researcher with the Wiltshire Victoria County History project.

Fiona McCall is an early modern historian, specializing in seventeenth-century religious and social history. She is a senior lecturer in history at the University of Portsmouth, a departmental lecturer in local and social history for the University of Oxford Department of Continuing Education and a fellow of Kellogg College, Oxford. Her first book was *Baal's Priests: the Loyalist Clergy and the English Revolution* (2013). She has since published several articles and chapters and is currently writing her second book, *Unruly People: Ungodly Religion in the English Parish, 1645–1660* for Routledge.

Sarah Ward Clavier is a senior lecturer in early modern history at the University of the West of England. She has a DPhil from the University of Oxford and has published on diverse subjects including seventeenth-century Anglicanism, royalist ballads, Welsh royalism, and seventeenth-century autobiographical and biographical writing. Her monograph *Royalism, Religion and Revolution: North-East Wales, 1640–1715* is forthcoming with Boydell & Brewer.

Rebecca Warren is an honorary research fellow at the University of Kent, specializing in the religious history of the British Civil Wars and the Protectorate of Oliver Cromwell. She is currently writing a monograph on 'The Interregnum Church in England, *c.*1649–1662'. She is an historical consultant to the Cromwell Museum in Huntingdon and has taught a range of early modern undergraduate and adult education courses at the University of Kent.

Helen M. Whittle is a freelance historical researcher and editor of *West Sussex History*, the journal of the West Sussex Archives Society. In 2019 she published *The Clergy of Sussex c.1635–c.1665*, based on her PhD research, and is currently working on a volume of abstracts of clergy wills of the period for Sussex Record Society.

Acknowledgements

This collection arose as a result of a British Academy-sponsored conference, 'The people all changed: religion and society in Britain during the 1650s', held at the University of Portsmouth on 15–16 July 2016. The aim of the conference had been to shine a spotlight on this somewhat understudied period of British history, as well as to broaden the research perspective on the period beyond the political. Many of the contributions here began as papers at this conference. Thanks are due to the British Academy for a research grant facilitating both my own research and the organization of this conference. Thanks are also due to the University of Portsmouth for further funding the costs of the conference, and of my own research over the last few years. I am especially grateful to Professor Bernard Capp, for agreeing to write the introduction to this volume, and for his very hands-on involvement throughout the process of editing the different contributions. I had been told beforehand that Bernard was a 'gent' and so it has proved. His willingness to provide detailed constructive assistance to the many early career researchers in this collection has been very much appreciated. Warm thanks also to Dr Andrew Foster, for editorial assistance throughout the process, and to all the members of his early modern studies group meeting at Chichester, for many opportunities to chew the cud over mid-seventeenth-century religion.

Abbreviations

A&O	*Acts and Ordinances of the Interregnum, 1642–1660*, ed. C. H. Firth and R. S. Rait (London, 1911)
Anglicanism	*The Oxford History of Anglicanism: Reformation and Identity, c.1520–1662*, ed. A. Milton (Oxford, 2017)
BA	Bristol Archives
BL	British Library
BL Add	British Library, Additional Manuscripts
Bod	Bodleian Library
CCED	*Clergy of the Church of England Database*
CR	A. G. Matthews, *Calamy Revised: Being a Revision of Edmund Calamy's Account of the Ministers and Others Ejected and Silenced 1660–2* (Oxford, 1934)
CRO	Cheshire Record Office
CSPD	Calendar of State Papers Domestic
DHC	Devon Heritage Centre
DOHC	Dorset History Centre
DRO	Denbighshire Record Office
Durston and Maltby, *Religion*	*Religion in Revolutionary England*, ed. C. Durston and J. Maltby (Manchester, 2006)
EHR	*English Historical Review*
ERO	Essex Record Office
ESRO	East Sussex Record Office
FSL	Folger Shakespeare Library
GA	Gwynedd Archives
HRO	Hampshire Record Office
LA	Lancashire Record Office
LPL	Lambeth Palace Library
LRRO	Leicestershire and Rutland Record Office
NLW	National Library of Wales
PA	Parliamentary Archives

ODNB	Oxford Dictionary of National Biography
RSLC	Record Society of Lancashire and Cheshire
SAC	*Sussex Archaeological Collections*
SCH	Studies in Church History
SHC	Somerset Heritage Centre
SRO	Staffordshire Record Office
Thurloe	*A Collection of the State Papers of John Thurloe*, ed. T. Birch (7 vols, London, 1742)
Trans. LCAS	*Transactions of the Lancashire and Cheshire Antiquarian Society*
TNA	The National Archives
VCH	Victoria County History
WAAS	Worcestershire Archive and Archaeology Services
Walker, *Attempt*	J. Walker, *An Attempt Towards Recovering an Account of the Numbers and Sufferings of the Clergy of the Church of England* (London, 1714)
WCRO	Warwickshire Record Office
WMS	Bodleian Library, MSS J. Walker
WR	A. G. Matthews, *Walker Revised: Being a Revision of John Walker's Sufferings of the Clergy During the Grand Rebellion 1642–60* (Oxford, 1948)
WSHC	Wiltshire and Swindon History Centre
WSRO	West Sussex Record Office
WYAS	West Yorkshire Archive Service

Introduction
Stability and flux: the Church in the interregnum

Bernard Capp

This book has a simple goal: to shed new light on the still shadowy world of the interregnum Church, primarily the established Church in its 1650s incarnation.[1] It does so through a series of focused studies drawing on the contributors' research that will, we hope, stimulate others to help answer the questions posed in Andrew Foster's chapter. The established Church of the interregnum presents a unique challenge for historians. The abolition of episcopacy in 1646 triggered the collapse of the entire structure of ecclesiastical administration, supervision and discipline, and the records it had generated in earlier periods were no longer created. Parish registers and churchwardens' accounts were still kept, if less systematically, and such accounts provide the basis for Rosalind Johnson's chapter exploring patterns of worship in the south-west. We have the church survey of 1650, the records of the patchy Presbyterian *classes*, and data on the work of Cromwell's Triers. But the absence of nationwide ecclesiastical institutions has made it impossible for historians to gain a clear picture of what was happening in the more than 9,000 parishes of England and Wales. To a remarkable degree, parishes were able to shape their own modus operandi, reflecting the tastes of the minister and leading parishioners. Local conflicts might have come to the attention of the central authorities, but most parishes handled their affairs with little outside scrutiny or interference. What is clear, however, is that the interregnum Church was able to contain former and future bishops and an archbishop, rigid Presbyterians, moderate puritans, strict Independents, and a handful of Baptists and Fifth Monarchists.[2] This was

[1] The best overview remains A. Hughes, '"The public profession of these nations": the national Church in Interregnum England', in *Religion in Revolutionary England*, ed. C. Durston and J. Maltby (Manchester, 2006), pp. 94–114; cf. A. Hughes, 'The Cromwellian Church', in *The Oxford History of Anglicanism: Reformation and Identity*, ed. A. Milton (5 vols, Oxford, 2017), i. 444–56.

[2] For the prelates Ralph Brideoak, George Bull, John Hacket, Robert Skinner, Robert Sanderson, Thomas Lamplugh and Richard Kidder, see *Oxford Dictionary of National Biography*; *WR*; K. Fincham and S. Taylor, 'Episcopalian identity, 1640–1662', in Milton, *Anglicanism*, pp. 457–82.

B. Capp, 'Introduction: stability and flux: the Church in the interregnum', in *Church and people in interregnum Britain*, ed. F. McCall (London, 2021), pp. 1–16. License: CC BY-NC-ND.

a very broad national Church or, more accurately, one that was flexible and localized.

Parliament's attempt to establish a Presbyterian structure had limited success outside London and Lancashire.[3] Even where *classes* were established, they operated on a voluntary basis, without power or much cohesion, and the system was plainly in decline as the 1650s advanced. In a national Church without an ecclesiastical hierarchy, the parish clergy became even more central figures, and they accordingly feature prominently in this collection. Control over appointments had undergone a massive change by the end of the 1640s. The patronage exercised by the crown and bishops was swept away, along with the rights of landowners sequestered as royalist malignants. In each case patronage was now transferred to the state, a theme explored in Rebecca Warren's chapter. It was impossible for the Rump's Council, or Cromwell as Protector, to give close attention to every vacant living. Cromwell played a very active role, but also relied heavily on recommendations by his chaplains and generally accepted suggestions from local petitioners. The ministers he appointed represented a range of religious positions, and only a minority were Independents. This was therefore a national Church that might satisfy the wishes of the parishioners, or at least the local godly, very well. They could hope to secure a minister to their taste, with little outside interference thereafter. In many parishes, this may well have been the case. Most contemporaries found the Cromwellian regime at least tolerable, in both its ecclesiastical and political incarnations. In many other places, however, the picture was less satisfactory or harmonious.

The clergy of the interregnum Church were a very heterogeneous body, as Maureen Harris and Helen Whittle demonstrate in their chapters on Warwickshire and Sussex. The Civil Wars had brought massive disruption. Ian Green has estimated that almost 3,000 ministers were ejected as 'scandalous' or 'malignant', mainly in the late 1640s, representing around twenty-eight per cent of benefices across England. Even that huge figure understates the scale of upheaval.[4] John Walker, the Anglican cleric collecting data half a century later, naturally had no interest in recording puritan ministers ousted by royalist soldiers in the areas under their control, and he overlooked or chose to ignore many of the Presbyterians ejected later. These ministers, having supported parliament during the war, recoiled from the radical shift that followed. The first years of the Commonwealth saw a purge of Presbyterian clergy who had condemned the regicide from

---

[3] Hughes, 'Public profession', pp. 95–6; E. Vernon, 'A ministry of the gospel: the Presbyterians during the English Revolution', in Durston and Maltby, *Religion*, pp. 115–36.

[4] I. Green, 'The persecution of "scandalous" and "malignant" parish clergy during the English Civil War', *English Historical Review*, xciv (1979), 507–31.

the pulpit and refused to take the Engagement, a pledge to live quietly under the new regime. A few dabbled in conspiracy, and one, Christopher Love, was beheaded for treason in 1651.[5] In Wales, the purge of 'malignants' belongs mainly to the years of the Commission for the Propagation of the Gospel in Wales, 1649–53, and historians have confirmed contemporary complaints that it left many parishes bereft. Sarah Ward Clavier's chapter explores their plight, and the anguish of those ejected.

The pattern of ejections in England varied from county to county. In London almost all livings were sequestered, and in several counties the figure exceeded fifty per cent, while in Lincolnshire it was only fifteen per cent. In areas predominantly royalist and anti-puritan, much depended on the presence of a nearby military garrison, while Trixie Gadd suggests in her chapter that factors related to the landscape and its impact on clerical incomes could also play a part.[6] The majority of parish ministers nonetheless survived in post, even if, as Maureen Harris shows, many had to fight off attempts to displace them. Those with puritan sympathies would have welcomed at least some of the changes the wars had brought. Traditionalists, far more numerous, accommodated themselves to the new order out of a sense of pastoral duty or to save their families from financial ruin, or both.[7] As a result, the interregnum Church contained many moderates who would have been at least equally happy to serve within an episcopalian Church, as indeed most were to do after 1660.

One consequence of the large-scale ejections during and after the Civil Wars was to leave many livings vacant, sometimes for many years. A survey of London in 1652 found that forty of the city's parishes had no settled minister at that point. At Cambridge, two years earlier, only three out of fifteen parishes had a settled minister in post. Cobham, briefly the site of the Digger experiment, had no permanent minister for thirteen years. Several Cornish parishes remained vacant for five or ten years, or even longer.[8] Another, and indirect, consequence was a high level of clerical turnover. Why did so many parishes find it hard to recruit ministers, and to hold on to those they did recruit?

Much of the answer clearly lies in the balance between supply and demand in these years. The Church needed to replace the hundreds of ejected ministers in addition to the normal wastage through deaths.

---

[5] B. Capp, *England's Culture Wars* (Oxford, 2016), pp. 40–4.

[6] F. McCall, *Baal's Priests: the Loyalist Clergy and the English Revolution* (Farnham, 2013), pp. 6, 130–1.

[7] Fincham and Taylor, 'Episcopalian identity', *passim*.

[8] Capp, *England's Culture Wars*, pp. 53, 111; M. Coate, *Cornwall in the Great Civil War and Interregnum 1642–1660* (Truro, 1963), pp. 336–7.

Demand thus increased, while supply fell. The flow of new entrants to the profession was affected by the disruption the universities suffered during and after the Civil War, including the large-scale purge of Fellows in the parliamentary visitations. Many young men must have viewed the Church as a very insecure career. For some years there was no clear machinery for the approval and ordination of new ministers. A Cromwellian ordinance of 1654 established a national body, which became known as the Triers, for the approbation of ministers. Its members proved energetic, examining and approving some 3,500 candidates over the next few years. Cromwell was proud of its record.[9] Ordination arrangements were less systematic. Many were carried out by Presbyterian *classes*, but very many new ministers preferred to be ordained clandestinely by one of the former bishops. Robert Skinner, formerly bishop of Oxford, claimed to have ordained between 400 and 500 over this period. Such activities cannot have escaped the government's notice, but it chose to turn a blind eye.[10]

The shortage of parish clergy also helps explain the pattern of rapid turnover. An educated minister, encountering opposition and divisions, might well respond positively to an invitation to move elsewhere. Some men escaped a divided and acrimonious flock by becoming parish lecturers in London, or state-funded public preachers in a former cathedral such as Hereford or Worcester. In such positions they could fulfil their evangelical calling, freed from intractable pastoral dilemmas. Paradoxically, the shortage of ministers also proved a lifeline for many ejected episcopalian and presbyterian clergy. Several hundred subsequently found another parochial living, albeit usually one of lower value. Anthony Tucker, ejected from a Cornish rectory worth £200 a year, was later appointed to another living, worth only £50. Some of the ejected ministers had been pluralists, and contrived to hold on to one of their livings, usually the poorest.[11] Many of the Presbyterian hardliners eventually made their peace with the Protectorate regime, recognizing that Cromwell, for all his crimes, was determined to uphold the national Church and the tithes on which it depended, and shared their commitment to the reformation of manners.

The character of parish life in these years depended, to a large degree, on the relationship between minister and people. An intruded cleric often faced opposition from the ejected minister or his friends, or both. Some

---

[9] Hughes, 'Public profession', pp. 97–9.

[10] K. Fincham and S. Taylor, 'Vital statistics: episcopal ordination and ordinands in England, 1646–60', *English Historical Review*, cxxvi (2011), 319–44; Hughes, 'Public profession', pp. 103, 106–7.

[11] Green, 'Persecution', p. 525; McCall, *Baal's Priests*, pp. 234–5; Coate, *Cornwall*, pp. 332–3, 338.

ejected ministers refused to give way or vacate the parsonage without a fight, and those who remained living close by became focal points for resistance. Many parishes contained inhabitants of strongly opposing views, on both religion and politics, and an intruded minister might find himself facing a sustained campaign to render his position impossible, not least by withholding tithes and fees. In one extreme case, the combative puritan Richard Culmer found himself struggling for years in a bitter war of attrition. At one point, his enemies seized the church key from the sexton, and locked him out. Culmer had to climb in through a broken window.[12] There were several other instances of radical preachers locked out of their own churches by hostile parish officers. With local society often deeply divided, few ministers could expect an easy ride, whatever their own position. Ministers could also come under fire from radical separatists, and lose parishioners to the Baptists, Quakers or other groups.

Another common feature of the interregnum Church was the dismay of idealistic young ministers at the level of ignorance and apathy they encountered in a rural parish. Richard Baxter's correspondence is full of letters from disillusioned younger ministers, inspired by him and eager to follow his pastoral methods, but quickly disheartened. Many complained that their parishioners were ignorant and indifferent, and failed to send their children and servants to catechizing. Isolated and frustrated, they soon became restless.[13] Ralph Josselin, vicar of Earls Colne in Essex, felt a stronger sense of pastoral responsibility towards his flock and remained in his post for over forty years. It is striking, nonetheless, that his diary records the concerns of only a handful of like-minded families in the parish, the rest of the parishioners remaining almost invisible. That reinforces the impression that many puritan ministers gave far more attention to the spiritual needs of the godly few than to those of the majority, a charge that some later admitted.[14] Such an approach risked alienating parishioners, leaving some to drift away or turn to the separatists. Ministers could then find themselves fighting on three fronts simultaneously: against the traditionalists, the worldly and profane, and disruptive radicals, such as Baptists and Quakers. The religious freedom of the 1650s had the effect of creating a fiercely competitive 'religious marketplace'. That led to the staging of several hundred public disputations, large and small, between champions of rival denominations, with such events swallowing up much

[12] McCall, *Baal's Priests*, pp. 202–5, 209–11; Capp, *England's Culture Wars*, pp. 1–3.

[13] *Calendar of the Correspondence of Richard Baxter*, ed. N. H. Keeble and G. F. Nuttall (2 vols, Oxford, 1991), i. 296–7, 326.

[14] *The Diary of Ralph Josselin 1616–1683*, ed. A. Macfarlane (London, 1976); Capp, *England's Culture Wars*, pp. 111–12, 129–30.

of the time and energy of moderate ministers. For some of the auditors, these could be life-changing occasions; for many, they were exciting verbal jousts where they cheered their champions and jeered their adversaries, and for others the effect may have been to leave them confused and perhaps sceptical.[15]

Zealous puritan ministers were partly to blame for the troubles they encountered. Some brought wholly unrealistic expectations, while others showed little interest in reaching out beyond the godly to the less responsive majority. Such attitudes became painfully apparent in disputes over access to the sacraments. The *Directory for Publique Worship* (1645) recommended that communion services should be 'frequent', but left open the timing and arrangements.[16] Abraham Pinchbeck, an Essex minister, decided that not one of his parishioners was worthy of admission to the sacrament. The ministers of Acton, Middlesex, similarly rigorous, decided that only two women in the town were sufficiently qualified – one of whom defected to the Quakers.[17] Such a policy was deeply misguided in a national Church, and inevitably bred resentment. At Durham, Joseph Holdsworth was reported to be 'generally disliked' by the entire parish.[18] Some independent ministers adopted a semi-separatist position, taking charge of a parish but creating a 'gathered church' of true believers within it. Thomas Larkham, who pursued this course at Tavistock, provoked bitter divisions among his congregation.[19] Most parishioners viewed access to communion as a right not a privilege, and resented what they saw as high-handed clericalism. Some responded by withholding tithes or complaining to the authorities, or even brought prosecutions. Few were willing to be examined by their minister on their spiritual fitness and many ministers, perhaps most, excluded only the notoriously reprobate. But the godly might well refuse to communicate alongside those they considered worldly and profane, and a minister who brushed aside their objections would forfeit the trust and support of his natural allies. Ministers thus often found themselves facing fierce criticism whatever position they adopted. Some ducked the issue by,

[15] B. Capp, 'The religious marketplace: public disputations in civil war and interregnum England', *English Historical Review*, cxxix (2013), 47–78; A. Hughes, 'The pulpit guarded: confrontations between orthodox and radicals in revolutionary England', in *John Bunyan and his England 1628–88*, ed. A. Laurence, W. R. Owens and S. Sim (London, 1990), pp. 31–50.

[16] *The Directory for the Publique Worship of God* (London, 1645).

[17] Capp, *England's Culture Wars*, p. 124; *CR*, p. 180.

[18] *CR*, pp. 272, 326.

[19] *The Diary of Thomas Larkham, 1647–1669*, ed. S. Hardman Moore (Woodbridge, 2011), pp. 14–28.

not holding communion services at all, and some parishes went for five or even ten years without one.[20]

Infant baptism proved similarly contentious. The *Directory* advised that baptisms should be public, at the close of Sunday morning service, but many Presbyterians imposed restrictions, insisting on examining parents they considered ignorant or profane, and refusing to baptize illegitimate children. Independents would baptize only the children of the godly, while a few radicals, such as William Dell, abandoned infant baptism altogether.[21] Disgruntled parents sometimes looked for a neighbouring clergyman willing to perform the office.[22] Access to the sacraments, moreover, was far from the only source of local contention. Another was bell-ringing 'for Pleasure or Pastime' on the Sabbath, a custom long opposed by puritans and banned by parliament in 1644. One Dorset minister who tried to suppress the practice received a death threat.[23]

The character of regular Sunday services demands further research. Many parishes had been reluctant and slow to abandon the Book of Common Prayer, but there is little evidence that it was still widely used in public services in the 1650s. Despite isolated pockets of defiance, prayer-book services were now generally clandestine, often held in private houses. Rosalind Johnson notes services held in a disused church in Bristol. In many places, 'prayer-book Protestantism' had become, in effect, a household religion.[24] Many ejected ministers became domestic chaplains to royalist families, and a few followed in the steps of Elizabethan Catholic 'hedge-priests' by operating as itinerants, finding temporary shelter with such families. Lionel Gatford, a former royalist army chaplain, travelled around Norfolk, Kent and Middlesex for several years in the 1650s.[25] Far more common was for traditionalist ministers to smuggle passages from the prayer book into their parish services. Clement Barksdale was complimented on prayers he had taken from that source, which many of his listeners thought he had composed himself. Though others doubtless recognized the words, memories of the old liturgy were fading, and copies of the prayer book itself

---

[20] Capp, *England's Culture Wars*, pp. 123–7; *CR*, pp. 215, 313.

[21] Capp, *England's Culture Wars*, p. 123; *CR*, pp. 161, 313.

[22] *CR*, p. 190.

[23] C. Marsh, *Music and Society in Early Modern England* (Cambridge, 2010), pp. 484–94; *CR*, p. 276.

[24] Capp, *England's Culture Wars*, pp. 119–22. J. Maltby, 'Suffering and surviving: the civil wars, the Commonwealth and the formation of "Anglicanism", 1642–60', in Durston and Maltby, *Religion*, pp. 163–4 and Fincham and Taylor, 'Episcopalian identity', pp. 472–3, suggest more widespread use of the prayer book.

[25] Thurloe, i. 707; *WR*, p. 334.

grew increasingly scarce. John Pelsant had to rely on a small pocket edition, and while Richard Kidder, a future bishop, was happy to see the old Church restored in 1660, it was another two years before he could secure possession of a prayer book.[26]

The success of the *Directory*, intended to replace the prayer book, remains unclear. Only a quarter of parishes appear to have owned a copy, but it went through fifteen editions and most copies may have been bought by the minister rather than the parish. The *Directory* prescribed only the broad outline of services, and did not provide a liturgical text. Services were to consist of extempore prayers by the minister, readings from scripture, a sung psalm and a sermon. Ministers without the skill to extemporize would compose prayers borrowed from the prayer book or another printed source. Psalms proved contentious, for radicals rejected the use of any set text in worship. Some churches were even partitioned, and at Hull, rival congregations worshipped at the same time, one rejecting psalms, the other singing with enthusiasm. The *Directory's* services were heavily clerical, and apart from psalms gave worshippers no scope to participate. Even the Lord's Prayer, if used at all, was to be spoken by the minister alone.[27]

A particularly unpopular change was the disappearance of services for marriage and burial. The *Directory* prohibited any religious ceremony at the burial of the dead, dismissing prayers and rituals as superstitious, and advised that a minister need not even attend. Many families found that deeply unsatisfactory, and some chose to use the forbidden prayer-book ceremony if they could find a minister to conduct it. Marriage underwent still greater transformation, with an act of parliament in 1653 making it now wholly secular. After public notice given by banns or proclamation in the marketplace, the marriage was to be conducted by a justice of the peace, without ceremony. Church marriage became illegal. Many couples doubted the legitimacy of the new procedures, however, and some arranged to be married twice, first by a magistrate to satisfy the law, and then privately by a minister, which alone they viewed as meaningful.[28] Other former ceremonies, such as confirmation and the churching of women after childbirth, vanished or, in the case of churching, survived only in clandestine

---

[26] *WR*, pp. 125, 307; Maltby, 'Suffering', pp. 163–4.

[27] J. Maltby, '"The good old way": prayer book Protestantism in the 1640s and 1650s', in *The Church and the Book*, ed. R. N. Swanson (Woodbridge, 2004), pp. 237–49; J. Maltby, '"Extravagencies and impertinences": set forms, conceived and extempore prayer in revolutionary England', in *Worship and the Parish Church in Early Modern Britain*, ed. N. Mears and A. Ryrie (Farnham, 2013), pp. 221–43, at pp. 221–4; Capp, *England's Culture Wars*, p. 122.

[28] C. Durston, *The Family in the English Revolution* (Oxford, 1989), ch. 4.

form, in private households. The great festivals of Easter and Christmas were now prohibited, and churches remained locked on Christmas Day. Reformers condemned such festivals as relics of paganism and excuses for profane licence. Attempts to make Christmas simply another working day proved futile, however, and the prohibition of services had the paradoxical effect of turning Christmas into a secular holiday.[29]

The interregnum also saw a wide-ranging campaign for moral reformation, addressing long-standing puritan concerns over the Sabbath, swearing, sexual promiscuity and drunkenness. Ministers campaigned on all these issues, but preaching was now almost their only weapon; the church courts had gone, and excommunication had lost its impact. Secular magistrates became responsible for driving forward the programme of moral reformation. The reformers enjoyed greatest success in urban contexts, operating through the borough courts and with individual justices also acting out of session. Cromwell hoped that his Major-Generals, appointed in 1655, would galvanize the work of reformation, and some did indeed share his sense of mission. Others had different priorities, and they all struggled to win the co-operation of suspicious local ministers and magistrates. Each had responsibility for a large area, making the overall impact patchy, and the new machinery survived for only a year and a half.[30] In Scotland, as Alfred Johnson demonstrates in his chapter, the kirk was able to continue disciplining offenders despite the presence of an English army of occupation.

Any assessment of the interregnum Church must also address the issue of church attendance. From 1650 there was no longer a legal requirement to attend the parish church each Sunday. Everyone was still required, in theory, to attend some place of worship, but there was no machinery of enforcement and no penalty for absentees. Some of the godly broke away to join the Congregationalists, Baptists or Quakers, though they may have numbered no more than five per cent of the population. Ministers complained that the worldly and profane simply stayed at home, and that England was sliding towards heathenism. A Newcastle minister complained that half the population spent the Sabbath drinking or idling. Such jeremiads were exaggerated. The Sabbath was more strictly enforced than ever before, limiting the scope for rival activities. Even on the eve of the Restoration, Samuel Pepys was unable to find an alehouse open in London in service-time. Levels of attendance may well have fallen, especially in the larger

[29] Capp, *England's Culture Wars*, pp. 19–24; R. Hutton, *The Rise and Fall of Merry England* (Oxford, 1994), pp. 210–16.

[30] Capp, *England's Culture Wars*, pp. 54–7; C. Durston, *Cromwell's Major-Generals* (Manchester, 2001), ch. 8.

urban centres. But in smaller rural communities, informal pressure and old habit may often have proved effective even without any formal machinery of enforcement. In some Northamptonshire parishes, officers reported that there were no absentees at all. In a few rural parishes, churchwardens still felt able to levy fines for non-attendance, though they no longer had legal authority to do so.[31]

Many church buildings had suffered serious damage during the Civil Wars, and the interregnum Church lacked the financial and administrative resources to undertake significant restoration. In some places, the situation deteriorated further. Petitioners from Wells explained in 1656 that the city's only parish church could not hold the 5,000 inhabitants, and that the cathedral, badly decayed, would soon be unusable. At Stow-on-the-Wold, the church could not be used in wet weather, and services had to be held in the schoolhouse.[32] There was very little new church building. One notable exception was at Plymouth, where a new church begun in 1640 was finally completed in 1658. The project had begun with a petition to the king in 1634, and the new interregnum Church and parish became known paradoxically as the Charles.[33] One novel phenomenon, unthinkable before or after the interregnum, was for some parish churches to be shared by separatist congregations for their own worship. The parish clergy generally resisted such arrangements, which often had to be enforced by orders from central government.[34]

As in all periods, the spiritual lives of ordinary parishioners remain largely hidden from us. The inner lives of the separatists, by contrast, are rather more accessible. Separatists were independent-minded people, almost by definition, and many led spiritually restless lives. The church-book of the Baptist congregation of Fenstanton, Cambridgeshire, offers many instances of members drawn away by Ranters or Quakers, while others questioned every received doctrine. One doubted that the Virgin Mary had ever existed, and rejected the idea that Christ had to die to satisfy God for the sins of mankind. Others defiantly married outside the faith, or drifted back to the parish church. One man asked for permission to attend both parochial and baptist services, striking testimony to the enduring pull of the parish church. John Blowes, a lay preacher, was disciplined in 1658 after missing a day of fasting and prayer to attend a football match, behaviour that was

---

[31] C. Durston, '"Preaching and sitting still on Sundays": the Lord's day during the English revolution', in Durston and Maltby, *Religion,* pp. 205–25; Capp, *England's Culture Wars,* pp. 100–9.

[32] *CSPD,* 1656–7, pp. 23, 278.

[33] R. N. Worth, *Cromwell's Major-Generals* (Plymouth, 1893), pp. 23–4, 62, 206, 253.

[34] *CSPD,* 1654, pp. 3, 32; *CSPD,* 1656–7, pp. 255, 299–300.

condemned as 'foolish and wicked'. Blowes refused to acknowledge that he had done anything wrong.[35] Not all separatists shared the Quakers' rejection of worldly pleasures.

Most of the chapters in this volume focus on rural parishes, so it may be helpful to look briefly here at the interregnum Church in the urban context. Leicester, a middle-sized town, and Norwich, a provincial capital, illustrate many of the challenges that faced urban communities, many with numerous small and poorly funded parishes. Leicester's five parishes had a combined income of only £93 *pa*.[36] The pluralist ministers of St Margaret's and St Mary's had been sequestered, and satisfactory replacements proved difficult to find. The new minister at St Mary's was twice seen drunk in the street in 1649 and a recruit for St Margaret's, sequestered from a Worcestershire living, faced similar allegations.[37] By the early 1650s, all five parishes were vacant, with services provided ad hoc by ministers from the surrounding countryside. The veteran town lecturer, John Angel, who had served for over twenty years, was also forced to step down in 1650 after refusing to take the Engagement.[38] Reformation was unlikely to make progress unless the ministry could be placed on a sounder financial foundation. The corporation made genuine progress, merging the five parishes into four, and seeking augmentations from the government to boost their value. It was awarded an augmentation of £200, to be shared equally between St Margaret's and St Martin's.[39]

Norwich faced a far greater challenge. The city had over thirty parishes, reflecting the economic status and religious practices of its medieval past but poorly suited to its seventeenth-century character. Most had no secure income above £10–£12 a year, and in 1647 over half had no settled minister.[40] Here too the corporation made progress in amalgamating small, poorly funded parishes. It was also energetic in promoting godly reformation, banning Christmas two years before it was abolished by parliament.[41] The

---

[35] *The Records of the Churches of Christ Gathered at Fenstanton, Warboys and Hexham 1644–1720*, ed. E. B. Underhill (London, 1854), pp. 8, 9, 41–4, 75, 173–4, 186–7, 242–5.

[36] LRRO, BR18/26A/144; *Records of the Borough of Leicester, 1603–1688*, ed. H. Stocks (Cambridge, 1923), pp. 339–40.

[37] *WR*, pp. 232, 234, 385; LRRO, BR18/26A/40; BR18/24B/367.

[38] LRRO, BR18/26A/52, 54; Stocks, *Records of the Borough of Leicester*, pp. 405–6.

[39] LRRO, BR18/26A/151, 198; BR18/26A/200, 209–11; BR18/28B/165, 244.

[40] J. Carter, 'The Wheel Turn'd', in J. Carter, *The Nail and the Wheel* (London, 1647), p. 99; J. Collinges, *Provocator Provocatus* (London, 1654), sig. B2v.

[41] J. T. Evans, *Seventeenth-Century Norwich* (Oxford, 1979), p. 165; A. Hopper, 'The Civil War', in *Norwich Since 1550*, ed. C. Rawcliffe and R. Wilson (London, 2004), pp. 89–116, at pp. 107–8; Evans, *Norwich*, p. 131.

city's magistracy included several fiery spirits such as Thomas Toft, who as sheriff had led zealots into the cathedral in 1643 to destroy monuments of superstition, smashing stained-glass windows and demolishing the altar. Toft became an alderman the following year and was chosen mayor in 1654.[42]

In both boroughs, however, puritans were deeply divided. At Leicester, the mayor begged the Council of State to appoint a new lecturer, explaining that the corporation was too divided to agree on any candidate.[43] An invitation to William Barton to serve St Martin's in 1656 also proved contentious. Barton, the author of a new version of the psalms, was described as 'grave and moderate', but quickly proved otherwise. The mayor complained that he had declared for the 'Congregational way', and was planning to bar everyone from the sacrament except those in church-covenant. Thirty-three leading parishioners joined the mayor in pressing for him to leave. They backed down when local MPs rallied to Barton's defence, urging compromise, but resentment lingered.[44]

Radical ideas had created divisions long before Barton arrived. George Fox, the future Quaker, visited the town in 1648 and joined in a rowdy public debate between Presbyterians, Independents, Baptists and 'Common-prayer-men'.[45] The following year, the baptist Samuel Oates was prosecuted under the Blasphemy Ordinance of 1648 for inflammatory preaching. Even more radical ideas gained a foothold. In 1650, a search prompted by government alarm over the Ranter phenomenon turned up scandalous pamphlets by Jacob Bauthumley, a Leicester shoemaker.[46] The radicals' activities inspired widespread fear and anger among the townsfolk. When Dr John Harding was invited to preach at St Martin's in June 1649, there was uproar before he could even begin. Believed mistakenly to be an ignorant tub-preacher, he was dragged from the pulpit by rioters who called for him to be put in the stocks or thrown in the river. The Council of State, appalled, demanded that the offenders be prosecuted at the assizes.[47] By the later 1650s, however, Leicester's magistrates had significantly improved clerical provision, and the radical voices had fallen silent. Young Dixie, a moderate puritan, now served St Margaret's and earned such respect that the corporation tried hard to retain him after the Restoration.[48] The lecturer's place had been filled

[42] Hopper, 'Civil War', pp. 102–4.

[43] LRRO, BR18/26A/149, 151.

[44] LRRO, BR18/28B/251, 290, 316, 323.

[45] *The Journal of George Fox*, ed. J. L. Nickalls (Cambridge, 1952), pp. 24–5.

[46] Stocks, *Leicester*, pp. 385–7.

[47] Stocks, *Leicester*, pp. 384–5; *CSPD*, 1649–50, p. 180. Harding was a DD and former fellow of Magdalen, Oxford: *CR*, p. 247.

[48] *CR*, p. 165; LRRO, BR18/30/21.

very satisfactorily, and William Barton had mellowed so far that he proved willing to conform in 1660.[49]

At Norwich, by contrast, divisions persisted. The reformers initially had grounds for optimism, with a group of very active puritan ministers, especially the veteran John Carter at St Peter Mancroft, and John Collinges, minister of St Saviour's from 1646.[50] On the key issue of Church government, however, the puritans were deeply divided. In June 1646, a group of eight ministers led by Carter urged the corporation to erect a Presbyterian system throughout the city, a plan that was thwarted by an alliance of Independents and anti-puritans. The Presbyterians also felt frustrated at the slow progress of reformation, and in 1647 Carter created uproar by a sermon berating magistrates for their failure to settle religion and curb profanity and vice.[51] Anti-puritan feeling was growing, and helped trigger serious rioting in spring 1648.[52] The Presbyterian clergy did not abandon their dreams, and enjoyed local success by erecting their model of Church government in St Peter Mancroft. Even there, however, they faced strong opposition, and in 1653 Carter's enemies forced him out by withdrawing financial support.[53] The successor they installed was of a very different hue. John Boatman, once a staunch Presbyterian ejected from Hull for refusing the Engagement, was now moving towards an episcopalian and royalist position. Attracting large congregations, he enraged the Presbyterians by celebrating communion on Christmas Day 1653, and inviting sinners to join in receiving the sacrament.[54] By 1655, the city's leading Presbyterian ministers were either dead or marginalized, and the puritan voice was muted. John Collinges, forced out of St Saviour's, lamented that most of the smaller parishes remained vacant, or were served by clergy hostile or indifferent to reformation, and with inhabitants still 'seasoned with the old leaven of ignorance and superstition'.[55] It was Boatman and open 'malignants' who now dominated the city's religious life.[56]

Despite efforts to place the urban ministry on a sounder financial footing, religious divisions proved major obstacles to godly reformation in both

---

[49] *CR*, p. 442; LRRO, BR18/26A/226–8; 26B/245–6, 252.

[50] Evans, *Norwich*, ch. 5; *CR*, p. 128.

[51] Carter, Wheel Turn'd, *passim*; Evans, *Norwich*, pp. 157–9, 167–70.

[52] Evans, *Norwich*, pp. 172–81.

[53] Collinges. *Provocator Provocatus*, sig. b3.

[54] Collinges, *Provocator Provocatus*, sig. c–d4v; Capp, *England's Culture Wars*, p. 38.

[55] Collinges, *Provocator Provocatus*, sig. b3.

[56] Thurloe, iv. 216–17, 257; v. 289.

Leicester and Norwich. While Leicester seems to have been moving towards accommodation, Norwich experienced continuing divisions and friction.

No simple model of the interregnum Church fits the entire country. The short-lived political regimes of the period all had a provisional flavour, and in the localities each had to work with whoever was willing to serve. Much the same was true of the interregnum Church. There was only a limited pool of committed puritan ministers, many of whom felt little affection for any of the interregnum regimes. While bishops and church courts had been swept away, the interregnum Church still needed the thousands of parish ministers who had remained in post and conformed, to varying degrees, and also had to draw on the services of many who had previously been ejected as scandalous or malignant. The result was a bewildering patchwork of parish and urban communities. In some towns and parishes reformation made significant advances. Puritans pointed proudly to the achievements of Richard Baxter in Kidderminster, Thomas Wilson in Maidstone, and to Rye, Exeter and Coventry. At Sedgehill, Staffordshire, Joseph Eccleshall was able to transform a community of coal- and lead-miners, and a new gallery had to be constructed to cope with the numbers.[57] In many other places, puritan reformation made little if any progress. Such contrasting outcomes reflected the interplay of several key variables: a community's experience during the wars, a local tradition of puritan influence, and the presence of a capable puritan minister and/or magistrate, along with a core of influential parishioners to provide support. Puritan reformers made little headway wherever an intruded minister faced determined opposition from supporters of a sequestered predecessor. In parishes with no settled minister, godly reformation was plainly impossible.

In assessing the interregnum, we should also note the things that did *not* occur. English Catholics must have feared that the puritan triumph would usher in a wave of ferocious persecution. In the event, Catholics fared far better than they could have anticipated. Anti-Catholic paranoia had faded, with no longer any suspicion of popish influence in Whitehall, while fears of a secret army of popish plotters had evaporated in the Civil War. When Thomas Edwards warned in *Gangraena* (1646) of a rotting disease that threatened to destroy all religion in England, he was referring to sectarianism, not popery. Cromwell respected the rights of the individual conscience, and had no wish to persecute English Catholics living peaceably. In the aftermath of the royalist risings in 1655, Catholics became liable to heavy fines if they refused a new oath of abjuration, but enforcement appears to have been patchy. Within the Catholic community, the Blackloist group

---

[57] Capp, *England's Culture Wars*, pp. 221–3, 232–56; *CR*, p. 179.

explored the possibility of reaching an accommodation with the regime, and the idea of toleration was growing within the regime itself.[58] Another striking non-event during the 1650s was the absence of any mass defection from the national Church. Levels of attendance may well have fallen, but most people continued to see the parish church as their religious home. Separatism appealed only to a relatively small minority, and old habits were reinforced by the elements of continuity within the interregnum Church.

We can only speculate how the Church might have evolved had the Cromwellian regime survived longer. The triumph of the post-Restoration Anglican model was by no means inevitable. It represented, as Judith Maltby has argued, only one strand within episcopalian thought in the 1650s.[59] The interregnum Church, for all its numerous shortcomings, was remarkably accommodating in both doctrine and practice, and would probably have evolved further towards a new Protestant *via media*. It could find room for Arminians like Richard Baxter and John Goodwin, and for anti-paedobaptists like John Tombes and William Dell. It also witnessed significant structural reform through the amalgamation of small urban parishes, the division of huge upland parishes in the north-west, and the augmentations awarded to poorly funded parishes to help attract and retain good ministers. Though it had no structures above the parochial level, except the Triers and Ejectors, the later 1650s saw the rise of voluntary bodies such as Baxter's Worcestershire Association, where moderates met to discuss issues, and examine and ordain new ministers. Over time, such bodies might have evolved to provide an acceptable ecclesiastical structure serving many of the functions of the old episcopalian hierarchy. The associations also reflected a wider recognition among puritan ministers that they had devoted too much energy to polemics, and not enough to the needs of ordinary parishioners. One prominent puritan minister wondered if it might even be advisable to devise set forms of prayer for parish worship.[60] The personal journeys of men like Barton at Leicester and Boatman at Norwich are at least suggestive. Had Cromwell accepted the offer of a crown, there might have been a further shift back towards traditional forms. There was obviously no substance to the rumours that Philip Nye and John Owen, two of his favourites, were to become archbishops of Canterbury and York, but they suggest contemporaries' sense of the direction of travel.[61]

---

[58] W. Sheils, 'English Catholics at war and peace', in Durston and Maltby, *Religion*, pp. 137–57, at pp. 147–50.

[59] Maltby, 'Good old way', pp. 246–7, 255–6.

[60] A. Milton, 'Unsettled reformations, 1603–1662', in Milton, *Anglicanism*, i. 63–83 at p. 78.

[61] *CSPD*, 1656–7, p. 318.

The established Church of the interregnum was an odd institution. A paucity of committed puritan ministers, the absence of hierarchical institutions, and Cromwell's tolerance in the operation of patronage resulted in what has been labelled 'religious localism', a situation partly accidental, partly deliberate.[62] Presbyterians and many episcopalians were willing to serve in it, as we have seen, and recent research has shown that many moderate Congregationalists were also willing to accept state funding, either as lecturers or in parish livings.[63] This was not a Church to inspire enthusiasm, but it was one that made accommodation remarkably easy.

[62] Maltby, 'Good old way', p. 255.

[63] Hughes, 'Cromwellian Church', p. 446, citing the research of Joel Halcomb.

The administration of the
interregnum Church

1. What happened in English and Welsh parishes c.1642–62?: a research agenda

Andrew Foster

Excellent work has been produced on this topic, yet there are still many assumptions to be tested, hypotheses to be explored and sources to be located, before we may gain a satisfactory answer to the big question of what actually happened in parishes across England and Wales during this turbulent period.[1] Parish life was disrupted – for many quite literally – during the course of the Civil Wars, but the whole 'parochial system' came under stress when between 1646 and 1660 the Church of England was technically dismantled. Bishops, archdeacons, cathedral deans and canons were abolished, and thus no longer involved in the oversight of the parochial duties of ministers, churchwardens and their associates.[2] Although this represented considerable change, it has been largely assumed that parish life continued much as before, and indeed, ministers and churchwardens continued to be appointed and to carry out customary duties, creating records in the process. This has been justly hailed as a sign of the strength of the parochial system.[3] Yet the contents of the parish chest were diminished: there was no longer any obligation to produce glebe terriers, registers of visiting preachers or inventories of church goods, or to copy out bishops' transcripts of the registers.[4] Ministers and churchwardens

---

[1] This chapter originated as an appeal for help made at a Network for Parish Research symposium held at Warwick in 2016 and repeated later that year at a conference held in Portsmouth. I am grateful to all present for constructive advice, and to Caroline Adams, Fiona McCall, John Hawkins, Helen Whittle and Kenneth Fincham, who have assisted me as I have since broadened the scope of what remains a call for help. Bernard Capp and Beat Kümin have been inspirations in this quest, as have Valerie Hitchman, Rebecca Warren, Joel Halcomb and Tim Wales.

[2] Bishops and archdeacons went first under an ordinance of 1646, while deans and chapters, along with their property, went in 1649.

[3] J. Merritt, 'Religion and the English parish', in *The Oxford History of Anglicanism, Reformation and Identity*, ed. A. Milton (5 vols, Oxford, 2017), i. 122–47 provides invaluable context to the discussion that follows.

[4] The obligations were removed, but many parishes continued to furnish some of these items, such as inventories of church goods.

were no longer subject to regular visitations by archdeacons and bishops, nor were they required to present cases to church courts. While the loss of authority and inspection routines may have brought comfort to some, there must surely have been some confusion and uncertainty at the local level. Much remains to be explored as to what was really entailed for local congregations during these critical years, and how they viewed what was happening.

This chapter focuses on the practicalities of religious life in parishes to raise questions about how ordinary people were affected during this turbulent period. While good work has been carried out on the 1640s and 1650s, attention has largely been focused on theological divisions, high politics, arguments between Independents, Presbyterians, Congregationalists and Quakers, and the explosion of uncensored religious literature produced in this 'world turned upside down'.[5] Latterly, attention has been drawn to the staying power of episcopalians and their continued influence on what may have happened across many parishes.[6] An excellent collection of essays edited by the late Christopher Durston and Judith Maltby set numerous hares running on subjects like preaching, Sunday observance, Catholics in the community, and the use of the prayer book.[7] This chapter is written quite frankly as an agenda for local historians, a call to arms – a confession of ignorance indeed – for we need more research at parish level to answer fairly basic questions about what happened during this period. What follows is essentially a range of those questions with some tentative responses aimed at drawing attention to where further research is needed, and where local historians in particular may be of assistance.

Many traditional parish records were lost, but were there any gains?

A running theme throughout this chapter will be noting how we are affected by loss of records, but also observing where some gains have been made. As noted above, there were some considerable losses that

---

[5] C. Cross, 'The Church in England 1646–1660', in *The Interregnum: the Quest for Settlement 1646–1660*, ed. G. Aylmer (London, 1972), pp. 99–120; J. Morrill, 'The Church in England, 1642–9', in *Reactions to the English Civil War 1642–1649*, ed. J. Morrill (London, 1982), pp. 89–114; C. Hill, *The World Turned Upside Down* (London, 1972); B. Capp, *England's Culture Wars* (Oxford, 2012); C. Durston and J. Maltby, *Religion in Revolutionary England* (Manchester, 2006); A. Hughes, 'The Cromwellian Church', in Milton, *Anglicanism*, i. 444–56.

[6] K. Fincham and S. Taylor, 'Episcopalian identity, 1640–1662', in Milton, *Anglicanism*, i. 457–82; C. Haigh, 'Where was the Church of England, 1646–1660?', *The Historical Journal*, lxii (2019), 127–47.

[7] Durston and Maltby, *Religion*, 2006.

historians will detect among traditional parish collections to be found in their local county record offices. Diocesan collections dried up quite rapidly after 1642 and even took some time to come back into existence after the Restoration in 1660.[8] Parish registers continued, but with what contents and scope will be discussed shortly. But all is not gloom and doom. Certain major caches of evidence appear in this period, which, because they are often found in central rather than provincial record offices, are worthy of brief comment here. Parliamentary surveys were conducted of the land held by bishops and cathedral chapters, and some of these are now finding their way into publication.[9] Declining interest in economic and social history has marginalized such material, yet there is no doubt that it provides rich pickings for those prepared to wade through the detail. Surveys of churches were conducted after 1650, the results of which have ended up in the archives of Lambeth Palace Library; they do not cover the entire country, but a fair proportion, and they too have been largely ignored owing to difficulty in use.[10] Only comparatively recently have the records of the Cromwellian Church come under close scrutiny in the work of Rebecca Warren.[11] These sources help to provide important information on the clergy appointed under Cromwell in the 1650s. Recent publications have given us more on the earlier phase of the ejection of scandalous ministers, following the pioneering work of Clive Holmes, while the editor of this collection is famed for her study of John Walker, on whose work all accounts of the clergy of this period lean so heavily.[12] In keeping with how that work was constructed, we are coming

[8] Fincham and Taylor, 'Episcopalian identity', in Milton, *Anglicanism*, i. 461–2 catalogued the varied chronology of loss of records.

[9] An early classic is *The Parliamentary Survey of Lands and Possessions of the Dean and Chapter of Worcester … 1649*, ed. T. Cave and R. Wilson (London, 1924); *The Parliamentary Surveys of the Cambridgeshire Properties of the Dean and Chapter of Ely 1649–1652*, ed. W. Franklin (Cambridge, 2018). These can offer useful details of properties to be found in the small parishes of early modern cathedral cities.

[10] *Catalogue of the Ecclesiastical Records of the Commonwealth 1643–1660*, ed. J. Houston (Farnborough, 1968); see Alex Craven's chapter in this collection.

[11] R. Warren, ' "A knowing ministry": the reform of the Church of England under Oliver Cromwell, c.1653–1660', (unpublished University of Kent PhD thesis, 2017); see Rebecca Warren's chapter in this collection and we look forward to her projected book, *The Interregnum Church of England and Wales, c.1649–1662*.

[12] *The Cambridgeshire Committee for Scandalous Ministers 1644–45*, ed. G. Hart (Cambridge, 2017); *The Suffolk Committees for Scandalous Ministers 1644–1646* (Suffolk Record Soc., 13, Ipswich, 1970), xiii; F. McCall, *Baal's Priests: the Loyalist Clergy and the English Revolution* (Farnham, 2013).

to learn more about the interregnum by looking back from the situation of the latter half of the seventeenth century.[13]

What happened to parish registers?

This was the starting point of my original appeal for help at the Warwick symposium, for although parish registers were maintained during this period, it is not clear how fully, or how widely across the country, and to what extent their keeping was disrupted.[14] A case study based on 154 parishes in West Sussex, basically the Archdeaconry of Chichester, suggests some degree of disruption to record-keeping in both the 1640s and the 1650s.[15] Some of the former may be put down to areas affected by warfare and turnover of incumbents, and these occur largely in more muddled entries often commented upon by later writers. Apologies were sometimes entered, as at New Shoreham, where in writing of 1646 it was recorded that 'this year was a total neglect of registering in this parish'.[16] And such apologies might remain in the memory much longer, for the new rector of Slinfold recorded on his appointment in 1683 that he would 'endeavour to keep the register in good order, it having been badly kept up to that date'.[17] Some of this was possibly a traditional problem with all registers, particularly in rural parishes – that of retaining scraps of paper for copying up later into the register. Occasionally, the problem can be traced to very physical disasters, as with the churches of St Bartholomew and St Pancras in Chichester that were both destroyed during the siege by Waller's parliamentarian troops in 1642.[18] Certainly, the most badly disrupted registers relate to the war years of the 1640s.

Legislation in 1653 brought changes that affected record-keeping greatly. Registrars, confusingly called 'registers', were appointed for each parish and

---

[13] 'Settling the Peace of the Church': 1662 Revisited, ed. N. Keeble (Oxford, 2014); K. Fincham, 'Material evidence: the religious legacy of the Interregnum at St George Tombland, Norwich', in Religious Politics in Post-Reformation England, ed. K. Fincham and P. Lake (Cambridge, 2006), pp. 224–40.

[14] I am grateful to those who responded to my appeals posted on the Parish Network, notably Marion Hardy for evidence of disruption to parish registers in Devon, while Patricia Cox alerted me to online databases for the Lancashire and Cheshire registers.

[15] This case study owes much to Caroline Adams, who helped me start investigating our hypotheses as we sought to assist Helen Whittle, whose research is captured in this volume.

[16] WSRO, Par 170/1/1/1, 39.

[17] WSRO, Par 176/1/1/1, fo. 46v.

[18] A. Fletcher, A County Community in Peace and War: Sussex 1600–1660 (London, 1975), pp. 255–89; R. Morgan, Chichester: a Documentary History (Chichester, 1992), pp. 8, 165–6, 184.

new registers were purchased in many cases; the appointments were to be signed off by local justices of the peace.[19] Given the complexity of religious views at the time, details of 'births' were now requested as opposed to 'baptisms', and to the delight of modern genealogists more detail was often given on parents. The Marriage Act of 1653 further complicated matters, for while banns were introduced formally, and now often recorded, justices of the peace conducted the marriages, at least until 1657 when the 'system' began to break down.[20] They were even provided with their own order of service.[21] These changes affected record-keeping in many places as hard-pressed ministers and 'registers' had to decide on what to record, in what books, and many marriages might have gone either unrecorded or appear in registers of key towns where justices of the peace (JPs) resided.[22] The appointment of new registrars is noted in a fair number of registers (as noted in the catalogues), some thirty-nine or around twenty-five per cent of the West Sussex sample. Many of the problems relate to confusion over marriages with banns being noted in registers, but no longer the marriages themselves.[23]

What this amounts to is that differing degrees of disorder may be detected in around ninety-six (sixty-two per cent) of West Sussex parishes; and this figure is broadly similar for both decades. The survey is based only on analysis of parish catalogues, and so findings are provisional, but it suggests that more might be done with these basic registers.[24] It is tantalizing to note that a small number of surviving parish registers are actually deemed to commence in and around 1654, suggesting that old registers were abandoned, or changed hands and were lost.[25] A similar spike in numbers for the commencement of the survival of registers appears for the early

[19] C. Chapman, *Marriage Laws, Rites, Records and Customs* (Dursley, 2008), p. 12.

[20] Chapman, *Marriage Laws*; D. Cressy, *Birth, Marriage and Death: Ritual, Religion, and the Life-Cycle in Tudor and Stuart England* (Oxford, 1997), p. 180; Rebecca Warren has reminded me that the original act was modified in 1657 before it was completely abandoned.

[21] Chapman, *Marriage Laws*, pp. 54–5.

[22] WSRO, Par 8/1/1/1 Arundel: the catalogue notes a tenfold increase in the recording of marriages in the 1650s; see later discussion of rites of passage.

[23] For more on marriages and the unpopularity of the new civil services (and hence doubts about registration) see C. Durston, *The Family in the English Revolution* (Oxford, 1989), pp. 57–86.

[24] This survey entailed wading through 14 thick A4 folders of the typescript catalogue of parish records held at WSRO; see also *Who are You? Family History Resources in West Sussex Record Office*, ed. C. Adams et al. (Chichester, 2007).

[25] A problem noted in a classic work that illustrates the value of local studies: H. Smith, *The Ecclesiastical History of Essex* (Colchester, 1933), p. 339; with thanks to Rebecca Warren.

1660s, suggesting that the Restoration marked a clearing of the books for some parishes. Whereas around sixty-five per cent of all parish registers in Sussex commence in the sixteenth century, forty-three or twenty-seven per cent date from later than 1640, and of those surviving from the 1640s, 1650s and 1660s (seventeen), for all bar two, we have surviving bishops' transcripts dating to earlier periods, confirming that registers had existed.[26]

It is possible to extend this kind of enquiry by analysing data drawn from the classic *Phillimore Atlas and Index of Parish Registers*.[27] Using county numbers of parishes based on contemporary estimates, the variation of parish register survival between counties is enormous and cries out for investigation to establish credibility and possible significance.[28] For counties mainly in the north, as many as half the parishes have registers that only survive from the 1640s and 1650s onwards, which may be a comment on later formation of parishes out of chapelries and weaker record-keeping. For southern counties like Sussex the figure is around eleven per cent.[29] It would be interesting to see how survival correlates with areas that saw fighting in the Civil Wars, and also with the work of different officials, including the Major-Generals, under the Cromwellian Protectorate. And of course, we would need to place this matter of the best keeping of registers into a much longer time-scale to check how unusual was the degree of disruption in the 1640s and 1650s.[30] This analysis of the survival of parish registers based on *The Phillimore Atlas* throws up a confusing picture. Checking just for those registers noted as commencing in the 1640s, 1650s and 1660s, it suggests an average across all counties of England and Wales of around 14.5 per cent. This is very crude for it is based on contemporary estimates of the number of parishes across the country. This mad, brain-numbing number crunching does however suggest there might be more in this for local historians to deduce in the regions.

---

[26] I wonder what might be gleaned from the variations in balance of surviving registers in different regions? Fiona McCall has also speculated if there might be a correlation here with livings where ministers were sequestered.

[27] *The Phillimore Atlas and Index of Parish Registers*, ed. C. Humphery-Smith (Chichester, 1995).

[28] Norfolk Record Office, ANW/21/8, fo. 322 contains a 17th-century formulary of parishes by county that suggests 9,317 for England and Wales.

[29] These figures are crude and need testing: Yorkshire (18%), Northumberland (51%), Lancashire (47%); the largest percentages for the midlands/south are Derbyshire (26%), Wiltshire (27%) and Cornwall (23%); the lowest is 5% for Kent.

[30] Kenneth Fincham and Bernard Capp emphasize the importance of this caveat.

What happened to parish records in general?

While parish registers survived in relatively good order for the majority of parishes in England – with the caveats noted – historians are faced with considerable losses in records for this period, hence some of our problems. Churchwardens continued to maintain their annual accounts, no doubt under pressure from their congregations, even if no longer scrutinized by archdeacons, diocesan chancellors and their officials. Yet the national database produced by Dr Valerie Hitchman on survival of churchwardens' accounts does reveal a slight blip in the numbers surviving for these two decades.[31] With a survival rate for early modern churchwardens' accounts of only around ten per cent for the whole country, and marked regional variations, this renders some of the past discussions of communion taking and survival of service practices and feasts, based largely on analysis of these records, rather tricky.[32] Yet churchwardens' accounts, where they can be found, obviously remain an invaluable source for local historians.

This period provokes fresh questions about the survival of churchwardens' accounts and their contents, over and above queries already raised about their use.[33] Local historians might usefully enquire as to how far the sets of accounts that survive for the interregnum represent a further skewed distribution to urban and wealthier livings. Such places as Devizes, for which we have a recent publication, had several reasons for keeping good records given the intertwinement of town and parish landholding; unsurprisingly perhaps, their records also maintained inventories of church goods.[34] Where

---

[31] See database compiled by Dr Hitchman on the website of the Network for Parish Research based at the University of Warwick under the direction of Professor Beat Kümin; on figures produced so far based on around 6,000 parishes covered, the survival of churchwardens' accounts suggests: 212 in 1640, 187 in 1645, 181 in 1650, 207 in 1655 and 218 in 1660; three years later it had gone up to 250. I am grateful to Dr Hitchman for discussion of these points and her words of caution about all of these figures.

[32] Morrill, 'The Church in England', pp. 89–114; J. Maltby, '"Extravagencies and impertinences": set forms, conceived and extempore prayer in revolutionary England', in *Worship and the Parish Church in Early Modern Britain*, ed. N. Mears and A. Ryrie (Farnham, 2013), pp. 221–43. A problem with these debates about communion lies with the relatively small sample numbers of churchwardens' accounts viewed.

[33] A. Foster, 'Churchwardens' accounts of early modern England and Wales: some problems to note but much to be gained', in *The Parish in English Life 1400–1600*, ed. K. French, G. Gibbs and B. Kümin (Manchester, 1997), pp. 74–93; *Views from the Parish: Churchwardens's Accounts c.1500–c.1800*, ed. V. Hitchman and A. Foster (Newcastle upon Tyne, 2015). In the light of Valerie Hitchman's sterling efforts to create a database, I have raised my estimate for surviving sets of accounts from 8 to 10% for the period 1559–1660.

[34] *The Churchwardens' Accounts of St Mary's Devizes 1633–1689*, ed. A. Craven (Wiltshire Record Soc., 69, Chippenham, 2016).

runs of accounts get broken at this date, it would be interesting to see if patterns emerge concerning types of communities or regions.

A big loss, however, is the church court material that would have been associated with the diocesan and archdeaconry courts. Here the assumption has been that much of that work would have transferred to quarter sessions, and indeed we pick up cases dealing with Catholic recusants, morals and disorderly behaviour – associated with campaigns for better godly behaviour conducted under the Protectorate and the work of the Major-Generals in particular.[35] Yet the increase in work for the justices of the peace cannot match the church courts in their heyday in the 1630s.[36] More research is needed on precisely how – and where – churchwardens worked with JPs between 1646 and 1660, and the nature of cases commonly presented.[37]

Other losses of records are also significant to different groups of historians; hence genealogists bewail the lack of bishops' transcripts, always valuable when crosschecking entries in parish registers.[38] Glebe terriers were no longer required, but major changes to Church property at this level were not common (although such documents would have been vital in determining parish amalgamations and augmentations), and material produced after 1660 restores our picture of Church landholding.[39] 'Registers of Strange Preachers' were perhaps a thing of the past, when authorities sought to control unlicensed preaching in the 1630s, and we rarely have much evidence on this score apart from presentments in visitations noting the neglect of keeping such registers.[40] It would be wonderful if we could

[35] See Fiona McCall in this collection; C. Durston, *Cromwell's Major-Generals: Godly Government during the English Revolution* (Manchester, 2001).

[36] M. Ingram, *Church Courts, Sex and Marriage in England, 1570–1640* (Cambridge, 1987); R. B. Outhwaite, *The Rise and Fall of the English Ecclesiastical Courts, 1500–1860* (Cambridge, 2006).

[37] My thanks to Caroline Adams for a wonderful example from Sussex records in which a minister, John Sefton, was cited in quarter sessions for not using the *Directory for Publique Worship*: WSRO, QR/W78, fo. 2.; Ken Fincham notes the need to distinguish between 'office' and 'instance' business, adding that tithe cases went to the Exchequer, while probate business was also separated out. Bernard Capp also notes how individual JPs acting out of session handled morality cases. There is clearly a need for more local research here.

[38] Our Sussex case study confirms the complete disappearance of bishops' transcripts for the parishes between 1640–1 and 1662.

[39] Glebe terriers survive most comprehensively in relation to metropolitical and primary Visitations, hence we possess a good number for Sussex in 1615 and 1636; survival is then patchy after 1660, with East Sussex doing better than West: *Diocese of Chichester: a Catalogue of the Records of the Bishop, Archdeacons and Former Exempt Jurisdictions*, comp. F. Steer and I. Kirby (Chichester, 1966), pp. 46, 115.

[40] Fiona McCall reminds me that we continue to see payments for visiting preachers in churchwardens' accounts for the 1640s and 1650s.

map the survival of records for this unique period, in order to provide context and provoke more ideas about regional differences and enforcement of official initiatives, by whom, when and why.

What happened to parish clergy?

Our knowledge of clergy active in this period is patchy, owing to the loss of particular sets of records at diocesan level. The now famous *Clergy of the Church of England Database* is based largely on evidence gleaned from institution act books, episcopal registers, *libri cleri* or call books, subscription books, exhibit books and licences to preach – all associated with records generated by episcopal and archidiaconal jurisdictions.[41] The loss of this type of record-keeping explains gaps in the database that can only be filled by painstaking work by hundreds of local historians.[42] The story is complicated by the work of various groups in the 1640s rooting out 'scandalous ministers' and later 'ejections' of clergy who did not meet the standards required by the Cromwellian ejectors.[43] The picture for clergy during this period is further confused now that evidence is coming to the fore of the work of several bishops carrying out clandestine 'ordinations' throughout the period, so enhancing the claims of earlier historians that as many as two-thirds of all clergy at this time were episcopally ordained.[44] Here is another topic on which local historians might be able to clarify the best dating of such remarks, for are we talking about the 1640s more than the 1650s?

Just to make matters even more complex, however, we are not sure exactly how many clergy were operating during this period. We know these were turbulent times with higher than usual turnover of ministers owing to expulsions and resignations. Between 2,500 and 3,000 ministers were apparently ejected from their livings during this period, although many

[41] *CCED.*

[42] See the chapter by Helen Whittle in this collection.

[43] See works edited by Clive Holmes and Graham Hart already cited, together with works by Ann Hughes and Fiona McCall; it is important to remember that expulsions from livings were going on throughout the 1650s, as well as the more commonly known 1640s (C. Durston, 'Policing the Cromwellian Church: the activities of the county ejection committees, 1654–1659', in *The Cromwellian Protectorate*, ed. P. Little (Woodbridge, 2007), pp. 188–205; I. Green, 'The persecution of "scandalous" and "malignant" parish clergy during the Civil War', *English Historical Review*, xciv (1979), 507–31).

[44] C. Cross, 'The Church in England', pp. 99–120, 224–5 and used by most later writers such as Ann Hughes, even though in her footnote for this figure Claire Cross herself raised doubts about the methodology through which it had been derived (225, fn. 16); K. Fincham and S. Taylor, 'Vital statistics: episcopal ordination and ordinands in England, 1646–60', *English Historical Review*, cxxvi (2011), 319–44.

found a way of moving elsewhere or getting back into livings later.[45] The Westminster Assembly may have interviewed as many as 5,000 ministers in the late 1640s, and a further 3,500 ministers were considered by the Triers in the 1650s.[46] These are much higher figures than usually proposed, and local knowledge is needed to clarify just how many clergy and parishes were affected, when one takes into account pluralism and non-residence, reasons given for many ejections in the 1640s.[47] It is little wonder that Joel Halcomb ended his appendix on the Westminster Assembly figures feeling that: 'The scale of our results points towards the need to conduct a fresh study of clerical appointments during the Civil Wars and interregnum, one that considers the individual experiences and reactions to parliament's reforms within a national and local context.'[48]

The rescinding of the requirement to attend parish church regularly on pain of fines in 1650 must have affected clerical/lay relations.[49] Tensions arose over matters like the taking of communion, 'baptisms', marriages and burials – when traditionalists might take issue with a new minister not using the form of words they wanted to hear.[50] Such tensions might lead to separation of parts of the congregation to join the newly emerging dissenting communities. In Lancashire and Essex, strong Presbyterian associations formed, examples of what had been hoped for briefly in the mid 1640s.[51] Some have claimed that godly clergymen of this period perhaps over-stressed the importance of preaching over other activities, notably their pastoral roles of hospitality, visiting the sick, leading catechism classes

---

[45] J. Maltby, 'Suffering and surviving: the civil wars, the Commonwealth and the formation of "Anglicanism", 1642–60', in Durston and Maltby, *Religion*, p. 167.

[46] I am grateful to Rebecca Warren and Joel Halcomb for advice on these figures; *The Minutes and Papers of the Westminster Assembly 1642–1652*, ed. C. Van Dixhoorn et al. (5 vols, Oxford, 2012), i. 217–26; see the chapters by Rebecca Warren and Helen Whittle in this collection.

[47] See Fiona McCall, Helen Whittle and Maureen Harris in this collection for discussion of complexities behind ejections.

[48] *Minutes and Papers of the Westminster Assembly*, p. 226.

[49] Act for the repeal of several clauses in statutes imposing penalties for not coming to Church (*A&O*, ii. 423–5).

[50] Examples of these tensions abound in the writings of Ann Hughes, Bernard Capp and Judith Maltby already cited.

[51] E. Vernon, 'A ministry of the gospel: the Presbyterians during the English Revolution', in Durston and Maltby, Religion, pp. 137–57; J. Eales, '"So many sects and schisms": religious diversity in Revolutionary Kent, 1640–60', in Durston and Maltby, *Religion*, pp. 226–48; *Church Life Pastors, Congregations, and the Experience of Dissent in Seventeenth Century England*, ed. M. Davies, A. Dunan-Page and J. Halcomb (Oxford, 2019).

and taking care of the poor and elderly.[52] Certainly, manuals published after the Restoration emphasized pastoral duties, possibly in reaction to things learned during the interregnum, and perhaps also in reaction to how well clergymen in the new dissenting groups fared in this regard.[53]

It is claimed that Walker's famous *Sufferings of the Clergy*, produced much later and based on oral testimonies, is reasonably accurate in picking up those clergy ejected during the 1640s.[54] This group may be usefully compared with those recorded by Calamy as having been forced out of the Church of England in 1660–2.[55] Both sets of accounts provide tantalisingly vivid details that suggest we can learn a lot about some ministers, yet they still need to be corroborated and placed in local context.[56] We need to pick up other 'ministers' whose existence as such was extremely transitory. Just as attention is now being paid to the notion of 'getting along', particularly in those communities that harboured Roman Catholic recusants, so we need to investigate how many moderate ministers were adopted by their congregations and enabled to find security after the Restoration without undue scrutiny of their ordination.[57] The period must surely have witnessed many kinds of compromises. The parish register and tithing book kept by Thomas Hassall of Amwell in Hertfordshire suggests continued recording of baptisms and careful concern for the rights of his church in troubled times.[58]

One theme that comes through in literature produced after the Restoration is complaints about the quality, education and experience of clergy appointed during this period, itself perhaps a comment on the high numbers required. In one tract published in 1663, Thomas Ken lamented 'five groans of the Church', one of which was that 'instead of the ancient fathers, we have children who are made priests in all lands'.[59] He also

---

[52] A. Hughes, '"The public profession of these nations": the national Church in Interregnum England', in Durston and Maltby, *Religion*, pp. 93–114.

[53] S. Degg, *The Parson's Counsellor* (London, 1676); S. Thomas, *Creating Communities in Restoration England: Parish and Congregation in Oliver Heywood's Halifax* (Leiden, 2013).

[54] *WR*; McCall, *Baal's Priests*.

[55] *CR*.

[56] See Helen Whittle and others in this collection.

[57] W. J. Sheils, '"Getting on" and "getting along" in parish and town: Catholics and their neighbours in England', in *Catholic Communities in Protestant States: Britain and the Netherlands, c.1570–1720*, ed. B. Kaplan et al. (Manchester, 2016), pp. 67–83; W. J. Sheils, 'English Catholics at war and peace', in Durston and Maltby, *Religion*, pp. 137–57.

[58] *The Parish Register and Tithing Book of Thomas Hassall of Amwell*, ed. S. Doree (Linton: Hertfordshire Record Publications, 5, 1989).

[59] T. Ken, *Ichabod: Or the Five Groans of the Church* (Cambridge, 1663), p. 26.

suggested that 1,342 'factious ministers' had been ordained without real care as to whether they could really be reformed.[60] He went on to catalogue the incidence of non-resident clergy by counties. The veracity of all these claims cries out to be checked in the localities, while also remembering that such complaints did have a long history.[61]

In considering the appointment of ministers, it is important to think about what happened to patronage during the interregnum and how clergymen came to be appointed without reference to bishops, ordinations and licensing. On the abolition of episcopacy in 1646, patronage of a large number of parish livings fell to parliament, which delegated matters concerning suitability of appointees to the Westminster Assembly. Likewise, the considerable number of livings that were under crown and ecclesiastical presentation fell to central authorities administered through the Committee for Plundered Ministers. Another portion of livings, such as those held by delinquent royalists, incumbents and patrons alike, also passed into the hands of the new authorities. As clergy were ejected or died, this thus put pressure on local communities who had to petition parliament for the appointment of a minister. What followed was first extensive work under the auspices of the Westminster Assembly, and later in 1654, in response to yet further petitions regarding the dearth of qualified ministers in the land, the creation of the Triers.[62] A group of trustees then presided over some appointments following nominations with testimonials. Most modern commentators have guessed that this system worked quite well, ensuring at least minimum standards of competence and orthodoxy among new clergy, and responding fairly and judiciously to local representation.[63] This optimistic assessment needs testing in the localities.

What happened to Church officials?

Ministers may have come and gone with greater rapidity than usual, as noted above, but questions need to be asked about how much continuity existed for those elected as churchwardens and appointed as overseers of the poor and parish constables.[64] Family traditions of service to the locality may have been

---

[60] Ken, *Ichabod*, p. 39.

[61] For pioneering work here see: R. O'Day, *The English Clergy: the Emergence and Consolidation of a Profession 1558–1642* (Leicester, 1979); I. Green, 'Career prospects and clerical conformity in the early Stuart Church', *Past & Present*, xc (1981), 93–103.

[62] See Rebecca Warren, '"A knowing ministry"'.

[63] A. Hughes, '"The public profession of these nations": the national Church in Interregnum England', in Durston and Hughes, *Religion*, pp. 93–114; a view endorsed by Rebecca Warren.

[64] See work on churchwardens already cited by Hitchman and Foster.

broken, first during wartime, and later by fresh divisions in the parish created by the arrival of new ministers. This would carry with it questions about the ability of those who came to serve the 'vestry', for many of the 'registers' of the 1650s were men of humble origin. The appointment of new registrars was not always welcome, nor timely. At Shermanbury in 1661, it was recorded that 'Robert Tredcroft was Rector … when this Register book was brought, but was denied the keeping of it by William Freeman and the rest of that rebellious crew.'[65] The names of such people appointed were often recorded in the parish registers, as already noted, and work could be done on tracking their parish affiliations, social status, and political and religious opinions.

In an important article on poor relief, Tim Wales has argued that 'this period forms a distinctive phase in the development of poor relief, involving significant changes in parochial practice: in levels of rates raised, of numbers relieved, of individual payments made. Not all of this survived significantly beyond 1660, but much did.'[66] He also drew attention to significant demographic and economic crises that peaked during this period, with particularly bad harvests over the latter half of the 1640s, all of which added pressure on the hard-worked overseers of the poor. Higher levels of parish expenditure may be detected all round owing to a 'double whammy' of higher taxation and demand for poor relief.[67] For Wales, the burden fell squarely on the shoulders of local parish congregations who found little help or leadership from a relatively new and inexperienced bench of justices of the peace, one consequence of a period that saw damage to the power of a predominantly royalist aristocracy and gentry. This research was based on Norfolk and is suggestive for what local historians might investigate elsewhere. Should we be talking about a sea change in how parishes thought about the poor and 'charity' as a result of this critical period?

What happened to Church services, customs and 'rites of passage'?

Big changes would have hit people when they were ordered to drop use of the Book of Common Prayer in 1645 in favour of the *Directory for Publique Worship*.[68] Huge question marks remain, however, as to how many copies of the *Directory* were actually purchased and available in parishes. Nor is it clear

---

[65] WSRO, Par 167/1/1/1, fo. 1r; Durston, *Family*, p. 78, noted that the appointment of 'registers' was not always timely.

[66] T. Wales, 'The parish and the poor in the English Revolution', in *The Nature of the English Revolution Revisited*, ed. S. Taylor and G. Tapsell (Woodbridge, 2013), pp. 53–80, at p. 54.

[67] Wales, 'The parish and the poor', pp. 76–7.

[68] *The Directory for the Publique Worship of God* (London, 1645).

how effectively use of this book was ever enforced, loose though its guidelines were. Surviving churchwardens' accounts for the period do not suggest that it was purchased in large numbers.[69] Indeed, many commentators since have noted plenty of examples where parishioners sought to hear services conducted with the Book of Common Prayer, and some clergymen who knew it by heart boasted of being congratulated on their ostensibly extempore services by ill-informed listeners.[70] In a reversal of the 'sermon gadding' common in the 1630s, the interregnum affords examples of people 'gadding' to those churches where they knew traditional services might be held; this was admittedly easier in urban settings with a variety of churches to choose from, or where house chapels were available. The popularity of the *Directory* is debatable: for some historians, it lacked familiar ringing phrases, and, it has been argued, changed the relationship between minister and congregation in services, affording the latter little real scope for participation.[71] On the other hand, it might have met with approval for the very scope it gave ministers.[72]

Even more difficult to gauge is how people sought to maintain customs now banned, like observing Christmas celebrations or parish feasts. What happened to parish customs traditionally used to aid the poor, such as perambulations held at Rogationtide or harvest festivals? A number of classic 'services' must have gone by the wayside, such as the practice of confirmation. Yet catechism classes apparently came back into fashion, having been criticized by puritans in the 1630s.[73] It is debatable as to how many churches continued to use baptism in the 1650s, when the registers now stressed 'births'.[74] Controversies erupted over the conduct of communion for all, marriages and even burials, as already noted, largely in relation to a given minister's predilections vis-à-vis members of the congregation over which service books to employ.

---

[69] J. Maltby, 'Suffering and surviving: the civil wars, the Commonwealth and the formation of "Anglicanism", 1642–60', in Durston and Maltby, *Religion*, pp. 158–80; see also her '"Extravagencies and impertinences": set forms, conceived and extempore prayer in revolutionary England', in *Worship*, ed. Mears and Ryrie, pp. 221–43. Bernard Capp feels that services frequently incorporated elements from the Book of Common Prayer, while Trevor Cooper cautions against seeing the *Directory* as unpopular for it went into several editions.

[70] Maltby, '"Extravagencies"', pp. 163–4.

[71] Maltby, '"Extravagencies"', p. 162.

[72] An opinion strongly asserted by Rebecca Warren.

[73] Capp, *England's Culture Wars*, ch. 6.

[74] Bernard Capp reminds me that baptism was still wanted by many people, as partly evidenced by the surge in numbers of young children getting baptized after the Restoration; as Joel Halcomb suggests, however, some of that surge could be taking the opportunity to record baptisms that had occurred before.

Genealogists have done sterling work investigating what the changes to registration entailed for 'births', deaths and marriages.[75] Ironically, although there are problems assessing loss of records, we probably have more data for these life events than for many years before or later. Less is known about associated 'rites of passage' such as the survival of catechism classes, churching of women, the impact of changes relating to marriage and confirmation. Demographers have been excited by the possibilities of a mini-population crisis in the mid seventeenth century, and also worked on birth–baptism intervals and what they may reveal.[76] Given what needs to be investigated about the completeness of parish registers during this period, it is sadly not clear how far this might turn out to be an optical illusion.

The *Directory* contained instructions for the key ceremonies concerning baptism, marriage and burials. Yet registration of births soon replaced baptisms and burial services were stripped of kneeling and processions, which had apparently been greatly abused.[77] Although various ordinances were issued concerning marriage, leading to the famous act of 1653, that act clearly confused registrars as to what they should record and where. It has been claimed that 'in many parishes, however, registers contain few marriage entries after 1642 and none after 1653 until 1660'.[78] It is a claim that once again cries out to be tested by local historians for it has great ramifications for demographers and family historians. My West Sussex case study suggests that there is something in the claim, for around eighty-two parish registers, approximately fifty-six per cent, have significant gaps in the recording of marriages in the 1640s and 1650s. On an associated theme, observance of the prohibited degrees of marriage was clearly a concern for the Commonwealth and Protectorate authorities, for acts were passed on the matter in 1650 and again in 1653.[79] How were such matters now checked by JPs, or was that left to ministers at the point at which banns were read?

What happened to the maintenance and repair of churches?

This is difficult to ascertain. After surveys from which we learn much about church interiors in the 1630s – usually associated with Laudian

---

[75] Chapman, *Marriage Laws*, pp. 10–13.

[76] D. McLaren, 'The Marriage Act of 1653: its influence on the parish registers', *Population Studies*, xxviii (1974), 319–27; D. Woodward, 'The impact of the Commonwealth Act on Yorkshire parish registers', *Local Population Studies*, xiv (1975), 15–31; D. Turner, 'A lost seventeenth century demographic crisis? The evidence of two counties', *Local Population Studies*, xxi (1978), 11–18.

[77] D. Cressy, *Birth, Marriage & Death*, p. 416.

[78] Chapman, *Marriage Laws*, p. 13.

[79] *A&O*, ii. 387–9, 715–18.

ceremonialism – we have less information on what happened in the 1640s and 1650s.[80] There are hotspots, however, associated with iconoclasm carried out in East Anglia under Dowsing in the 1640s, particularly in Cambridge colleges where altars and rails were pulled down and stained-glass windows smashed.[81] Conversely, we also know of one or two churches actually built during this period, usually with strong gentry involvement, such as the chapel of Staunton Harold in Leicestershire.[82] We know that parliament was concerned about the condition of churches as an ordinance was passed on the matter in February 1648, interestingly coupled with instructions on payments through churchwardens, possibly suggesting the need to reinforce the continuity of that function.[83] There were also the important surveys of churches carried out for parliament in 1650, the records of which have yet to be fully exploited.[84] These were used to guide instances where poor livings were augmented, usually from funds coming from royalist fines, confiscations or cathedral and episcopal estates. They were also used to inform decisions made in a number of cases, many relating to the reduction in number of poor city livings, as in Chichester, through amalgamations.[85] Few of these changes survived the Restoration and it remained for Queen Anne's Bounty much later to try to deal with the poverty of so many livings within the Church of England.[86]

Only where we have surviving churchwardens' accounts are we likely to find answers to what happened to items like the royal coat of arms after 1649, and to what extent incidents of iconoclasm occurred in parish churches as well as in the more famous cases of Oxbridge colleges and cathedrals. In the church of Maids Moreton in Buckinghamshire, the rector recorded that

[80] *Church Surveys of Chichester Archdeaconry 1602, 1610, 1636*, ed. J. Barham and A. Foster (Sussex Record Soc., 98, Lewes, 2018).

[81] *The Journal of William Dowsing Iconoclasm in East Anglia during the English Civil War*, ed. T. Cooper (Woodbridge, 2001), pp. 47–55, 155–91.

[82] *The Buildings of Britain Stuart and Baroque: A Guide and Gazetteer*, R. Morrice (London, 1982), reveals just a handful of churches that experienced major renovations during this period: Staunton Harold in Leicestershire, Holy Trinity in Berwick-upon-Tweed, Carsington in Derbyshire and Brightwell in Suffolk stand out. Roger Davey has kindly pointed out one exceptional case of restoration to the west end of Carlisle cathedral that occurred in 1652 after damage by the Scots.

[83] *A&O*, i. 1065–70.

[84] See the chapter by Alex Craven in this collection.

[85] A. Fletcher, *A County Community in Peace and War: Sussex 1600–1660* (London, 1975), pp. 109–10; C. Welch, 'Commonwealth unions of benefices in Sussex', *Sussex Notes and Queries*, xv (1958–62), 116–20, at p. 119.

[86] For the classic work on this: G. Best, *Temporal Pillars: Queen Anne's Bounty, the Ecclesiastical Commissioners, and the Church of England* (Cambridge, 1964).

'the windows were broken, a costly deske in the form of a Spread Eagle guilt, on which we used to lay Bpp Jewells Works, hewed to pieces as an abominable Idoll'; he also noted that they managed to hide a number of items, including the register, hence it 'is not absolutely perfect for divers years'.[87] Where money could be found for work on church interiors, we know that it was spent on providing pulpits and galleries rather than fittings around an altar. That this was in response to local need and relatively popular may be deduced from the survival of such galleries after the Restoration.[88] In a general account of iconoclasm in this period, Julie Spraggon noted that after initial attacks on altars and communion rails in the early 1640s, 'responses to the 1643 and 1644 ordinances are harder to come by in parish accounts'.[89] This fits well with what John Walter found for the period 1641–2, but more work is needed by local historians around the country to give a fuller answer to the question posed by Spraggon on the enforcement of iconoclastic legislation in the localities and what happened later.[90]

How were parishes financed during this period?

In theory, much should have remained as before: ministers would have been paid out of fees for services, tithes, lived off their own glebe land if they were fortunate enough to possess such property, and other customary perquisites of office such as gifts at Easter. In practice, much of this came into dispute during the period as first there might be problems with ejected ministers refusing to give up residences and perquisites of office; and as time wore on, with fewer levers available for enforcement of practice, payment of tithes might become a problem in certain areas.[91] One of the very last acts of this period, which was passed in March 1660, related to tithes and other sources of grievance in Wales.[92] Certainly, this was a thorny issue that many hoped would be resolved by reforms proposed in parliaments held in the 1650s, yet it never happened. To what extent tithe disputes continued through quarter sessions is another question that requires more research. Classic articles by

[87] I owe this choice example to Ken Fincham: Buckinghamshire Record Office: PR 139/1/1, p. 21.

[88] Fincham, 'Material evidence', pp. 224–40.

[89] J. Spraggon, *Puritan Iconoclasm during the English Civil War* (Woodbridge, 2003), p. 102.

[90] J. Walter, 'Popular iconoclasm and the politics of the parish in eastern England, 1640–1642', *The Historical Journal*, xlvii (2004), 261–90.

[91] Bernard Capp reminds me that two new issues would have arisen affecting payment of tithes, one the appearance of Quakers who flatly refused to pay them, and the other, non-payment as a weapon to get rid of an unwanted minister.

[92] *A&O*, ii. 1467–9.

Paul Carter, Rosemary O'Day and Ann Hughes provide ample signposts for further work that is required on this murky topic of finance, whether talking about income or expenditure.[93]

What happened to 'Church/state relations' during this period?

To say that relations changed between Church and state would be an understatement. With the authority of the crown, bishops and archdeacons removed – the hierarchy above the parishes was lost and replaced by secular authorities. Committees of parliament, the trustees, Triers and ejectors, local justices of the peace and the Major-Generals, all came to play a strong part in the life of parishes. Yet it is difficult to see how this worked in practice, such as, for example, compliance with orders to the churchwardens to present cases to quarter sessions. We know from literature produced by many divines at this time that a fierce debate ensued as to how far episcopalians should comply with the new regime; there were debates about 'where was the Church of England without its bishops, or indeed, their king?'[94] While the balance of power may have swung away from the clergy and towards the laity and secular functions of the parish, it is worth remembering just how new and inexperienced some JPs and military authorities would have been in the face of parish traditions.[95]

One considerable – and yet possibly undervalued – loss might have been that of clerical representation in parliament. Bishops might never have been particularly robust advocates on parochial concerns, but they did sit in the Lords. Examples can be found of their advocacy in very particular cases, as when Bishop Neile spoke up against a bill to split two poor livings in Kent in 1610.[96] The whole apparatus of Convocation that used to sit

[93] R. O'Day and A. Hughes, 'Augmentation and amalgamation: was there a systematic approach to the reform of parochial finance, 1640–60?', in *Princes and Paupers in the English Church 1500–1800*, ed. R. O'Day and F. Heal (Leicester, 1981), pp. 167–94; P. Carter, 'Clerical taxation during the Civil War and Interregnum', *Historical Research*, lxvii (1994), 119–33.

[94] Haigh, 'Where was the Church of England', 127–47, at p. 127; Bernard Capp points out that Presbyterians and moderates faced the same dilemma, especially after the regicide in 1649.

[95] I am grateful to Tim Wales for this reminder, yet Rebecca Warren warns that we should not exaggerate the inexperience of JPs, all of whom would have been brought up to understand the significance of parishes' customs. Bernard Capp also points out that the loss of experienced JPs would have affected some areas of the country more than others.

[96] A. Foster, 'The function of a bishop: the career of Richard Neile, 1562–1640', in *Continuity and Change: Personnel and Administration of the Church of England 1500–1642*, ed. R. O'Day and F. Heal (Leicester, 1976), p. 43; *Proceedings in Parliament 1610*, ed. E. R. Foster (New Haven, Conn., 1966), pp. 111–12.

alongside parliamentary sessions did provide opportunities for discussion of parish affairs as proctors were appointed from dioceses to the lower house.[97] Visitations brought clergy together from deaneries fairly regularly. Rural deans were significant administrators in some large dioceses, and an important link between clergy and their archdeacons.[98] One wonders how isolated many clergy operating the 'parochial system' – as it was shorn in the 1640s and 1650s – may have felt, and how they might have viewed the attractions of a Presbyterian *classis*, or a network of Congregationalists, or the voluntary associations of Worcestershire.

How did people feel about these changes?

This is very difficult to gauge. We have much literature about the religious debates of the times, evidence of growing tensions, and a feeling that the end of the world was nigh in some areas. At the parish level, one wonders how traumatic the events of the times must have felt. Parishes had existed within a well-defined structure that was now abandoned: they related to rural deaneries in many areas, to the larger units of archdeaconries which handled probate affairs and court cases in their own right, and to dioceses with bishops to whom they could appeal. Unless they were in peculiar jurisdictions – another category of parishes whose experiences need to be investigated – they were not necessarily as isolated as we may have thought. It was common still for many wills in the seventeenth century to leave gifts for the 'mother church' of the cathedral. How did people react when they learned that several cathedrals had been sacked and looted by troops during the wars, clergy turned out, books and goods pillaged, and lands confiscated for other uses? No wonder that the more literate and those associated with bishops speculated on the nature of the Church without bishops, and what that might entail. Was the Church now really just a 'community of the faithful'?[99]

A common theme in the writings of historians about this period is a sense of heightened tensions and anxieties. Godly preachers now had an

---

[97] *Records of Convocation, vii, Canterbury 1509–1603*, ed. G. Bray (Woodbridge, 2006); sadly, the archive for Convocation is rather slim and formal, so we cannot tell how often parish affairs might have registered with those present.

[98] Note how rural deans seem to have been appreciated in the literature of the day when bemoaning the size of some of the old dioceses and searching for an administrative unit that cared more for souls than for geographical space: H. Ferne, *Episcopacy and Presbytery Considered...* (London, 1647); J. Ussher, *The Reduction of Episcopacie...* (London, 1656) and R. Baxter, *Five Disputations of Church Government* (London, 1659) also noted the advantages of employing suffragan bishops and rural deans.

[99] C. Haigh, 'Where was the Church of England', p. 144.

opportunity to preach without restraint and must have challenged – or delighted – many of their parishioners. There was a new determination to enforce Sabbath-day observance and control of behaviour: drinking, alehouses, gambling and sports. All of this represented a threat to how many went about their lives. The very appearance of new sects with radical views must have been disturbing. With the loss of sanctions, many of the worldly in the parishes must have wondered about the necessity to attend church. With one form of loose identity lost, namely the whole Church structure, it is little wonder that people clung to new forms of identity based around their congregations, often willing to draw new lines regarding inclusion and exclusion.[100]

How can we get towards a fuller picture?

As should be clear by now, research on this period is difficult. While we have suffered losses in parochial records, we have also made gains in material kept largely in central repositories. This presents new challenges to local historians, but there is much to be gained and good case studies exist to light the way, as chapters in this volume also illustrate.[101] Painstaking work will one day reveal much more about the clergy and the officers who served their parishes. Concepts like 'getting along' might be more profitable lines of enquiry than those that have hitherto suggested conflict, even though there were clearly parishes in which major disturbances occurred. While strife-torn areas often produce the most compelling evidence, it is harder to distinguish what was happening in communities where people compromised. Local studies can helpfully provide timescales for events that modify the picture as viewed from London, and reveal how different groups in the parishes – whether dissenters or Catholics – fared.

Difficult as this agenda might be, it could be very rewarding. It affords a chance to look again at our parish communities during troubled times, to see what worked for them, and think about how they were subtly affected by those years without a supreme governor and bishops. 'Identity' is a fragile thing, and although we see how swiftly the restored Church was welcomed back by some, many cracks with long-standing implications may have appeared below the surface. It was not the *same old* Church of England. Ministers were forced to think about how they related to their congregations; rival views came into existence of what was entailed in

---

[100] For fuller discussion of this possible 'cultural turn' see B. Capp, *England's Culture Wars.*

[101] J. Eales, '"So many sects and schisms": religious diversity in Revolutionary Kent, 1640–60', in Durston and Maltby, *Religion*, pp. 226–48; chs. by Helen Whittle and Maureen Harris among others in this collection.

pastoral care. Not everyone welcomed the return of the Church of England, and many gains made in the interregnum were now lost. It was to take some time before events of these troubled times were forgotten. To end on yet more questions: to what extent did puritan reformers achieve what they had hoped for in the 1640s? How far were traditionalists able to hold on to their old ways, old services and old ministers that they liked? How disruptive was this period for ordinary parishioners? Research on the Church of England post Restoration is now needed to look back on the legacy of the interregnum with fresh eyes.

2. 'Soe good and godly a worke': the surveys of ecclesiastical livings and parochial reform during the English Revolution

Alex Craven

In the course of a few short years, the Long parliament dismantled the traditional apparatus of the English Church, abolishing episcopacy and replacing the Book of Common Prayer with the *Directory for Publique Worship*.[1] The abolition of bishops in 1646 and of cathedral chapters in 1649 left the state in possession of land, tithes and advowsons across the country. Much of this estate was sold by a regime ever hungry for money, but tithes and other ecclesiastical revenues were reserved for the improvement of clerical wages. Nevertheless, the haphazard augmentation of livings during the 1640s demonstrated that the committees charged with regulating the Church had no clear idea of the value of its property, the quality of its ministers or the condition of the parishes.[2]

Consequently, parliament ordered a survey of the Church to be made. Local juries were to catalogue the resources in each parish, evaluate their clergy and consider the need for the union or division of parishes. Returns are extant for thirty-five counties, produced between 1650 and 1659. They provide an essential snapshot of the state of the Church during the English Revolution. The recommendations made in these documents would have dramatically redrawn the parochial map, redistributed resources and rooted out incompetence. Nevertheless, few of the proposed reforms had been implemented by the time they were reversed by the Restoration. This chapter will examine the surveys of six counties – Dorset, Gloucestershire, Lancashire, Middlesex, Norfolk and Wiltshire – made between 1650 and 1657, to analyse the state of the Church in the 1650s, assess the problems facing ecclesiastical authorities and evaluate the effectiveness of the successive bodies appointed to reform the Church during the Commonwealth and Protectorate.

---

[1] *The Directory for the Publique Worship of God* (London, 1645).

[2] A. Craven, 'Ministers of state: the established Church in Lancashire during the English Revolution, 1642–1660', *Northern History*, xlv (2008), 51–69.

The parochial structure of early modern England and Wales was part of the Church's medieval inheritance, reflecting the wealth and pattern of settlement of an earlier age. Parishes were established in the late Saxon period, and their numbers had grown rapidly thereafter, but the rate of expansion slowed from the thirteenth century as parish boundaries became fixed. The uneven distribution of parishes, probably numbering about 8,800 by the sixteenth century, presented different problems in different regions. In the south and east, many small parishes were too poor to attract a learned ministry. In the uplands of the north and west, very large parishes were once sparsely populated but now the dispersed congregations had swollen far beyond the capacity of many parish churches.[3]

The contrast was observed in 1641 by one Lancashire man, who compared the populous counties of south-east England to the district of Furness, 'which for spacious compasse of ground is not much lesse than Bedfordshire or Rutlandshire, [yet] it hath onely eight parish churches'.[4] The spiritual needs of Lancastrians were served by just sixty parishes in 1640, and the average parish measured 20,000 acres (thirty-one square miles). Twelve were over 30,000 acres (forty-seven square miles), and the gargantuan parish of Whalley measured some 108,140 acres (169 square miles).[5] Only Northumberland had larger parishes than Lancashire, and only the small counties of Westmorland and Rutland had fewer parishes.[6] By contrast, parishes in many southern counties were smaller and more numerous. For example, it has been estimated that at least 928 parish churches existed in Norfolk between the eleventh and the sixteenth centuries, sixteen times as many as Lancashire's total, while a fifteenth-century survey of the same county recorded 782 parishes. Discounting the forty-six parishes of Norwich, this would give an average area of 1,752 acres for the county's parishes. Norfolk was an extreme example, but elsewhere in eastern England there were 415 parish churches in Essex and 580 in Suffolk.[7]

---

[3] N. J. G. Pounds, *A History of the English Parish* (Cambridge, 2000), pp. 3–40, 67–112; R. N. Swanson, *Church and Society in Late Medieval England* (Oxford, 1989), pp. 4–5; D. M. Palliser, 'Introduction: the parish in perspective', in *Parish, Church and People: Local Studies in Lay Religion 1350–1750*, ed. S. J. Wright (1988), pp. 5–28.

[4] G. Walker, *An Exhortation for Contributions to Maintain Preachers in Lancashire*, ed. C. Sutton, in *Chetham Miscellanies: New Series, Vol. I* (Chetham Soc. new ser., 47, Manchester, 1902), p. 16.

[5] The mean area was 19,756 acres, the median area 13,420 acres (21 square miles), based on the figures returned for the 1831 census: *Abstract of the Population Returns of Great Britain, 1831* (Parl. Papers, 1833 (149) xxxvi), pp. 284–385.

[6] C. Haigh, *Reformation and Resistance in Tudor Lancashire* (Cambridge, 1975), p. 22.

[7] N. Batcock, *The Ruined and Disused Churches of Norfolk*, East Anglian Archaeology Report 51 (Dereham, 1991), p. 1; *VCH Norfolk*, ii. 235; *Population Returns 1831*, pp. 384–425.

The provision of parish churches was no less uneven in the urban environment. Cities that had been large from an early date often had many more parishes than were necessary by the sixteenth century – forty-six at Norwich and Lincoln, forty at York – while the growing towns of the late middle ages had to squeeze their expanding population into a solitary parish church, or were served by chapels of ease that remained subordinate to ancient mother churches.[8] Liverpool, Weymouth and Sunderland were all supplied by chapels of ease, while all six of the churches of Kingston-upon-Hull were technically chapels. Indeed, some urban chapels outdid parish churches in their wealth and splendour. William Worcestre described the church of St Mary Redcliffe, near Bristol, as 'like a cathedral', and Elizabeth I called it 'the fairest, goodliest and most famous parish church in England', yet it was only a chapel of ease until the eighteenth century.[9] Chapels were also common in the countryside. Their number is difficult to ascertain because they were often poorly documented, but they tended to be established where large distances, rugged terrain or hostile weather made attending the parish church difficult. Chapels supplied some of the deficiencies of the English Church, but their existence was a constant cause of friction and disputes. They provided regular worship for communities outside the parish church, but other pastoral services were often jealously reserved as the exclusive right of the mother church, to preserve the fees of the incumbent. Meanwhile, the congregation of a chapel had the double burden of maintaining both it and the parish church.[10]

Addressing the deficiencies of the Church by founding new chapels had proved attractive because altering the established parochial structure risked upsetting vested interests: creating new parishes deprived their former incumbents of their tithes and fees; consolidating parishes upset the privileges of their patrons. Formal reorganization required the permission of the respective incumbents and patrons of each parish, as well as a licence from the

---

[8] Swanson, *Church and Society*, p. 4; N. P. Tanner, *The Church in Late Medieval Norwich 1370–1532* (Toronto, 1984), p. 3; D. M. Palliser, 'The union of parishes at York, 1547–86', *Yorkshire Archaeological Journal*, xlvi (1974), 87–102.

[9] F. Neale, 'William Worcestre: Bristol's churches in 1480', in *Historic Churches and Church Life in Bristol*, ed. J. Bettey (Bristol, 2001), pp. 28–55; J. Collinson, *The History and Antiquities of the County of Somerset* (3 vols, Bath, 1791), ii. 285.

[10] C. Kitching, 'Church and chapelry in sixteenth-century England', in *The Church in Town and Countryside*, ed. D. Baker (Studies in Church History, 16, Oxford, 1979), pp. 279–90; N. Orme, 'Church and chapel in medieval England', *Transactions of the Royal Historical Society*, 6th ser., vi (1996), 75–102; N. Orme, 'The other parish churches: chapels in late-medieval England', in *The Parish in Late Medieval England*, ed. C. Burgess and E. Duffy (Donington, 2006), pp. 78–94.

bishop, although informal unions could be achieved by nominating the same cleric to two parishes, especially if both benefices shared the same patron.

Where parochial reform was undertaken before the 1650s, it was a haphazard process resulting from local initiative rather than the product of a coordinated national plan. In the absence of any systematic effort to reform the parochial structure before the middle of the seventeenth century, individual changes were local responses to particular circumstances. The demographic crises of the fourteenth century had left many benefices unviable, and many depopulated parishes were subsequently united. It has been estimated that nationally there was a net reduction of seven per cent of the total number of parishes, from around 9,500 to 8,800, between the Black Death and the Reformation.[11] In those counties already possessed of an overabundance of parish churches, the decline was more marked. In Norfolk, where typically seven churches were closed every fifty years between 1100 and 1500, this rate doubled in the second half of the fourteenth century.[12]

During the sixteenth century, parliament was introduced into the question of parochial reform, beginning with legislation passed in 1545 which allowed for the union of two churches within a mile of each other if one was worth less than £6 a year, although such unions still required the consent of the incumbents, patrons and bishop to take effect.[13] This certainly had an impact in those areas that were oversupplied with parish churches. In Norfolk, 112 parish churches were abandoned during the sixteenth century, mostly as a result of the consolidation of poor parishes with their near neighbours.[14] Further acts were obtained for the reorganization of specific places, including York in 1547, which eventually enabled the closure of fourteen churches and the consolidation of two more parishes.[15] A later opportunity to consolidate unviable parishes in other corporate towns and cities was lost when parliament was prorogued in April 1563.[16] Nevertheless, the involvement of parliament in parochial reform for the first time did not yet represent a systematic approach to parochial reform, the various acts only serving to encourage and enable further local initiatives.

Although Tudor legislation contemplated the union of small and poor parishes, none addressed the problem of large parishes in counties like Lancashire. While it had been possible to close unwanted parish churches

---

[11] Swanson, *Church and Society*, pp. 4–5.

[12] Batcock, *Disused Churches of Norfolk*, pp. 7, 181.

[13] 37 Henr. VIII, c. 21.

[14] Batcock, *Disused Churches of Norfolk*, pp. 7, 181–3.

[15] 1 Edw. VI, c. 9; D. M. Palliser, 'Parishes at York', 87–102. There were also acts for Lincoln and Stamford in 1548: 2 & 3 Edw. VI, c. 48, 50.

[16] *Commons Journals* [*CJ*], i. 72; *Lords Journals* [*LJ*], i. 617–8.

as the population collapsed after the Black Death, responding to a growing population proved more difficult, and few new parishes were established in the century before the Civil War. The population of Lancashire is thought to have grown by two and a half times between 1377 and 1563, to about 95,000 in that year, and was estimated to be approximately 150,000 by 1640.[17] In the same period the average Lancashire congregation rose from 630 in 1377 to 1,700 in 1563, and to 2,500 by 1640. As with previous centuries, founding chapels remained the easiest way to fill gaps in the parochial structure, and in Lancashire the number of chapels increased from sixty-one in c.1500 to ninety-nine by 1548, and to 128 by 1640.[18] Many of these new chapels were founded in the large cloth-producing parishes of the east of the county, where population growth was highest: by 1640, Blackburn had seven chapels, Manchester nine and Whalley twelve.[19] By contrast, only two new Lancashire parishes were created during the sixteenth century, Deane in 1541 and Hawkshead in 1578.[20]

Parochial reform remained a low priority in the early seventeenth century. Efforts to create new parishes at Blindley Heath (Surrey) and Melcombe Regis (Dorset) through legislation came to nothing in 1604, while bills to make St Mary's in Lichfield a separate parish were lost in 1621 and 1626.[21] The meeting of the Long parliament presented new opportunities for the reorganization of the parochial structure, although these were initially restricted to the reform of individual parishes. Legislation introduced in 1641 resulted in the separation of the Lancashire chapels of Hoole and Upholland from their respective mother churches. Both examples emphasize the importance of well-connected local men to the success of establishing new parishes. The chapel at Hoole was only established in 1628, endowed by the mercantile brothers Andrew and Thomas Stones.[22] Through their influence, Hoole was divided from Croston in 1641, the act installing the Stoneses as patrons of the new rectory.[23] The process of separating Upholland from the parish of Wigan was more drawn out. A bill introduced in 1641 was initially resisted

---

[17] For the demography of early modern Lancashire: C. B. Phillips and J. H. Smith, *Lancashire and Cheshire from AD 1540* (London, 1994), pp. 5–12; J. K. Walton, *Lancashire: A Social History, 1558–1939* (Manchester, 1987), pp. 7–35.

[18] G. H. Tupling, 'The pre-Reformation parishes and chapelries of Lancashire', *Trans. LCAS*, lxvii (1957), 7–10; Haigh, *Reformation*, pp. 22–3, 31; B. G. Blackwood, *The Lancashire Gentry and the Great Rebellion 1640–60* (Chetham Soc. 3rd ser. 25, Manchester, 1978), p. 3.

[19] *VCH Lancs.* iv. 174–338; vi. 235–560; G. H. Tupling, 'Pre-Reformation parishes and chapels', 9.

[20] *VCH Lancs.* v. 3; viii. 370.

[21] *CJ*, i. 198, 224, 605, 819.

[22] *VCH Lancs.* vi. 153.

[23] *CJ*, ii. 172, 223; *LJ*, iv. 338, 349.

by John Bridgeman, bishop of Chester and rector of Wigan, but passed the Commons in April 1642. Nevertheless, it remained overlooked for over a year until an ordinance was finally passed in September 1643. In the case of Upholland, the influence of the godly landowner Henry Ashhurst and his MP son William was instrumental.[24] Elsewhere, Plymouth was divided into two parishes by an act of 1641, but other bills initiated in 1641 – to divide the large London suburban parishes of St Andrew's Holborn, St Giles' Cripplegate, St James Clerkenwell, St Margaret's Westminster, St Martin in the Fields and Stepney, and to make Newport in the Isle of Wight a separate parish – all fared less well.[25]

Instead of such ad hoc reorganization, the Commons turned its attention to a more general reform of the Church. The Committee for Plundered Ministers, established in 1642 to relieve clerical supporters of parliament who had been ejected from their livings by royalists, was soon given further powers to augment clerical wages, to sequester royalist clergy and to appoint approved ministers to vacant benefices. Initially the committee sought to improve clerical livings from local resources, making grants from sequestered tithes to improve poor livings within the same county.

The committee continued this work until the dissolution of the Rump in 1653, yet at first it had no certain knowledge of where the need was greatest or what resources it could draw upon, and so long as it was reliant upon sequestrations, temporary in nature, the system would remain insecure and inefficient.[26] The need for a survey of benefices had first been suggested in April 1642, when committees considering the maintenance of the ministry and reform of Church government were combined, but the project stalled following the outbreak of war.[27] Parliament returned to parochial reform in April 1646, when another committee was appointed to consider the settling of a preaching ministry throughout England and Wales, and directed, among other things, to contemplate the necessity of altering parishes and erecting new churches.[28] The abolition of the episcopal hierarchy later that year provided parliament with a vast estate with which to endow the parochial clergy, further enlarged in 1649 with the estates of abolished cathedral chapters.[29]

---

[24] *CJ*, ii. 148, 155, 348, 415, 523; *LJ*, vi. 233–4; J. Lowe, 'The case of Hindley Chapel, 1641–1698', *Trans. LCAS*, lxvii (1957), 63; *VCH Lancs*. iv. 98–100.

[25] *CJ*, ii. 162, 177, 184, 200, 255, 259, 329, 351, 461, 516; *LJ*, iv. 331. Covent Garden was finally made a separate parish in 1646: *CJ*, iv. 398.

[26] W. A. Shaw, *A History of the English Church during the Civil Wars and under the Commonwealth, 1640–1660* (2 vols, London, 1900), ii. 185–97.

[27] *CJ*, ii. 549; Shaw, *English Church*. ii. 248.

[28] *CJ*, iv. 502.

[29] *A&O*, i. 887–904; ii. 81.

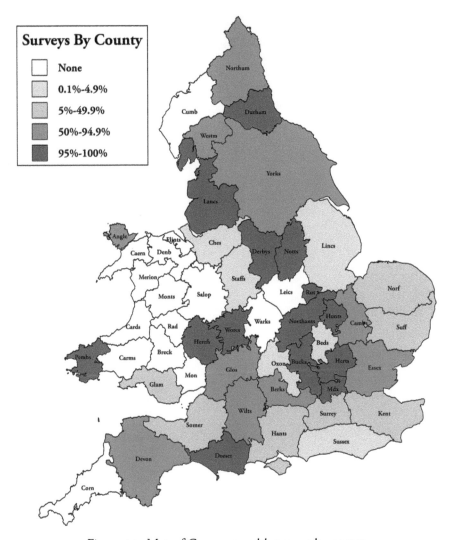

Figure 2.1. Map of Commonwealth surveys by county.

An Act for the Maintenance of Preaching Ministers was not passed, however, until June 1649. This created a new body of thirteen trustees who were to take possession of these properties and to apply their revenues 'for providing of a competent maintenance for supply and encouragement of Preaching-Ministers'. The stated goal of the act was to bring the value of each benefice up to a minimum of £100 a year. Commissioners were to survey the state of the Church throughout England and Wales, returning the value of each benefice, the identity of its incumbent, how they served the cure, what they were paid, and whether it was desirable to unite or divide

Table 2.1. Table of Commonwealth surveys by county and date

County	Year(s) of survey	Number of parishes[a]
Anglesey	1650	29/36 (81%)
Bedfordshire	1659	2/122 (2%)
Berkshire	1655	109/144 (76%)
Buckinghamshire	1650	200/204 (98%)
Cambridgeshire	1650, 1659	138/141 (98%)[b]
Cheshire	1656	3/147 (2%)
Derbyshire	1650	120/120 (100%)
Devon	1650	330/431 (77%)
Dorset	1650, 1656	220/239 (92%)
Durham	1650	64/67 (96%)
Essex	1650	379/405 (94%)
Glamorgan	1657	48/124 (39%)
Gloucestershire	1650	253/287 (82%)[c]
Hampshire	1650	31/249 (12%)[d]
Herefordshire	1655	193/196 (98%)
Hertfordshire	1650, 1657	126/128 (98%)
Huntingdonshire	1650	91/94 (97%)
Kent	1650	84/411 (20%)
Lancashire	1650	61/62 (98%)
Lincolnshire	1656	4/601 (1%)
London	1658	4/108 (4%)
Middlesex	1650	69/70 (99%)
Norfolk	1655–7	259/734 (35%)
Northamptonshire	1657	270/280 (96%)
Nottinghamshire	1650	193/203 (95%)
Oxfordshire	1656	2/198 (1%)
Pembrokeshire	1650, 1658	137/141 (97%)
Rutland	1650	43/43 (100%)
Somerset	1650	139/408 (34%)
Staffordshire	1658	1/122 (1%)
Suffolk	1650	199/492 (40%)
Surrey	1658	38/126 (30%)

(continued)

Table 2.1. (Cont.)

County	Year(s) of survey	Number of parishes[a]
Sussex	1656	2/299 (1%)
Westmorland	1656	23/32 (72%)
Wiltshire	1650, 1656	225/294 (77%)[e]
Worcestershire	1650	151/151 (100%)
Yorkshire, East Riding	1651	166/173 (96%)
Yorkshire, North Riding	1658	1/156 (1%)
Yorkshire, West Riding	1650	219/224 (98%)

[a] No definitive list exists for the number of parishes in each county during the 1650s, and it is not always certain what constitutes a parish, or when a church was parochial and when it was not. These figures have been derived from the analysis of several sources, principally F. A. Youngs, *Local Admin. Units of England* (2 vols, London, 1979) and R. J. P. Kain and R. R. Oliver, *Historic Parishes of England & Wales: An Electronic Map of Boundaries before 1850 with a Gazetteer and Metadata* (Colchester, 2001), as well as antiquarian histories and the volumes of the *VCH* for each respective county.

[b] Figures do not include the Isle of Ely.

[c] The city of Gloucester and the parishes surrounding it were treated as a separate county, known as the Inshire. Excluding this, the figures for the rest of Gloucestershire are 250 of 256 parishes surveyed (98 per cent).

[d] Comprises the six parishes of Southampton and twenty-five of the twenty-six parishes of the Isle of Wight.

[e] 145 parishes were surveyed in 1650, and another 80 parishes in 1656.

the parish.[30] MPs were instructed to nominate suitable commissioners in December, and the first commissions were issued in February 1650.[31] Over the course of the next twelve months, surveys, some only partial, were undertaken in at least twenty-four counties (see Table 2.1). Once returned to chancery, though, these surveys seem to have languished.

At the same time, an Act of April 1650 transferred responsibility for augmenting clerical livings to the Committee for the Reformation of the Universities, who immediately initiated a review of all existing augmentations. It is not clear whether the 1650 surveys were consulted as

[30] *A&O*, ii. 142–8; *CJ*, vi. 359; Shaw, *English Church*, ii. 210–4; *Lancashire and Cheshire Church Surveys 1649–1655*, ed. H. Fishwick, RSLC, i (1879), pp. xviii–xix.

[31] *CJ*, vi. 334–6, 354, 365.

part of this task, but the committee was abolished in April 1652.[32] Its powers were transferred to the Committee for Plundered Ministers in February 1653, two months before that committee's own termination upon the dissolution of the Rump. This left only the Trustees for the Maintenance of Ministers, upon whom all of the previous committees' powers were devolved by an act of September 1654.[33] The trustees were to send for the surveys of 1650 and to commission new surveys to be undertaken where necessary. The 1654 act went further than the earlier acts, empowering the trustees themselves to unite or divide parishes as they thought appropriate. As a result, surveys were produced of parishes in London and seventeen counties between 1655 and 1659, including six counties already surveyed in 1650. These numbers include eight returns comprising no more than a handful of parishes surveyed in advance of intended unions. In total, partial or complete parochial surveys produced between 1650 and 1659 are extant from thirty-five English and Welsh counties, and the city of London (see Table 2.1 and Figure 2.1).

These surveys vary in their nature. Many of the parchment originals of these surveys are still to be found among the records of chancery at the National Archives.[34] A number are now badly damaged and difficult to read, so it is fortunate that the trustees had paper copies made in 1654, preserving some surveys for which no original now survives. Their archive, now held by Lambeth Palace Library, also contains several original parchment surveys produced after 1654.[35] The Dorset returns of 1650 are singular. Although the act required that the returns be enrolled on parchment, instead the commissioners returned the paper presentments of each individual parish. The diversity within the surveys is reflected not just by differences in the form but also in the content of the surveys, sometimes even within the returns from the same county. While some jurors gave expansive answers, others restricted themselves to very limited comments. Some took up the task of recommending the reorganization of parishes enthusiastically, with Lancashire's jurors often detailing new boundaries down to individual households, but others were much more hesitant to recommend changes. Many jurors drew upon their knowledge of local topography, their local archives and communal memory to make the case for change; elsewhere jurors did little more than list the names and salaries of incumbents.

---

[32] A&O, ii. 369–78; Shaw, *English Church*, ii. 216–19.

[33] A&O, ii. 1000–6; Shaw, *English Church*, ii. 219–25, 230.

[34] TNA, C 94/1–4. In addition, two stray fragments (for Huntingdonshire and Rutland) have been filed amongst the State Papers: TNA, SP 46/96, fos. 122–123.

[35] LPL, COMM. XIIa/1–21; COMM. XIIb/1–12.

Unsurprisingly, those called upon to serve as commissioners tended to be drawn from the new wave of men who made up the backbone of the republican regime, many of whom had only come to prominence during the 1640s. Although twenty-one of the twenty-two Lancashire commissioners were either assessment commissioners or magistrates in 1650, thirteen had not served on a county committee before 1648, and only three had sat on the bench magistrates before 1642. Four of the six Gloucestershire men who presided over the county's survey were among the most active in the county during the 1640s or 1650s. Wiltshire's commissioners included the clerk of the peace and members of the corporation of Salisbury, and Dorset's commissioners included townsmen of Bridport, Gillingham and Sherborne. Nevertheless, there were also men from well-established families, 'of undoubted position in the country'. The Lancashire commissioners included four MPs and five interregnum sheriffs, the MP Thomas Hodges was a commissioner in Gloucestershire, and the Dorset commissioners included the MPs Anthony Ashley Cooper and Sir John Trenchard.[36] In some counties, the commissioners apportioned the separate divisions of their respective counties between themselves. Ten Lancashire commissioners dealt only with the southern half of the county, and nine only with the north.[37] In Wiltshire, nine commissioners concerned themselves only with the Salisbury division, while another five dealt exclusively with the Chippenham division.[38] This partition between different groups of commissioners may explain why some counties, such as Wiltshire, made only partial returns of the survey.[39] It was not true of all counties, however, and in Gloucestershire a single group of commissioners apparently received the presentments of all four divisions of the county during a single sitting at Gloucester.[40]

By surveying their counties according to quarter-sessions divisions, the commissioners used the familiar structures of county government. The act drew further upon this traditional apparatus, requiring sheriffs to call together juries, whose names we can usually learn from the individual returns. A single warrant survives from Lancashire, empanelling

---

[36] *CJ*, vi. 365; *Lancashire Church Surveys*, pp. xix, 1; *A&O*, ii. 301; Lancs. Archives, QSC/52; *List of Sheriffs for England and Wales*, PRO List and Indexes, ix (1963), p. 73; *VCH Wilts.* v. 90; vi. 119; A. R. Warmington, *Civil War, Interregnum and Restoration in Gloucestershire* (Woodbridge, 1997), pp. 92, 102.

[37] Three more Lancashire commissioners did not act: TNA, C 94/1, fos. 37–65.

[38] TNA, C 94/3, fo. 45; C 94/4, fos 50–3; LPL, COMM. XIIa/14, fos. 306–497.

[39] In 1656 an entirely different group of commissioners was responsible for surveying the Marlborough division of the county; TNA, C 94/3, fos. 29–44.

[40] TNA, C 94/1, fos. 28–32.

twenty-four men to act as jurors, from whom seventeen were sworn.[41] The numbers sitting in juries in Lancashire varied between twelve and seventeen. Where jurors can be identified, as might be expected, they were leading men within their own communities who held parochial office during the 1650s. Lancashire jurors included Ralph Worsley of Platt, father of the future Major-General and a former member of the sub-committee of accounts for Lancashire, and John Gilliam, who would be added to the assessment committee in November 1650. They also included men who would serve as high constables during the Commonwealth, borough reeves of Manchester and Salford, and a common councillor of Liverpool. Not all Lancashire jurymen were of unquestionable conformity to the new regime, however, including as they did the sequestered delinquent Richard Blackburn of Brindle.[42]

The returns exposed the divisions within the parishes of the nation. Rival factions within parishes saw the survey as another opportunity to pursue particular agendas, while neighbouring communities made competing claims upon each other's resources. In Shaftesbury, the parishioners of St Peter's called for the demolition of the neighbouring parish of Cann, described dismissively as a chapel, and its materials to be used to enlarge their own church, a suggestion unsurprisingly rejected at Cann. In Salisbury, the corporation hoped that the former cathedral would be converted into another parish church.[43] No doubt, many of these incidents were simply another episode in a longer history of friction. Antagonism between neighbouring parishes, or between chapels and their mother church, might be ancient in origin. Elsewhere, conflict might be the result of more recent conflict. The proposal to unite the two parishes of Abingdon (Berkshire) was later said to have been a ploy by the godly parishioners of St Helen's to dissolve the royalist congregation of St Nicholas, while Peter Heylyn strove successfully to resist the plan in order to provide shelter to the royalist clergyman.[44] The returns expose antagonism within communities as well, such as at Toller Porcorum (Dorset), where the parishioners refused to sign a document that was said not to represent the views of the majority of the parish. Some communities simply rejected the authority of the

[41] Lancs. Archives, DDKe/3/99.

[42] *Lancashire JPs at the Sheriff's Table, 1578–1694*, ed. B. W. Quintrell, RSLC, cxxi (1981), pp. 100, 186; Lancs. Archives, DDHk/2/1/4, fo. 2.

[43] TNA, C94/2, fos. 4, 10, 25; C 94/4, fo. 51.

[44] J. Barnard, *Theologo-Historicus, or the True Life of the Most Reverend Divine and Excellent Historian Peter Heylyn* (London, 1683), pp. 229–35. I am grateful to Fiona McCall for this reference.

commissioners, with complaints in both Gloucestershire and Wiltshire that parishes had not appeared when ordered to do so.[45]

One key task given to the church surveyors was the evaluation of the abilities and conformability of the various ministers of the nation's parishes. Elrington suggested that the nuances of the descriptions applied to each minister were intended to be meaningful, but the repetitive nature of many answers seems more formulaic than nuanced.[46] It is certainly interesting to note, for instance, that the Lancashire surveyors could regard both John Pollet of Milnrow and John Harrison of Ashton-under-Lyne as 'orthodox' ministers, Harrison being a strict Presbyterian while Pollet had been accused of malignancy and a scandalous lifestyle. The curate of Newton-in-Makerfield was described as a godly preaching minister despite having been ejected three years earlier.[47] The jurors of Burcombe (Wiltshire) only noted blandly that their minister Samuel Maniston preached twice each Sunday, although he had been accused six years earlier of kissing girls and offering to be 'unchaste' with them.[48] Nevertheless, jurors could also be scathing of their minister's abilities. In Wiltshire, where the jurors usually made bland statements, they dismissed the curate of Maddington as 'no fitt man for the ministerye', and Roger Flower of Castle Combe as one who 'maketh use of other mens workes by reading them in the pullpit'. At Buckland (Dorset) the congregation bemoaned the 'slender guiftes in preachinge' of the vicar, observing that 'ther cannot be constant preaching of such that hath not any books especially a bible, such preaching is morr prating'. They complained that he neither catechized the young nor visited the sick, and that he employed a curate who 'liveth a very disorderly & debased course of life'. The situation was so poor that many parishioners resorted to other churches.[49]

Elsewhere it was apparently the manner of an incumbent's appointment into a parish which caused dissatisfaction. The congregation of East Smithfield (Middlesex) complained that their minister had been appointed by the Committee of Plundered Ministers 'not only without the knowledge or consent of one hundredth part of the inhabitants, but without their

---

[45] TNA, C 94/1, fo. 28; C 94/4, fo. 52.

[46] C. R. Elrington, 'The survey of Church livings in Gloucestershire, 1650', *Transactions of the Bristol and Gloucestershire Archaeological Society*, lxxxiii (1964), 87.

[47] TNA, C 94/1, fos. 40r–40v, 45; *Minutes of the Bury Presbyterian Classis, 1647–57*, ed. W.A. Shaw (Manchester: Chetham Soc. new sers., 36, 1896), pp. 48–50, 53–61; *WR*, pp. 228–9.

[48] TNA, C 93/4, fo. 45; BL Add 22084, fo. 138; *WR*, p. 377. I am grateful to Fiona McCall for this reference.

[49] TNA, C 94/2, fo. 201; C 94/3, fos. 45, 50.

approbation … by which means the people are not only deprived of Christian fellowship, but of sacramental communion, contrary both to the law of God and this present Commonwealth'. The criticisms of the parishioners of Long Crichel (Dorset) were particularly severe both on their minister and the parliamentary administrators, lambasting their minister as 'one of those that runs: that [he] was never sent by Christ but by the Committee: For wee conceve that Christ never sends forth a messinger without a message to deliver'. In Lancashire, the criticism of the rector of Middleton by his parishioners was so strong that the county's commissioners felt compelled to send separate certification of his conformability to the Committee of Plundered Ministers.[50]

In passing judgement upon the clergy, the surveyors were considering political as well as religious inclinations. Clerics in Lancashire, Middlesex and Wiltshire refused to observe the official days of fasts and thanksgiving.[51] The rector of Sapperton (Gloucestershire) had been ejected from the benefice for his disaffection to parliament but continued to receive its profits, while the vicar of Lower Swell was 'a man disaffected' who officiated 'by intrusion without authority'. The rector of Stour Provost (Dorset) was accused of employing disaffected ministers to serve the cure in his place. In Lancashire, the curate of Cartmel Fell was dismissed as 'an old malignant', the curate of Burtonwood 'constantly [made] marriages contrary to the directions and rules appoynted by order of parliament', and the curate of Blackley had railed against the republic's Engagement oath. In Wiltshire, ministers at Alton Priors and Boscombe still used the Book of Common Prayer.[52] We should not assume that accusations against ministers were always disinterested, however. Obediah Wills, the rector of the neighbouring parish of Alton Barnes, was accused of informing against the minister at Alton Priors because he hoped to have the two parishes united, a recommendation made by the Wiltshire jurors in 1650 and 1656.[53]

The surveys underlined just how unequally the resources of the Church were distributed. Population growth and rising prices meant that the rectors of many of Lancashire's large parishes enjoyed an income at least equal to

[50] TNA, C 94/1, fos. 40v–41v; C 94/2, fo. 95; C 94/3, fo. 8; SP 46/95, fo. 254.

[51] TNA, C 94/1, fos. 38, 40, 42, 45, 46v–47v, 50, 52v, 56; C 94/3, fos 7v–8; LPL, COMM. XIIa/14, fos. 336–340.

[52] TNA, C 94/1, fos. 29, 31, 38, 46, 62; C 94/2, fo. 47; C 94/4, fo. 52; LPL, COMM. XIIa/14, fos. 336–340. Rather than deny the charge, John Gregson, the minster at Alton Priors, is supposed to have told the Wiltshire commissioners that 'it could not be called Common Prayer when, as he thought, he alone of Wiltshire ministers then read it'; WR, p. 373.

[53] WMS, C8.159v. I am grateful to Fiona McCall for this reference; TNA, C 93/3, fo. 43; C 93/4, fo. 52.

the regime's target. Seventeen of twenty-four rectors earned £100 a year or more, and the average value of a Lancashire rectory was almost £200, although this was inflated by very wealthy benefices such as Winwick, worth £660 a year. In Middlesex, rectors of suburban parishes could benefit from the inflated land values. St Clement Danes was worth £300 a year, and the new parish of Covent Garden £250. However, although the average value of the county's rectories was £113 a year, only nine of Middlesex's twenty-two rectories were worth at least £100. In other counties, the small size and population of many parishes reduced the value of rectories. The average income of Gloucestershire's 128 rectors was £79, and only thirty-two could expect at least £100; in Dorset 152 rectors enjoyed an average income of £77, of whom forty-three received at least £100. By contrast, forty-four parsonages in Gloucestershire and fifty-six in Dorset were worth £50 or less; the Dorset rectory of Castleton was valued at just £6 a year. In Norfolk, where returns were made for approximately one-third of the county's parishes, the 160 rectories surveyed were worth an average of only £48; only nine were worth at least £100, and forty-eight were worth less than £50 a year.

Many rectories were impropriated, their tithes diverted from the incumbent of the parish into the hands of laymen. Where the surveys recorded the value of impropriations, in Lancashire twenty-four out of thirty-one impropriated rectories were worth £100 or more, in Dorset eighteen out of thirty-one, and in Middlesex twenty-six out of forty.[54] Where the vicars of these parishes had extensive glebe, valuable small tithes or a share of the rectorial tithes, they had also benefitted from rising values, but where the vicars received only a stipend or customary rents, these were often fixed at ancient values, depreciating in real terms over time. Across all six counties only twenty-one vicars had an annual income of at least £100, while the livings of forty-three vicars were worth no more than £10.[55]

Some of the most egregious examples of the poverty of vicars were to be found in parishes with valuable impropriations. In Middlesex, where the inhabitants of East Smithfield complained that their tithes had been increased by four or even eight times their ancient value by the impropriator, to a total of £500, their vicar at St Botolph without Aldgate was endowed with just £5 or £6 a year. Unsurprisingly, the living was vacant.[56] The

[54] Although 73 Dorset rectories surveyed in 1650 were impropriated, their values were only recorded in 31 instances. In Middlesex, values were given for 40 of the 50 impropriations, and in Gloucestershire the values of only 3 of 123 impropriations were recorded.

[55] £100 or more:- Dorset: 6; Gloucestershire: 1; Lancashire: 2; Middlesex: 4; Norfolk: 0; Wiltshire: 8. £10 or less:- Dorset: 7; Gloucestershire: 12; Lancashire: 7; Middlesex: 4; Norfolk: 7; Wiltshire: 10.

[56] TNA, C 94/3, fo. 8.

vicarage of Cartmel was one of three Lancashire vicarages with no fixed income, even though its impropriated rectory was worth £350.[57] Worse still were the circumstances of curates of chapels of ease, many of whom relied upon nothing more than voluntary contributions by the congregation. In Lancashire only eight of 127 chaplains could count upon a certain income of £20 or more, and forty-five chapels had no endowment at all. Small wonder then that forty of Lancashire's chapels, and another four of its poorest vicarages, were vacant in 1650.[58] Seventeen of Dorset's forty-three chapels had no fixed income, and twenty were without a minister; fifteen of Gloucestershire's thirty-six chapels were unendowed, and twenty-four were vacant.

Although the authorities had spent the previous decade trying to eradicate pluralism, it was an obvious solution where benefices were of low value. In Norfolk, where so many parishes were of small size and little value, at least fifty of the 259 parishes surveyed were held in plurality with near-adjacent neighbours. Through this informal unification the average income for these twenty-five ministers was raised to £72, although the results were still uneven. The wealthy livings of North and West Lynn when combined were worth £125, five times as much as the combined total of Little Bittering and Longhorn. The poorest living in Dorset was Wareham St Mary's, worth just £2 10s. Its vicar combined the benefice with Holy Trinity and St Martin's in the same town, to make a total income of £118 (including an augmentation of £30), from which he employed a team of assistants to help him manage the spiritual needs of the town and its neighbourhood.

In order to address these structural problems, the surveyors were to consider how to redraw the parochial structure to meet contemporary needs. They were to recommend where to unite or divide parishes, to transfer areas from one parish to another, or to establish new parishes and build new churches. Across the country, changes were recommended to rationalize parochial boundaries, with individual farms or entire hamlets being moved to neighbouring parishes. No doubt these recommendations reflected existing practice, with the intention that those who already resorted to a more convenient church than their own should also contribute towards the maintenance of that building. Unsurprisingly, in Lancashire the jurors often identified the size of the parish and the distance of many parishioners from any place of worship as a problem, and they seem to have intended that, where possible, no congregation should be further than three miles from its parish church. In other parts of the country, the concern seems to

[57] The others were Hawkshead and Lytham: TNA, C 94/1, fos. 62, 64.

[58] I differ with Fishwick, who noted only 38 vacancies: *Lancashire Church Surveys*, pp. xx–xxv.

have been to ensure that parishioners did not have to travel further than a mile to worship.

Many communities emphasized the size of their population to resist their incorporation with their neighbours or to reinforce their demands for independence. Although the chapel of Salford was less than a quarter of a mile from its mother church at Manchester, yet it had 'a competencye of inhabitants and communicants there within itselffe'.[59] In Middlesex, the suburban communities closest to the capital struggled with swollen populations. The inhabitants of the Middlesex portions of the London parishes of St Andrew's Holborn, St Botolph Aldgate, St Dunstan in the West, St Giles Cripplegate and St Sepulchre complained that their parish churches could not accommodate them, as did the congregation at Stepney. The Middlesex parishioners of St Sepulchre had also been excluded from the vestry. The populous market town of Uxbridge was left unsupplied, the endowment belonging to its chapel too small to attract a settled minister, but the parish church at Hillingdon was too small to contain the whole 'multitude of people'. A similar situation was only averted at Brentford, a chapel of Hanwell, for so long as a generous augmentation from the Committee for Plundered Ministers was continued.[60] Yet it was not only urban communities which had outgrown the cramped confines of their parish churches. The population of fourteen Lancashire chapelries, including three in the parish of Blackburn and eight in the parish of Whalley, comprised 200 families or more, more than many parishes elsewhere in the country.[61] At the opposite end of the scale were the decayed parishes with tiny populations, whose resources were eyed hungrily by neighbouring congregations. Compton Greenfield (Gloucestershire) comprised only six families but had tithes and glebe worth £30, while Winterborne Farringdon (Dorset) was occupied by just three families and no longer had a church but its tithes amounted to £40, both tempting acquisitions for neighbouring parishes.[62]

Where parish boundaries did not follow topographical barriers, communities might be prevented from attending their church by poor weather and dangerous conditions. In Lancashire, the inhabitants of Tarleton and Hesketh-with-Becconsale could only travel to their parish church at Croston by boat, but even this was impossible during the winter

[59] TNA, C 94/1, fos. 37r–37v.

[60] TNA, C 94/3, fos. 1, 7–8, 10.

[61] The other three were Bispham (Poulton-le-Fylde), Broughton (Preston) and Lund (Kirkham): TNA, C 94/1, fos. 63–65.

[62] TNA, C 94/1, fo. 28v; C 94/2, fo. 45.

'by reason of the greate inundacon of the said waters there'. The congregation at Arkholme could not pass the river Lune to their parish church of Melling 'without danger of life', while those living near Overton chapel were 'so surrounded by the flowing sea twice in twenty foure howers that they cannot pass to their parish church' at Lancaster. In Dorset, West Orchard was separated from its mother church at Great Fontmel for much of the winter, and the people of Stanton St Gabriel's hoped to be made a separate parish because 'the way ioyneinge to the sea is exposed to all violence of winde & weather insoemuch as many amongst us can very seldome repaire to any other church especially in the winter tyme'. The congregation at Tytherton Lucas (Wiltshire) complained that the minister often could not reach their chapel because he was 'prevented by the rysing of the waters many times so hapning that he cannot come thither for three weekes together'.[63] Elsewhere, congregations suffered from the depredations of the recent conflict. At Weymouth, most of the town's chapel was destroyed during a siege, and what remained was still in use as a sentry post. Its repair would be costly, complained the townsmen, who emphasized the potential dangers if the population of a garrison and port town were forced instead to travel far from home to worship. Another Dorset chapel, Hamworthy, had been demolished during the siege of Poole. However, no mention was made by the Wiltshire jurors of the church at Westport, demolished during the siege of Malmesbury.[64]

The recommendations of the Lancashire jurors would have divided the county's sixty-two parishes into at least 185 parishes. The huge parish of Whalley was to be divided into sixteen, while Blackburn would be separated into eight. The scheme would have necessitated the erection of twenty-eight new churches and chapels, and the relocation of some existing buildings. The jurors ordered the building of new churches at Litherland and Ince Blundell, 'the want of such churches being the cause of loytering and much ignorance and poperie'. The Ulverston chapels of Blawith and Lowick were to be united into a single new parish, and the two chapels replaced with a new church 'in an indifferent place'. The churches of Halton and Burtonwood were to be moved to the centre of their respective parishes to better serve their congregations. The inhabitants of Overton and Middleton were prepared to build a new church in the latter town at their own expense if Overton chapel were made into a parish. The ruined ancient chapels at Garston and Lathom were also to be rebuilt and made parish churches. Nevertheless, although the chapel of Tatham Fell stood 'quite

---

[63] TNA, C 94/1, fos. 57, 60–61; C 94/2, fos. 23, 168; C 94/4, fo. 50.
[64] TNA, C 94/2, fos. 26, 113; C 94/4, fo. 50; *VCH Wilts.* xiv. 238.

beyond any inhabitant of the said parish very inconveniently', no remedy was suggested.[65]

Unsurprisingly, in a county as well endowed with parishes as Norfolk the only recommendations were for their unification. The jurors recommended that 136 parishes, more than half those surveyed between 1655 and 1657, should be united to create sixty-four parishes, reducing the number of parishes by twenty-eight per cent, from 259 to 187. Had this been replicated across the whole county, it would have reduced Norfolk's 734 parishes to a new total of 528. Of the twenty-five parishes already informally united in the person of the incumbent, fourteen were to be formally united, although Little Bittering and Longham (which shared a minister) were to be united to two other parishes instead. In most cases the reasoning for the proposed unions was the proximity of the churches, many of which were less than a mile apart. The Norfolk commissioners expressed surprise, however, that the jurors had not seen fit to unite Repham and Whitwell parishes, the churches of which were 'as fit for union as any other in the hundred because the meeting houses stand both in one yard'.[66] Nevertheless, a greater distance need not prevent unification with neighbours. Although Horsey was two miles from any other church, the poverty of the vicarage, worth just £6, necessitated its union with Waxham and Pauling. The church at Brunstead was said to be 'fallen downe & ... very little', despite which the parishioners were described as 'being so averse to union' with their neighbours at Ingham that the jurors instead recommended the union of the latter with Sutton and Stalham.[67]

Elsewhere, the picture was more mixed. The jurors recommended the union of eighteen Dorset and thirty-two Gloucestershire parishes, creating nine and fifteen parishes, respectively. They also recommended the division of seventeen Dorset parishes into thirty-five, and of ten Gloucestershire parishes into twenty-one. Further changes were recommended to the boundaries of thirteen Dorset parishes and sixteen Gloucestershire parishes. The two surveys of Wiltshire, together comprising more than three-quarters of the county's 294 parishes, returned recommendations that forty-nine parishes be united into twenty-three, fourteen parishes be divided into thirty-three, and changes be made to the boundaries of seventy-three parishes. In Middlesex, four parishes were to be united into two, eleven parishes (including four London parishes) were to be divided into twenty-four, and boundary changes were made to four more.

[65] TNA, C 94/1, fos. 46, 49v, 52, 54v, 60–61, 63, 65.
[66] LPL, COMM. XIIa/20, fo. 8v.
[67] TNA, C 94/3, fo. 16.

In Gloucestershire, the large parish of Henbury was to gain the neighbouring small parish of Compton Greenfield, and lose its chapels at Aust and Northwick, which together would form a single new parish. Three parishes bordering Bristol – Westbury-on-Trym, Horfield and Clifton – were to be united into a single parish, although Westbury's detached chapel at Shirehampton was also to be separated. The extra-parochial district of Eyford, occupied by just two families, was united to Upper Slaughter, while the nine families of Shipton Sollars were to unite with Shipton Oliffe. No extra provision was made for the populous towns of Tetbury, Cirencester and Tewkesbury, however, despite each having only a single parish church serving respectively 500, 700 and 1,000 families.[68]

In suburban Middlesex, the parishioners of St Andrew Holborn recalled the former deliberations by the Long parliament over the division of their parish, and they were keen to accomplish the project. The parishioners of St Giles Cripplegate hoped to adapt the disused Fortune playhouse to public worship until a more appropriate venue could be erected. New churches were demanded at Smithfield (St Sepulchre) and East Smithfield (St Botolph Aldgate). The large parish of Stepney was to be divided into four, Wapping was separated from Whitechapel, and the large market towns of Brentford, Hammersmith and Uxbridge were made distinct parishes. Meanwhile, the poorly endowed parishes of Paddington and Marylebone were to be united, with the demolition of both ancient churches and the erection of a new church at Lisson Green.[69]

The surveys of the 1650s demonstrated the pressing need for parochial reform. Many benefices were left vacant for want of resources, while numerous parishes were too large or populous to meet the needs of their inhabitants. Despite this, progress towards parochial reform was limited by the end of the decade. The Committee for Plundered Ministers was focused solely upon the augmentation of existing livings, and the dissolution of the Rump in 1653 brought its work to a close without it having made any changes to the parochial system. This left the Trustees for the Maintenance of Ministers as the only body overseeing the administration of the Church, but they too were initially preoccupied with augmentations. By this time many of the augmentations granted in the previous decade had failed, either through overestimation of the available revenues or their loss through the lifting of sequestrations. Parochial reform represented the means to make a more permanent settlement. Early in 1655 the trustees issued commissioners for new surveys to be made, including some counties already surveyed

[68] TNA, C 94/1, fos. 28v–29, 30.
[69] TNA, C 94/3, fos. 1, 7–8, 10–2.

five years earlier, and the first orders for the union or division of parishes followed later in 1655.[70]

Overall, the achievements of the trustees were moderate. Where reforms had the support of local inhabitants, a reorganization of local benefices could be achieved quickly. In Norfolk, fifty-one parishes were united to create twenty-three parishes, with few complications. In Middlesex, although petitions were received for the division of St Andrew's Holborn, St Pancras, Staines and Stepney, the trustees accomplished nothing.[71] In Lancashire, despite the apparently egregious need for reform of the parochial structure, the only changes achieved by May 1658 were the establishment of Kirkby and Liverpool as new parishes. Further orders that year would have divided the eight parishes of Blackburn, Bury, Croston, Kirkby Ireleth, Kirkham, Middleton, Prestwick and Rochdale into thirty-seven parishes, but came too late to be completed before the Restoration.[72] In Gloucestershire, ten parishes were combined into five and three parishes were divided into six, a net reduction of two parishes, and in Dorset the division of one parish and the union of two others left the county with the same number of parishes.[73] In Wiltshire the orders of the trustees would have produced a net reduction of just four parishes. Eleven parishes were united with neighbours to form five parishes. Chapels at Brokenborough and Charlton were made independent, the large market town of Calne was united with Blackland but its chapel at Berwick Bassett was made a parish church, and the extra-parochial Savernake forest, 'likelie to increase with inhabitants', was to become a parish with a new church.[74] Presumably, positive action by the trustees was a response to local initiative, as with augmentations.[75] With resources dwindling, petitions for an augmentation might be greeted instead with a proposal for the unification of the benefice with a vacant neighbour, as was found by the London parishes of St Martin's Ironmonger Lane and of St Olave Silver Street.[76]

---

[70] LPL, COMM. XIIc/1, fos. 1–8; COMM. XIIc/2.

[71] LPL, COMM. XIIc/2, fos. 17, 23, 28, 41, 55, 85, 170, 186, 192, 195, 244, 345–346.

[72] LPL, COMM. XIIc/2, fos. 458, 464–468, 494–499, 501–505, 550–553, 569–573.

[73] LPL, COMM. XIIc/2, fos. 1–2, 39–40, 59, 115, 174, 406–407, 476, 500; COMM. XIIc/3, fos. 12–16, 29–31, 74–8, 251–254.

[74] LPL, COMM. XIIc/2, fos. 126–128, 333; COMM. XIIc/3, fos. 45–51, 65–67, 70–72, 123–125, 131–133, 220–221.

[75] Craven, 'Ministers of State', 61.

[76] LPL, COMM. XIIc/2, fos. 391, 562.

Where opposition to reorganization was encountered, the trustees encouraged the two sides 'to indeavour an accomodation among themselves if it may bee'. Hearings concerning the union of All Hallow's Honey Lane and St Mary le Bow in London were suspended so that the two parishes 'may make an amicable & neighbourly agreement in this matter between themselves'. Nevertheless, resistance or delay by influential opponents to proposed reforms was often enough to prevent their success. Patrons prevented unions with neighbours at South Pickenham and at Pattesley in Norfolk, at the latter by promising voluntarily to raise the value of the living to £100. Parishioners at Shaftesbury St Rumbold's similarly promised to increase the stipend to £100 if it remained separate.[77] The opposition of the incumbent of Stepney was sufficient to block the separation of Poplar and Blackwall from his parish in 1656, and the division of Shadwell from Stepney was frustrated two years later when objections were raised to defects in the surveys. Defective surveys were also obstructive at Marlborough and Cerne Abbas.[78] The trustees were so frustrated by objections to several Lancashire surveys that they ordered those opposed to their proposals to pay for new surveys and to contribute towards the costs of the other side.[79] The proponents of parochial reform were not infallible, however; the proposed union of Hill Deverill and Brixton Deverill in Wiltshire was dismissed because its promoters failed to appear before the trustees to argue the case.[80]

In large cities overloaded with too many poor parishes, the corporations were often empowered to undertake parochial reform directly. Committees of the House of Commons were established in 1645 to consider the reorganization of the parishes of Bristol and Gloucester, but it was not until 1648 that an ordinance was passed for Gloucester. This condensed the city's ten parishes into four and endowed the new parishes with estates formerly belonging to the cathedral chapter.[81] Of the six disused churches, one had been demolished during the Civil War, four were subsequently demolished or converted into public buildings, and a school was established in the sixth.[82] The Rump returned to the question of urban parishes while it was debating the bill for the maintenance of ministers in 1650. Prompted by a

---

[77] LPL, COMM. XIIc/2, fos. 93, 108–11, 546–547, 560.

[78] LPL, COMM. XIIc/2, fos. 55, 346, 350–351, 366, 483, 525–526.

[79] LPL, COMM. XIIc/2, fos. 571–572.

[80] LPL, COMM. XIIc/2, fo. 424.

[81] *CJ*, iv. 381, 398; *LJ*, viii. 14–15; x. 173–5.

[82] Gloucestershire Archives, GBR/B3/2, pp. 459, 583, 628, 677, 700, 753, 815, 862–2; *VCH Glos.* iv. 100–1, 292–311.

petition of Norwich corporation in December 1649, a bill for uniting that city's parishes was introduced in February 1650, when the Bristol bill was also resurrected. Passed in April 1650, it differed from the earlier Gloucester Act by commissioning aldermen and citizens to survey and consolidate the city's parishes themselves.[83] An act for Coventry was passed in March 1651, and another for Exeter in June 1657 led to the closure of all but four of the city's churches, but the Norwich bill came to nothing despite the continued pressure of the corporation until 1656.[84]

Meanwhile, although the Bristol commissioners had used their powers to appoint ministers, they had done nothing else.[85] Perhaps stirred into action by the arrival late in 1656 of John Desborough, Major-General for the south-west, a new act was secured in 1657, appointing commissioners who recommended the reduction of Bristol's seventeen parishes into twelve. A new rate introduced by the act would have raised the average value of the livings to £76, although the actual sums received by each minister would range between £20 and £120. The new rates proved too unpopular, however, and in 1659 the corporation instead ordered augmentations of £20 each be paid to four ministers from the city's funds.[86]

The ambitious objective of successive regimes to reorganize the Church to create a secure, better-endowed clergy was only partially achieved. Nowhere did the Trustees for the Maintenance of Ministers come close to completing the reforms proposed in the surveys of the 1650s. Even where they did make changes, they frequently fell short of the aim of raising the value of benefices to at least £100. Only in five of the forty-eight cases where the estimated value of a new benefice was recorded did it match or exceed this sum, while eight were still worth less than £50. Even after unification, the new benefice of Biddestone St Nicholas, Biddestone St Peter and Slaughterford in Wiltshire was only worth £23 a year, and that of Matson and Upton St Leonard in Gloucestershire just £36.[87] Nevertheless, in Gloucestershire, Lancashire, Norfolk and Wiltshire, the average annual value of the new parishes was

---

[83] *CJ*, vi. 354, 370, 443, 458, 551; *CJ*, vii. 474, 488, 513, 553; BL, Thomason, E 1060 (92); Coventry Archives, BA/H/17/F8/3/5; W. Cotton and H. Woollcombe, *Gleanings from the Municipal and Cathedral Records Relative to the History of the City of Exeter* (Exeter, 1877), p. 169.

[84] J. T. Evans, *17th Century Norwich: Politics, Religion, and Government 1620–90* (Oxford, 1979), pp. 196–7.

[85] *The Records of a Church of Christ in Bristol, 1640–1687*, ed. R. Hayden (Bristol Record Soc., 27, Bristol, 1974), p. 103.

[86] *CJ*, vii. 475, 477, 516, 543, 576–7; *A&O*, i. civ; BA, M/BCC/CCP/1/5, pp. 122, 125, 135, 142–4, 150, 168, 182; C. Durston, *Cromwell's Major Generals* (Manchester, 2001), pp. 163–4.

[87] LPL, COMM. XIIc/3, fos. 131–133; COMM. XIIc/3, fos. 14–16.

between £65 and £69. This compared favourably with the values of ancient benefices recorded in the church surveys: slightly lower than the Wiltshire average of £73, slightly higher than the Gloucestershire average of £59, and much higher than the Norfolk average of £40. In Lancashire, the average value of a parish church had been £110 in 1650, but more significantly the average value of their chapels had been just £6, less than a tenth of the value of the new parishes created from them. In Wiltshire, the average income of the county's chaplains amounted to £18 a year, almost a quarter of the anticipated value of the new benefices.

The slow progress of the trustees highlights the difficulties of reforming the Church during the 1650s. Each new change of regime or innovation in government cast doubt upon the legitimacy of the decisions of predecessors. One of the first orders of the trustees in 1655 reiterated a command previously made in 1646, to divide Motcombe from Gillingham in Dorset.[88] As was often the case during the 1650s, reforms were frequently a response not to the greatest need but to the loudest clamour of local protagonists. Where there was no opposition to, or indeed where there was active support for, reform, the trustees could effect changes with relative speed, to the satisfaction and benefit of those concerned. However, as had been the case long before the 1650s and would remain so long afterwards, vested interests often prevented reform, no matter how urgent the apparent need. Patrons, impropriators and incumbents represented a potent impediment to the reorganization of the Church, careful to protect their property and rights, but the opposition of parishioners, unwilling to lose their independence or unable to fund the building work entailed by many of the proposals, was also instrumental. While successive parliamentary regimes were unwilling or unable to contemplate more fundamental reform of the property of the Church, ambitious aims to reorganize the Church's medieval structure and provide a better-endowed preaching ministry were doomed to failure.

---

[88] LPL, COMM. XIIc/2, fos. 1–2.

3. The ecclesiastical patronage of Oliver Cromwell, c.1654–60[1]

Rebecca Warren

Between 1653 and 1658, Oliver Cromwell was the single most powerful ecclesiastical patron in the history of the post-Reformation English Church. When he became Lord Protector in late 1653, all the patronage that had previously been exercised by the recently abolished crown and the episcopalian administration of the Church – making up perhaps forty per cent of the livings in England and Wales – devolved directly into his hands, along with that of numerous other livings that were under sequestration.[2] And yet, despite the vast extent of this ecclesiastical portfolio and his many other duties as head of state, Cromwell chose not to delegate his ecclesiastical patronage to others, but to exercise it personally up until his death in 1658. Evidence of the scale and nature of his patronage has, hitherto, been buried within the records of clerical appointments that were maintained during the Protectorate but, combined with contemporary comment, it reveals that he not only appointed seven times more clergy than the next most active patron, but also that he presented ministers to benefices in every county of England and Wales.[3] Moreover, the breadth of the churchmanship of those clergy whom he chose demonstrates that he adopted a pragmatic approach to recruitment, which outweighed his personal leanings towards independency. The transformation of Britain into a godly state has long

---

[1] Papers on this subject were given at the University of Portsmouth in 2016 and the University of Oxford in 2017. I am grateful to all those who discussed it with me on both occasions. Cromwell's ecclesiastical patronage is discussed in R. Warren, '"A knowing ministry": the reform of the Church under Oliver Cromwell, c.1653–1660' (unpublished University of Kent PhD thesis, 2017) [later: Warren] and in my *The Interregnum Church in England and Wales, 1649–1660*, currently under preparation.

[2] For estimates of crown and Church patronage, see R. G. Usher, *The Reconstruction of the English Church* (London, 1910), i. 110–11; D. R. Hirschberg, 'The government and church patronage in England, 1660–1760', *Journal of British Studies*, xx (1980), 111–12.

[3] The Trustees for the Maintenance of the Preaching Ministry were the next most active patron, presenting roughly 165 ministers and corroborating the presentations of a further twelve.

R. Warren, 'The ecclesiastical patronage of Oliver Cromwell, c.1654–60', in *Church and people in interregnum Britain*, ed. F. McCall (London, 2021), pp. 65–83. License: CC BY-NC-ND.

been recognised as one of Cromwell's most cherished objectives but, thus far, the extent of his personal input into this process has been more difficult to quantify. Detailed attention has thus focused more upon his political activities than his reforms to the Church. The evidence presented here seeks to rebalance this focus to reflect the importance that Cromwell himself gave to the consistent and considered exercise of his ecclesiastical patronage, placing it at the very heart of his role as Lord Protector.

Ecclesiastical patronage during the revolution has received little scholarly attention.[4] In part, this reflects the turmoil and confusion of the 1640s and 1650s, decades which experienced unprecedented levels of clerical turnover and substantial disruption to ecclesiastical and legal record-keeping. To this social and administrative turmoil must be added the frequent sales or temporary gifts of advowsons and rights of presentation that took place throughout the early modern period, a practice which, as Rosemary O'Day has noted, 'completely invalidates any estimates of lay and ecclesiastical patronage based on the ownership of advowsons'.[5] These factors have coalesced to create a perfect storm of research challenges and have hitherto prevented detailed scrutiny of Cromwell's personal role as a patron.[6] It is, nevertheless, possible to build a relatively robust picture of his activities from the registers of the Commissioners for the Approbation of Public Preachers,

[4] The subject has received only limited attention across the wider early modern period. The most detailed coverage is found in: R. O'Day, 'Ecclesiastical patronage: who controlled the Church?', in *Church and Society in England: Henry VIII to James I*, ed. F. Heal and R. O'Day (Basingstoke, 1977), pp. 137–55; R. O'Day, 'The law of ecclesiastical patronage in early modern England', *Journal of Ecclesiastical History*, xxvi (1975), 247–60; D. J. Lamburn, 'The influence of the laity in appointments of clergy in the late sixteenth and early seventeenth century', in *Patronage and Recruitment in the Tudor and Early Stuart Church*, ed. C. Cross (York, 1996), pp. 95–119; C. Hill, *Economic Problems of the Church from Archbishop Whitgift to the Long Parliament* (London, 1971), pp. 50–73. See also F. Heal and C. Holmes, *The Gentry in England and Wales: 1500–1700* (Basingstoke, 1994), pp. 322–33. For post-1660 patronage, see Hirschberg, 'Church patronage', 109–39. Studies of individual patrons are largely restricted to holders of major political or Church offices: R. O'Day, 'The ecclesiastical patronage of the Lord Keeper, 1558–1642', *Transactions of the Royal Historical Society*, xxiii (1973), 89–109; K. Fincham, 'William Laud and the exercise of Caroline ecclesiastical patronage', *JEH*, li (2000), 69–93.

[5] R. O'Day, 'Who controlled the Church', p. 153. The best analysis of the legislation that affected patronage in the revolution remains W. Shaw, *A History of the English Church during the Civil Wars and under the Commonwealth, 1640–1660* (2 vols, London, 1900), ii. pp. 263–79. Otherwise scholars must turn to studies of particular patrons or localities, such as Alice MacCampbell's investigation of London patronage: A. MacCampbell, 'Incumbents and patronage in London, 1640–1660', *Journal of Church and State*, xxv (1983), 299–321.

[6] Exceptions are J. Collins, 'The Church settlement of Oliver Cromwell', *History*, lxxxvii (2002), 18–40, at p. 31; J. Murphy, 'Oliver Cromwell's Church: state and clergy during the Protectorate' (unpublished University of Wisconsin-Madison PhD thesis, 1997), pp. 84–117.

or 'Triers'.[7] The Triers were established early in 1654 to interview all aspiring clergymen, to ensure that they met acceptable standards of godliness and preaching ability. The names of those ministers whom they approved were entered into a series of registers, along with their intended livings and the names of their patrons. The extent and pattern of Cromwell's patronage is thus embedded within these registers, and from them it is possible to reconstruct something of his personal input into the construction of a preaching ministry after 1654.

Cromwell exercised his patronage formally from the earliest days of his Protectorate but, like other parliamentary grandees, he began informally promoting ministers before his assumption of power.[8] In November 1653 he had written to Henry Weston, the patron of Speldhurst in Kent, acknowledging his own 'presumption in moving for, and your civility in granting the Advowson of Speldhurst to one Mr. Draper'.[9] Around the same time, he had sought to persuade Nicholas Bernard, one of his own chaplains, to reject a presentation offered to him by the royalist peer, John Egerton, Second Earl of Bridgewater, for the living at Whitchurch in Shropshire. Writing to Bridgewater after he became Protector, however, he acknowledged the earl's superior right of presentation to the benefice, adding that he would accept Bridgewater's candidate, so long as 'you should intend the reall good of the people in your choyce'. The only condition, he noted, was that Bernard must gain the approval of the newly established Triers in Whitehall.[10] In neither case did Cromwell claim legal authority for his intervention, a fact he openly acknowledged. Nevertheless, his position of power gave his actions a weight that brought them dangerously close to constituting state interference in private patronage.

The bulk of Cromwell's patronage when he became Protector in late 1653 derived from three sources: the livings formerly controlled by the crown and the episcopalian administration of the Church devolved to him via a complex series of transfers between government committees and the Commissioners of the Great Seal that took place during the years of the Commonwealth. The justification for these transfers seems to have derived from the Instrument of Government. Clause III devolved 'writs, processes,

[7] LPL, COMM. III/3–7.

[8] These included Sir William Brereton in Cheshire and the Earl of Manchester in East Anglia. Cromwell's first formal presentation in the registers was approved in late April 1654: LPL, COMM. III/3, *lib.1*, fo. 3.

[9] W. C. Abbott, *The Writings and Speeches of Oliver Cromwell* (4 vols, Cambridge, Mass., 1945), iii. 120–1.

[10] Huntingdon Library, MS. Ellesmere 8044 [reproduced by kind permission of the Duke of Sutherland].

commissions, patents, grants, and other things' from the Keepers of the Liberty of England (the title that had itself replaced 'Commissioners of the Great Seal') to the Lord Protector.[11] Clause XXXI vested delinquents' lands in the Protector's hands.[12] Neither clause referred to ecclesiastical patronage specifically but it may have been deemed that they offered sufficient legislative backing to allow the pragmatic reassignment of these rights.[13]

Cromwell also presented ministers to a third, loosely defined cohort of livings, where either the minister or the patron had been sequestrated or ejected as a result of allegations of political, doctrinal or behavioural delinquency.[14] Nearly three-quarters of such livings noted in the registers were subsequently filled by ministers chosen by Cromwell, yet his acquisition of these livings had a complex genesis.[15] In some cases, the presentation right must have devolved to him legally through lapse, but in others the justification seems to have been largely pragmatic, his personal input becoming widely regarded, and used, as a means of settling disputed claims.[16]

Overall, the Triers' registers reveal that Cromwell acted as patron in roughly one-third of the approximately 3,500 interviews recorded by the Triers.[17] Since some livings reappeared several times in these registers, this figure equates to nearly forty per cent of the *unique* livings that were entered in the records, and it represents just over ten per cent of all the livings

[11] 'Instrument of Government', in S. R. Gardiner, *Constitutional Documents of the Puritan Revolution* (Oxford, 3rd ed., 1906), p. 406; 'Act of this present Parliament for the Alteration of several Names and Forms heretofore used in Courts, Writs, Grants, Patents', in *A&O*, ii. pp. 1262–3.

[12] Gardiner, *Constitutional Documents*, pp. 414–15.

[13] Shaw, too, struggled to explain the transfer legally: Shaw, *English Church*, ii. 276–8.

[14] Robert Frampton lost his living at Bryngwyn, Monmouthshire, in 1654, when the estates of his patron, the Catholic royalist Marquis of Worcester, were sequestrated. Frampton was not himself delinquent: J. Knight, *Civil War and Restoration in Monmouthshire* (Almeley, 2005), pp. 132–3.

[15] This reflects all those livings noted in the registers as 'sequestrated'; however, the status of livings was not always recorded by the Triers' clerks, so the total number of sequestrated livings that appeared in the registers may have been higher.

[16] The Triers' Ordinance required patrons to present within six months: 'Ordinance for appointing commissioners for approbation of publique preachers', in *A&O*, ii. 857. Legislative backing may have been believed to exist in Clause XXXI of the Instrument of Government but the equation was not straightforward and numerous anomalies can be identified.

[17] This excludes those few livings for which Cromwell corroborated a presentation by a different patron. Although his role was termed both 'patron' and 'nominator', these terms did not always reflect different mechanisms behind his appointments.

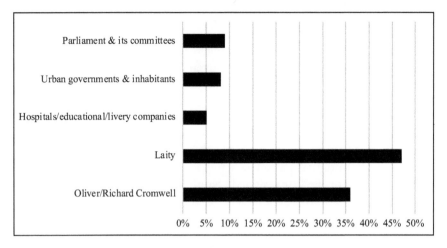

Figure 3.1. Presentations recorded in the Triers' registers by patron type, 1654–60.[a]

> [a] The totals in this chart are approximate and aggregated from a wider range
> of patrons. Note: The final entry in the registers dates from just
> before the return of the Rump parliament in May 1659.

in England and Wales.[18] Yet even this enormous amount of patronage did not reflect the theoretical extent of his dominance. The Triers' registers record only those livings for which they approved a new minister, or where an existing minister had applied for a financial augmentation and been approved; livings that did not fall into either category did not appear in the registers.[19] Had Cromwell lived longer, therefore, more ministers would have changed livings and the registers would have shown more parishes for which he was patron; thus, the extent of his theoretical – or unexercised – patronage must have been even greater. Even so, he presented to far more livings than any other class of patron except for the aggregated class of 'lay patrons', none of whom individually controlled more than twenty benefices.

[18] The total number of parishes for which ministers were required is taken here to be approximately 10,000. This figure is above the widely quoted totals of 8–9,000 recorded in some Jacobean surveys, which have not been securely identified as comprehensive and could not take into account the increasing numbers of chapels-of-ease for which the Cromwellian regime sought ministers: BL, MS. Stowe 570/3, fo. 91; BL, Harleian MS. 280/29, fos. 157–72; BL, Lansdowne MS. 459/1; Warren, Appendix. E.

[19] Moreover, recent analysis suggests that perhaps ten per cent of the changes in minister may not appear in the Triers' registers: Warren, '"A knowing ministry"', p. 152; Welsh livings may have been especially under-recorded; see T. Richards, *Religious Developments in Wales (1654–1662)* (London, 1923), p. 35.

Cromwell used the authority of both his seal manual and the great seal in his patronage but over time he favoured the great seal.[20] This trend was particularly evident in his patronage of sequestrations. In 1654, all his presentations to such livings were given under his seal manual, but by 1658 they were all given under the great seal.[21] This probably reflected the widespread concern about the insecurity of ecclesiastical titles bestowed during the Protectorate; in the eyes of opponents, the perceived illegitimacy of the regime conferred an equal illegitimacy upon presentations made under its authority. Moreover, sequestrated livings were known to be particularly insecure, as the original patron was free to present a new minister if the ejected incumbent died or resigned. Numerous godly ministers who had served sequestrated livings since the 1640s did indeed find themselves suddenly ousted after years of service. Despite the passing of the 'Act for quiet enjoying of Sequestred Parsonages' in 1657, which reinforced the titles of intruded ministers, disputes continued to take place.[22]

In any case, Cromwell's patronage of sequestrations was often temporary. In March 1655, for example, he presented John Bird to Bulmer in Essex, where the original patron, Nicholas Daniell, was under sequestration for recusancy. Nine years before, in 1646, the elderly incumbent John Donnel had died and been replaced by John Chamberlain, presented by Thomas Bayles, who had acquired the right of presentation. Yet when Chamberlain left Bulmer in 1655, it was Cromwell who stepped in to present Bird, presumably on the basis of Daniell's sequestration. When Bird left the living in 1658, however, it was Thomas Bayles who presented his successor, Thomas Bernard; probably Chamberlain had resigned the living or died, an event which returned the patronage to the patron.[23]

Nominating ministers for sequestrated livings was the only mechanism through which Cromwell routinely expropriated private patronage, which otherwise continued to operate unmodified throughout the interregnum, wherever the patron was not judged delinquent. There were a number of other occasions, however, when he became involved in the exercise of

---

[20] Fifty-five per cent of his presentations were under the great seal, forty-five per cent under his seal manual and for five per cent, no seal was recorded.

[21] The great seal was also used in a small number of other presentations, including some from private patrons, for example: LPL, COMM. III/4, fo. 562 (Runwell).

[22] 'Act for the quiet enjoying of sequestered Parsonages and Vicarages by the present Incumbent' (1657), in A&O, ii. 1266–7. See, for example, Edward Fletcher's disputes at Bagenden in 1658: TNA, SP 18/183, fo. 209.

[23] LPL, COMM. III/4, fo. 193; LPL, COMM. III/7, fo. 140; H. Smith, *The Ecclesiastical History of Essex under the Long Parliament and Commonwealth* (Colchester, n.d.), p. 297; *WR*, p. 147. Death or resignation of the sequestrated incumbent returned the patronage to the original patron, if not him/herself under sequestration.

private patronage through his corroboration of presentations. Most of these instances were in response to disputes over titles, indicating that he was aware of the frequent legal challenges to intruded ministers from their ejected predecessors. In 1657 he stepped into the fraught situation at Great Rissington in Gloucestershire, where the royalist patron, Sir Edmund Bray, had already failed to gain the Triers' approval for two ministers whom he had recently presented. Cromwell presented Abraham Drye under his seal manual, an act which antagonized Bray further. Drye's situation must have become so awkward that some months later he petitioned Cromwell for additional support, since he subsequently reappears in the registers with a second presentation from the Protector for Great Rissington, this time given under the great seal.[24]

Cromwell's right to present to Church and crown livings, however, especially using his seal manual, was never universally accepted and even after his death his actions continued to be challenged. In November 1659, Timothy Baldwin petitioned the Commissioners of the Great Seal for the rectory of Llandrillo, Denbighshire, noting,

> Now in regard that some doubt had ben made of grants of this nature made in the tyme of the said lord protector your petitioner humbly desires your lordshipp to give unto your petitioner a grant of the said rectory under the present greate seale.[25]

Moreover, in April 1660, on the eve of the Restoration, Philip Nye, one of the Triers, showed the Commissioners of the Great Seal a legal judgement in support of John Loder's claim to the disputed living of St Bartholomews Exchange in London, to which he had been presented by Cromwell in 1656. The judgement accredited the Protector's seal manual with equal authority in such matters to that of the Great Seal, '... but the Lords Commissioners denied it and said the Protector could not dispose of that, which was their right to bestowe And that Mr Loder's title ... was voyde ...'[26]

Besides demonstrating the uneasiness over Cromwell's use of his seal manual and a preference for the authority of the great seal, the commissioners' denial of his right to present to the living suggests also that the original transfer of ecclesiastical patronage from the commissioners to the Protector had been neither smooth nor, indeed, clear cut.

---

[24] Walker, *Attempt*, p. 174; TNA, SP 29/440, fo. 129; TNA, SP 29/36, fos. 87, 90; LPL, COMM. III/6, fos. 37, 174; TNA, SP 29/36, fo. 90.

[25] BL Add. MS. 36792, fo. 1. Note: the rectory was separate from the vicarage of Llandrillo.

[26] *The Vestry Minute Books of the Parish of St Bartholomew Exchange in the City of London 1567–1676*, ed. E. Freshfield (London, 1890), pp. 73–4. St Bartholomews had been a crown living: Shaw, *English Church*, ii. p. 268.

Cromwell presented ministers in every county of England and Wales. Numerically, most of these were in the south-east, south-west and east of the country but, as a percentage of those settled by the Triers, his input was greatest in London, the north-west and the north-east. Critically, however, the Cromwellian regime did not operate a policy of emptying pulpits to allow the Protector or any other patron to intrude new clergy. Only where ministers were found to be delinquent at a hearing did the County Ejection Commissions remove them from their parishes, and by no means all hearings resulted in ejection.[27] In fact, the total number of ejections during the Protectorate was low, probably only two to three hundred.[28] Thus the geographical occurrences of Cromwell's presentations were essentially random, influenced by the number and location of former crown and Church livings and of sequestrations, and by the number of times individual benefices changed hands. In London, for example, he was a major patron, making thirty-one presentations to twenty-six livings. Only three of these were to sequestrations, but twenty-one of the twenty-six had been in the gift of the crown or Church before the Civil Wars. Elsewhere, however, the proportions were strikingly different. In Essex roughly a quarter of his presentations were to livings where the former incumbent was recorded in the registers as ejected or sequestrated; in Norfolk the proportion was a third, yet in Cumberland none of his presentations were to sequestrations.[29] Thus the distribution of his patronage was highly variable and this defeats attempts at rationalization on geographic grounds.

Cromwell remained an active ecclesiastical patron throughout his Protectorate. Even in the last year of his life, beset by impending financial catastrophe, his own poor health and the death of his favourite daughter, he still made 160 presentations over just eight months, a quarter of all the appointments approved by the Triers in 1658.[30] His greatest input, however, was in 1656, when forty-five per cent of the Triers' approvals were

[27] Local hostility may also have driven some ministers from their livings, but such instances were not at the instigation of the regime.

[28] The total number of ejections throughout the revolution has been variously calculated at between roughly 2,500 and 3,600: I. Green, 'The persecution of "scandalous" and "malignant" parish clergy during the English Civil War', *EHR*, xciv (1979), 507–31, at p. 508; R. Bosher, *The Making of the Restoration Settlement, 1649–1662* (London, 1951), p. 5.

[29] But note: the registers did not always record the sequestration or ejection of an incumbent. Further research suggests that in Essex, for example, the figure may be closer to one-half than one-quarter. Moreover, some sequestrated livings had also been in the gift of the crown or Church, so multiple factors may have accounted for Cromwell's acquisition of some livings.

[30] It is likely, of course, that some of his presentations were made by his close associates at times of personal crisis.

of presentations made by him. This was almost certainly a consequence of the royalist uprisings of 1655, which culminated with Penruddock's rebellion in the south-west of England. The resulting clampdown on known or suspected rebels included new legislation against royalist clergy, which triggered the ejection of a considerable number of ministers from their livings. Moreover, it involved the identification and sequestration of other political delinquents, some of whom were also ecclesiastical patrons.[31] This resulted in an increase in the turnover of livings, for many of which Cromwell nominated a replacement minister. The peak in his patronage months later, in 1656, reflects the time lapse between the political turmoil and the consequent legislation and its effects, followed by the slow process of identifying, presenting and approving suitable clergy.

The sheer extent of Cromwell's ecclesiastical patronage alongside his numerous other duties begs the question of the extent of his personal participation in the process. How closely involved was he in the exercise of his patronage? And what mechanisms underpinned his identification and choice of ministers? There is surprisingly little direct testimony of his role in individual appointments, but it seems very likely that he was heavily reliant upon others to locate suitable ministers on his behalf. Chief among these scouts must have been the loose group of personal chaplains who surrounded him, not only leading churchmen such as John Owen and Thomas Manton, but also lesser-known ministers, among whom were Nicholas Bernard and William Hooke. Representing a range of denominational sympathies, these men had connections across the spectrum of godly practice and, crucially, within the universities.[32] It is probable that, like Charles I before him, Cromwell expected them to bring aspiring ministers to his attention when necessary. Certainly, he often asked them for informal judgements on ministers awaiting his approval. Thomas Manton and Jeremiah White both interviewed the previously ejected minister Peter Samways, when he petitioned Cromwell for re-admittance to the Church in 1658, reporting back that he was 'of unquestionable abilityes' and 'very great merrit'.[33]

More formally, Cromwell responded to personal petitions from parochial congregations in need of a minister. In April 1654, the parishioners of Mashbury in Essex asked him to present Abraham Pinchbecke, 'whom [your petitioners] had unanimously made choyce of' after a vacancy of two years.

[31] A&O, ii. 1025–6; TNA, SP 18/100, fos. 310–311.

[32] Owen was an independent, Manton a Presbyterian, Bernard a protégé of James Ussher, archbishop of Armagh and espoused a similar openness towards 'reduced episcopacy'; Hooke had spent some years in New England and another of his chaplains was the Baptist Daniel Dike.

[33] TNA, SP 18/182, fos. 8v, 11.

He complied with their request.[34] Shortly after that, he agreed to present John Firth to Mansfield, in response to a similar petition from the inhabitants of the town which, they claimed, had been without a minister 'by the space of five years and upwards'.[35] Occasionally, he instructed parishioners to find a suitable minister themselves, as he did at Maidstone, where he offered the congregation 'the liberty to spy out a man fit for them'.[36]

Cromwell also stepped in to support the parishioners of Brickhill in Buckinghamshire, where the right to present to the living had been contested since 1653 by the hereditary patron, John Duncomb and George Cockayn, who held a grant of next presentation. While both men argued, the parishioners had chosen themselves a new minister, Matthew Mead, on whose behalf they successfully petitioned Cromwell for a formal presentation, pointing out that the living had briefly lapsed to the Commissioners of the Great Seal and thus that it had devolved to him. Even so, the dispute over the patronage dragged wearily through the civil courts for several years until finally Cromwell ordered the hereditary patron, John Duncomb, to hand over his presentation, allegedly saying that he would otherwise 'make him the poorest Duncomb that ever was in England and that he would make Brickhill too hot for him'.[37] Not surprisingly, Duncomb finally complied and Cromwell was recorded in the registers as Mead's patron for Brickhill.[38]

Not all of the petitions Cromwell received, however, resulted in his compliance. In October 1654, some of the parishioners of St Botolph's Without Bishopsgate, London, sent in a petition requesting an interim minister while the existing incumbent, John Simpson, was under investigation for delinquency.[39] Shortly afterwards, Daniel Nichols was installed with Cromwell's confirmation, but this move divided the parish, prompting a counter-petition in favour of a different candidate, Samuel Lee. In response, a third faction within the parish petitioned Cromwell, requesting that either Simpson or Nichols be retained instead of Lee. Although Lee was known to be unwilling to take up the position, Cromwell personally persuaded him to accept it, a move which must have infuriated a number of the parishioners.[40]

---

[34] TNA, SP 18/70, fo. 80; LPL, COMM. III/3, *lib.1*, fo. 42.

[35] TNA, SP 18/73, fos. 61, 63; LPL, COMM. III/3, *lib.1*, fo. 41.

[36] *Calendar of the Correspondence of Richard Baxter* (Oxford, 1991), ed. N. H. Keble and G. F. Nuttall (2 vols), i. 136–7 (letter 177).

[37] WMS C4.39.

[38] LPL, COMM. III/4, fo. 146.

[39] Simpson was a radical Fifth Monarchist, at this point in opposition to Cromwell.

[40] TNA, SP 25/92, fos. 51, 77; TNA, SP 18/99, fo. 194.

The conclusion from Brickhill and St Botolphs Without Bishopsgate is that Cromwell was not above using the authority of his political position to intervene in disputes and bring about the resolution that he thought right. Nevertheless, his involvement in these cases, and that at Whitchurch in 1654, highlights a paradox in his role as an ecclesiastical patron.[41] Where he felt that the needs of congregations were suffering as a result of disagreements over patronage, he was at times prepared to act over and above the disputing parties to achieve a settlement. On the other hand, he also sought consistently to work within the legal framework governing clerical appointments. Having presented Matthew Mead to Brickhill, for example, he did not try to override the legal caveats entered by Duncomb and Cockayn against Mead's claim to the living, which left the latter with a valid presentation but without the necessary Instrument of Approval, until Duncomb finally withdrew his presentation – a move which, eventually, Cromwell had to precipitate.[42] Cromwell also insisted that those clergy, such as James Potter, whom he approved personally as fit to re-enter the ministry after an earlier sequestration, must, nevertheless, also satisfy the Triers.[43]

Petitioning was a tried and tested means for congregations to influence the choice of incumbent for their parish but if the process was unexceptional, the degree of Cromwell's personal engagement in this process was not. In 1657, Marchmont Nedham, the newspaper editor and political commentator, noted of Crowell's presentations that,

> He seldom bestoweth any of them upon any man whom himself doth not first examine and make trial of in person; save only that at such times as his great affaires happen to be more urgent than ordinary, he useth to appoint some other to do it on his behalf.[44]

Nedham's comment was part of a flattering justification of the Protector's religious programme and must be understood within this context, but his point about Cromwell interviewing his candidates is not without corroboration. A year or so earlier, Sebastian Pitfield, minister of Caundle Marsh in Dorset, tried to arrange for a fellow minister, whom Cromwell was presenting to a nearby living, to be examined locally in Dorset rather than London. Writing to a colleague about it, Pitfield noted that his request

[41] For Whitchurch, see p. 120 above.

[42] WMS C4.38–9.

[43] TNA, SP 18/77, fo. 75; TNA, SP 25/75, fo. 607.

[44] M. Nedham, *The Great Accuser Cast Down* (London, 1657), p. 103.

was 'a favour of the largest size … it is his Highnesses custom to examine whom he presents himself, before he presents them'.[45]

This comment supports Nedham's assertion. And indeed, Cromwell's willingness to become personally involved in other parochial matters suggests that such a practice would have been in keeping with his character. In 1654, for example, he personally requested that a number of parishes in East Anglia supply him with detailed information on their individual circumstances, in response to an earlier petition they had submitted exposing their 'low estate'.[46] There is also extensive evidence of his direct role in approving augmentations to parochial incomes to ensure that parishes were not deprived of the word of God through their own poverty.[47]

The Triers' registers show that Cromwell presented between 150 and 300 ministers in each year of his Protectorate.[48] If he interviewed most of those whom he presented, even allowing for some delegation when necessary, this constituted a very significant workload. Thus in 1656, his busiest year as a patron, he presented nearly 300 ministers, which meant (hypothetically) one man on every working day for eleven months and two men every working day of the final month.[49] While some presentations may have involved only a brief reading of a petition and personal recommendations, his own conscience and natural verbosity may have meant that those whom he interviewed in person found themselves in his company for much longer.[50]

Cromwell's close involvement in his presentations may be corroborated by a letter that he received from a minister following up queries that had arisen during a mutual conversation. The writer elaborated on his conversion experience and then his certainty about the nature of his vocation: 'I study not for wordes or formes, or ostentation of learning, but to divide

---

[45] Letter from Sebastian Pitfield, undated and now lost, quoted in A. Bayley, *The Great Civil War in Dorset, 1642–1660* (Taunton, 1910), p. 439.

[46] J. Nickolls, *Original Letters and Papers of State Addressed to Oliver Cromwell* (London, 1743), pp. 155–9.

[47] Cromwell personally approved many augmentations, and indeed his input at some Council meetings seems restricted to making such approvals: see TNA, SP18/126, fos. 6 (13), 311 (3); TNA, SP 25/114, fo. 83 (2, 3). See also TNA, SP 25/78, fo. 858 for his intervention in the dispute between John Wells and George Hopkins in Worcestershire.

[48] Note: these figures reflect the numbers and dates of the Triers' approvals, not the date when Cromwell bestowed his presentations, which was rarely recorded. Where his presentation dates *were* recorded, however, the majority of his ministers were presented and approved on the same day.

[49] The actual intervals between his presentations are not known.

[50] The minister Richard Baxter noted witheringly on several occasions Cromwell's 'slow and tedious' speaking: R. Baxter and M. Sylvester, *Reliquiae Baxterianae* (London, 1696), lib. 2, p. 205 (58).

the word aright, so as it may bring most glory to God, and edification to his people.' He added that he recognized God's providence in placing Cromwell in power and that both he and his parishioners had subscribed their allegiance to him. He concluded with a detailed explanation of the various scriptural interpretations of the apostle Peter's phrase, 'To the answer of a good conscience towards God, by the resurrection of Jesus Christ from the dead.'[51] It seems likely, perhaps probable, that this letter was sent by one of those ministers interviewed by Cromwell prior to receiving his presentation, continuing or confirming points raised in conversation between them. The topics covered – proof of his conversion experience and his pastoral vocation, his political loyalty, and his understanding of, and familiarity with, the scriptures – suggest that this encounter had been an interview, rather than simply a debate. These matters were also similar to the questions asked by the Triers at their own ministerial interviews and imply that the correspondent had been subjected to a fairly lengthy and searching examination by Cromwell.[52]

It was widely believed by Cromwell's opponents that his regime favoured the appointment of Independents, especially to wealthier livings.[53] In 1660, Seymour Bowman recorded the views of a fellow MP, Sir Thomas Meeres, who, 'moved against the Tryers at Whitehall who put in persons of Anabaptisticall principalls sayinge that they would put in anybody into mean livings but none but those of their own humour into a great one'.[54]

The accusation that the Cromwellian regime gave rich livings only to men of 'Anabaptisticall principalls' – a term often used scathingly for all forms of independency – is not supported by the evidence, although such pairings did occur sometimes. In 1657, Cromwell backed John Robotham's move to the living of Upminster in Essex, worth £130 *pa*. Robotham moved

[51] The letter is anonymous and undated: Nickolls, *Original Letters*, pp. 152–3; Murphy, *Oliver Cromwell's Church*, p. 93.

[52] A. Sadler, *Inquisitio Anglicana* (London, 1654), pp. 8, 11–13; WMS C1.327; Walker, *Attempt*, pp. 172–5. It should be noted that the few records of actual Triers' interviews were all written by those whom they rejected, so the Triers' questions in these reports are perhaps unusually dominated by the concerns the interviewed ministers aroused, such as signs of Arminianism.

[53] 'Independents' here is used broadly for those men called elsewhere both Independents and/or Congregationalists, who sought the essential autonomy of the congregation, while accepting *or* rejecting membership of a national Church. The precise terminology for such men was contested, then as now. For a helpful recent discussion, see J. Halcomb, 'A social history of congregational religious practice during the puritan revolution' (unpublished University of Cambridge PhD thesis, 2009).

[54] Diary of the proceedings of the House of Commons [by Seymour Bowman], 18 June–18 Aug., 1660: Bod., Dep. f. 9, fo. 104.

within Cromwellian circles, as an army chaplain and preaching assistant to the Independent minister, Joseph Caryl, one of the Triers, and he had been a member of an Independent congregation in Stepney in 1656.[55] Cromwell also presented another Independent, Theophilus Polwhele, to one portion, worth £280 *pa*, of the rich living of Tiverton in Devon, and he presented Matthew Mead to Brickhill, worth £130 *pa*, but the majority of his presentations were to livings whose values were considerably less than the £100 *pa* that parliament had deemed to be an adequate ministerial income in 1649.[56]

In fact, Cromwell presented Independents to some remarkably impoverished benefices too. One such was Samuel Alexander who, in 1654, was given the sequestration of Stanfield in Norfolk, valued three years later at only £25 *pa*.[57] Almost immediately, the parishioners of neighbouring Godwick, which had no minister, decided to join themselves to his congregation and begged money from the Council of State in order to retain him. He was finally granted a £10 augmentation in 1657.[58] Woodborough in Wiltshire, to which Cromwell presented Isaac Chauncy, and Rothwell in Northamptonshire, to which he presented John Beverley, were also poor; both were impropriated livings, the former offering a ministerial salary of £6 *pa*, the latter £6, 13s, 4d, although here, at least theoretically, Beverley was granted a modest augmentation around the time of his appointment.[59]

Yet the Protector also presented Presbyterian ministers to livings offering an equally diverse range of values: in Essex alone, he gave the impropriated living of Bulmer to John Bird in 1655, where in 1650 it had been noted that the incumbent was currently receiving £16 *pa*, and in 1658 he presented John Smith to Rickling, which had an income of £28 *pa*, and had been unserved for the last seven years, 'the lyving being so small that noe man would accept thereof'.[60] In 1656, however, he had presented Francis Chandler to Theydon Garnon, offering £170 *pa* in 1650 and Martin Alderson to Latchingdon, worth £159 *pa*.[61] Further north, in Huntingdonshire, he presented another

---

[55] S. Wright, 'John Robotham', in *Oxford Dictionary of National Biography* (2004), <https://doi.org/10.1093/ref:odnb/23896>.

[56] 'Act for Maintenance for Preaching Ministers, and other Pious Uses', in *A&O*, ii. 142–8.

[57] LPL, COMM. XIIa/20, fo. 9.

[58] Nickolls, *Original Letters*, p. 159; TNA, SP 25/78, fo. 375.

[59] TNA, SP 25/77, fo. 437. This augmentation seems to have been reduced from the £30 *pa* granted in 1656.

[60] LPL, COMM. XIIa/8, fos. 455–456.

[61] Chandler participated in the Presbyterian ordination of Edmund Calamy the younger in 1658: Smith, *Essex*, pp. 367–8; Alderson was named a member of the 8th Essex *classis* in 1648: Shaw, *English Church*, ii. 383.

Presbyterian, James Bedford, to Bluntsham-cum-Earith, worth £180 *pa*. The evidence suggests, then, that Cromwell settled both Independent and Presbyterian ministers in wealthy livings, a practice which did not prevent later critics from cherry-picking a few examples on which to base a legacy of unsubstantiated complaint.

The Triers' registers demonstrate, in fact, that Cromwell and his regime appointed men from across the orthodox godly spectrum. Indeed, roughly ninety per cent of the ministers presented by the Protector espoused, or at least leant towards, Presbyterianism, or fell into Richard Baxter's category of 'dis-engaged, faithful men', unaligned to any clearly identified denomination.[62] Just under five per cent are currently identified as having been Independents. These figures are in line with the overall proportions of appointments to the Cromwellian Church; of the *c*.3,500 ministers approved by the Triers, only two per cent have been securely identified as Independents.[63] On the other hand, Cromwell was personally responsible for presenting sixty-five per cent of all the Independent ministers approved by the Triers.[64] It is unclear whether this reflected a deliberate policy of favour or whether the vast extent of his patronage simply gave him many more opportunities to present Independents than any other patron. Indeed, it may be that his own Independent sympathies encouraged a higher proportion of ministers who shared his outlook to ask for his support. No doubt his belief that essential godliness was more important than minor differences in its form and practice underpinned the breadth of his sponsorship but even had he wished to promote only Independents, the small number of such men available would have made this impossible.

Intriguingly, approximately five per cent of the ministers presented by Cromwell were men who chose to undergo illegal episcopalian ordination after the abolition of the bishops in 1646, although only a third of these did so *before* he presented them.[65] Cromwell's regime must have been aware that such ordinations were still taking place – after the Restoration,

[62] These men are suggested by A. G. Matthews to have been 'Presbyterians, or ordained by presbyters though not convincedly of that pursuasion' and 'political presbyterians', who eschewed rigid categorization: *CR*, pp. x, lxvii; Baxter, *Reliquiae, lib. 1*, p. 148.

[63] These percentages have been calculated using A. G. Matthews's identification of 'congregationalists' in 1662, although more probably remain unrecognized: *WR, CR*, p. lxvii. See also n.56 above. The Triers Commission at its inception in March 1654 comprised eighteen Independent ministers, fourteen Presbyterian, Baptist or unaligned ministers and six men who were not ministers, at least two of whom were Independents.

[64] One of these, John Skynner, was a Baptist: LPL, COMM. III/4, fo. 554; *WR, CR*, p. 444.

[65] The identification of post-1646 to 1660 episcopal ordinations comes from a draft list drawn up by S. Taylor and K. Fincham; it is likely that more remain unidentified.

Robert Skinner, former bishop of Oxford, claimed to have ordained several hundred ministers at his house close to the city – but whether the identities of individual ministers were known is unclear.[66] Cromwell had investigated some degree of accommodation for moderate episcopalians within the godly Church in the early 1650s although, when the Instrument of Government was issued at the outset of the Protectorate, it had specifically prohibited those practising 'prelacy' from benefiting from the state's protection.[67]

In fact, Cromwell's approach to episcopalians remained pragmatic, generally avoiding outright confrontation except in circumstances where they were believed to be a threat to the security of the regime.[68] Did he know that some of those whom he presented had been ordained by former bishops? It seems unlikely. Most of these men were evidently minor clergymen with obscure referees, who may have stayed below the radar of the authorities in Whitehall. One or two, however, moved in more august circles but these men were able to call on the support of some impeccably godly referees. John Houseman, presented by Cromwell to Great Thurlow in Suffolk in 1656, was secretly ordained in Norwich in 1651 by Robert Maxwell, former bishop of Kilmore in Ireland. Yet Houseman provided nine testimonials at his interview, including three from prominent Presbyterian Cambridge academics, John Arrowsmith, Anthony Tuckney and Lazarus Seaman, the first two of whom were themselves members of the Triers' Commission in Whitehall.[69]

In some cases, Cromwell chose to present men of similar religious views to those of their predecessors for his livings, but it seems unlikely that this was a deliberate policy. Throughout the Protectorate there were more empty benefices than available ministers and an overwhelming ratio of Presbyterian or unaligned ministers to Independents. Thus it was inevitable that he would often present Presbyterians to livings formerly served by Presbyterians. Yet there were, of course, instances when Cromwell sponsored Independents in

[66] K. Fincham and S. Taylor, 'Vital statistics: episcopal ordination and ordinands in England, 1646–60', *EHR*, cxxvi (2011), 319–44, at p. 332.

[67] Ralph Brownrigg later told William Sancroft, future archbishop of Canterbury, that talks were faltering owing to Presbyterian recalcitrance, although 'the Independents are of a more moderate disposition': H. Carey, *Memorials of the Great Civil War in England from 1646 to 1652* (2 vols, London, 1842), ii. 415; Bosher, *Restoration Settlement*, pp. 9–10; Gardiner, *Constitutional Documents*, p. 416.

[68] The royalist uprisings of 1655, for example, resulted in a clampdown on episcopalian clergy: *Orders of the Protector and Council for Securing the Peace of the Commonwealth* (1655) in TNA, SP 18/100, fos. 310–11.

[69] LPL, COMM. III/5, fo. 20. Arrowsmith was Master of Trinity College from 1653; Tuckney, Master of St Johns; Seaman, Master of Peterhouse from 1644 and Vice-Chancellor of the university in 1653–4.

succession. In early 1656, he presented Nathaniel Mather, one of a number of Independent ministers recently returned from New England, to the sequestration of Harberton in Devon. When Mather moved to Barnstaple a year later, Cromwell presented another Independent, George Mortimer, to Harberton.[70] In 1655, however, he had presented Nathaniel's brother Samuel, also an Independent, to Gravesend, but when Samuel did not take up the living, Cromwell presented a Presbyterian, Philip Sharpe, shortly afterwards.[71]

Moreover, Cromwell sometimes deliberately overruled a congregation's choice of minister. In 1654 he rejected Richard Henchman, nominated by the parishioners of Christchurch in London, in favour of Seth Wood, a young Independent whom he sponsored several times during his Protectorate.[72] Henchman's mild Presbyterianism was perhaps tinged with episcopalian sympathies, which may have contributed to Cromwell's preference for Wood.[73] It would appear, then, that Cromwell could not, and did not, operate a strict policy of copying denominational loyalties within livings; and indeed, a rigorous segregation along such lines would have sat uneasily with his personal tolerance of godly diversity and his drive for godly unity.

Cromwell's patronage record reveals the existence of a number of loose clerical networks that provided support for each other when seeking appointments in the Church and who benefitted from his favour. One of these comprised Independent ministers who had recently returned from New England, men such as Isaac Chauncey and the Mather brothers, Nathaniel and Samuel, who discovered 'what an advantage to preferment it is to have been a New English man'.[74] Cromwell presented at least eight 'New England men' to livings, including Edward Fletcher, who was also able to call upon another network of Independents favoured by Cromwell. Based largely in Gloucestershire, this group included William Tray, William Becket, Simon Moore, Carnsew Helme and Stephen Ford, all of whom he presented during the 1650s and who provided each other with references for their Triers' interviews, alongside several other local Independents.[75]

[70] LPL, COMM. III/4, fo. 563; LPL, COMM. III/6, fo. 184.

[71] Mather was in Ireland at the time: LPL, COMM. III/3, *lib. 3*, fo. 139; LPL, COMM. III/4, fo. 133.

[72] LPL, COMM. III/3, *lib.2*, fo. 158.

[73] Henchman was nephew of Humphrey Henchman, future bishop of Salisbury, and conformed to the restored episcopalian Church in 1662.

[74] N. Mather to J. Rogers, 23 Dec. 1650/1 in *Collections of the Massachusetts Historical Society*, (1868), 4th series, viii. 5.

[75] Eg, LPL, COMM. III/6, fo. 49 (Buckland), LPL, COMM. III/4, fo. 374 (Oddington).

Similar Presbyterian networks also existed. Simeon Ashe and Edmund Calamy, for example, worked continuously together providing references for Presbyterian ministers, men such as Thomas Case. When Cromwell presented Case to St Giles in the Fields in London, Calamy and Ashe provided him with testimonials alongside the Presbyterian ministers Elidad Blackwell, George Smallwood and John Webb.[76] The previous year Case, Calamy, Ashe and Smallwood had all signed Simon Patrick's Presbyterian ordination certificate and frequently acted together to promote their colleagues within the Cromwellian Church, many of them benefiting from the Protector's patronage.[77] Such networks of men reappear throughout the Triers' registers, and probably provided another means by which potential ministers may have come to Cromwell's attention other than through his chaplains.[78]

Cromwell's participation in the exercise of his ecclesiastical patronage indicates that, for him, the transformation of Britain into a godly nation was not a distant aspiration but a daily activity, an ongoing process which required and received constant attention. Moreover, his close engagement with the construction of a preaching ministry was a personal crusade: the ministry was the means through which he could achieve his overriding objective – the unity of the godly. In 1655, he had railed at MPs for not

> settling of such matters in things of religion as would have upheld and given countenance to a godly ministry, and yet would have given a just liberty to godly men of different judgements, though men of the same faith with them that you call the orthodox ministry in England – as it is well known the independents are, and many under the form of baptism, who are sound in the faith only may perhaps be different in judgement in some lesser matters ...[79]

Analysis of his work as an ecclesiastical patron demonstrates that this principle was one upon which he acted throughout his Protectorate in carrying out his duties as an ecclesiastical patron. After all, verifying the orthodoxy and suitability of those whom he presented could have been left to the judgement of his chaplains and the Triers, yet he chose to devote his

---

[76] LPL, COMM. III/3, *lib.* 2, fo. 252. Calamy, Ashe and Blackwell were members of the 12th London *Classis*, Webb belonged to the 2nd Essex *Classis* and Smallwood was minister of St Mildreds, Poultry, in the 6th London *Classis* where Calamy was a *classis* Trier.

[77] Bod, MS. Tanner 52, fo. 6.

[78] Such networks existed beyond London: in Sussex, Francis Cheynell, John Tredcroft, George Vinter, John Chatfield and Robert Fish frequently supported each other, Vinter Fish and John Tredcroft offering testimonials for Tredcroft's relation, Nathaniel, when Cromwell presented him to Horsham in 1657: LPL, COMM. III/6, fo. 126.

[79] Abbott, *Writings of Oliver Cromwell*, iii. 586.

own time to ensuring that his presentees were worthy of the responsibility laid upon them. At the same time, his commitment also signalled his proactive response to a national ministry in crisis. During 1653, parliament had received petitions from several counties begging for support for the ailing national Church.[80] There was widespread concern at the number of livings without incumbents or subject to rapid clerical turnover, situations aggravated by the collapse of the mechanisms for appointing new clergy. Thus his engagement in settling ministers must have served both his spiritual conscience and the political and personal imperative of improving parochial provision. The judicious use of his ecclesiastical patronage lay at the centre of his understanding of his role as Lord Protector.

After Cromwell's death in 1658, Richard Cromwell took over his father's ecclesiastical patronage. At the restoration of the monarchy, however, some of those put into livings by Cromwell were ejected from their benefices by returning royalist incumbents or dissatisfied parishioners. A further cohort of ministers, whose consciences would not allow them to work within a restored episcopalian Church, were forced out by the requirements of the Act of Uniformity in 1662. Yet the flexible boundaries of Cromwell's godly Church had unexpected consequences. Overall, less than a third of those ministers whom he presented left the ministry in 1660–2. The others found ways to accommodate their beliefs and personal circumstances within the Restoration Church and to continue their pastoral missions. This meant that over seven hundred ministers chosen by Cromwell were able to preach the word of God in parish churches across England and Wales after 1662. Whether Cromwell would have seen this as a positive or negative outcome is, of course, debatable. What is clear is that despite the almost total demolition of the ecclesiastical administration constructed by the Protector's regime, the godly ministry – the very heart of Cromwell's Church – continued to have an input into public worship long into the reign of Charles II.

---

[80] *The Cryes of England to the Parliament* (London, 1653), pp. 4, 6–8.

The clergy of the Commonwealth

4. The impact of the landscape on the clergy of seventeenth-century Dorset

Trixie Gadd

Introduction

Drawing on data from a broader study of the effect of economic, social, political and geographical issues on clerical prosperity in Dorset throughout the century, this chapter examines how the county's landscape and topography impacted on seventeenth-century clergymen's prosperity, security and mobility.[1] Having first established the broad context of Dorset's parochial landscape and income, it then relates these issues specifically to clergymen's experiences in the turbulent 1640s and 1650s. In this respect, the 1650 parliamentary surveys of parochial livings are a particularly valuable source, revealing connections between the landscape and persecution. These are complemented by data from the 1535 *Valor Ecclesiasticus* and a later glebe survey, which provide more detailed breakdowns of ecclesiastical income, while evidence from glebe terriers, wills and inventories sheds light on incumbents' actual land usage and other sources of income.[2] Patterns of sequestration, ejection and survival between the Civil Wars and Restoration are then examined in the context of landscape differences.

The Dorset landscape and its impact on parochial experiences

In a well-known description of seventeenth-century southern England, John Aubrey distinguished between two major types of landscape, 'chalk' and 'cheese'. According to Aubrey, in the downland or chalk country 'the shepherds labour hard; their flesh is hard, their bodies strong', whereas in

---

[1] T. Gadd, '"Tis my lot by faith to be sustained": clerical prosperity in seventeenth-century Dorset' (unpublished University of Leicester PhD thesis, 2019).

[2] TNA, C 94/2 Surveys of Church livings, 1650; Anon., *Valor Ecclesiasticus Temp. Henry VIII Auctoritate Regia Institutus* (6 vols, Burlington, Ont., 2013), i; C. B. Stuart-Wortley, 'Return of glebe lands in England and Wales', *House of Commons Papers*, 64 (1887), Paper no. 307, pp. 162–8.

T. Gadd, 'The impact of the landscape on the clergy of seventeenth-century Dorset', in *Church and people in interregnum Britain*, ed. F. McCall (London, 2021), pp. 87–109. License: CC BY-NC-ND.

the 'dirty clayey country' where 'they only milk the cowes and make cheese ... their persons are generally plump and feggy'.[3] David Underdown's study of cultural and political differences in seventeenth-century Somerset, Wiltshire and Dorset was based on this distinction between sheep-corn (chalk) and wood-pasture (cheese) husbandry.[4] However, his analysis of popular allegiances revealed that although the 'chalk' areas were more likely to be royalist and the 'cheese' areas parliamentarian, north Dorset was atypical, and as Ann Hughes observed, this basic dichotomy 'cannot do justice to the complexity of English economic and settlement patterns'.[5] This chapter therefore presents a more detailed analysis of parish-level landscape differences.

Thomas Gerard's *Survey of Dorsetshire*, written in the 1620s, followed each river from west to east, 'even from their Springs and Fountaines, untill they take up their Lodgeing in the Ocean'.[6] Nevertheless, in common with other county histories written with influential patrons in mind, he focused on manorial rather than topographical issues, ignoring obvious landscape features. The most extensive early description of Dorset at a parochial rather than county level was by John Hutchins (1698–1773), a clergyman himself, whose familiarity with the landscape is evident.[7] For example, he observed that the soil of the downland parish of Bradford Peverell 'consists of gravel and chalk, arable and pasture, but near the river is much meadow ground', while Buckland Abbas in Blackmore Vale 'is mostly arable land, and pasture for sheep, but the lower part is used for grazing and dairies and is much inclosed'.[8]

The mixed geology of Dorset creates a wealth of different landscapes in a comparatively small area (around ninety kilometres east to west and sixty kilometres north to south). Forty-six per cent of parishes are mono-geological: many downland settlements lie on largely undifferentiated chalk soils, while the heathlands around Poole harbour are almost entirely sandstone based. However, in the north, the low-lying land is clay but is pierced by limestone ridges, where most settlements are situated. The south

---

[3] J. Aubrey, *The Natural History of Wiltshire* (London, 1847), p. 11.

[4] D. Underdown, *Revel, Riot and Rebellion* (Oxford, 1985); D. Underdown, 'The chalk and the cheese: contrasts among the English clubmen', *Past & Present*, lxxxv (1979), 25–48.

[5] A. Hughes, 'The "chalk" and the "cheese": David Underdown, regional cultures and popular allegiance in the English Revolution', *History Compass*, xi (2013), 373–80, at p. 376.

[6] T. Gerard, *A Survey of Dorsetshire* (London, 1732), p. 8.

[7] J. Hutchins, *History and Antiquities of the County of Dorset* (4 vols, London, 3rd ed., 1861–73).

[8] Hutchins, *History and Antiquities*, i. 443, 233, 144; ii. 252.

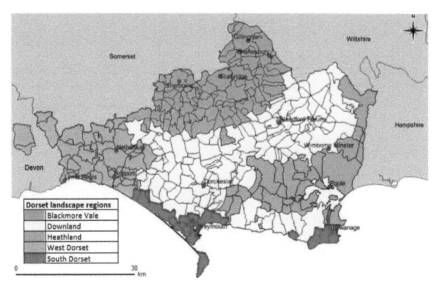

Figure 4.1. Map of Dorset's landscape regions and main towns.[a]

[a] Author's own calculation based on DigiMapGB-250 data.

coast from Portland to Bridport is similarly mixed, and the Isle of Purbeck has a spine of downland separating heath from clay.

For this study, detailed examination of the predominant geology of the 289 seventeenth-century Dorset parishes resulted in their classification into five landscape regions: Blackmore Vale (84 parishes), West Dorset (39), downland (120), heathland (27) and South Dorset (19) (see Figure 4.1).[9]

Blackmore Vale, a 'cheese' area of wood-pasture husbandry, still has deep lanes and the small fields characteristic of former woodland. Gerard described it as 'verie subject to Durt and foule Wayes', and John Leland's journey between Caundle Marsh and Sherborne was '3. miles by enclosid and sumwhat hilly Grounde meately welle woddyd'.[10] West Dorset, the other 'cheese' area of clay landscape, was described by Gerard as 'rich and well stored with Woods, by means whereof it affordeth convenient dwellings'.[11] The largest landscape area is the 'chalk' downland, which stretches in a wide

[9] DigiMapGB-250 [ESRI Shapefile geospatial data], scale 1:250,000, British Geological Survey, UK, using: EDINA Geology Digimap Service, <http://digimap.edina.ac.uk/> [accessed 24 Jan. 2017].

[10] Gerard, *Survey*, p. 3; T. Hearne, *The Itinerary of John Leland the Antiquary* (Oxford, 3rd ed., 1769), p. 109.

[11] Gerard, *Survey*, pp. 3, 13.

band across the county, with settlements along the valleys of the Cerne, Piddle, Tarrant and Allen, and along escarpments where springs emerge. There were few habitations on the open downland where sheep-corn husbandry was practised, and following the dissolution, major landowners amassed very large flocks of sheep, leading to the desertion of many downland villages. For example, Gerard described Winterborne Farringdon in 1634 as 'a lone Church, for there is hardlie anie house left in the Parish, such of late hath beene the Covetousnesse of some private Men, that to encrease their Demesnes have depopulated whole Parishes'.[12] The south-east of the county around Poole harbour and the Isle of Purbeck consists mainly of heathland, described even in the early nineteenth century as 'a most dreary waste' used for 'the support in summer of a few ordinary cattle and sheep, and the heath which is pared up by the surrounding villages for fuel'.[13] Finally, the South Dorset region, comprising the south of Purbeck, the Isle of Portland and the villages close to the south coast from Portland to Burton Bradstock, lies on a mixture of limestone and clay but is hillier than Blackmore and is exposed to the maritime air.

Impact of parish terrain

In Blackmore Vale, winter flooding was a major issue. Hutchins referred to the church at Caundle Bishop as standing 'in a very dirty, watery place, far distant from any other'.[14] The 1650 parliamentary surveys provide several indications of Blackmore parishioners' problems in getting to church during adverse weather conditions. The chapel of West Orchard sought separation from the mother church of Fontmell Magna because 'by reason of the height of waters in the winter season … the passage betweene them two is impassible'.[15] Several chapelries, situated wholly on wet clay land in the middle of Blackmore Vale and watered by tributaries of the River Stour, had been established as chapels of ease because in wet weather it was so difficult to get to the mother churches of Fontmell Magna and Iwerne Minster, which were situated on higher ground on the periphery of the Vale. However, the parishioners of Iwerne Minster complained about the proliferation of chapels: 'wee have more Churches built alreddy than wee are able to maintaine'.[16]

---

[12] Gerard, *Survey*, p. 73.

[13] G. A. Cooke, *Topographical and Statistical Description of the County of Dorset* (London, 1802), p. 50.

[14] Hutchins, *History and Antiquities*, i. 343.

[15] TNA, C 94/2, fo. 12, West Orchard.

[16] TNA, C 94/2, fo. 24, Iwerne Minster.

A similar problem was experienced by the villages of East and West Stour, between which was 'a great river that often overflows, whereby there is noe convenient passage from one place to the other', so 'the Minister cannot serve both Cures at seasonable times'.[17] Motcombe, another Blackmore chapelry, sought to be established as a parish church, 'there being noe other church or chappell nearer to it then the said Church of Gillingham, the road thereunto from Motcombe in winter season by reason of floods is unpassable'.[18] At Kington Magna, too, part of the parish was 'a mile away from the church and inaccessible when the waters are high'.[19]

In more extensive or elongated parishes, parishioners expressed difficulty in getting to church owing to its distance from their homes rather than the terrain. For instance, at Folke in 1635, 'most parishioners do not come to divine service on holy days in regard their houses are too far distant from the church'; and in nearby Haydon, five people were presented for non-attendance in 1619 because 'they dwell three miles from the church', and two in 1628, who 'inhabiting att Boy's Hill, within the precincts of our parish and distant from our parish Church about fower miles, doe very seldome frequent our parish Church ... but onely frequent the parish Churches which are neere adjoyning with them'.[20]

Some problems were no doubt attributable to incumbents' failure to appoint curates to outlying chapels where travelling was difficult. For example, in 1684, John White, vicar of Yetminster (not the famed Dorchester 'patriarch'), was presented by the churchwardens at the dean of Salisbury's visitation for not celebrating divine service in the chapels of Leigh and Chetnole every Sunday, but only 'on every other Sunday, except when he was sick, from home or the waters up'.[21] There was evidently some tension between amalgamating parishes to enable suitable preaching ministers to serve the cure, and employing curates to maintain weekly services.

It was also clearly no coincidence that the dean of Salisbury's visitations took place in July when the roads were more passable. Indeed, in 1560, the archdeacon of Dorset had delayed visiting until summer, 'when both the

---

[17] TNA, C 94/2, fo. 229, East Stour; fo. 231, West Stour.

[18] E. A. Fry, 'The augmentation books (1650–1660) in Lambeth Palace Library', *Proceedings of the Dorset Natural History and Antiquarian Field Club*, xxxvi (1915), 48–105, at p. 90.

[19] TNA, C 94/2, fo. 113, Kington Magna.

[20] WSHC, D5/28/35, fo. 86, Folke churchwardens' presentment, 1635; D5/28/20, fo. 83, Haydon churchwardens' presentment, 1619; D5/28/28, fo. 65, Haydon churchwardens' presentment, 1628.

[21] WSHC, D5/22/19 fos, 7v–15, depositions in the case of William Harris, churchwarden of Yetminster against John White, vicar of Yetminster for neglecting the cure of the chapel of Leigh, 1684.

time of the yere and also opportunite for that purpose will serve better'.[22] Even so, the journey to attend visitations was not always easy. Robert Lane, rector of Hermitage in Blackmore Vale, sent his apologies to the dean in 1638, since 'at the last visitation in this place, I adventured to ryde on a side sadle ... but I was not able to endure the miles ryding homeward'; he was taken down from his horse, which was led home while he had to 'creepe home ... in great payne & misery alone there after'.[23]

The 1650 survey responses for West Dorset, the other clay area, reveal fewer examples of travelling difficulties than in Blackmore. However, the 250 inhabitants of Shipton Gorge, a chapelry of Burton Bradstock, claimed that they were 'not able to travell to Burton Church ... the waies thither unpassable at winter by reason of dirt'. Similarly, at Stanton St Gabriel, the parishioners were struggling to attend the mother church of Whitchurch Canonicorum more than two miles away, 'along a road exposed to such violence of wind and weather'.[24]

In contrast to the two wood-pasture areas, parishes in the remaining landscape regions reported no travelling difficulties in 1650, indicating that such problems were confined largely to the 'cheese' areas.

Value and use of glebe land

Clergymen were intimately bound up with the landscape through their entitlement to glebe land. During the middle ages, 'there were very few parishes, apart from those of recent creation, which did not have at least five or ten acres of glebe', which would have constituted a small peasant holding.[25] The 1650 surveys sought overall valuations rather than descriptions of glebe land, seeking to ensure that the income was sufficient to support able ministers, although some responses do provide more detail. For instance, in the downland region, Bincombe had 'glebe land of meadows, arable and pasture', and at Askerswell there were six acres of pasture 'upon the gleabe' and fifteen acres of arable 'in the Common field upon the same gleabe'.[26]

Further detail can be gleaned from two relatively complete valuations of glebe land. In the first, the *Valor Ecclesiasticus* of 1535, sixty-eight per cent of parishes in Dorset were recorded as having at least some glebe land, although glebe terriers reveal that, for some, this consisted of no more than the parsonage house and a small garden, as in the West Dorset village of

[22] Corpus Christi College Cambridge, Parker MS. 97, fo. 148v.

[23] WSHC, D5/28/38, fo. 18, Hermitage presentment, 1638.

[24] TNA, C 94/2, fo. 118, Shipton Gorge; fo. 82, Stanton St Gabriel.

[25] N. J. G. Pounds, *A History of the English Parish* (Cambridge, 2000), p. 216.

[26] TNA, C 94/2, fo. 84, Bincombe; fo. 91, Askerswell.

Burstock.[27] The second full glebe survey was not carried out until 1887, by which time some glebe had been augmented by Queen Anne's Bounty, and some had been altered through enclosure, often converting strips of common-field entitlements into closes.[28] Although the 1887 survey does not specify how glebe land was actually used, it does reveal that its yield varied considerably between landscape types: almost £3 per acre in West Dorset and around £2 in Blackmore Vale and South Dorset, but only £1 10s per acre in heathland and downland parishes. Therefore, both the location and quantity of glebe land had a significant impact on clergymen's income.

Two major sources of evidence, glebe terriers and inventories, shed light on individual clergymen's land usage rather than income. Of the 102 Dorset parishes for which seventeenth-century terriers or similar documents survive, the majority were produced for the archbishop of Canterbury's metropolitical visitations in 1612 and 1634. There was also a spate of terrier production in the early 1660s as incumbents sought to re-establish parochial entitlements following the Restoration. These terriers list land and property belonging to the Church which incumbents could either farm themselves or rent out. Many specify land use in terms of arable, meadow, pasture and woodland, and disclose whether the landscape was enclosed or still had common fields.

The terriers reveal that all glebe land in West Dorset was enclosed, as it was in Blackmore Vale except for a few rights to common pasture at Minterne Magna, Stockwood and Sutton Waldron, and common fields in Marnhull and Over Compton. In contrast, the glebe in most downland and South Dorset parishes was in common fields, sometimes in numerous pieces. Common-field farming survived longer in the chalk parishes, raising issues for clergy whose glebe was distributed in small parcels across different fields. For example, the terrier for Cattistock lists twenty-two parcels in the north, middle and south fields, as well as pasture for sheep and cattle on the down. At Langton Long Blandford, another downland parish where the rector had one small close of pasture, the rest of the glebe consisted of meadow land in the 'Town meadow', various acres of ground in the north, middle and south fields, and common pasture for cattle and horses in the marsh and for sheep on the downs.[29]

In heathland parishes, glebe was more mixed, with both common and enclosed land, as well as sizeable coppices at Bloxworth and Morden. For

[27] WSHC, D28/10/22, Burstock terrier, 1612.

[28] Stuart-Wortley, 'Return of glebe lands', pp. 162–8; N. J. G. Pounds, 'Terriers and the historical geographer', *Journal of Historical Geography*, xxxi (2005), 373–89, at p. 377.

[29] WSHC, D28/10/24, Cattistock terrier, 1612; D28/10/76, Langton Long Blandford terrier, 1633.

example, the rector of Studland had four small closes of glebe land, two small areas of meadow and twenty acres of arable in two common fields, plus common of pasture for 120 sheep 'to have their feeding in the fields and heath' and horses and rother cattle 'in the heath, so many in the summer as he can winter'.[30] Like other heathland parishes, he could take as much furze and turf as he needed for fuel, and was also allowed 'frith from the wood'. The mixed nature of his glebe and the fuel allowance were advantageous; however, glebe had accounted for only six per cent of the parish valuation in 1535, and his total income amounted to only £50 in 1650, confirming the poor yield on heathland.[31]

Terriers provide a snapshot of land use at a particular time, but do not usually indicate whether the incumbent was farming the glebe land himself, or indeed making any profit from it. In this respect, probate inventories, which were drawn up post mortem to establish the value of individuals' estates, can be used to determine the types of activities in which they were engaged, in terms of farming implements and stores of grain and other crops, as well as wealth in leased property and debts owing. Annabelle Hughes found that between a half and a third of Sussex clergy inventories listed stock and/or crops. She noted that this must relate to farming of the glebe, but cautioned that their amount would have been affected by when in the agricultural year the inventory was taken.[32] Margaret Spufford also cautioned of the limitations of inventories since they list only leased land and property, whereas if a corresponding will also survives, this may specify land and property actually owned by the individual.[33] Inventories survive for only six downland parishes out of 120, and for very few heathland or South Dorset parishes. Many more survive for the Blackmore Vale and West Dorset 'cheese' regions, indicating that the incumbents of these parishes were wealthier and left more substantial estates.

One downland parish for which relevant evidence does survive is Blandford St Mary, one of the more valuable livings in Dorset. In common with most other downland parishes, it had little glebe, accounting for only 5.43 per cent of the value of the living in the 1535 parish valuation.[34] However,

[30] WSHC, D5/10/1, Bloxworth terrier, 1613; D28/10/89, Morden terrier, 1631; D28/10/127, Studland terrier, 1634.

[31] WSHC, D28/10/127/1, Studland terrier, 1634; TNA, C 94/2, fo. 36, *Valor Ecclesiasticus*, Studland.

[32] *Sussex Clergy Inventories, 1600–1750*, ed. A. Hughes (Lewes, 2009), p. xviii.

[33] M. Spufford, 'The limitations of the probate inventory', in *English Rural Society, 1500–1800*, ed. J. Chartres and D. Hey (Cambridge, 2006), pp. 139–74, at p. 142; M. Overton, 'Probate inventories and the reconstruction of agricultural landscapes', in *Discovering Past Landscapes*, ed. M. A. Reed (London, 1984), pp. 167–94, at p. 169.

[34] *Valor Ecclesiasticus*.

William Sutton's inventory, taken in 1635, lists arable, meadow, pasture, woodland and rights to common pasture, and in his will, he bequeathed to his children large sums of money, as well as 'small quilletts of land I have purchased in Dorset'. This land, rented to various tenants, comprised at least sixty acres of arable, as well as several acres of meadow and pasture, common pasture for 264 sheep, fifteen cattle and three horses, and various closes, meadows, leazes, pasture, woods and underwoods.[35]

Sutton's successor, John Crooke, held multiple livings and several administrative posts in Winchester, and had family connections with the patrons of the living.[36] John Pitt, who succeeded Crooke in 1645, remained there until his death in 1672, by which time he had acquired the advowson. In his will, he entrusted all lands, tenements, debts, goods, reversions and chattels to his brothers to dispose of at their discretion among his children, indicating that his property was considerable.[37]

Other inventories from downland parishes confirm that, perhaps because these livings had little glebe land, their incumbents tended to derive personal wealth from other sources, as well as serving more than one cure. For example, Abel Selley, rector of Winterborne Tomson for twenty years until his death in 1661, left an inventory totalling £110, of which the most valuable items were books worth £10, plus £45 due to him on bonds and other debts.[38] At Spetisbury, William Zouch's estate was valued in 1680 at the huge sum of almost £4,000, most of which comprised ready money and various types of credit; and Zouch's successor, Benjamin Crosse, formerly vicar of Holy Trinity Cork, was owed over £1,200 in bills, bonds and debts in London and Ireland.[39]

At Maiden Newton, William Huish's 1685 inventory lists the impropriate tithes of Dunsford, Devon worth £170, a house in Maiden Newton worth £60 and debts of £69 owing to him, as well as farm goods. Also listed, alongside some ricks of hay and a dung cart, is a coach. This and an unspecified number of horses suggest some opulence, as these were

---

[35] TNA, C 94/2, fo. 13, Blandford St Mary, 1650; C 142/720/15, inventory post mortem of William Sutton, clerk, 1635; PROB 11/162/658, will of William Sutton, clerk of Saint Mary Blandford, 1632.

[36] 'Crooke, John' (*CCED* Person ID 54441)', Clergy of the Church of England Database (*CCED*) (accessed 17 July 2019); J. R. Childs, *Reliques of the Rives (Ryves)* (Lynchburg, Va., 1929), p. 6.

[37] TNA, PROB 11/339/308, will of John Pitt, clerk of Blandford Saint Mary, 1 July 1672.

[38] WSHC, P5/1661/54, administration bond, commission and inventory of Abel Selley, clerk of Winterborne Tomson, 1661.

[39] TNA, PROB 4/19863, inventory of William Zouch, clerk of Spetisbury, 20 May 1680; PROB 11/378/255, will and inventory of Benjamin Crosse, 1684.

'trappings of affluence', and records of clergy owning them are rare.[40] For example, Peter Heylyn owned a coach and horses, and initially held onto them when sequestered, but subsequently had to sell them to survive.[41] The evidence from downland parishes thus suggests that their incumbents tended to be sponsored by wealthy local gentry or had influential family members, enabling them to purchase property, while close ties with local gentry were characteristic of the strength of manorial authority in downland villages.[42]

Similarly to the downland parishes, those in West Dorset tended to have little glebe land. For example, Chardstock had none, and its tithes were worth only £40 a year in 1650. Nevertheless, James Keate, rector from 1669 until his death in 1704, left the 'lease of the new parks in the parish of Chardstock', valued at £150, and property in several other locations.[43] At Wambrook in 1685, John Chase left a large inventory of goods at properties in Dorset, Devon and Somerset valued at £461, and was owed £267 in debts. Chase had succeeded his father at Wambrook, and had certainly profited from his family wealth despite sequestration in 1645.[44] These West Dorset parishes had little glebe land, whereas the 1650 survey for Symondsbury, the most valuable parish in Dorset, lists about 146 acres of glebe to the value of £120, with tithes worth another £190 per year. The advowson was purchased for Walter Newburgh by his mother in 1618 before he had even taken clerical orders, and in addition to being born into an armigerous family, Newburgh married (successively) the daughters of two MPs, and bequeathed various lands and rented properties in Dorset.[45] As for the downland areas, the

[40] A. Milton, *Laudian and Royalist Polemic in Seventeenth-Century England: the Career and Writings of Peter Heylyn* (Manchester, 2007), p. 134.

[41] J. Barnard, *Theologo-Historicus, or the True Life of the Most Reverend Divine and Excellent Historian, Peter Heylyn DD* (London, 1683), p. 204.

[42] J. Bettey, 'Downlands', in *The English Rural Landscape*, ed. J. Thirsk (Oxford, 2000), pp. 27–49, at pp. 29–30.

[43] WSHC, P14/101, administration bond, commission, inventory, renunciation and will of James Keate, vicar of Chardstock, 1705; D5/29/4, fo. 16, dean of Salisbury's visitation book, 1671; D5/28/46, fo. 39, churchwardens' presentment, Chardstock, 1668; TNA, C 94/2, fo. 74, Chardstock.

[44] *The Minute Books of the Dorset Standing Committee, 1646–1650*, ed. C. H. Mayo (Exeter, 1902), pp. 462, 476–7 & 542–3; TNA, C 94/2, fo. 73 Wambrook; PROB 4/11139, inventory of John Chase of Wambrook, 1685.

[45] 'Newboroughe, Walter (*CCED* Person ID 13880)' and 'Newburgh, Walter (*CCED* Person ID 55009)', *CCED* (accessed 7 March 2017); TNA, C 94/2, fos. 78–79, Symondsbury; J. G. Bartlett, *The Ancestors and Descendants of Thomas Newberry of Dorchester, Norfolk, Massachusetts* (Boston, Mass., 1914), pp. 24–6; F. Thistlethwaite, *Dorset Pilgrims* (London, 1989), p. 51; TNA: C 142/762/150, inventory post mortem of Walter Newburgh, clerk, 1632; PROB 11/162, will of Walter Newburgh, 1631.

evidence for West Dorset thus indicates that most incumbents had little glebe land on which to rely, and that those who thrived had wealthy family and invested in land and property.

Many more inventories survive for Blackmore Vale than for other regions, including a series for three successive rectors of Beer Hackett. John Downton, appointed in 1577, was a local man. Although his will includes bequests of land and property in two neighbouring parishes, his inventory lists only a few household items valued at £20, with no animals or farm equipment. His successor, Nicholas Jefferies, was appointed in 1626, but two years later the churchwardens reported that 'our parson is not resident uppon his parsonage'. Jefferies' inventory of 1636 lists estate to the value of £79, including wheat and oats growing upon the ground worth £40, as well as animals, various plough stuff, and a cart and wheels. He was clearly involved in farming, although he may not have been resident in Beer Hackett.[46] Hugh Strode succeeded Jefferies in 1637, and was sequestered in 1646, having allegedly been plundered of the enormous sum of £5,000 in money and 'an incredible quantity of plate and jewels' (this may have been exaggerated, but nevertheless indicates considerable wealth). He was restored in 1660, but died two years later. His inventory, totalling £31, includes £14 in bonds, £4 for a mare, and 'a parcell of small bookes which the plundering rebells left him'.[47] Neither Downton nor Strode were graduates, but both were local men who had amassed land and money, although Strode had been stripped of most of his. Jefferies' family background is unknown, and his inventory lists no property, but he appears to have been personally involved in farming.

Few inventories survive for heathland parishes. Bere Regis has some higher land but comprises predominantly heathland, and in 1650, total income from the living was estimated at below the median value of £60 for Dorset parishes. Thomas Bastard, vicar of Bere Regis from 1593, had led a chequered career. At Oxford, he had been described as being 'a most excellent epigrammatist, and being always ready to versify upon any subject, did let nothing material escape his fancy'.[48] Having been accused of libel and forced to leave the university, he received support from the Earl of Suffolk for appointments to two heathland parishes, Bere Regis and Almer. Yet despite trying to supplement his income by publishing epigrams, including one bemoaning his poverty, he died in debt in Dorchester prison

---

[46] WSHC, D5/28/28 fo. 68, Beer Hackett churchwardens' presentment, 1628; P5/1636/35, account, administration bond, commission, inventory of Nicholas Jeffries, clerk of Beer Hackett, 1636.

[47] *WR*, p. 137; WSHC, P5/1662/94, inventory of Hugh Strode, clerk of Beer Hackett, 1662.

[48] A. à Wood and P. Bliss, *Athenae Oxonienses* (London, 1813), ii. 228.

in 1618, leaving an inventory valued at only £16, half of which was for '133 books in a chest'. A study of books was also the most valuable item left by Thomas Basket, another incumbent of Bere Regis, in 1665. His inventory mentions no farming equipment or produce, apart from 'Three thousand of turffes', which would have been dug from the heathland.[49] The evidence for heathland parishes is therefore scanty, although the absence of surviving inventories suggests that the incumbents left little wealth. There are no surviving inventories for seventeenth-century incumbents of South Dorset parishes.

In summary, those incumbents of downland and West Dorset parishes for whom inventories were made tended to have influential patrons or wealthy family, enabling them to invest in property and engage in money lending and other activities. The absence of glebe meant that most did not engage directly in farming. The survival of a larger number of wills and inventories from Blackmore Vale suggests that a greater proportion of incumbents in this region were sufficiently wealthy to have property to bequeath. Self-sufficiency was perhaps easier here, given the enclosed nature and higher yield of the glebe land. In contrast, incumbents of heathland parishes derived little income from the land, and either lived in relative poverty or, like Thomas Bastard, turned to more creative ways of supplementing their income.

Tithe income

Few 1650 survey returns distinguish between glebe and tithe income, but details of the latter are given in the *Valor Ecclesiasticus*. Total tithe income amounted to 68.24 per cent of all Dorset income recorded in the *Valor*, whereas glebe income accounted for only 9.21 per cent, the remainder being received from oblations and pensions.

Table 4.1. Tithe income by landscape region in Dorset

Landscape	Median	Maximum
Blackmore Vale	£6 13s 4d	£28 0s 0d
Downland	£8 9s 8d	£34 6s 8d
Heathland	£7 0s 0d	£20 8s 0d
West Dorset	£5 2s 8d	£31 12s 0d
South Dorset	£7 13s 3d	£24 7s 4d

[49] WSHC, P5/1665/8, administration bond, commission and inventory of Thomas Baskett, clerk of Bere Regis, 1665; 'Baskett, Thomas (*CCED* Person ID 13728)', *CCED* [accessed 7 March 2017].

In Blackmore Vale, the median value of parish tithes was £6 13s 4d, with a maximum of £28 at Stalbridge where tithes accounted for eighty-one per cent of the rector's income. In the downland parishes, the median was higher, and several parishes yielded more than £25 in tithes, but fortunes in this area were more variable, as five vicarages produced no tithe income for the incumbent at all since the tithes were payable to impropriate rectors. The median for heathland parishes was only £7, with no parish yielding more than £20 8s per annum, and that for South Dorset was £7 13s 3d, with only one parish worth more than £16 in tithes. These figures are broadly in line with expectations, given the previously mentioned variations in yield in the different landscape regions. However, surprisingly, West Dorset had the lowest median tithe valuation, at only £5 2s 8d. The populous parish of Netherbury provided tithe income of £31 12s but the rest as little as £1, although all parishes in this region had at least some tithe income.

Terriers for several parishes note that monetary payments were customary in lieu of tithes. In some cases, tithes relating to specific lands or farms had been commuted. For example, in the West Dorset parish of Pilsdon, all tithes were paid in kind except for those from the manor farm, worth £13 6s 8d per annum in 1535 and reputed to be worth £8 out of a total parochial income of £30 a year by 1650.[50] The rector therefore relied heavily on payments by a single farmer, which might be risky in case of any dispute, but would be advantageous if these payments were reliable since it meant chasing fewer individual tithe payers. At Buckhorn Weston in Blackmore in 1634, five shillings were paid annually 'in lieu of all tithes of certain grounds called Cowparke', but this accounted for only a small proportion of the total income of around £50.[51] In the downland parish of Portesham, two farms nearly three miles east of the village made fixed annual payments: in 1650, the parishioners noted that Friar Waddon farm paid 'but 40s yearly', whereas Corton farm paid in kind at the rate of three lambs and three fleeces.[52] Again, this may have been advantageous to the vicar since it would have been difficult for him to monitor and enforce payments from more distant residents.

More commonly, tithes in kind were substituted with flat rates on specific types of tithable produce, known as moduses.[53] These were prone to reduce in value as a result of inflation, as acknowledged by John Cowell in 1607,

---

[50] WSHC, D28/10/101, Pilsdon terrier, 1634; *Valor Ecclesiasticus*; TNA, C 94/2, fo. 166, Pilsdon.

[51] WSHC, D28/10/19, Buckhorn Weston terrier, 1635.

[52] TNA, C 94/2, fo. 125, Portesham.

[53] W. Stevenson, *General View of the Agriculture of the County of Dorset* (London, 1812), p. 96.

who observed that monetary payments were 'very unreasonable in these daies, when both lamb and calves are growne four times dearer, and more then they were when this price was first accepted'.[54] Moduses in Dorset were most frequently agreed in lieu of milk from cows and heifers. In the dairying regions of Blackmore Vale and West Dorset, parishioners paid two or three pence per cow and somewhat less for a heifer. For example, Matthew Perry, rector of Silton in Blackmore, confirmed in a 1637 terrier that there was 'an absolute perfect Custome for cowe white' of two pence per cow and one penny per heifer.[55] By contrast, downland parishioners tended to pay only one penny per cow, confirming their lower milk yield, and there are no recorded instances of moduses applied to any other produce in this region, apart from one penny per garden plot at Godmanstone. Surviving terriers for heathland parishes mention no moduses and are relatively unspecific about particular types of produce, referring only to corn, wheat and hay. Similarly, terriers for South Dorset parishes do not mention types of produce, apart from detailed arrangements for fish caught in Portland, but tend to name specific farms and holdings from which tithes were due.

Much more information is provided by terriers for the 'cheese' regions, which frequently list a wide range of produce, including apples, hemp, flax, hops, turnips, honey, wax, geese, ducks, turkeys, eggs, pigs, lambs, sheep, kine, horses and colts. As a perishable form of produce, eggs appear to have been a particular source of annoyance for incumbents. Some parishes specified that a penny was due annually for eggs, often at Easter. At Buckhorn Weston, tithe eggs were due 'on Good Friday if demanded', suggesting that the rector might not insist on his entitlement; whereas at Sutton Waldron, the rector claimed he had never received tithe eggs for thirty-two years, and had then been paid for two years together, at three eggs for a cock and two for each hen.[56] He did not record how many eggs this amounted to, but it had been sufficiently irksome for him to note it in the parish register. Despite the wooded nature of the 'cheese' regions, only one terrier, for Hazelbury Bryan, mentions tithe of 'stock or board wood', in this case as an exception, as the rector was allowed only three pence per acre rather than its true value.[57]

The 1650 parliamentary surveys are generally silent on the nature of tithe produce, except where special arrangements had been made. For example,

---

[54] J. Cowell, *The Interpreter* (Cambridge, 1607).

[55] WSHC, D28/10/117/2, Silton terrier, 1637.

[56] WSHC, D28/10/19, Buckhorn Weston terrier, 1682; DOHC, PE/SWN/RE1/1, Sutton Waldron parish register, 1721.

[57] DOHC, D/392/1, Hazelbury Bryan terrier, 1614.

the chapelry of West Milton in West Dorset received tithes due from the sinecure of Witherstone on wheat, rye, barley, oats, beans, peas, thatch, hemp, flax, hay, cow white (milk, butter and cheese), calves, sheep, wool, hogs, colts, apples, hops and gardens.[58] It appears, therefore, that the greater detail of Blackmore Vale and West Dorset tithe entitlements may have resulted from the potential for evasion owing to the more diverse nature of the tithable produce and the distributed settlements in this landscape, whereas produce from the nucleated villages of the downlands was more easy to survey, with fewer small landholders.

In a few cases, subsequent incumbents managed to reverse disadvantageous modus agreements. At Buckland Newton in Blackmore, William Lister succeeded in revoking an unusual modus allegedly introduced by the parishioners in a 1634 terrier, by which cheese was due in lieu of all tithe of cow white from three tithings, 'to be delivered when stiff and fit to be carried'.[59] Nathaniel Napier, appointed rector of the previously mentioned Blackmore parish of Sutton Waldron in 1686, recorded a long list of tithe customs in the parish register in order to safeguard the rights of future incumbents, writing that 'experience has confirmed to me, which I communicate to you, viz. that twill be much to your disadvantage to be over-familiar with your neighbours at first coming'. For example, he had succeeded in renegotiating tithes on milk and calves: 'The parishioners have pleaded a Custome of paying 2d per Cow for milk; the left shoulder for a Calfe kild at home; but we are now agreed that the Rector shall receive 1 shilling for each Cow in lieu of Milk and Calfes.' He advised his successors 'at yr Perill to make yrselfe truely M^r of these Directions that so you may not be abused or foold by these unmannerly Clowns'.[60] However, despite their potentially declining value, moduses may have been more convenient in terms of both collection and disposability of income. They were certainly easier than the experience of William Hastings, rector of Burton Bradstock in West Dorset, who died in 1635 as a result of an argument while trying to claim his tithe lambs.[61]

[58] TNA, C 94/2, fo. 71 West Milton.

[59] TNA, E 134/2/Anne/East16 & Trin4 Lister v Foy & Hopkins, Buckland Newton tithes. According to one definition, 'cow white' was 'a customary payment in lieu of tithe milk of a cow ... called in this county "cow white money", or simply "cow white"' (E. Boswell, *The Ecclesiastical Division of the Diocese of Bristol* (Sherborne, 1826), p. 73); however, in this case, the context indicates that it meant the combined tithe due on milk, butter and cheese, to be delivered as a portable cheese.

[60] DOHC, PE/SWN/RE1/1, Sutton Waldron parish register, 1721.

[61] J. Bettey, *Casebook of Sir Francis Ashley, 1614–35* (Dorchester, 1981), p. 120.

Persecution

Having examined variations in clerical income by landscape region, this section investigates the extent to which the landscape may have affected clergymen's experiences during the 1640s and 1650s. Seventy-five incumbents were sequestered from eighty-five of Dorset's 289 parishes between 1642 and 1659, amounting to approximately twenty-nine per cent of the total (see Figure 4.2), over half of whom (forty-four) had been restored to the same living by 1662.

Furthermore, three sequestrations in Blackmore Vale were for very short periods. Edward Davenant, rector of Gillingham, was sequestered in 1645 but restored by the county committee two years later, and William Bisson's sequestration from Shillingstone, purely on account of his old age and sickness, was also overturned.[62] The most surprising case was of Thomas Bravell, rector of Compton Abbas, who was sequestered 'for joininge with the Country in the clubb business', having allegedly led a rising of 4,000 Clubmen on Hambledon Hill on 4 August 1645. Clubmen were groups of countrymen who rose up against the depredations of both royalist and parliamentarian soldiers, whom they accused of damaging crops and looting local inhabitants. According to a parliamentary source, the Clubmen of

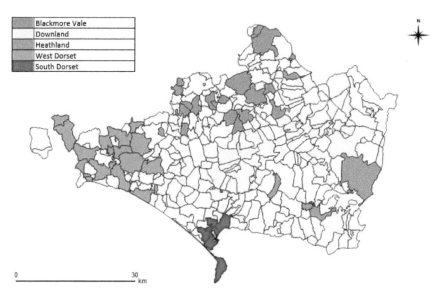

Figure 4.2. Parishes from which Dorset incumbents were sequestered, 1642–59.

[62] Mayo, *Minute Books*, p. 202; *WR*, p. 128.

Hambledon Hill carried banners on which were written 'sentences of Scripture, profanely applied by their Malignant Priests, who were the principal stirrers up of the people to these tumultuous assemblies'. Those arrested and questioned claimed that Mr Bravell himself had issued the warrant for their gathering.[63] However, the following year he was awarded a doctorate from the University of Oxford, and in April 1647 was restored to his living on the testimony of three godly divines.[64]

Some of those sequestered – six from downland parishes, three from West Dorset and three from Blackmore Vale – managed to secure alternative cures while awaiting the Restoration. In Blackmore, Richard Gillingham, ousted from Lillington, was permitted to serve the cure of Pulham; while Matthew Perry, sequestered from Silton in 1647, was reported to be still officiating there in 1650, 'but by whose permission we knowe not being an outted minister; Mr Parry makes use of the glebe, and the tythes are sequestered into the hands of two officers'.[65]

Overall, analysis of the percentage of parishes affected by sequestration in each landscape region suggests that incumbents in South and West Dorset were much more likely to be sequestered (with thirty-seven and thirty-eight per cent of parishes affected, respectively) than those in other parts of the county (between twenty-two and twenty-nine per cent). The figure for Blackmore Vale drops from twenty-nine to twenty-seven per cent if the three aforementioned short-term sequestrations are discounted, while the heathland parishes were generally rather poor livings, as previously discussed, perhaps reducing the incentive for sequestration. The relatively high figures for South and West Dorset might suggest that there was greater support in the south and west of the county for puritan values and the new emphasis on preaching. However, the parishes of South Dorset were close to the garrisons of Portland and Weymouth, and West Dorset was within the purview of forces at Lyme Regis, by whom Gamaliel Chase, rector of Wambrook, was plundered, supporting Ian Green's suggestion that sequestrations were more prevalent in the vicinity of parliamentary garrisons.[66]

Nevertheless, twenty-eight Dorset incumbents survived in the same livings from prior to the outbreak of war through to the Restoration (see

[63] J. Sprigge, *Anglia Rediviva* (London, 1647), p. 80.

[64] Mayo, *Minute Books*, p. 232.

[65] TNA, C 94/2, fo. 114, Silton.

[66] WMS C2.365, cited in F. McCall, *Baal's Priests: The Loyalist Clergy and the English Revolution* (Farnham, 2013), pp. 157–8; I. M. Green, 'The persecution of "scandalous" and "malignant" parish clergy during the English civil war', *EHR*, lxiv (1979), pp. 507–31, at p. 523.

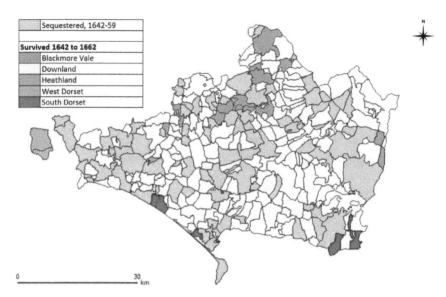

Figure 4.3. Parishes in which Dorset incumbents remained
from pre-1642 until after 1662.[a]

[a] Gillingham is included as a parish where the incumbent survived, since Edward
Davenant was sequestered for only a short time. In the two other short-term
sequestrations previously mentioned, the incumbents died before the Restoration.

Figure 4.3). A geographical pattern of survival is clearest in Blackmore Vale,
where twelve incumbents (fourteen per cent) survived throughout this
period. Although based on fewer parishes, the survival rate in South Dorset
parishes (twenty-six per cent) is surprisingly high. Away from the port
towns, other coastal parishes remained relatively unaffected. In contrast,
only one incumbent survived in a heathland parish (West Parley), and two
(five per cent) in West Dorset. The latter were the small parish of North
Poorton, and Stockland with Dalwood chapel, which was a Dorset enclave
surrounded by Devon.

Following the Restoration, sixty-two ministers were ejected from their
livings (see Table 4.2). In twenty-three cases, this resulted from the return
of a formerly sequestered incumbent, and a further twelve also departed
in 1660 or 1661. Twenty-seven were ejected in 1662, undoubtedly for non-
conformity, since all who were still alive in 1672 applied for non-conformist
licences.[67]

[67] F. Bate, *The Declaration of Indulgence 1672: a Study in the Rise of Organised Dissent*
(London, 1988), pp. xxiv–xxvi.

Table 4.2. Number of ejections, 1660–2

	Sequestered minister restored	No returning minister – year ejected				Percentage of parishes affected
		1660	1661	1662	Total	
Blackmore	4	2		4	**10**	12
Downland	8	1		11	**20**	17
Heathland	2	2		3	**7**	26
West Dorset	6	1	4	8	**19**	49
South Dorset	3	2		1	**6**	33
Total	**23**	**8**	**4**	**27**	**62**	**22**

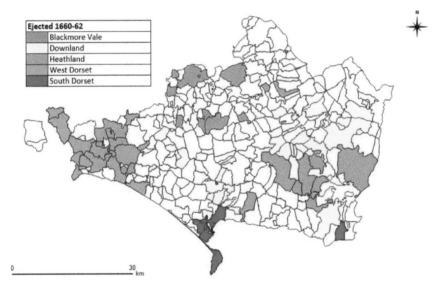

Figure 4.4. Parishes from which Dorset incumbents were ejected, 1660–2.

Figure 4.4 illustrates the preponderance of ejections in West Dorset, affecting forty-nine per cent of parishes in this area, with a high proportion also in South Dorset. Furthermore, in West Dorset, six sequestered incumbents were restored, and a further five ministers were ejected in 1660 and 1661, outnumbering the eight who departed as a result of their failure to subscribe to the Oath of Uniformity in 1662; and in South Dorset, five out of six of those ejected departed in 1660, with only one expelled in 1662. This strongly suggests that, in these regions, unwelcome 'intruders' who had been placed in parishes during the interregnum were ousted as soon as possible at the Restoration.

With regard to the effect of garrisons, the South Dorset parishes of Portland and Wyke Regis quickly removed their intruded ministers, yet George Thorne, in the adjoining parish of Radipole and Melcombe Regis, remained there until 1662 and was the only South Dorset minister ejected for refusing the Oath of Uniformity. In West Dorset, Ames Short also held on until 1662 in Lyme Regis where, 'Being much respected by the neighbouring gentry he was often and strongly urged to put aside his scruples.'[68] Thus, although the presence of garrisons may have influenced sequestrations in the 1640s, by the 1660s some ministers subsequently appointed to these parishes had gained local support.

The percentage of ejections was very much lower for Blackmore Vale, at only twelve per cent. This was perhaps because some replacements for sequestered incumbents had been nominated by the patrons of the living rather than being inserted by the county committee, making them more acceptable to the parishioners.

Three long-standing incumbents who survived the Civil Wars and interregnum in the same parish lost their livings for failing to take the Oath of Uniformity in 1662. These were William Benn, rector of Dorchester All Saints since 1629, Henry Martin, vicar of Tarrant Monkton since 1627, and Hugh Gundry, rector of Mapperton in West Dorset since 1640. Benn had been a stalwart of Dorchester's puritan regime, and in a post-Restoration pamphlet listing what might be viewed as divine punishments on those refusing to use the Book of Common Prayer, he was said to be suffering a 'monstrous chin-cough, which would make any that hears him, doubt theres a shrewd core at his consience, for his subscribing to the Kings tryall ... and other hainous crimes, besides his great slip at Oxford, that all his Hah-hings cannot remove'.[69] Benn was clearly unpopular with the new regime, and Daniel Sagittary later reported that he had stolen a plate from Queen's College and had remarked on the Restoration 'Lord send us better News of Heaven yn we had by the Post, or we are all undone!'[70]

Gundry had also been in favour during the interregnum, having received a payment of £10 from the county committee in March 1647 for his 'constant

---

[68] W. Densham and J. Ogle, *The Story of the Congregational Churches in Dorset* (Bournemouth, 1899), p. 144.

[69] Anon., *An Anti-Brekekekex-Coax-Coax, or, A Throat-Hapse for the Frogges and Toades that Lately Crept Abroad, Croaking Against the Common-Prayer Book and Episcopacy* (London, 1660), pp. 5–6.

[70] WMS C4.112, letter from Daniel Sagittary to John Walker. My thanks to Fiona McCall for this reference.

and paynefull labours', but was ejected in 1662 following a visitation by the dean of Salisbury, when he failed to produce his ordination papers and refused to subscribe to the oath.[71] Mapperton had had puritan-inclined rectors for over half a century. In the late 1590s, Gundry's immediate predecessor, George Bowden, had been presented by his parishioners for refusing to wear a surplice and not standing at the name of Jesus, and in 1607 the parishioners had complained that 'Our parson does not wear any cappe according to the latest canon.' These were indications of puritan leanings, yet Bowden had continued to serve the cure, despite being censured by the dean of Salisbury.[72] Gundry's appointment in 1640 followed in the same tradition. However, it was one thing to have puritan tendencies in a remote parish prior to the Civil Wars, but Gundry's active patronage by the interregnum regime made him more visible to both judicial and ecclesiastical authorities. Having raised his head above the parapet of relative seclusion, the new political climate of 1662 brought about his ejection.

Cross-county mobility

Earlier in this chapter, some evidence was presented relating to parishioners' and clergymen's experiences of travelling relatively locally, including Robert Lane's difficulty in returning from a visitation. However, William Huish must have used his coach to travel further afield, and Hugh Gundry's payment of £10 from the county committee in 1647 also suggests the necessity for clergymen to travel beyond their own parishes. In Gundry's case, the county committee recorded that 'through and by reason of plundringe his goods and losse of the profitts of his parsonage for his affeccon to the Parlyarment in these late troubles [he] hath not an horse to ride on'.[73]

Nevertheless, evidence from 215 wills and inventories suggests that clergymen in West Dorset, where Gundry lived, were less likely to own horses than in the downland and heathland parishes. Horses, saddles or riding apparel appear in only four out of thirty-five West Dorset records (11.43 per cent), compared with twenty per cent of heathland and sixteen per cent of downland parishes. None of the eight available wills and inventories for South Dorset mention horses, and the figure for Blackmore Vale is just under fourteen per cent. Thus, horse ownership appears to have

---

[71] Mayo, *Minute Books*, p. 201; WSHC, D5/29/2, fo. 17v, dean of Salisbury visitation book, 1662.

[72] WSHC, D5/28/7 fo. 2, Mapperton churchwardens' presentment, 1597–9; D5/28/9, fo. 54, Mapperton churchwardens' presentment, 1607; M. Ingram, 'Puritans and the church courts, 1560–1640', in *The Culture of English Puritanism, 1560–1700*, ed. C. Durston and J. Eales (Basingstoke, 1996), pp. 58–91, at p. 79.

[73] Mayo, *Minute Books*, p. 201.

differed by landscape type, with heathland and downland perhaps being more conducive to keeping and riding the animals, particularly given the relatively unenclosed nature of the landscape. This is confirmed by evidence from glebe terriers. In Blackmore Vale, only five terriers mention provision for horse pasture, and the vicar of Sherborne, whose glebe amounted to only his house, garden and stable, was 'permitted to keepe his horse in the Churchyard, Abby Lytten or Abby greene'.[74] Similarly in West Dorset, the only mention of horses is in Wambrook, where the outhouses included 'a stable to conteyne ffower horzes', and where the rector, Christopher Marraker, left his 'baye Mare' to his wife.[75] Wives are also mentioned in two heathland wills, with a wife's 'pillion Saddle and Saddlecloathe' at Owermoigne and 'my wife's Riding Suite and best wastcoate' at West Parley.[76] However, only one heathland terrier, for Studland, makes reference to horse pasture on the heath, whereas several South Dorset terriers mention commons for horses, although the latter probably included animals for ploughing rather than riding.[77] Horse commoning occurs much more frequently in downland terriers, often providing for two or three horses in the common fields or leazes, although once again, rather than for riding, the terrier for Bradford Peverell specifies 'the depasturing of fower Hallers [haulers], whether they be Horses or oxen ... in all Commons, pastures, meades and stubbles'.[78]

An interesting indication of the extent of cross-county communications in Dorset during the interregnum is given in a letter from Dorset MP John Bingham, of Melcombe Bingham in Blackmore Vale, to secretary Thurloe in 1655. Writing to report suspicions of conspiracy against the Cromwellian regime, he suggested that people were gathering from as far afield as Beaminster in the west and Canford in the east. In particular, they were drinking at Cashmore Inn near Blandford and watching cockfighting in Wimborne. Many of the participants were 'yong blades, well horsed, habited, and each a man waiteinge on them', but the older gentry and clergy were also involved, including Thomas Bragge, vicar of Horton. According to Bingham, 'At yong squire Hid's at Horton, 8 miles from Blandford, is one Bragg ... He it was, that betrayed Portland castel to the caveleers at the

---

[74] WSHC, D5/10/2, Sherborne terrier, 1669.

[75] WSHC, D28/10/139, Wambrook terrier, 1612; TNA, PROB 11/138, will of Christopher Marraker, Wambrook, 1620.

[76] TNA, PROB 11/124, will of Leonard Parry, Owermoigne, 1614; PROB 11/335, will of John Sherren, West Parley, 1671.

[77] WSHC, D28/10/127, Studland terrier, 1634.

[78] WSHC, D28/10/14, Bradford Peverell terrier, 1634.

first of our wars.'[79] Bragge's predecessor at Horton had died in 1647, and he had been presented to the living by Giles Greene, a puritan sympathizer. However, Greene died in 1655, and Bragge was sequestered the following year, having lost his protective patron. All the parishes mentioned in this letter, apart from Beaminster, are in the downland and heathland regions. This confirms the potentially greater mobility of incumbents in these areas, but perhaps also their greater visibility and susceptibility to surveillance where enclosure was less common.

Conclusion

This chapter has focused on the extent to which the landscape was a potential determinant of clergymen's prosperity, through a more fine-grained analysis than a simple chalk/cheese dichotomy. The nature of the landscape evidently affected clergymen's experiences, in terms of the ease with which they themselves could get around their parishes and further afield, and parishioners' church attendance. Classifying the landscape in this way has also highlighted other landscape-related factors, such as the productivity of glebe land and the yield and collectability of tithe income. The analysis has revealed that the values of livings and clergymen's ability to live on income from agricultural activities varied considerably by region, as did the availability of alternative sources of income. Patterns of sequestration, ejection and survival were also partly attributable to the nature of the landscape itself, in terms of soil type and topography, which affected the value of livings and the social structure of parishes. Poorer heathland livings may have been less attractive targets for sequestration, whereas incumbents in South and West Dorset were much more likely to be sequestered, perhaps owing to their proximity to garrisons. Nevertheless, South Dorset also harboured the highest proportion of interregnum 'survivors'. Overall, stability was greatest in Blackmore Vale, where there were relatively few sequestrations and ejections and more long-term survivors. Little surprise, then, that despite the difficult terrain, and the military depredations that led to the Clubmen uprising in this area, an old Dorset native in the mid-twentieth century was heard to say that 'Cromwell could not conquer this part of the country, "Dirty Do'set"'.[80]

---

[79] Letter from J. Bingham to secretary Thurloe, Jan. 1655, Thurloe, iii. 117–34.

[80] G. E. Fussell, 'Four centuries of farming systems in Dorset, 1500–1900', *Proceedings of the Dorset Natural History and Antiquarian Club*, lxxiii (1951), 116–40, at p. 119.

5. The clergy of Sussex:
the impact of change, 1635–65

Helen M. Whittle

The following analysis is based on twelve years' research into the county of Sussex from *c.*1635 to *c.*1665, looking at ways to measure the degree of change or impact experienced by the inhabitants as a result of the Civil Wars, interregnum and restoration of the monarchy. There is, as yet, no single source for information of this nature; in order to facilitate the analysis a database was compiled from many sources – for example, the Protestation Returns, the Return of Contributions to the Relief of Irish Protestants, Calamy's *Nonconformist's Memorial,* Walker's *Sufferings of the Clergy,* and Matthew's *Calamy Revised* and *Walker Revised,* as well as parish and county histories, *Sussex Clergy Inventories* and the *Clergy of the Church of England Database (CCED).*[1] The only previous substantial studies of the county for this period are Charles Thomas-Stanford, *Sussex in the Great Civil War 1642–1660* (1910) and, more recently, Anthony Fletcher's *A County Community in Peace and War.*[2] Other work has been done for the county as part of more general work, for example Timothy McCann's chapter on religious observance in *An Historical Atlas of Sussex.*[3]

Looking outside Sussex, work has previous been done by, in particular, Fiona McCall and Rosemary O'Day, as well as by Clive Holmes, John Morrill and others, but the subject of the clergy who served during this period of disruption is only now emerging as a topic requiring serious, in-depth study.[4] Where previous work has been done, the analysis of figures

[1] *East Sussex Contributors to the Relief of Irish Protestants 1642,* ed. M. J. Burchall (comp.) (Sussex Genealogical Centre Occasional Papers No. 10, Brighton, n.d.). Original returns in the Parliamentary Archives; E. Calamy, *The Nonconformist's Memorial* (London, 1775); Walker, *Attempt*; *WR*; *CR*; Sussex Record Society [SRS], xci.

[2] C. Thomas-Stanford, *Sussex in the Great Civil War 1642–1660* (London, 1910); A. Fletcher, *Sussex 1600–1660: a County Community in Peace and War* (London, 1975).

[3] K. Leslie and B. Short, *An Historical Atlas of Sussex* (Chichester, 1999), ch. 28.

[4] F. McCall, *Baal's Priests: the Loyalist Clergy and The English Revolution* (Farnham, 2013); R. O'Day, *The English Clergy: Emergence and Consolidation of a Profession, 1558–1642* (Leicester, 1979).

seems to indicate that there was almost certainly a wide difference in experience between local areas, but whether this is due to factors influenced by geographical location, differences in prevailing local ideology, or simply variations in the available data is something that will require a much wider study than is possible here.

Part of my project set out to identify as many clergy who served Sussex between 1635 and 1665 as possible (so as to include those in post at the outbreak of the Civil Wars and those in post after the dust had settled post Restoration). Names were located from a wide miscellany of sources as they came to light.[5] Some 724 individual clergy were identified but this cannot be assumed to be exhaustive. New names come to light from time to time, but these almost certainly represent a tiny fraction of those who served the county at the relevant time and are unlikely to skew the conclusions arising from the research.

Methodological issues

There are some issues with the sources. The writings of Walker, Calamy and Matthews are often contradictory.[6] For example, Walker provided what appears to be a vivid account of John Edsaw of Chailey:

> He was … of the family of the Edsaws of Chainton …The occasions of his sufferings were … his reading the King's Declarations, and sending his eldest son to serve as a volunteer in His Majesty's Army. He was imprisoned … His living also was sequestered, his children turned out of doors, … He had … six children, none of which … came to want; … the eldest son having … married a Lady of good fortune … Mr. Edsaw, … just lived to see the Restoration, but was prevented by Death from re-possessing his own living.[7]

This gives an example of the 'sufferings' of one clergyman. However, it states that he lived to see the Restoration, whereas other sources indicate that he

---

[5] Additional sources include the *CCED*, the *Alumni* of Oxford and Cambridge, the National Archives catalogue, the catalogues of wills proved in the various Sussex courts (Archdeaconries of Chichester and Lewes and the Peculiars of Battle, Chichester, Pagham and Tarring and South Malling), the series of volumes published by Sussex Record Society and Sussex Archaeological Society and the two major works on Sussex during this period, Thomas-Stanford, *Sussex* and A. Fletcher, *Sussex*.

[6] Much of Matthews's information for Sussex was compiled by Thomas Newcomb, who was apparently not a very reliable correspondent. See F. McCall, *Baal's Priests*, pp. 42–3.

[7] No place name in Sussex can be identified with 'Chainton' unless this is intended as a reference to the Chancton or Chanctonbury area, the administrative district around Storrington and Washington. The Sussex Marriage Index indicates that the surname was well represented in those parishes. Walker, *Attempt*, p. 238; *WR*, p. 355. Walker's information was supplied by Edsaw's son, who was a small child when his father died, and presumably his recollection of events was vague.

had died by 1647. The strongest evidence must be his PCC (Prerogative Court of Canterbury) will, made and proved in 1647.[8] John Abbot served the parish of Hollington for many years and is relatively easy to trace in the records. However, the name John Abbot recurs in the parishes of New Fishbourne, South Stoke, New Shoreham and Midhurst but he is not listed in any of these parishes on *CCED* and the references are taken from Calamy.[9] If John Abbot of Hollington died in 1644/5, the remaining entries must be a different man and it seems likely that they relate to one individual who ended up at South Stoke after the Restoration, having been ejected from New Fishbourne. Walker gave William Cox DD, prebendary, as being sequestered in 1643 and dying in 1647, having joined the royal court at Oxford. However, there is evidence that Cox was the same William Cox who was at Felpham in 1640 and Bolney 1641–62. It is likely that this latter date is purely indicative of the next appointment to this parish and does not preclude Cox having died in 1647, but emphasizes the need for caution. The likelihood of confusion is increased by the probate of the will of William Cox DD of Petworth in 1657, raising the likelihood that there were several of this name.[10]

Some clergy had been Sussex incumbents for decades before 1641, others who were reinstated or conformed after the Restoration continued for decades after 1660; many more came and went within months as the local situation changed during the 1640s and 1650s. A note from the Ardingly parish registers is just as relevant to the majority of parishes: 'These yeares that is to [say] 1643, 1644 and 1645 are imperfect in this register by reason of the change in ministers.'[11] In many Sussex parishes the registers are defective or missing altogether for the period 1642–60, and the bishops' transcripts were also not kept (the post of bishop having been abolished).

Puritanism

Puritan influence in the county had been strong long before 1641. The major towns of Rye and Lewes were important areas of puritanism. Mayhew stated that 'the growth of Protestantism in Rye owed much to the geographical

[8] TNA, PROB11/203/76.

[9] Midhurst was in fact a chapelry of Easebourne at this period; Calamy, *Nonconformist's Memorial*; *CR*, p. 1.

[10] TNA, PROB11/274/155. He requests to be interred in 'some place of Christian burial without any other ceremony since the use of the book of Common Prayer and other rites of the Church of England (whereof I die a member) are interdicted'. The will is dated and proved in 1657.

[11] Ardingly Parish Registers, SRS, xvii, p. 29.

situation of Rye and its function as a port, in particular to the impact of new Protestant ideas coming in from outside, which found an echo in an earlier nonconformity, for which the town's northern hinterland was well-known'.[12] Godfrey wrote that 'there are many records of the troubles of the Nonconformists ... Lewes became a centre for the conference of many of the ejected ministers of the County, and the more prosperous tradesmen of the town seem to have been their supporters'.[13] Adamson commented on how 'liberating, gentry-empowering puritanism confronted authoritarian, clericalist Laudianism' and how 'even zealous Puritanism [could be] regarded as scarcely more than a means of social control'.[14] However, Underdown stated that 'the Sussex Clubmen voiced the same religious orthodoxy as their western counterparts [complaining that] "Mechanics and unknown persons" had replaced orthodox clergy at the whim of a single committee-man'.[15]

There is a useful survey of conformity by Timothy McCann in the *Historic Atlas of Sussex*.[16] He shows that, while the greater part of the county was conformist, there were significant levels of non-conformity in a number of parishes, while there were concentrations of recusants at West Firle, Racton, Clapham, West Tarring and Burton as well as the major community at Midhurst/Easebourne.[17] There was also a significant Catholic community in Chichester which produced its own martyr, Thomas Bullaker, hanged, drawn and quartered at Tyburn as late as 1640.[18]

Clergy origins

Using the data extracted for this chapter it is possible to conclude that the clergy serving the county across this period were drawn from a diverse cross-section of backgrounds but, where the relevant details have been recorded, the greatest number identifiable were Sussex-born (see Figure 5.1).[19]

Birthplaces were identified for 388 of the 724 clergy studied. These show that nearly a fifth of the clergy studied were known to be born in the county, representing around two-fifths of those whose origins are known, while a

---

[12] G. Mayhew, *Tudor Rye* (Brighton, 1987), p. 55.

[13] *Lewes: The Official Guide to the Historic County Town*, ed. W. Godfrey (Lewes, 1932), p. 11.

[14] J. Adamson, *The English Civil War* (Basingstoke, 2009), p. 12.

[15] D. Underdown, 'The chalk and the cheese: contrasts among the English clubmen', *Past & Present*, lxxxv (1979), 25–48, at p. 43.

[16] Leslie and Short, *Historical Atlas*, pp. 56–7.

[17] That is, close to Cowdray, seat of the Montague Brown family.

[18] P. Gill and A. McCann, *Walks around Historic Chichester* (Chichester, 1980), p. 3.

[19] Birthplace information was gleaned from entries in the *Alumni*, the *Oxford Dictionary of National Biography*, information in wills or anecdotal evidence in local and other histories.

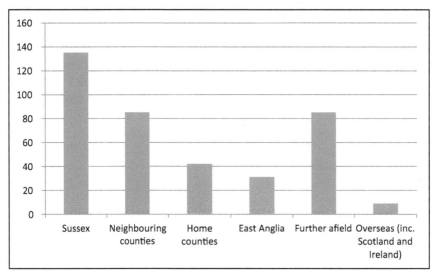

Figure 5.1. Birthplaces of Sussex clergy.[a]

[a] For clergy whose birthplaces could be identified.

similar number were drawn from adjacent counties and London and the 'Home Counties'. A considerable number (similar to those from the nearer area) came from much further afield, including Scotland, Ireland, the Channel Islands and overseas.

There is evidence from the wills examined of various clerical 'dynasties' in the county, as well as inter-marriage between clerical families and strong friendships between the clergy of neighbouring parishes. One such 'dynasty' is the Frewen family, commencing with John Frewen of Northiam, father of Accepted Frewen, Thankful Frewen and John Frewen, and grandfather of Thomas Frewen.[20] There are also instances of recurring surnames where the rarity of the name indicates a connection. The Independent brothers Isaac, Andrew and Samuel Wilmer are almost certainly connected with another Independent, Thomas Wilmer.[21]

[20] John Frewen, rector of Northiam 1583–1613; Accepted Frewen (1588–1664) who rose to be archbishop of York, 1660; Thankful Frewen (1591–1636), secretary to Lord Keeper Coventry; John Frewen (1595–1653), rector of Northiam 1628–1641; Thomas Frewen, rector of Northiam 1670–7, appointed there 10 June 1654. Stephen Frewen, brother of Accepted and John, was patron of the living and owner of Brickwalls House.

[21] At Coombes, Clapham, Clapham and Patching and Pagham, respectively.

The King family are another notable 'dynasty'. Henry King, bishop of Chichester 1642–69 was chaplain to James VI & I and Charles I. Walker stated him to have been 'puritanically affected and was promoted to [the bishopric of Chichester] to please that party, yet when the rebellion broke out he was most barbarously treated by them'. He made his will in 1653 but did not die until 1669.[22] It is strange he did not revise the will after 1660 as the document is full of his despair at the change in fortune following the wars. He stated that he was 'bred up in the reformed Protestant Church of England … I professe myself to dye a sincere member of the English Church.'[23] His father was a former bishop of London, his grandfather's uncle was bishop of Oxford. Despite the change in his fortunes he still had a large estate to leave. He mentioned his books: 'a small remainder of a large library taken from me at Chichester contrary to the condicion and contract of the Generall and Counsell of Warre at the taking of that Citie'; various pieces of plate given to him by Queen Anne; debts running into thousands of pounds owed him. He left various modest legacies totalling about £150 as well as £100 to the poor of Wornholt, Buckinghamshire, his birthplace. The money was to be used to purchase land to provide a dole of bread. There is no surviving inventory for his estate so it is not possible to know whether his estate recovered after the Restoration but he was obviously more 'comfortably off' than many of his clergy.

There are numerous other examples – the Blaxtons and Goffes are easy to identify and there are almost certainly further generations earlier or later. Daughters of clergy seem to have regularly married incumbents of neighbouring parishes or their fathers' curates, possibly signalling the difficulty of finding suitable matches in rural areas when their fathers were unable to provide large portions for them. Such arrangements were equally attractive to the husbands – a clergy daughter would not expect lavish entertainment and would know the duties expected of her as a clergyman's wife.

Next in importance to Bishop King must be Bruno Ryves or Reeves. Although not a native of Sussex (he came from Dorset) and most of his appointments were outside the county, his experience of this period is partly concerned with Sussex. He was deprived of St Martin in the Fields in January 1642 and later sequestered of Stanwell, Middlesex. Charles I appointed him to the deanery of Chichester and he was appointed Master

---

[22] TNA, PROB11/331/371.

[23] It is interesting that he added 'the first' after 'King Charles', given the date of the will; the monarchy had not yet been restored and although Charles II had been accepted as such by his followers, he was living in exile and England was officially a republic.

of Chichester Hospital.[24] A Mr Rook of Bradninch in Devon later described to Walker what is said to have happened:

> Dean Reeves (for so he spells it, tho' I take him to be this same person) was, with … all his family, taken out of their beds at midnight, turned out of doors, all his goods seized, and all that night lay under a hedge in the wet and cold. Next day my Lord Arundel hearing of this barbarous usage done to so pious a gentleman, sent his coach, with men and horses; where he was kindly entertained for some time.[25]

Education

In the same way it is possible to examine the standard of education of the greater part of the clergy who served in this period, with details available for 553 of the 724 studied. This breaks down as shown in Figure 5.2.

There is evidence of a widespread lack of education among the county clergy at an earlier date. An early seventeenth-century document in the collection of manuscripts at Hatfield House refers to conventicles involving

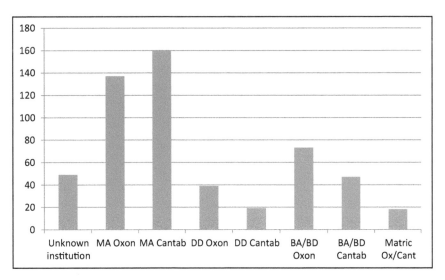

Figure 5.2. Levels of education of Sussex clergy.[a]

[a] Data in the graph represents all ascertainable information for the 724 clergy studied.

[24] At the Restoration he was appointed chaplain to Charles II and Dean of Windsor.

[25] Walker, *Attempt*, p. 56; *WR*, pp. 12, 175, 345.

Samuel Norden, parson of Hamsey, John Pearson 'a lay minister', Healy, Goldsmith, Frewen (presumably John Frewen of Northiam), Goffe (presumably Stephen Goffe of Stanmer), Ebury (all ministers) and others.[26] The unsigned document concludes:

> Since the three petitions were examined, a fourth was brought to my hands, contrived also by the ministers … sundry of these hot reformers and learned ministry never saluted any university, some of them departed with the lowest degrees and continue Bachelors of Arts, and the best of them in Sussex is but Master of Arts, yet they control degrees, orders and ordinances.

Various commentators on the 'sufferings' of the ejected royalist clergy indicate that lack of education was claimed. Richard Halsey of East Dean was turned out of his living 'upon a pretence of insufficiency' and was prohibited 'even from keeping an English school' at a penny a week, even though this meant that his nine children would starve.[27] Walker's opinion is that the 'insufficiency' was not so serious but that Halsey was not learned enough for the ministers who decided his fate. He was later restored to his living after the Restoration and Walker describes him as 'a very honest and industrious man'.

There is at least one instance of a sequestered living being taken up by someone with no apparent academic attainment. A letter in the Bodleian Library John Walker Archive states that, in 1642, the living of Steyning was procured by Benbrick, an Anabaptist, for Robert Childes, a coachman.[28] Childes held the living until the Restoration when 'being conscious of his having no right or title but by usurpation, [he] thought fit to withdraw'. He presumably had strong local support to have held the living for almost twenty years.[29]

Although the most common qualification in this study was MA Cantab, overall more clergy attended Oxford (250 against 226 Cambridge). A total of 298 were qualified to master's level – a little under half of the entire study with fifty-eight holding a DD and 120 only a BA or BD. Forty-nine are recorded as holding a degree but are not recorded in *Alumni Oxon* or

[26] Historic Manuscripts Commission, 9, Hatfield House Library & Archives, MS. 583, p. 262, dated after 18 Oct. 1603.

[27] Walker, *Attempt*, p. 357; *WR*, p. 275. Halsey held the degree of MA but the 'insufficiency' may relate to his skills (or absence of) as a preacher or the level of pastoral care he provided.

[28] F. Sawyer, *Proceedings of the Committee of Plundered Ministers relating to Sussex* (*SAC*, xxxvi, 1880), pp. 139–40; WMS C1.381.

[29] Sawyer indicates that he may already have retired as early as 1656; Charles Blackwell was recorded being disturbed as minister on 20 Dec. 1647, see WSRO, QR/W90, no. 19, 1657.

Cantab.[30] A few of these are noted as having attended Leiden, Dublin or other named institutions but they are too few to separate out. A proportion of those where no qualifications are known may also have studied overseas but, in turn, these are balanced out by those who achieved only matriculation at Oxford or Cambridge. Overall, the picture is that the county clergy were relatively well educated and that the traditional 'legend' of parishes being seized by uneducated, itinerant, fanatical preachers is not borne out. Only one story of such an incursion was found during the course of the study, with the suspicion that local men may have served as preachers in one or two further instances (see previous paragraph).

Yet there were variations in Sussex clergy's levels of education. Some were perhaps little more literate than their parishioners; others achieved academic recognition before appointment or during periods of exile from their parish duties. George Edgeley attained DD at Oxford in 1643, was prebendary of Heathfield and rector of Nuthurst.[31] Walker conjectures his sequestration from Nuthurst and states 'He ... hath expressed his Loyalty, by his active services, and passive sufferings in these times of hostility, for the defence of his Majesty's person, religion and laws.' Edgeley appears to have been succeeded as prebendary by William Oughtred, likely to be the mathematician of that name, a son of Benjamin Oughtred, registrar of Eton College.[32] William is stated to have attained an MA at Cambridge but is also shown as BD in Walker. In 1605 he was appointed to Shalford in Surrey but seems to have been known more for his mathematical work. According to Walker he expired from an 'excess of joy' in 1660 upon hearing that parliament had voted to restore the monarchy.

The earliest clergy studied died in 1635; the latest lived well into the eighteenth century. Obviously some of the men who died in the 1630s would have been of great age while others had been ordained for just a year or two. The same applies later but those at the end of the period will have been incumbents from at least 1662. It is difficult to generalize, as they were from all shades of the confessional spectrum, but it is fair to say that those who evidenced the highest degree of education were mostly those who were ordained closest to the beginning of the period, while those who had been ordained prior to the 1630s were generally less well educated.

---

[30] J. A. Venn, *Alumni Cantabrigiensis* (Cambridge, 1922–54); J. Foster, *Alumni Oxoniensis* 1500–1714 (London, Oxford, 1887–8). Many of the wills refer to the testator as being 'DD' or 'Master of Arts'. Other sources of information as status were gleaned from the parish registers at induction or burial, from memorial inscriptions or from local histories, although such were often written many years after the event.

[31] Walker, *Attempt*, pp. 13, 238; *WR*, p. 355.

[32] Walker, *Attempt*, p. 352; *WR*, pp. 14, 159.

Those ordained after the Restoration seem to be more uniformly products of the universities, but were (perhaps) of a slightly lower social status.[33] While there is no such thing as the 'average' person, most Sussex clergy of the period were MA Oxbridge and, as shall be shown in the next section, held an estate of between £100 and £500 including a substantial number of books and some form of real property. Around 7.5 per cent could be counted as extremely wealthy by the standards of the time, having estates valued in excess of £500 in addition to real property and valuable goods.

Wealth and wills

As noted, there are a large number of wills for Sussex clergy. The figures presented contain brief details of the wills and inventories (see Figure 5.3). In all, 268 wills and grants of administration (admons) were found in the Prerogative Court of Canterbury (PCC), Chichester and Lewes (including Battle and South Malling) courts. There were another six wills found in courts further afield and there may be others to be found, particularly in Kent, Hampshire and Surrey. There may be a few omitted from Lewes as the indexing of these is not sufficient to enable easy finding of clergy, although nominal searches were made where it seemed likely a will should be found. Grants of administration were not examined as the information

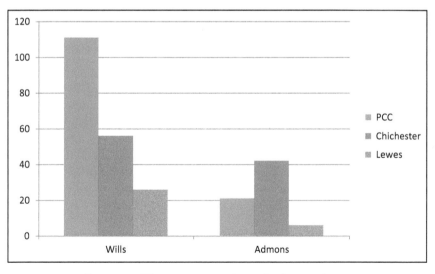

Figure 5.3. Testamentary evidence for Sussex clergy.

---

[33] See also I. Green, 'Career prospects and clerical conformity in the early Stuart Church', *Past & Present*, xc (1981), 93–103.

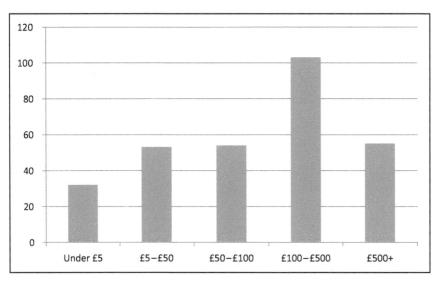

Figure 5.4. Monetary values in Sussex clergy wills.

obtainable was unlikely to have added to the study. In all 199 clergy wills were examined and details extracted. In addition, there are ninety-two surviving clergy inventories which were also examined.[34] A proportion of these are additional to wills but a number are the only surviving record of an estate.

The following figures show the ascertainable financial values (Figure 5.4) and numbers of clergy leaving books, plate and land (Figure 5.5)

From Figure 5.4 it appears that the greater number of clergy (103) were able to leave cash sums of £100–£500, but a comparable number (107) left only £5–£100 and thirty-two less than £5. A further fifty-five were able to leave sums greater than £500, often well into four figures.

Most bequests of plate amounted to a modest number of named pieces and larger bequests were mostly confined to clergy who went on to hold high office. A small number directed that specific sums of money should be expended to purchase items of plate in the same way that many left money for the purchase of mourning rings. Real property was mentioned in 166 of the 199 wills examined, indicating a high level of property ownership.[35] Many refer to recent purchases of property, presumably made in order to provide security for their families, who might otherwise find themselves homeless if reliant on parish accommodation.

[34] Mostly taken from SRS, xci.

[35] 'Real property' here includes freehold land, leases, copyholds etc.

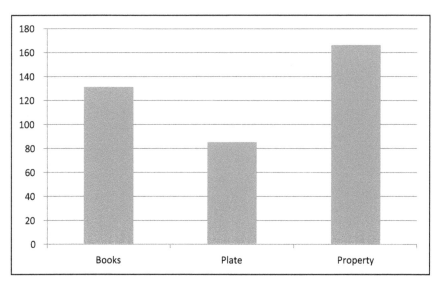

Figure 5.5. Sussex clergy wills mentioning books, plate and real property.

Where they are mentioned, details of gifts to the poor and references to 'libraries' or books are noted.[36] Unsurprisingly, given the level of education, nearly half the estates examined mentioned books in the will or inventory. Some appear to own only a handful, others refer to their 'libraries' or 'studies' of books and a handful left detailed catalogues. A greater number specifically directed that their books should be used to found a library or school or to replace libraries looted during the wars. While an omission of references to books cannot be taken as proof that they either owned none or were not interested in them, where specific books are referred to many of these would have been of considerable value. Many refer to books in Hebrew, Latin and Greek, indicating that they had sufficient acquaintance with those languages to be able to read the books in the original. Many list farming and/or brewing equipment, indicating that some were able to partly support themselves by growing food and brewing ale. Others mention monies placed out in the form of loans.

Some wills cast light on the personal beliefs of the testators. Joseph Henshaw of East Lavant, Stedham and Heyshott and later bishop of Peterborough used his will to express his thoughts 'after so great a persecution and usurpation both in Church and State as was not many years since in this land under which wicked times many holy and excellent

[36] Eg TNA, PROB11/413/51, George Benson, prebendary of Wisborough; PROB11/360/91, John Buckley of Shipley; PROB11/264/321, Joseph Hawkesworth of Burwash.

persons did resist with blood and I have been as a brand snatched out of the fire…).[37] William Cox[e] DD of Petworth, in his will proved in 1657, requests to be interred in 'some place of Christian burial without any other ceremony since the use of the Book of Common Prayer and other rites of the Church of England (whereof I die a member) are interdicted'.[38] John Scull of Slinfold left the large sum of £80 to the poor of various parishes and further gifts in excess of £350, clothing (including clerical gowns) and books. He also left £100 for the re-edifying of the cathedral 'provided that my Executrix first see whether the parliament will dissolve Deans and Chapters', in which case the gift would be withdrawn.[39] This reference to dissolution is interesting as the will was proved in 1641, when the upheavals of the war were only just beginning and parliament was not in uncontested control of either Church or state. Christopher Elderfield, minister of Burton, appears to have been considerably wealthier than average, mentioning plate, gowns, rings, bibles, books (including law books) and gifts amounting to over £400.[40] In his will proved in 1653 he leaves £36 to 'be bestowed upon godly poor ministers cast down by these times'. Some of his books are left to the 'publique library of Oxford'. In 1650, Elderfield had published *The Civil Right of Tythes*; 'the great pains he took with his second book, *Of Regeneration and Baptism, Hebrew and Christian*', published posthumously in 1653, 'are believed to have cost him his life'.[41] This is one of the longer clergy wills, running to five full pages, whereas most are little over one full page.

Henry Kent, 'Minister of God's word', Selsey, states 'I do believe the Bible to be the word of God, and the doctrine of the Church of England concerning matters of salvation to be grounded upon the holy scriptures and that by faith salvation is therefore to be had.' He also requests sermons to be made by Mr Speed or Mr Callowe or some other godly minister.[42] At the end of the document he leaves a book to his uncle titled *The Anatomy of Arminianism*, 'which heresie and a few ceremonies hath brought all this misery of warre upon this kingdome and I am the willinger to leave the world because the people are for bloody cruel and heart hardened'. Interestingly, this is dated as early as 1642, but not proved until 1645. Thomas Jackson,

[37] TNA, PROB11/361/4.

[38] TNA, PROB11/274/155. See further comment on Coxe above.

[39] TNA, PROB11/188/111; his executrix was his mother.

[40] TNA, PROB11/227/49.

[41] This story appears in the *Dictionary of National Biography* but is not repeated in the *ODNB*.

[42] TNA, PROB11/193/569; possibly John Callow of Sidlesham.

ejected from West Stoke in 1662 for non-conformity (will dated 1669), 'profess[es] that I die in the true Christian faith as it is held forth by all the Protestant churches, the Church of England particularly in that which the Assembly of Divines held forth in their Confession and Catechism'.[43]

Looking at so many wills enables a number of observations relating to the Sussex clergy across the period of study. Many are comparable to those of any other contemporary gentlemen, mentioning similar possessions and properties and making similar bequests to the poor and to kin. However, there are also a large number which indicate that the testator possessed only the clothes he stood up in. Some indicate inherited lands, others humble beginnings, such as Oliver Penicod of Graffham, clerk.[44] He mentions his children and the children of his brothers whom he describes as 'illiterate'. However, he was MA Oxon. and left legacies approaching £700 and a £10 annuity. His will was proved in 1653.

There are similar disparities with regard to real estate; many of the clergy were obviously landless and presumably relied on their parish for accommodation. Others, such as Christopher Elderfield, minister of Burton (mentioned above), appear to be considerably wealthier than average, mentioning plate, gowns, rings, bibles, books and gifts amounting to hundreds of pounds.[45] Giles Moore of Horsted Keynes demonstrates the uncertain experiences of clergy in the county:

> The Parsonage was left to mee in so ruinous a state that it cost mee £240, before I could make it fit to dwell in. Should I leave a widow behind mee, let ... my successor ... deale alike kindly by her as I have done by Mistresse Pell ... Mrs. Pell had the whole years tythes ending at Lady Day 1656, though her husband dyed at the beginning of the harvest.[46]

While only a handful of men came from gentry families in Sussex (Ashburnham, Middleton, Pelham and possibly Morley), it is evident that several others from outside the county were also from wealthy backgrounds as their wills mention large landholdings and considerable amounts of expensive goods, plate and other assets. Table 5.1 shows the number of identifiable wills made by Sussex clergy during the pre-war period, the war years, the interregnum and the year immediately following the Restoration. After 1661, the numbers dropped significantly, the greatest number for any

---

[43] WSRO, V24/52b.

[44] TNA, PROB11/240/226.

[45] TNA, PROB11/227/49.

[46] *The Journal of Giles Moore*, ed. R. Bird (Lewes, Sussex Record Soc., 68, 1971), p. 64. We can deduce that he had been a chaplain in the royalist army as he is noted as a prisoner of Essex's Regiment of Horse.

Table 5.1. Wills of Sussex clergy executed and proved in the PCC and Sussex courts

Dates	PCC	Sussex
1633–40	26	16
1641–6	22	9
1647–52	23	4
1653–60	57	0
1661	4	7

single year being five to six (many years being zero) whereas in 1652, 1657 and 1658 the numbers per year were ten and over.[47]

It would not be safe to assume that the data drawn from the wills can be projected across the clergy for whom no evidence survives. Many will be among the numbers who were ejected from their livings and financially ruined. Many will also have died long before the Restoration and any hope of restitution. We must now look at the levels of disruption experienced in the county.

Ejections and displacement

Changes were already occurring in the nature of the clergy before 1642. By that date a number of puritan clergy had already been appointed, some having been established in their parishes for a number of years by 1641, either due to the inclinations of the patrons of the living or due to particular local conditions (e.g. Rye and its 'commonwealth').[48]

Between 1642 and 1646 there was a fairly brief period when a large number of clergy were ejected, sequestered or deprived.[49] Using information drawn from the database it was possible to compile a table of removals between

[47] From 1653 to 1660 all wills were proved centrally in London and the records are now held with those of the Prerogative Court of Canterbury (PCC). A few were proved in the royalist court at Oxford and are also now held at TNA under class PROB10. Table 5.1 shows the dates the wills were made rather than the dates of grants of probate.

[48] Thomas-Stanford, *Sussex*, pp. 23–7; Fletcher, *Sussex*, pp. 62–71; J. Lowerson, *A Short History of Sussex* (Folkestone, 1980), pp. 104–5. See also Mayhew, *Rye*, ch. 2, which deals with the development of puritanism there in great detail.

[49] The data is drawn from a variety of sources, although the bulk comes from *Calamy*, *Walker* and *WR*, supplemented by *SAC*, xxx-xxxiii and anecdotal information in local histories and litigation cases which appear in TNA *Discovery*. My database shows clergy deprived pre-1640, presumably as a result of the Laudian reforms. Removes became more frequent in 1642–6. More upheavals occurred in 1650–4, though in far smaller numbers, and then again in 1660–3, but again in smaller numbers than in the 1640s.

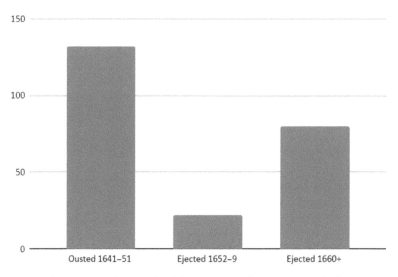

Figure 5.6. Removals of Sussex clergy from 1641 until after 1662.[a]

[a] The first column 'Ousted 1641–51' shows parishes whose incumbent was stated
to have been sequestered, ejected or driven out or where their successor was
stated to have intruded on or supplanted their predecessor. The figures labelled
'Ejected 1660+' list parishes whose clergy were last recorded in their parishes
in the period 1660–2, not all of whom may have been formally removed.

1641 and 1662. As shown in Figure 5.6, over forty per cent of parishes appear
to have suffered an enforced change of incumbent during or immediately
after the first period of disruption (1641–50/1).

Of the 724 clergy studied, fifty-two were appointed during the period
1650–9, thirty-seven were ejected c.1662 and twenty-nine conformed.
This table may, however, underestimate the figures affected in the second
two columns. The numbers shown in the first column include all those
stated to have been sequestered, ejected or driven out. Where someone
is stated to have intruded or otherwise supplanted an incumbent, it has
been taken to indicate that the previous minister has been ousted. This
tells us that the parish has been disrupted. In the first period 131 parishes
(out of 325) appear to have suffered at least one change of incumbent other
than by 'natural turnover'. Stated ejections in the second and third period
appear to be far fewer but this may be due to lack of clear evidence of
ejection as much as a lesser degree of disruption. As the sum of those
who were ejected and conformed is higher than those known to have been
officially appointed, it would appear that the numbers must include others
who had arrived either pre-1650 or without official sanction.

Much displacement took place during the period, not only due to ejection and sequestration but also for the clergy who attached themselves to the armies of both sides. Some of these were chaplains to gentry commanders but others left their parishes to follow their chosen allegiance voluntarily.[50] It is likely that some clergy who were turned out of their livings after 1642 would have attached themselves to the royalist armies, and a proportion of the 'new clergy' who supplanted them may have previously been attached to the parliamentarian armies.[51] For others there is no way of knowing how they came to be in the 'front line'. Dr William Chillingworth, Fellow of Trinity College, Oxford, accompanied Hopton's army and was taken prisoner after the siege of Arundel in December 1643. He was removed to the Bishop's Palace at Chichester where he died on 30 January 1644. He is commemorated in a memorial in the cathedral.[52] William Stanley of West Tarring admitted on sequestration that he had gone to the royalist garrison at Arundel in 1643, having been promised a commission as a captain of dragoons, and that he had urged men to enlist and prevent the enemy from crossing the Shoreham ferry. Despite this he was discharged in 1645/6

---

[50] Eg Thomas Twiss, chaplain to the Earl of Essex's train of artillery, admitted rector of East Horsley in Surrey in 1643 and rector of Old Alresford, Hampshire in 1644, who despite being in his seventies was recorded with the army in Scotland in 1653, when he left the army to return south on a family matter. He was recorded as deceased in the Hampshire quarter sessions records of 1654, HRO Q1/3, fo. 244. John Allen was presented to the living 31 Jan. 1654 'on death of previous incumbent'.

[51] See I. Green, 'The persecution of "scandalous" and "malignant" parish clergy during the English Civil War', *English Historical Review*, xciv (1979), 507–31, at p. 513. Green suggests that it was a minority but it was an option for displaced clergy, particularly those who were unmarried and had no other access to accommodation or protection. Thomas Bridge, rector of Tillington, was an active royalist during the siege of Chester and others are noted in the royalist camp at Oxford, eg William Cartwright, prebendary of Sutton and Hove, who died there in 1643, see *WR*, pp. 14, 88.

[52] See also F. Cheynell, *Chillingworth Novissima* (London, 1644) and *ODNB*. R. Hagedorn, *Arundel at War* (Kibworth Beauchamp, 2018), p. 136 listed Chillingworth, 'Mr. Payne' and 'another Minister' (possibly William Stanley of West Tarring, see *WR*, p. 361) among the royalists who surrendered following the siege of Arundel. Both Thomas-Stanford and Fletcher stated that the Chichester cathedral clergy aligned themselves with the royalist gentry. Thomas-Stanford, *Sussex*, p. 55–6 stated that they were 'dealt with' in 1643 by the commissioners appointed to sequestrate royalist estates and mentioned Bishop Henry King, the dean, Bruno Ryves and John Gregory, Bracklesham prebendary, but I have found no other direct evidence to identify clergy caught up in the siege of Chichester. Thomas-Stanford, *Sussex*, pp. 135–50, mentions the treatment of a number of Sussex clergy on both sides and states that several compounded for their personal estates under Articles of War granted at Oxford and Exeter, indicating that they had joined the garrisons of those places following ejection from their parish livings.

when the county committee failed to reply to the Committee for Plundered Ministers.[53]

In a number of parishes the parishioners were happy to supply evidence against the incumbent to secure his ejectment should he not share their particular wishes as to liturgy and ordering of the church, as in the case of Randolph Apsley of Pulborough, whose removal was procured by allegations of (*inter alia*) drunkenness and was summoned to give an account 'before some ruling men'.[54] On the first occasion he was cleared but was later 'seen in a public alehouse' and accused of being a scandalous liver and thrown out 'almost to the ruin of his family', his children being kept by the charity of his relations. After the Restoration he regained his living but died in 1663. William Hine of Fittleworth was said to have been deprived for having employed a tailor to sew a button on his breeches on the Sabbath.[55] Others, such as Thomas Allcock of Tillington, were forced to resign 'partly by threats, partly by promises, afterwards unfulfilled'.[56]

Anthony Hugget, of Cliffe and Glynde, was sequestered of both livings and charged with offences ranging from severity to parishioners for going to other churches to domestic violence and being seen with the royalist army, but his successor thought the charges to be groundless, Hugget having made enemies due to his strictness in his role as Surrogate.[57] Similar treatment was given to John Large of Rotherfield, despite accusations being rebutted by a petition by almost the whole parish.[58] Richard Taunton/Teinton of Ardingly was 'voted out of his late Parsonage by the Hnble Committee of the House of Commons in Parliament August 16, 1643'.[59] In a note inside the cover of the parish register the clerk wrote: 'The cause why he was thus Voted is manifest to the world. He the said Richard was ejected Novemb. 29 by a Companie of Dragoniers sent by the command of Captain Symon Querendon de Lewis.'[60]

[53] *WR*, p. 361. Thomas Bayly DD, prebendary of Lincoln and subdean of Wells, also became a royalist officer before fleeing to exile.

[54] Similarly Thomas Heny of Arundel. See Walker, *Attempt*, p. 357 and *WR*, p. 275.

[55] A. Poole, *Fittleworth 1540–1840* (Gravesend, 2019), p. 127. According to Poole, this accusation was made by Francis Cheynell (see above).

[56] *WR*, p. 353.

[57] *WR*, p. 276; Walker, *Attempt*, p. 358.

[58] See lengthy narrative in *WR*, pp. xliii, 299; Walker, *Attempt*, p. 358. See also M. Reynolds, 'Puritanism and a Sussex clerical scandal in the 1630s and 1640s', *SAC*, cliv (2016), 227–41, and J. White, *The First Century of Scandalous, Malignant Priests* (London, 1643). Hugget is no. 67.

[59] Ardingly Parish Register, quoted in *SRS*, xvii, 197.

[60] Presumably dragoons.

It would be misleading to suppose that all ejections occurred due to ideological differences. An attempt was made in 1644 to remove Thomas Bainbrigg from Icklesham, which he had held since 1618, for being absent for twenty-five years and employing scandalous curates. His absence was due to his tenure as Master of Christ's College, Cambridge and he was allowed to retain Icklesham on condition that he appointed a curate acceptable to the committee.[61]

In examining the accounts of the 'sufferings' of the clergy in Sussex, a picture seems to emerge of a progressive 'tightening of the screw'. In the beginning a large number of those examined and ejected were those who were obvious targets – that is, those who were overt in their support for the king, the rule of law and order, the Anglican/Laudian Church etc., as well as pluralists and those allegedly guilty of living a less than godly life but, as the years passed, the targets seem to grow less obvious. Rye was already a 'godly commonwealth' as early as the previous century, so it was surprising to find that the vicar, Brian Twyne, was himself sequestered in 1644. He had been the incumbent there since 1614 and by 1644 the process of 'cleansing' had been underway for some time, more than long enough for the parishioners to have decided on his sufficiency or otherwise. His non-residence at Oxford, and the influence of sectarianism in Rye, which also impacted his successor and was complained about by John Bastwick, probably decided his case.[62]

Although there is evidence that many clergy were willing to compromise to retain their livings, particularly those appointed during the interregnum, there are also some cases where clergy were finding a greater struggle with their consciences. Richard Carpenter became a Benedictine monk before returning to Anglicanism and being appointed to Poling. After 1642 he reverted to Rome before joining the Independents and preaching at Aylesbury. He later reverted to Rome once again.[63]

More upheaval occurred in the 1650s when the system of Triers and Ejectors came into being. As there were no longer bishops, there could be no episcopal ordinations, and a process had to be devised by which parish clergy could be approved or ejected.[64] This seems to have subsequently been devolved to local committees. While the level of ejectment in Sussex appears to be lower than in the first decade, it seems clear that clergy were

[61] WR, p. 353.

[62] See J. Bastwick, The Utter Routing of the Whole Army of All the Independents and Sectaries (London, 1646), epistle; see Twyne's entry in the ODNB.

[63] Venn, Alumni, i. 294

[64] Although there is at least one reference to an ordination by the 4th London Classis – see the case of Thomas Goldham below.

removed for a variety of reasons and some references suggest that men holding a profitable or otherwise 'comfortable' benefice were occasionally removed to make way for a protégé of the committee or other influential person.[65] The rectory of Pulborough became the subject of a dispute in 1658. The county commissioner, Colonel John Downes, appointed William Cooper on 24 September. On 19 November Matthew Poole was appointed by Thomas Henshaw the younger, under-sheriff, but on 8 December he in turn was replaced by Jeremiah Dyke, also appointed by Downes. Fiona McCall discusses this theme further in *Baal's Priests*. Walker states that Aquila Cruso's living was worth £80 *pa* and his sequestration is thought to have been dubious. John Large's living was thought to have been worth £300 *pa* and he was also sequestered.[66]

Often supplanting ministers were themselves removed within a short time. Sometimes a minister who had 'intruded' with little or no official authority was challenged by the community or by official intervention. At Aldingbourne, Daniel Thompson was replaced by John Goldsmith in 1644. By 1645 Thompson had returned, under the impression that sequestration had ended. Goldsmith appealed to the Committee for Plundered Ministers who ordered Thompson's removal but he refused to leave. Goldsmith himself was removed, leaving Thompson in place. At Hurstpierpoint, Christopher Swale was removed by the Westminster Assembly, who appointed Morgan Haine in his place. He in turn was replaced by Humphrey Street, who had previously served Hove and Preston. He was then replaced by Leonard Letchford, but the parishioners demanded the return of Street. The outcome of this dispute has not survived.[67] Similar scenarios occurred in other

---

[65] E. H. Dunkin, 'Admissions to Sussex benefices (temp. Commonwealth) by the Commissioners for the Approbation of Public Preachers', *SAC*, xxx–xxxiii, records appointments which were either not finalised, not taken up or cancelled within days or weeks of being made. Thomas-Stanford, *Sussex*, pp. 144–7 quotes a 'joke of the time' (source WMS C5.23v), that John Large, rector of Rotherfield, was ejected not for his bad life, but for his good living, worth £300 *pa*. Large himself alleged that the evidence against him was 'through a secret plot and combination of John Russell, Edward Russell and John Calle, who … wanting a living [for a kinsman] drew up these articles against him'; see Walker, *Attempt*, ii. 279.

[66] This account is also supplied by Thomas Newcomb (WMS C3.377) – see note above. WMS C5.219, 220; C3.377. See also *SAC*, xxxi, p. 178 and Fletcher, *Sussex*, p. 107. McCall, *Baal's Priests*, discusses valuation of livings in some detail, p. 100 and ch. 4.

[67] *SAC*, xxx, pp. 123–4. Letchford was especially unpopular with the Quakers, whom he appears to have treated particularly harshly (*ODNB*, Ambrose Rigge). *CCED* has a gap between Swale in 1641/2 and Minhard Shaw in 1674/5, although Letchford is also shown, but without any date attached. See also ESRO, QR/86, fo. 41–42, presentment of Thomas Swan nuper de Hurstperpoynt, clericus for entering the close of Richard Whitepayne, 3 Nov. 1649; Henry Deane is named as minister there in 1658, ESRO, QR/121, fo. 7.

parishes, occasionally accompanied by violence as either candidate sought to impose their entitlement. An ejected minister might still retain local support. William Fist of Wiston and Ashurst was sequestered *c*.26 February 1645/6. On 1 July 1647 the committee received a complaint that he had, with the help of three others, 'thrust himself into the pulpit and prayed there by force'. John Goff[e] of Ripe was accused of fomenting a party against the intruding minister, Fairfull.[68]

Supplanting 'clergy' were not necessarily more blameless than those they replaced. At East Lavant, Joseph Henshaw was supplanted in 1653 by Richard Bettsworth. The parish register contains the following:

> 29th Oct 1653. Richard Betsworth of the parish of East Lavant was approved of and sworn to be Parish Minister for the said Parish according to an Act of parliament in that case made and provided. ... He was a man ... very violent for the rebels and a plunderer of the Royalists, particularly of the Morley family. He had some learning, a great deal of chicanery though seldom more than one coat which for some time he wore the wrong side out only on Sundays its right side was seen til it was almost worn out and then he had a new one which he used in same manner.[69]

The register also indicates that Bettsworth was replaced in 1658 by Robert Parke, who continued there until 1660.[70]

Some parishes appear to have suffered more uncertainty and disruption than others. A small number of parishes experienced repeated changes within a short period – Ninfield has seven names associated with it in 1635–65 and Peasmarsh ten in the same period. John Giles had held both parishes, along with Penhurst, until he was sequestered in 1644/5. When he died at Penhurst ten years later, he left money for sermons to be preached in all three parishes on the anniversary of his death. This is not unique in the county by any means. Such frequent disruptions must have been, at the very least, unsettling for parishioners, particularly during a time of war.

Even where they disappeared from Sussex, clergy may have retained livings across the county boundaries in Kent, Surrey or Hampshire. It is difficult to unravel the precise dates when incumbencies changed, especially where the parishes concerned were in different counties. Even where someone subsequently died in one of 'his' parishes, it does not necessarily imply

---

[68] There is a document at LPL, COMM2/285, 11 Jan. 1659, appointing Robert Fairfull to Fivehead, Somerset. See also C. Durston, '"Unhallowed wedlocks": The regulation of marriage during the English Revolution', *Historical Journal*, xxxi (1988), 45–59.

[69] WSRO, Par 120/1/1/1. This note may have been written by Thomas Gumble, instituted to the parish in 1663.

[70] Other sources indicate 1662.

that he was still incumbent and there is often evidence to the contrary, suggesting that he either retreated to private property in the area or sought refuge with a sympathetic parishioner.[71]

It is evident from the records of (*inter alia*) the Committee of Plundered Ministers that as early as 1646, large sums of money, raised from sequestrations of royalist estates, were used by parliament to engineer the nature of the clergy throughout the county.[72] An order of 3 June 1646 allotted the sum of £150 from the income of the cathedral 'for … the maintenance of three learned and orthodox divines appointed to officiate in the City of Chichester'.[73]

Not only did the nature of the clergy change between 1642 and 1653, but so did its function. Conduct of marriages was removed to state control in 1653. Ardingly parish register recorded the change:

> a Certificate under the hands of divers of the inhabitants of the Parish of Ardingly that Thomas Bassett …, Tayler, is … elected to be the parish Register for the said parish; …. Witnessed … 27th daye of February … 1653. Tho. Challoner.[74]

The wording of this and a similar entry in 1655 indicates that the registrars were elected by the parishioners, but whether this was by popular vote or that of the vestry or some form of parish council is unclear.

It is difficult to gauge how rigorous the enforcement of measures against the clergy was in Sussex. Incumbents were forced from their livings, but what proportion of this was due to a general strategy and how much down to their popularity or otherwise is another matter.[75] There are fragments of evidence of action being taken against ministers for infringements of the

---

[71] Numerous examples of this were found during the course of research. John Sefton was assisted by locals after ejection from Burton before fleeing to the West Indies. John Wilshaw of Selmeston was assisted by John Nutt, who was himself sequestered from several livings held in plural, allegedly as punishment for his assistance to Wilshaw; see *WR*, p. 362. Richard Francke, whose will stated that he was 'of Hastings', may also be one of these – there were at the time two separate parishes in Hastings, All Saints and St Clements. As Francke did not state which parish it seems probable that he had been ejected when he made his will in 1646, dying in 1648.

[72] *SAC*, xxxvi, pp. 144–5.

[73] Before the Civil War there were at least eight separate parishes in Chichester.

[74] 'According to the directions of the late Act of Parliam't Intitled an Act touching Marriages and the Registring thereof, & also touching Births & Burialls', WSRO, Par 231/1/1/3.

[75] See table in McCall, *Baal's Priests*, p. 130. McCall suggested the overall rate for Sussex was twenty-six per cent, just below average. My figures [see below] suggest a slightly higher turnover overall.

new procedures, but often the records do not show whether these measures were ever completed. In 1655 the quarter sessions ordered that 'a warrant be issued forth against Mr. William Rogers, Minister of Chiddingly, … for marrying of divers persons without certificate contrary to the late Act'.[76] At the Lewes session on 4 October there was a warrant against John Cooke and Thomas Plains, constables, for not executing a warrant against William Rogers. There is no further reference and it would appear the matter was allowed to drop. *CCED* has no reference to William Rogers at Chiddingly. The only William Rogers found was at Chailey, removed from there c.1650. If the Chiddingly man had been ignoring the statute this might indicate that he is the same one, but in the absence of further information this cannot be proved. The two parishes are not far apart and Rogers may have held both in plural, retreating to Chiddingly when he lost Chailey.[77]

There is no clear picture of what happened in the first few years after the Restoration. There were twenty-four references to clergy being restored to parishes from which they had been ousted and only eight who appear to have remained undisturbed throughout the war and the interregnum and post 1660.[78] Many clergy had of course died or otherwise vanished in 1641–60, leaving space for a large number of incomers. There is only one reference to a man being ordained during this period, Thomas Goldham, minister of the chapel of East Chiltington in 1646, who was ordained minister by the Fourth London Classis on 31 January 1648/9.[79] He is listed at Hartley Wespall (Hampshire) in 1650 and later Burwash, where he kept the grammar school before being ejected for non-conformity in 1662.[80] He seems to have remained in the area as he was buried there in 1691. There were further upheavals after the restoration of the monarchy and a significant number of clergy who had acquired livings during the Civil Wars and interregnum found themselves removed from their parishes if they refused to conform or in order to make way for an incumbent previously ousted.

[76] ESRO, Q/1/5/3, quarter sessions order book, fo. 5, 26 April 1655.

[77] *WR*, p. 360; C. Robertson, *Hailsham and its Environs* (London, 1982), p. 95 shows that seventy couples married there in a three-year period instead of a more usual two to three per year. The parties came from parishes in Sussex as well as the adjoining counties of Surrey and Kent, while a number of parishes recorded no marriages at all during the currency of the Act. However, Robertson named the vicar as Robert Baker who was also at Rottingdean and Kemsing (Kent).

[78] Rosemary O'Day quotes a 'natural turnover' of two per cent per year; my figures suggest a much higher turnover in Sussex during this period. R. O'Day, *The English Clergy: Emergence and Consolidation of a Profession, 1558–1642* (Leicester, 1979), pp. 8–12.

[79] *SAC*, xxxvi, 159; *CR*, p. 226.

[80] *CR*, p. 226.

Conclusion

So what patterns emerge overall from this chapter? The figures show that there was a higher level of disruption in Sussex than has previously been acknowledged, a product more likely of the degree of religious polarization in the county than of any proximity or otherwise to areas of actual disruption attributable to the wars and their aftermath. But the picture of the religious complexion of the county across this relatively short period is complex. It is too much of a simplification to state that the 'religious colour' was more Catholic/Arminian in the westernmost part and more puritan/reformed Protestant in the easternmost parts. Pockets of 'resistance' to this simple picture occur in various locations across the county, although it is fair to say that there are no obviously ultra-'reformed' parishes in the western half and the pockets of 'Catholic/high Church Anglicanism' that occur in the eastern half can be associated with the beliefs of local magnates such as the Gages at Firle, despite their location close to Lewes, a centre of non-conformity. There were wide variations of experience, not only regionally but even within much smaller localities. There is no discernible pattern in the distribution of clergy according to their own leanings and it would require a parish-by-parish examination to map any clusters, although a conclusion can be drawn from many of the wills that many of the men were on close terms with, or related by marriage to, the incumbents of neighbouring parishes. This must surely indicate some congruity of belief or ideology.

Levels of affluence among the Sussex clergy were highly variable, education less so. In general, in line with trends identified by Ian Green, Sussex clergy ordained from the 1630s onwards appear to have been better educated than those appointed in the earlier part of the century. A significant number came from outside Sussex and the south-east generally, some from a considerable distance. Was it easier for local people, already unsettled by the rapid religious changes in the locality, to accept a 'stranger' than someone who had originated closer to home? But did this 'strangeness' perhaps leave incumbents with a less secure hold over their livings in more turbulent times? The chapter shows numerous instances of clergy whose tenure of a parish was obviously not tranquil, either for themselves or their parishioners. Comments in wills reveal a number of men whose experience had obviously left its mark. Some are just a passing reference to the 'troubled times' but others are much longer lamentations of loss and privation.

Enforcing godly ideals

6. 'Breaching the laws of God and man': secular prosecutions of religious offences in the interregnum parish, 1645–60

Fiona McCall

In 1645 the Church of England was radically reformed, its hierarchy abolished, the Book of Common Prayer prohibited and Church lands put up for sale. Conservative clergy were being removed and replaced. For those who considered the Church only half-reformed, these were changes long demanded. Yet what followed was not what was hoped for and the end result one least expected in the early 1640s. Traditionalist Church practice, then so utterly vilified, was restored little changed in 1662, albeit now with a non-conformist minority determined to practise religion outside it.

Different explanations have been offered for this surprising turn of events. Loyalist Hugh Todd, writing in 1704, dismissed the attempts to impose godly religion in Cumberland, saying that the 'people, generally, had no great likeing' for 'New-lights' and preferred the old ways.[1] But Exeter non-conformist George Trosse remembered interregnum religion with nostalgia:

> There were very good Laws against the Prophanation of the Lord's-Day, and good Magistrats to put them in execution ... Religion was in its Glory ...[2]

Historians are equally divided. Derek Hirst contended that godly religion failed to appeal on an emotional level to most people; Christopher Durston concurred, while conceding that efforts towards moral reformation made progress in a few localities.[3] Elliot Vernon, in contrast, found evidence of a continuing 'evangelical spirit', assessing the 'puritan gloom' quoted by Hirst

---

[1] WMS C7.2v.

[2] G. Trosse, *The Life of the Late Reverend George Trosse* (London, 1714), pp. 37, 81.

[3] D. Hirst, 'The failure of Godly rule in the English Republic', *Past & Present*, cxxxii (1991), 33–66; C. Durston, 'Puritan rule and the failure of cultural revolution, 1645–1660', in *The Culture of English Puritanism*, ed. C. Durston and J. Eales (Basingstoke, 1996), pp. 210–33, at p. 220.

---

as no more than a conventionalized line of complaint.[4] John Morrill's work on churchwardens' accounts emphasized the continuation of traditional practices; Ronald Hutton's saw traditionalism as a declining phenomenon, confined to a privileged semi-secret minority.[5] More recently, Bernard Capp highlighted the vigorous efforts of parliamentary reformers and city leaders towards further godly reformation throughout the 1650s, hardly suggestive of a cause given up for lost.[6]

It is also debatable in what sense the Church as an institution could be said to have continued into the 1640s and 1650s. As Ann Hughes pointed out, many puritan ministers certainly felt that their interregnum ministry operated within a national Church tradition, even if, in practice, she suggested, we should think of Cromwellian churches in the plural.[7] Alex Craven maintained that there was indeed a 'functioning, national, established Church', although he did concede that it had a 'very different form' from what preceded it.[8] Many loyalists considered the Church of England to have been utterly swept away: 'mangled to death', according to Christopher Hindle, preaching in 1650, 'by the sons of her own bowels'.[9] Presbyterians had a different conception of an institutional Church, but by the late 1640s, their fears for its future matched the loyalists'. 'The great designe', warned *Vox Norwici*, was 'to take off all the Orthodox Ministers, and fixed Starres of the Church of England … and to leave us in a scattered condition'.[10] References to the 'Church of England' are uncommon in contemporary legal records. The period from 1648 to 1660 has been described as a period of ecclesiastical confusion.[11] Yet there were considerable elements of stability in religious practice, for example in the way the church was served and paid for. Parish churches remained, served by clergy of varying persuasions: closet traditionalists, Presbyterians who sought a national form of Church government, and Independents or Baptists who did not.

---

[4] E. Vernon, 'A ministry of the gospel: the Presbyterians during the English Revolution', in Durston and Maltby, *Religion*, pp. 115–36, at p. 130.

[5] J. S. Morrill, 'The Church in England 1643–9', in *Reactions to the English Civil War 1642–1649*, ed. J. S. Morrill (London, 1982), pp. 89–114; R. Hutton, *The Rise and Fall of Merry England* (Oxford, 1994), pp. 213–15.

[6] B. Capp, *England's Culture Wars* (Oxford, 2012), ch. 12.

[7] A. Hughes, 'The Cromwellian Church', in Milton, *Anglicanism*, i. 445–56, at pp. 444–5.

[8] A. Craven, 'Ministers of State: the established Church in Lancashire during the English Revolution, 1642–1660', *Northern History*, xlv (2008), 51–69, at pp. 54, 69.

[9] WMS C3.4r.

[10] *Vox Norwici* (London, 1646), preface.

[11] W. A. Shaw, *A History of the English Church during the Civil Wars 1640–1660* (London, 1900), ii. 98.

In practice, an Erastian form of Church government evolved, with central initiatives and ultimate authority resting with the state.[12] In this era, the idea of state control over the Church was not seen as problematic: 'One and the selfsame people are the Church and the Commonwealth', wrote Richard Hooker.[13] Even those whose chief aim was to defend the godly ministry against tithe-defaulters were careful to state that they 'own'd' 'the power of the Magistrate in matters of Religion'.[14] More at issue was who was meant by the 'Civil Magistrate', and the precise nature of their remit; under the monarchy the supreme governor had not claimed the powers of a priest, but only the power of jurisdiction.[15] But ideas concerning legal jurisdiction were themselves subject to change and debate during the 1640s, from the exclusion of many MPs from parliamentary law-making, to the abolition of several major courts of law including all the ecclesiastical courts and overturning of legal decisions by the Committee of Indemnity.[16] Sometimes adverse comment was made on the pace of change. 'Bootes over Bookes'; there was 'noe law' now, cried those who evicted Mary Swanne from her messuage in Carley, Cheshire in 1649.[17] Military influence on the state was powerful, legal jurisdiction unclear, and magistrates and ministers often in disagreement over Church organization, yet they found more in common around the goal of effecting a godly reformation of morals and manners. With the Church hierarchy and ecclesiastical courts gone, this programme had to be driven forward by secular authorities. Many changes to religious practice were implemented via acts or ordinances of parliament, and an expanded role emerged for judges and justices in interpreting and enforcing them. This chapter explores their work.

Study of legal records offers a means to deepen our understanding of how new religious practices and an accompanying godly reformation of manners and morals were received at ground level, by moving beyond the

---

[12] C. Cross, *The Church in England* (Hassocks, 1976), p. 213.

[13] H. M. Carey and J. Gascoigne, *Church and State in Old and New Worlds* (Leiden, 2010), p. 8.

[14] *Cryes of England to the Parliament for the Good Continuance of Good Entertainment to the Lord Jesus his Embassadors* (London, 1653), p. 1.

[15] L. F. Solt, *Church and State in Early Modern England, 1509–1640* (Oxford, 1990), pp. 207–11.

[16] F. L., *Considerations Touching the Dissolving or Taking Away the Court of Chancery and the Courts of Justice* … (London, 1653); R. Ashton, 'The problem of indemnity 1647–1648', in *Politics and People in Revolutionary England*, ed. C. Jones, M. D. D. Newitt and S. Roberts (Oxford, 1986), pp. 117–40; J. Shedd, 'Legalism over revolution: the parliamentary committee for indemnity and property confiscation disputes, 1647–1655', *Historical Journal*, xliii (2000), 1093–1107.

[17] CRO, QJF 77/1, Easter 1649, fo. 42r.

Table 6.1. Legal records analysed

County	Quarter sessions records indexed	Quarter sessions petitions, informations, examinations, depositions indexed	Assize records indexed
Cheshire	531	287	151
Yorkshire	506	5	104
Sussex	269	29	14
Somerset	264	154	1
Devonshire	231	53	8
Essex	104	70	54
Hampshire	126	43	2
Lancashire	92	73	2
Kent			57
Northamptonshire	44		
Nottinghamshire	44		
North Wales	36	16	
Other counties	17	10	28

stereotypical sources frequently cited as evidence. This chapter considers the priorities of local justice with regard to religion from the end of the First Civil War to the Restoration and the patterns of prosecution observed, based on a large-scale study of over 2,500 extant assize and quarter sessions records for this period, from several counties. Although these records have previously been cited by historians, most notably Christopher Durston and Bernard Capp, such a systematic investigation of these records has never previously been attempted. They include over 400 assize records, mainly indictments giving only summary information about each case, plus some depositions from the Northern Circuit. The remainder are taken from quarter sessions order books and rolls from several counties (see Table 6.1) and include presentments and indictments, warrants and orders, with around thirty per cent including detailed petitions, examinations, informations or witness depositions. Capp reminds us that these statistics can tell us little or nothing about the 'dark' figure of summary punishments imposed by magistrates or officers on their own authority which went unrecorded, or whose records have not survived.[18] Thus, what is presented and discussed here is more indicative of the regime's religious priorities than a definitive record of all its actions, some of which we only know about through other sources, contemporary publications, state papers or accounts of religious suffering, for example.

The cases looked at here all relate to religious practice or belief in its broadest definition. These were usually only a small proportion of the sessions' business, much of whose efforts were occupied with crimes relating to property or secular violence, dealing with vagabonds, illegally erected cottages, apprentices, unlicensed artificers, maintaining highways and bridges, along with the administration of assessments, payments to maimed soldiers and poor relief. Particularly at assizes and at times of heightened political uncertainty, they also include reports of disaffection to the state. Cases relating to sexual activity, alehouse regulation or drinking were numerous, too much so for the scope of this chapter, so these are considered only where they relate to religion: adultery, an offence against the Decalogue, or sexual misbehaviour or drinking in churches, on the Sabbath or involving clergy or church officers, for example. Individual appeals for poor relief are not incorporated, only wider concerns expressed about church officers' practices or probity.

This chapter examines the most common types of offences prosecuted over the fifteen-year period from the Church's disestablishment in 1645 to Charles II's Restoration in 1660. As shown in Table 6.2, prosecution rates varied considerably, reflecting the increasing activity and security of legal process year on year up to 1658, the number of surviving records of religious cases for each year in the mid–late 1650s being more than four times that in 1645–6 when the legal process was recovering from civil war.

It was mainly the laity who used the law as a mechanism for dealing with religious concerns: in only around a quarter of cases were clergy involved in any way, and in less than four per cent were they prosecuting or informing against others. Yet there was no lack of godly mission in evidence, based on assumptions that the 'laws of God and man' were intertwined. 'The Captaine of our Salvacion is highly dishonord' by the number of alehouses, claimed fifty-four male petitioners to the Cheshire magistrates in 1645, 'The nurseries of all ryott …and idleness', the thrones of Satan, 'a growing evill', a 'Gangrene' endangering the 'whole body'.[19]

---

[18] B. Capp, 'Republican reformation: family, community and the state in Interregnum Middlesex, 1649–60', in *The Family in Early Modern England*, ed. H. Berry and E. Foyster (Cambridge, 2007), pp. 40–66, at p. 47.

[19] CRO, QJF 73/3, Michaelmas 1645, fo. 76r.

Table 6.2. Number of legal cases analysed by year[a]

Year	No. of cases
1645	56
1646	59
1647	127
1648	113
1649	130
1650	135
1651	169
1652	177
1653	190
1654	256
1655	277
1656	306
1657	247
1658	260
1659	127
1660	29

[a] Only cases before 29 May 1660 are included for 1660.

The possibility of establishing a Christian Commonwealth seemed at hand: 'I beseech you to consider wee in this nation have long prayed for reformation, and complained for want of it, and most of our talke hath beene about it,' wrote Major-General James Berry to the Welsh Commissioners in December 1655. Paralleling God's final judgement to contemporary legal process, he argued that those who were neglectful now would 'have cause to blush' when they came before God 'with their petition'. He prayed that God would stir their hearts to be zealouse for him' as a 'terrour to evill doers'.[20] This belief that current religious policy represented God's mission articulated via the state meant that although much of it was enforced via new regulations, there was consistency in what was prosecuted across the country, although particular offences were not always pursed with equivalent vigour everywhere.

[20] GA, XQSH1656/14.

Table 6.3. Legal cases by type (all counties)

Type of case	No. of cases
Parish finances	374
Sabbath-day observance	316
Swearing or cursing	281
Church repairs	204
Catholicism	176
Adultery	173
Disruption of church services	146
Witchcraft	122
Anti-clerical abuse or violence	120
Non-attendance at church	103
Quakers	68
Aggressive behaviour by clergy or their families	67
Church seating	41
Use of the Book of Common Prayer	27
Blasphemy	25

Profaning the Sabbath

The need for strict observance of the Lord's day had been one of the 'core beliefs' of puritans since the early seventeenth century.[21] Thus, profanation of the Sabbath – drinking, visiting alehouses, sexual misbehaviour, working or travelling – became one of the most commonly prosecuted religious offences between 1645 and 1660 (see Table 6.3). Parliamentary success in the field in the autumn of 1645 galvanized hopes for parallel success in an accompanying moral crusade. Puritan ministers in Essex demanded constables and churchwardens make monthly presentments of profane swearers, those who did not 'sanctify the Lords day' and 'religiously observe' days of fasting or thanksgiving, who absented themselves from 'publick ordinances' or were disorderly therein.[22]

Prosecutions peaked in 1648 and then again in 1654–8, although the former represented a higher proportion of the religious-related offences for that year (see Figure 6.1). Yet their very frequency attests to the impossibility of the

---

[21] Durston, 'Puritan rule', pp. 213–14.

[22] ERO, Q/SBa 2/58, Michaelmas 1645.

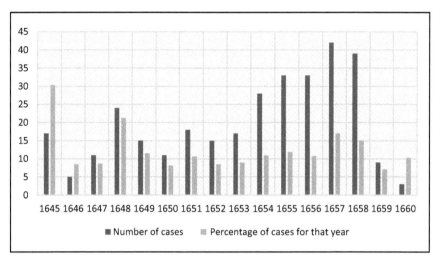

Figure 6.1. Offences related to Sabbath-day observance by year.

undertaking. A 1647–8 petition from Hale in Cheshire complained bitterly that the 'worke of reformacion' had made little progress, due to continuing profaneness: 'the Actors' 'grow more audacious every day'.[23] Alehouses were said to be 'excessive' and 'increasing' in an April 1649 Hampshire petition, corrupting youth and encouraging the poor to idleness.[24] Attempts to prevent Sabbath-day drinking encountered acts of resistance varying from the immediately verbal or physical to the more calculated. Presented in 1648 for keeping a disorderly alehouse at Alvanley in Cheshire on Sabbath days and fast days 'when Ministers have beene in Exercise', Ellen Collier expressed defiance; a few months later, Dorothy Bradbury of Mobberley was in trouble for striking Simon Stewarte after he rebuked her for being in an alehouse at sermon time.[25] At Overton in 1647, Robert Cockhill had lately come to town and sold ale without a licence, causing disorder, fighting and gaming on the Sabbath. But no-one would complain after he stabbed one of them.[26]

Although attempts were made to pull people out of alehouses in many areas, this could prove counter-productive when those targeted intermixed with church-goers. In Tedburn St Mary in Devon in January 1650, people reportedly drank between the morning and afternoon services at Walter

[23] CRO, QJF 75/4, fo. 42r.
[24] HRO, Q1/2, fo. 275r.
[25] CRO, QJF 76/2, Trinity 1648, fo. 13r; QJB 2/6, 19 Oct. 1648.
[26] CRO, QJF 74/4, fo. 18r.

Berry's alehouse, then came in drunk and full of 'spleen' to the afternoon service, 'defiling' the church and treading down the churchyard fences.[27] In Cheshire in October 1649, there were complaints that people either stayed at home, went to alehouses or stayed talking in the churchyard rather than paying any regard to the church service. Constables were ordered to note down offenders.[28] But not a lot appeared to have changed by 1651, when drunken individuals spewing in a chapel and churchyard were reported at Church Hulme and Clive, respectively.[29]

In September 1648, the Cheshire bench ordered constables to give strict account of alehouses, seeking advice from the minister, churchwardens or 'the most religious and discreet Inhabitants'.[30] Initially, puritan clergy keenly monitored Sabbath-day drinking. In July 1649, a group of 'painful and Laborious Ministers' complained of the 'great prophanacion of the Lords Day' throughout Yorkshire's North Riding.[31] In October the same year Benjamin Barnard, intruded rector of Warnford, petitioned the Hampshire bench to close two out of the three inns he claimed were causing Sabbath-day disorders there.[32] But such efforts could backfire. After Thomas Gilbert, parson of Cheadle in Cheshire, certified in 1647 that Hugh and Anne Hooley were unfit to run an alehouse, the Gilberts found themselves arrested twice over. On the second occasion the charges were grave, with Gilbert ordered in mid-1650 to London to give satisfaction touching his affection to the present government, after some ill-advised remarks about the Scots got reported to the authorities, requiring the intervention of local JP Colonel Robert Duckenfield to extricate him.[33] When in 1652 William Prytherch, minister of Aber in Caernarfonshire, reported an unlawful assembly on the Lord's day, the response was more physical: those charged, he claimed, with 'staves and fists and feet fell upon him with effusion of blood and bruises'.[34]

Clergy learned to conduct themselves more gingerly. In the summer of 1655, John Salter reportedly came into the church at Wraxall in Somerset drunk during an afternoon service and made 'strange ugly, mimicall faces and gestures' at the preacher Thomas Gorges, 'pointing' with his finger and

---

[27] DHC, QS/1/8, Jan. 1649/50.

[28] CRO, QJB 1/6, 9 Oct. 1649.

[29] CRO, QJB 2/6, QJF 79/2, Trinity 1651, fo. 100r; QJB 2/6, fo. 109v.

[30] CRO, QJF 76/3, fo. 22r.

[31] NYRO, QSM 2/8, fo. 153v.

[32] HRO, Q1/2, fo. 277r.

[33] CRO, QJF 75/1 fos. 38r, 101r, Easter 1647; QJF 78/3, fos. 73, 77r, Michaelmas 1650.

[34] GA, XQS 1652/32, 12 April 1652.

raising his fist at him. But it took a second incident several months later, when Salter and his wife disrupted the choosing of churchwardens and overseers on Easter Monday, to make Gorges resort to the higher authorities.[35] One reason for caution was the lack of certainty that parish officers would endorse prosecutions. At Heathfield in Sussex in 1653, the officers were said to have connived at allowing five alehouses to continue profaning the Sabbath. Alehouses 'were again sett up as often as they were pulled downe'.[36] In 1656, Chester churchwardens circumvented the regulations, reportedly disposing of fines paid by Sabbath-breakers to their own children's use.[37] The constable Randle Whitakers was one of the men found drinking at Hugh Brotter's disorderly alehouse at Hunsterson in Cheshire on a Sunday in June 1655, all of whom wore in their hats hairs pulled from Brotter's wife Joane's 'privy parts'. Joane herself was described as 'very drunke'.[38]

Some parishioners were openly antagonistic towards sabbatarianism. At Wiveliscombe in Somerset in 1654, William Davye apparently ran through the streets on the Sabbath, crying out against 'Independent rouges' reading chapters of the Bible in their houses, 'that the divell will have them all'.[39] There was much fun to be had in subverting the new religious imperatives. At Hurdsfield in Cheshire in 1649, gentleman Edward Morecroft was cited for dancing to music on the Lord's day. Knocking his knees together, he 'cutt the Stroke with his foot, and said a Curse a god on the Parliament, a pox a god upon the Parliament', at least thirty times, according to the husbandman and collier's wife who reported him.[40] Complaint was made in Somerset in 1650 that several persons gathered at Winsham church on Sabbath days to 'ringe in peale for pleasure and pastime', pretending to call people to church, contrary to the laws of the Sabbath.[41] A similar practice was used two years later at Wookey to drown out a soldier who attempted to preach in the absence of the minister.[42]

In Hampshire in 1656, Sabbath-day 'helpe Ales and merry meetings' were reported, with barrels of beer in private houses.[43] 'Merry nights' were denounced in Lancashire in 1647; 'private clubbing for ale' in West Yorkshire

[35] SHC, Q/SR/93/171.

[36] ESRO, QR/102, fo. 9r.

[37] CRO, QJF 84/3, fo. 18r.

[38] CRO, QJF 83/2, Trinity 1655, fo. 70r.

[39] SHC, Q/SR/89/55.

[40] CRO, QJF 78/1, 20 March 1641.

[41] *Quarter Sessions Records for the County of Somerset*, ed. E. H. Bates-Harbin (London, Somerset Record Soc., 1912), iii. 157.

[42] SHC, Q/SR/85/55.

[43] HRO, Q1/3, p. 292.

in 1656.[44] One of these meetings apparently took place in October 1657 at an alehouse in Soughton, where John Caulverley esquire led revellers from Chester twelve miles away in fiddling, piping, dancing and shouting at James Dunne's alehouse from Saturday night until after sunrise on Sunday morning, disquieting the neighbours. When one complained, he was badly beaten, and the offenders continued playing music 'as ever' they had done, profaning 'the lords holy day'.[45]

Along with the many presentments for Sabbath-day drinking were numerous presentations for Sabbath-day travelling or working. Reported in particularly tedious detail were the exact circumstances in which John Prichard David Lloyd of Gwernor and Eline wife of Owen ap Richard on 18 April 1655 drove a mare bearing two 'winchesters' of corn a mile to Elizabeth John Prichard's house in Llanllyfni.[46] Many of those prosecuted were ordinary people trying to earn a livelihood: by baking bread in Devon and Kent, loading a barge with stones at Topsham in Devon in 1648, selling tobacco at Weare in Somerset in 1650, working at a lime kiln in Pitminster in Somerset in 1651, selling boots and shoes at Chiltington in Sussex in October 1654, trimming hair in Exeter the same year, walking in the fields in Middlewich and sweeping the streets in Nantwich in Cheshire in 1655, selling cloth in Drewsteignton in Devon in 1651, and dressing it in West Bergholt in Essex in 1657. Even in the spring of 1660, as Charles II looked set to return, there were presentments for selling mutton on the Sabbath at Basing in Hampshire and of two Essex men for being drunk and travelling.[47]

The highest prosecution rate for Sabbath-day offences was in Cheshire; rates in Devon were much lower, although the Exeter quarter sessions order book reveals a particularly determined battle to detect any illicit Sunday behaviour there. In March 1657, an Exeter constable discovered a pair of weavers working behind the locked doors at Wilmott Mather's house in Castle Lane. Entry had been at first denied, 'not withstanding they often knockt'. A couple of months earlier another weaver was fined £10 for being found at 'sermon tyme' hiding 'uppon the barr' of a chimney, presumably attempting to escape detection for not being in church.[48]

---

[44] LA, QSB/1/288/22; WYAS, Quarter Sessions Order Book, 15 April 1656, pp. 185–6.

[45] CRO, QJF 85/3, Trinity 1657, fo. 76; now called Sychdyn and in Wales.

[46] GA, XQS/1654–1655/22.

[47] J. S. Cockburn, *Calendar of Assize Records: Kent Indictments 1649–1659* (London, 1979), p. 280; DHC, QS/4/54, 57; QS/1/9; ECA, fos. 141r, 385r, 262r; SHC, Q/SR/83/69; Q/SO/ 5, fo. 256r; TNA, ASSI 35/99/2/31; CHES 21/4, fo. 332v; CRO, QJF 84/1, fo. 31r; ESRO, QI/EQ2, fo. 11v; *Scarborough Records 1640–1660*, ed. M. Y. Ashcroft (Northallerton, 1991), p. 229; HRO, Q4/1, fo. 146v; ERO, T/A/465/2 1647–87, 9 April 1660.

[48] DHC, ECA, fos. 342v, 351v.

Prosecutions in the peak years of 1655–8 ran at around twice the rate of those in 1649–54. But they continued to meet spirited opposition. The 'crying noyce' of wickedness was now 'rendring our parts' like 'Sodome', urged a petition to the Cheshire bench in 1657; it was 'high time for all … that would have peace here and glory hereafter to bend their bow against it'.[49]

Along with drinking, some took the opportunity of others' absence at church for illicit sex or opportunistic thefts from neighbours' empty houses. In May 1652, labourer Peter Mudge of Whitchurch in Devon, 'haveing lost many small thinges out of his house', stayed away from church purposely during the morning service to see if he could discover the thief. Concealed in his chamber and looking through a hole, he saw his neighbour, widow Dorothy Spiller, unlock his house door and take away 'a dish of gerts', using a key she later surrendered to the constable.[50] Outdoor theft and poaching was particularly reported in Sussex. In 1655, Sabbath-day hare hunting was investigated at Caulfield in July, at snowy Barcombe in November, Sabbath-day evening rabbit hunting with dogs in the grounds of Mr Conert at Slaugham in October, and in September 1656 'searching for ferrets in the howse of John Rease gent'.[51]

Servants, teenagers and adults often found the time on the Sabbath when other people were at church useful for other purposes than religious devotion. Quaife found that forty per cent of illicit conceptions in Somerset for 1600–60 were claimed to have taken place on a Sunday.[52] Examined in September 1647 about her pregnancy, Anne Lande admitted that she had had sex with James Smith, fellow-servant to Henry Howell of Balsdean in Sussex on a Sunday evening, in her master's malthouse, and again on a Sunday morning, in his house.[53] At Stockport in August 1652, alderman Francis Harpur accused labourer John Wood of visiting his house on the Sabbath at 'the tyme of devine Service', on purpose to abuse a teenage girl's chastity. Wood countered that he had been 'fetched by Anna Harpur … in Sermon tyme', 'to get forth mucke forth of the Stable', and that she had then encouraged him to touch and kiss her.[54] In an adultery case from Rothsterne in Cheshire in 1655, John Warburton testified that Thomas Finlowe did not attend church but 'almost every Sunday' went instead 'about

49 CRO, QJF 85/4, fo. 123r.
50 DHC, QS/4/57.
51 ESRO, QR/110, fos. 11–13, 70r; QI/EQ2, fos. 17v, 20v.
52 G. R. Quaife, *Wanton Wenches and Wayward Wives* (London, 1979), p. 87.
53 ESRO, QR/79, fo. 43r, 30 Sept. 1647.
54 CRO, QJF 80/3, fo. 30.

Church tymes' to Margery Blackburne's house until 'church was donne' and then returned home, 'but what he did there', Warburton commented darkly, he could not say.[55] Not everyone was so ready to use the Sabbath to contravene the seventh commandment. In a 1648 Cheshire case, Martha Malmeck testified that Randle Grafton had suggested she go with him to the stable 'and hee would give her content' but she 'bade him goe into the Church for his wife'.[56]

Because of swearing, the land mourneth

The degree of effort by local authorities in prosecuting swearing, with 281 recorded cases here, seems extraordinary to modern eyes, and it seems some contemporaries agreed. When John Witcombe was set in the stocks at Barton (St) David in Somerset in July 1657 for swearing, the minister Mr Horsey brought him a pot of beer and, referring to a statute book in his hand, told his weeping mother not to fret, 'for by the statute no justice can punish him after twenty daies, and the statute will allow him Five pounds for every hower and I will see that he shall have it'.[57] Yet our modern insensitivity to

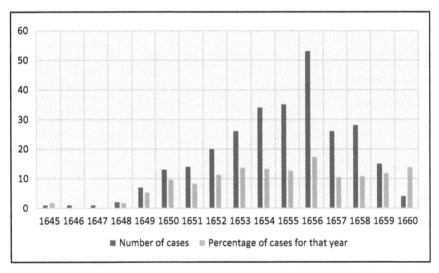

Figure 6.2. Offences related to swearing and cursing by year.

[55] CRO, QJF 83/3, fos. 89–92.

[56] CRO, QJF 76/2, fo. 44r.

[57] SHC, Q/SR/95/197.

bad language, explained by the eighteenth-century philosopher Giambattista Vico as a natural tendency for language to transform from the sacred to the conventional, obscures our understanding of how much such words troubled contemporary auditors.[58] In a largely oral society, anxieties about speech lay in its power to promote action, and its unpredictable, uncontrollable, shape-shifting path beyond the first thoughtless utterance. Reprobation of 'sins of the tongue' was commonplace, dating back to the fourteenth century; and 'substantially unchanged', argued Bodden, through to the seventeenth century, although the increasing inclination to apply legal sanctions was a newer development.[59] Laws against it were first enacted in England in James I's Act of 1624, with a fine of twelve pence or three hours in the stocks for anyone over twelve and unable to pay, or whipping for the under-aged.[60]

Charles I ratified his father's legislation: there was a fair degree of consensus against the offence, with tracts denouncing it across all sides of the religious spectrum.[61] Objections rested on three counts. First, it did injury to sacred things. 'The oyle wherewith the tabernacle and the arke of the testament ... was holy' wrote William Perkins, 'no man might put it to any other uses ... we much more ought to tremble at the word of God, not to make our selves merrie with it.'[62] Second, swearing offended others: 'His words are but so many vomitings cast up to the loathsomenesse of the hearers,' wrote John Earle in his 'Character of a profane man' in 1628.[63] But most importantly, the tongue was a 'two-edged sword', harming the offender most of all, alienating him from God, to become, in Perkins's view, a 'child of the devill'.[64] 'Because of swearing, the land mourneth,' preached John Parker at Bovingdon in Hertfordshire in February 1654, following a popular choice of biblical text on the subject, albeit one which suggests a somewhat different interpretation in modern translation.[65] Stories abounded of the divine punishments inflicted upon swearers and blasphemers, affecting the whole wider community.[66] On 19 May 1644,

---

[58] G. Hughes, *An Encyclopedia of Swearing* (London, 2015), p. xxiv.

[59] M-C. Bodden, *Language as the Site of Revolt in Medieval and Early Modern England* (Basingstoke, 2011), pp. 8–21.

[60] A. Montague, *The Anatomy of Swearing* (London, Macmillan, 1973), pp. 157, 162, 167.

[61] Montague, *Anatomy*, p. 159.

[62] N. Vienne-Guerrin, *The Unruly Tongue in Early Modern England: Three Treatises* (Madison, N.J., 2012), p. 83.

[63] J. Earle, *Micro-Cosmographie* (London, 1650), p. 125.

[64] Vienne-Guerrin, *Unruly Tongue*, pp. 31, 73.

[65] Jeremiah 23:10; W. J. Hardy, *Hertfordshire County Records* (Hertford, 1905), i. 101.

[66] Vienne-Guerrin, *Unruly Tongue*, p. 31.

royalist Edward Symmons blamed the failure at building ramparts at Shrewsbury on 'such cursing and such swearing', even by women and children, 'as did I never heare'. Did they but reform their habits, their works 'would stand the better'.[67]

During the First Civil War, royalist clergy attempted to stem the tide of swearing among royalist soldiers, while a parliamentary army formulating its own self-identity in opposition to the habits of the 'goddamee' 'cavaliers', 'Irish rogues and English monsters' sometimes inflicted severe punishments on swearers, condemning one impious quartermaster to have his tongue bored with a red-hot iron, according to Bulstrode Whitelocke.[68] In 1645, the Scottish parliament made cursing punishable by death.[69] In this context, the English penalties for swearing enacted in 1650 appear comparatively mild, if of questionable deterrent value given the spirited responses from those denounced. The statutory fine had been increased three-fold to 3s 4d for a first offence for those of ordinary estate or three hours in the stocks for those unable to pay.[70] But at Wincanton in Somerset in July 1653 when John Lane was set in the stocks for swearing six oaths, the bystanders, who included the tithingman and churchwarden, defiantly celebrated and toasted him.[71] Perhaps perceiving his household honour besmirched on being fined for his wife's swearing, in 1655 Robert Lincole of Chard in Somerset gave the constables a brass half-crown as payment, berating the parish overseers as knaves and fools when, in the churchyard on a Sunday morning, they attempted to get him to exchange this for legal tender.[72] Bernard Capp has noted the tendency for those accused of swearing to retaliate with counter-accusations against their accusers.[73] In the summer of 1656 officious puritan Nathaniel Durant, minister of Cheriton Fitzpaine, took issue with Christopher Gill of Cadbury for swearing 'god's lie' on the public highway, repeating the words twice in reproof. Gill informed local justices that Durant himself had used the oath.[74] This ruse was well travelled: it was also

---

[67] E. Symmons, *A Militarie Sermon* (Oxford, 1644), p. 32.

[68] E. Woodward, *A Good Soldier* (London, 1644), p. 22; W. Prynne, *A True and Full Relation of the Prosecution … of Nathaniel Fiennes* (London, 1644), p. 86; B. Whitelocke, *Memorials of the English Affairs* (Oxford, 1853), iii. 162.

[69] Montague, *Anatomy*, p. 171.

[70] *An Act for the Better Preventing and Suppressing of Prophane Swearing and Cursing* (London, 1650).

[71] SHC, Q/SR/86/155.

[72] SHC, Q/SR/92/53.

[73] Capp, *England's Culture Wars*, p. 98.

[74] DHC, QS/4/58.

employed at Rowton in Cheshire in May 1659 against a puritan constable in a dispute over a maypole.[75]

Swearing prosecutions, prosecuted not just at quarter sessions but sometimes at assizes too, rose year on year through the interregnum towards a peak in 1656, dropping by half as soon as the rule of the Major-Generals was over (see Figure 6.2). They reduced again by 1659, although some maintained their enthusiasm: long lists of swearers were made by Presbyterian Thomas Bampfield in Devon in July 1658, January 1659 and March 1660, while in Somerset, Major Henry Bonner was also vigilant and, along with other military JPs Colonel John Pyne and Captain John Barker, contributed to a 'Certificate of Convictions for Swearing' in 1650 and 1655.[76] At Ilchester in late 1658 and early 1659, several people were charged with swearing multiple oaths, each on the evidence of a single accuser.[77]

A late-medieval wall-painting at St Lawrence, Broughton in Buckinghamshire 'represents the injury done to the Body of Christ by those who swear by God's wounds, God's bones, etc., a common medieval habit', wrote M. R. James.[78] William Lambarde's *Eirenarcha* (1579), a set of instructions for JPs, also condemned the practice, for similar reasons.[79] Catholic-type oaths relating to the body of Christ such as God's wounds, blood or flesh, either singly or in combination, abounded in Cheshire; but were less commonly reported elsewhere. Use of 'by God' was commonly reported everywhere, but 'by Christ' only three times. There was a significant category of reported oaths relating to judgement or vengeance: 'upon my soul', 'God judge me' or 'damn me'. Oaths of 'upon my life' were reported six times in Devon, but nowhere else, hinting at specific knowledge of what was taken as actionable by this county's commissioners.[80] Interestingly, 'By faith' and 'by troth', which Charles I considered an 'asseveration' not an oath, use of which had however commonly been considered a cause to remove clergy in the early 1640s, only appear in a handful of prosecutions of the

---

[75] CRO, QJF 87/2/2, fo. 111r.

[76] DHC, QS/4/63–4; History of parliament <http://www.historyofparliamentonline.org/volume/1660–1690/member/bampfield-thomas-1623–93> [accessed 8 April 2020]; SHC, Q/SR/91/53, 64, 65; Q/SO/5, fo. 280v; Q/RCC/1, Box 1.

[77] SHC, Q/SR/98/88.

[78] M. R. James, 'The iconography of Bucks', quoted in J. Edwards, 'The wall paintings of St Lawrence's Church, Broughton', *Records of Buckinghamshire*, xxvi (1984), 44–55, at p. 46.

[79] S. Bardsley, 'Sin, speech, and scolding in late medieval England', in *Fama: the Politics of Talk and Reputation in Medieval Europe*, ed. T. S. Fenster and D. L. Smail (London, 2003), pp. 145–64, at p. 151.

[80] DHC, QS/1/9, 10 July 1655, 8 July & 30 Sept. 1656, 7 Apr. & 6 Oct. 1657.

laity.[81] Diseases were wished on others, the pox or the plague, 'of God' in some cases, and perhaps the reason these were considered actionable. Likewise, as the terms of the legislation were against blasphemous swearing, scatological oaths were sometimes reported but were not generally the focus of prosecution.

Witnesses keenly noted when and where the offence took place, and counted the number of oaths. Multiple offenders included Wynfrid Coles, set in the stocks for three hours at Bridgwater in 1650 for swearing thirty oaths by God's wounds and blood, and Peter Harrar, indicted at assizes for swearing sixty oaths in Midsummer 1654 in an alehouse at Acton Common in Cheshire.[82] But when in July 1655 constable Ambrose Hare came to Robert Chedzoy's house at Curland in Somerset to demand payment of his fine for swearing twenty oaths, Chedzoy refused to pay, followed Hare for a quarter of a mile and used 'uncivill language', that Hare 'should kisse his [ ]',[83] 'hee did not care a turd' for him, 'Nor the justice of the peace neither'.[84] Other 'common swearers' seemed oblivious to the offence caused. In 1658, William Turner, constable of Matley in Cheshire, was prosecuted for swearing repeatedly in praise of his horse, 'by God this is a good horse, as god judge mee, by my faith and troth, yes by the masse', 'and so continued all along his discourse', twenty-four oaths in total, reported the witness.[85]

The charge of swearing often acted as mere corroborative detail in an overall pattern of misdemeanour, with violent language mirroring claims of physical aggression. Reports of violence and swearing also commonly accompanied claims of political disaffection, usually intended to ramp up the perceived seriousness of the offence and invite official notice. 'Even mundane quarrels could become charged with political tensions that individuals exploited to shape their authority within communities and amidst personal squabbles,' wrote Caroline Boswell.[86] An argument between Mrs Mary Barrett and her neighbour John Johnson at Withinlee in Cheshire on 7 February 1659 illustrates both tendencies clearly. It centred on Johnson's taking impertinent advantage of Barrett's husband's absence at church to water his two horses in a hole in the ice used by Mary to fetch

---

[81] M. Griffin, *Regulating Religion and Morality in the King's Armies: 1639–1646* (Leiden, 2004), p. 24; see BL Add. MS. 5829 & 15672, University of Leicester MS. 31, WMS Cii, for charges of swearing against clergy.

[82] SHC, Q/SO/5, fo. 245v; TNA, CHES 21/4, fo. 306v.

[83] Left blank in the original.

[84] SHC, Q/SR/91/65.

[85] CRO, QJF 84/2, 1656, fo. 9r.

[86] C. Boswell, *Disaffection and Everyday Life in Interregnum England* (Woodbridge, 2017), pp. 95, 239.

water for cooking and drinking. Mary's account reformulated the offence as sedition. 'God blesse my Lord Protector hee should water noe horses there,' she claimed to have cried, Johnson responding, 'by God hee did not care if the Lord Protector were hanged', 'for hee would water his Horses there'. 'Noe trator should water his horses there,' Mary unwisely continued, before Johnson brought the argument to a swift conclusion by breaking her head with a shovel.[87]

Swearers were also frequently cited in the process of resisting arrest or remonstrating at legal process. Watching John Spooner replevining a cow her husband had taken at Stockport in April 1656, Anne Hooley was said to have sworn six oaths 'by Gods wounds that she would stone him'.[88] Told to be quiet in the Protector's name, she said she would stone the Protector.[89] Placed in the stocks in September 1654 for drunkenness while pregnant, Anne Jeyeson cursed the whole town of Nantwich, wishing the 'pocks of god' on the lot them.[90] Although around three-quarters of those convicted of swearing were male, eighty-four female swearers were listed; cursing was more of a women's crime; although men still formed the majority of the accused, around forty per cent were women.

Accusations of swearing were surprisingly skewed towards the elite, who paid higher fines according to the schedule in the statute. Where status was given, over forty per cent were described as gentleman, esquire or mister, yeomen, clergy (or their wives) or office-holders such as constables or overseers, far out of proportion to their numbers among the population. In 1653, Robert Dacy, interregnum incumbent at Offwell in Devon, recklessly denounced the son and heir of royalist baronet Sir Richard Grenville for swearing five oaths, despite (or perhaps in retaliation for) all the intimidation Dacy and his wife had already faced from royalists in the parish.[91] Grenville was fined fifty shillings. But Dacy could take small comfort for he was soon forced out of the parish.[92] Several clergy were listed among the swearers, including the sequestered rector of Forscote in Somerset, William Parsons, convicted of swearing eight profane oaths by Major Henry Bonner in October 1655.[93] In January 1660, Thomas Hanson, rector of Llanllyfni, was accused of swearing

[87] CRO, QJF 86/3, fo. 26r.

[88] *OED*: replevin: the recovery by a person of goods or chattels distrained or confiscated, giving a surety to have the matter tried in court and to return the goods if the case is lost.

[89] CRO, QJF 84/2, fo. 215r.

[90] CRO, QJF 82/3, fo. 102r.

[91] DHC, QS/1/9 1652–1661, 4 Oct. 1653; spelled Grynvile in the original.

[92] WMS C2.226; DHC, QS/1/8, Michaelmas 1649, petition of Anne Dacye.

[93] SHC, Q/RCC/1, Box 1.

five profane oaths at Caernarfon, and 'provoking words' for calling 'all good people of the Commonwealth' 'knaves and assess and puppies'.[94]

Keeping a close eye on adulterers

Another frequently cited offence was adultery, with 173 cases, suggesting a need for a reassessment of historical arguments downplaying the significance of the Adultery Act of 1650.[95] True, as has been argued, female offenders were rarely executed, but this did not prevent their neighbours from reporting their misbehaviour in prurient detail. The fact that there was so much other sexual crime being prosecuted may have something to do with it, although few cases related to bastardy claims as was often the case with other sexual offences.

The highest number of cases recorded was in Cheshire (sixty-two cases), where the rich survival of depositions means we hear about reported cases that never went beyond an accusation, followed by Yorkshire (thirty-five cases) and Devon (thirty cases). This supports the work of Bernard Capp on Middlesex, who also found many more accusations than trials, suggesting these in themselves were used as tools by authorities to exert lower-level pressure on reported offenders.[96] Despite the statutory capital penalty for female offenders after 1650, only forty-five cases come from assize records. As expected, accusations of adultery rose significantly after the passing of the Adultery Act, in 1651–2, but actually peaked in 1656 and did not significantly reduce until 1659.

Only in three cases did clergy (half-heartedly) endorse accusations.[97] At Prestbury in Cheshire in 1653, it was only after parishioners pressurized him that minister John Brereton took action against Elizabeth Upton, a married woman said to be committing adultery with her employer. He refused to baptize her child, and reported her to the authorities.[98] At Siddington in Cheshire in July 1658, there were rumours about George Lowe's behaviour towards his daughter-in-law Sarah. Lowe tried to persuade the minister Edmund Burtinshaw to quash them, but Burtinshaw demurred: 'His Judgement and Conscience tould him hee might not doe it.'[99]

---

[94] GA, QXS 1660/2.

[95] Durston, 'Puritan rule', p. 220; K. Thomas, 'The puritans and adultery: the Act of 1650 reconsidered', *Puritans and Revolutionaries*, ed. D.H. Pennington and K. V. Thomas (Oxford, 1978), pp. 257–83; F. A. Inderwick, *The Interregnum* (London, 1891), pp. 33–9.

[96] Capp, 'Republican reformation', pp. 49–55; see also details of cases from the Exeter quarter sessions in Capp, *England's Culture Wars*, p. 248.

[97] ERO, Q/SBa 2/76, 15 July 1651.

[98] CRO, QJF 81/2, fo. 283r; QJF 81/3, fo. 14r.

[99] CRO, QJF 86/3, Michaelmas 1658, fo. 24.

Around thirty per cent of accusers or witnesses were women, higher than their participation levels for other religious offences. Accusers came from across the social spectrum: gentry, yeomen, husbandmen, labourers, a constable, a cutler, a carpenter, a blacksmith and a servant included. The middling sort, yeomen and craftsmen, were disproportionately targeted, accounting for nearly half of all those accused. Gentry were rarely denounced, suggesting accusers feared the ramifications of accusing their social superiors for something that was by its nature more doubtful than the public offence of swearing.

Such persons as refuse to pay their dues

Parochial financial disputes were another ubiquitous cause at quarter sessions: refusal to pay church leys, clergy stipends or tithes or irregularities in church accounting. These represented over a fifth of religious-related complaints to quarter sessions or assizes during 1647–9, when there was widespread resistance to paying dues in the wake of clergy ejections and many churches needing repair, dropping dramatically in 1650, but thereafter returning to around twenty to thirty complaints per year between 1651 and 1659 (see Figure 6.3). Resistance to paying tithes was widely reported and wages of clergy, schoolmasters and parish clerks often difficult to extract. At Barking in April 1649, the parish clerk Richard Hutchinson complained that despite being chosen by 'joint consent' five years ago, with an agreed yearly allowance from the minister, 'chief inhabitants' and 'several house holders', 'divers people takeinge advantage of the present distracions and

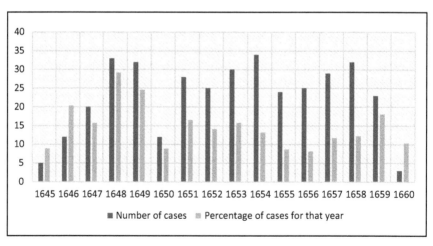

Figure 6.3. Legal cases relating to parish finances by year.

aimeinge att theire owne ends doe refuse and delay' to pay him because there was no longer any commissary to recover them by 'Ecclesiasticall proceedings' as formerly.[100] At Flixton in Lancashire in 1651, the parish clerk John Loe, describing himself as a 'poor labouring Man' with a wife and six children, complained that ten of the fifty parishioners with plough lands refused to pay him but 'Can alledge No Just or reasonable Cause'.[101] In 1655, parishioners at Congresbury in Somerset even contested the pitiful sum of four pence yearly due to Edmond Watts after twenty years as parish clerk.[102]

The motivations for such behaviour were often clear enough. Economic conditions were difficult and the financial demands on the populace unprecedented. Aware that parishioners were finding it difficult to meet the sums demanded, Cheshire clergy sometimes tried to alleviate demands on parishes. In 1653, the minister and churchwardens of Wybunbury complained of the 'almost Constant Collections in our Congregations', claiming that some of the so-called poor were not in need.[103] But others thought rate-payers were taking advantage: the churchwardens of Lower Peover complained in 1651 that 'the burthen is layd on some few, and the rest will not contribute'.[104] Assault was an occupational hazard for those collecting arrears or distraining goods on the orders of justices or assize judges to pay for them. In 1654 when the churchwardens attempted to collect a sixpence church ley from a Nantwich shoemaker, he attacked them with a 'great log of wood'.[105] This was a parish suffering severe social problems. In 1650 the churchwardens claimed that over 800 people sought poor relief, 'much augmented' by the soldiers in the 'late wars' 'at which tyme the Statute Lawes were not at all put in Execucion'.[106] So many collections were held that many avoided church services or 'Came not till after the … Colleccions'. In 1651 when Anne Bowry, widow of the town's minister, petitioned Cheshire quarter sessions for arrears of her husband's stipend, all the churchwarden could extract from the parishioners was seven pounds in 'Course clipped money'.[107]

[100] ERO, Q/SBa 2/64, 6 April 1649.

[101] LA, QSP/44/20.

[102] SHC, Q/SO/5, fo. 437v.

[103] CRO, QJF 81/3, fo. 104r.

[104] CRO, QJF 79/1, fo. 125r.

[105] CRO, QJF 82/1, fo. 115r.

[106] CRO, QJF 79/4, fo. 81r: soldiers' dependants presumably increased the number of the poor.

[107] CRO, QJF 79/2, fo. 126r.

In North Petherton in Somerset, the continuing presence in the parish of the sequestered incumbent John Morley and his family perhaps discouraged compliance: a John Morley was bound over in both 1651 and 1654.[108] In July 1649, the tithingman was assaulted and robbed by two men who threatened to sink his body in a ditch.[109] Tattenhall in Cheshire, sequestered from Dr Edward Morton, had similar problems. Intruded 'by force', his first replacement Francis Smyth was reportedly 'disliked' in the parish; his successor Josias Clarke fared little better.[110] In 1651, Clarke complained to quarter sessions that the churchwarden George Edge neglected his office, neither attending church for twelve months, making collections for the poor nor doing anything to repair the 'much broken' church, leaving it 'exposed to unseasonable weather'.[111]

To loyalists refusing to pay tithes to disliked new ministers were added those refusing them on self-interest proclaimed as principle. At harvest time at Stanton Drew in Somerset in 1650, Richard Addames was said to have ordered his servant to fetch back forty-two sheaves laid out for the parson, saying that the parson had no right to them.[112] Complaints about parish finances peaked in 1654 after a year of anti-tithe agitation; assize depositions reveal serious problems in Yorkshire around this time, detailing at length a conspiracy in the North Riding in July 1653 led by Thomas Elsylott Esquire, with Richard Bickerdike acting as his agent, to gather people to resist paying tithes and assessments, claiming authority from the army. At Knottingley in the West Riding, the constable William Sykes signed a petition against tithes, describing them as robberies.[113]

Necessary repairs to church or churchyard were often contested. In areas like Cheshire, fought over during the Civil Wars, there were many damaged churches, requiring additional rates from a population little inclined or able to pay. At Pulford, '8 bayes of building' 'and all other combustible matter' about the parsonage and church had been burnt by parliamentary soldiers. Describing the parishioners as 'verie few' and the incumbent's means as 'verie small', in 1646 the minister, Richard Houlford, pleaded for sequestration money to provide glass and slate for the chancel and to make the house 'habitable with glasse and doors and stayres'.[114] At Audlem in 1646, the issue

---

[108] SHC, Q/SO/5, fos. 301v, 454v.

[109] SHC, Q/SR/81/16.

[110] BL Add 33937, fo. 32.

[111] CRO, QJF 78/4, fos. 35–37.

[112] SHC, Q/SR/82/212–4.

[113] J. Raine, *Depositions from the Castle of York* (Surtees Soc., London, 1861), nos. l, lvi. pp. 54–5, 59–62.

[114] CRO, QJF 74/4, Epiphany 1646/7, fo. 22r.

of church repairs provoked physical violence: the churchwardens reported 'many severall abuses dayly Comitted both in the said Church and Steple ... the fflores pulled up the belropes and wheles broken in peeces and the clocke in great decay'. For mending what was broken, John Turnor incurred the 'hatred and malice' of 'one Jane Pickstocke', who bit him on the ear and sung 'a lybell or Ryme' against him, while William Gilbert threatened to stab him.[115]

Requests for orders to secure funds for church repairs peaked around 1648, following the parliamentary ordinance for the repair of churches.[116] The Cheshire quarter sessions minuted on 11 January 1649 'divers' petitions complaining of parishioners refusing to contribute towards repairing churches 'ruinde and decayed' 'in the time of the warres' on 'Pretence that there is nowe noe lawes' to compel them.[117] At Tarvin, although it was understood that the parishioners' vicinity to Chester and Beeston Castle had made them 'greater sufferers in the tyme of warre by quarter and plunder', repeated petitions in 1649 and 1651 demanded action against those who refused to fund repairs to a church in which a 'great parte of the Roofe' had fallen down. As at Barking, there was nostalgia for the old ecclesiastical regime, the 'Concestory Courte ... wherein such persones as refused to pay theire Church dues, where [sic] punished for theire neclecte [sic] and Compelled to pay'. The bench was now 'the onely place as wee conceave for the present to releeve us'.[118]

The situation was similarly dire in other former war zones. At Poulton in Lancashire, 1646–7, the 'fower and twenty' avoided meeting to avoid paying for repairs to a church, decayed since these 'troublesome times', needing new glass and repairs to a badly damaged roof.[119] But at Kirkham in July 1653, it was the '30 men' who petitioned, saying that all the things there were in a 'posture of confusion', with churchwardens elected at Easter refusing to take office, no poor rates, communions or registering of infants, and both church and school facing 'utter ruen' because of disrepair.[120] Churches in the south and south-west also suffered. Bedminster church in Bristol had been burnt down by Prince Rupert's soldiers in 1645 and become 'unserviceable'. But the inhabitants could never bear the 3,500 pounds cost to repair it: many

[115] CRO, QJF 74/2 Trinity 1646, fo. 46r.

[116] Ordinance for repairing churches and paying of church duties within the kingdom of England and Wales, 9 Feb. 1647/8, <https://www.british-history.ac.uk/no-series/acts-ordinances-interregnum/lix-lxvi> [accessed 8 April 2020].

[117] CRO, QJB 2/6, 11 Jan. 1648/9.

[118] CRO, QJF 79/2 Trinity 1651, fos. 645, 135r.

[119] LA, QSB/1/283/20.

[120] LA, QSP/82/9.

of their own houses had also been burnt down.[121] According to Thomas Holdsworth, a later rector at North Stoneham in Hampshire, Lewis Alcock, the octogenarian rector sequestered after the Civil War, had contributed £400 towards the rebuilding of the church earlier in his incumbency.[122] But by 1649 the church required rebuilding anew at a cost of £700. The cruel treatment of the charitable Alcock, described by Holdsworth, could hardly have cultivated warm feelings within the parish; disputes persisted throughout the interregnum, with churchwardens at one stage arrested and forced to request the intervention of House of Commons speaker William Lenthall.[123]

Particular individuals were often blamed for their neglect of church maintenance. Most commonly complained about were ways or paths leading to churches, followed by chancels, which it was the responsibility of the minister or impropriator to maintain and which were thus more likely to be impacted by lay or clerical sequestrations. One of the most flagrant cases was that of Middlesex resident Colonel Edmund Harvey, who bought the fee farm of Bromborough church in Cheshire and in 1656 stubbornly resisted paying the four pounds per annum due for repairing the chancel and the preacher's stipend.[124] Deficient churchyard fencing was also commonly reported. At Hillfarrance in Somerset, the churchyard had been maintained by 'particular persons', but, decayed since the 'late wars', in 1655 lay as 'open common'. The justices ordered the matter to be settled by amicable mediation, 'if they can'.[125]

Unrepaired civil war damage was still being dealt with well into the 1650s, with the highest number of cases recorded in 1658. As late as 1657, the chapel at Exmouth was described as having rotten timberwork and seats 'burnt and destroyed' 'during the late wars'.[126] The same year, the private chapel at Manchester belonging to the royalist earls of Derby was evidently open to the street, making it 'liable to Defilementt by the poorer sort of people and other Rude men who in the night time Creepe and Lodg therein'. Roofs, steeples and towers naturally caused the greatest concern. Royalist soldiers under Sir Ralph Hopton had been quartered at Crondall in Hampshire during the siege of Farnham in 1643.[127] In 1658, the justices,

---

[121] Harbin, *Somerset*, pp. xxix, 202.

[122] WMS C3.119–20; N. Pevsner and D. Lloyd, *Hampshire and the Isle of Wight* (London, 1967), p. 357.

[123] HRO, Q1/2, fo. 235r; Q1/3, pp. 10, 171, 178, 238, 245.

[124] CRO, QJF 84/4, fo. 99r.

[125] Harbin, *Somerset*, p. 270.

[126] DHC, QS/1/9, 13 Jan. 1656/7.

[127] E. Archer, *A True Relation of the Red Trained Bands of Westminster* (London, 1643), p. 8.

having consulted with 'experienced artyficers', concluded that the tower and bell loft were 'exceedingly ruinous' and dangerous; at a previous Sunday morning service, the congregation had been 'soe terrified and amazed' with fear of the tower falling 'upon their heads' 'that they all ran out of the Church to avoid the danger'.[128]

Disorders in church

At Bedminster in July 1655, the minister John Moon was driven away by local youths throwing stones, a disorder directly connected with the deplorable state of the church fabric there, which had made such projectiles available.[129] Disruptions to church services and conflicts in church or churchyard, sometimes violent, were regularly prosecuted by the secular authorities throughout the 1640s and 1650s. Earlier on, these might relate to opposition to new ministers: at Paignton in Devon, the sequestered incumbent David Davies was presented to the grand jury, but found ignoramus, for disturbing new minister Nathaniel Terry on 28 Februrary 1647.[130] Or they might be politically motivated: at Ingleton in Yorkshire on 27 February 1652, gentleman Thomas Baynes used the church as a forum to protest at his own sequestration for delinquency and recusancy.[131] At Kirby Usborne in Yorkshire in March 1653, former royalist Robert Watters, 'on purpose to picke a quarrell' with parliamentarian Thomas Dickinson, climbed over and sat in the Dickinson's pew, and had to be removed by a constable.[132] At Goostrey chapel in Cheshire, political factionalism continued into the mid-1650s. When the names of the churchwardens previously chosen at a meeting of the minister and chief inhabitants were read out on the Sabbath day 13 May 1656, certain members of the congregation, 'who by their notorious delinquencie and vicious Course of Life are rendered uncapable of haveinge any votes ... in the election', objected 'in a riotous and turbulent manner' 'pretending' an order from two JPs to the contrary.[133]

The number of reported disturbances was higher from 1652 onwards, as Quakers became the main agents of disruption. In 1655, Christopher Bramley was presented to assizes for repeatedly disrupting the services at Ouseburn in Yorkshire, challenging people in the church porch as they came in, and the preacher Josiah Hunter during the service, and for creating

[128] HRO, Q1/4, p. 12.
[129] SHC, Q/SR/91/60.
[130] DHC, QS/4/54, Midsummer 1647.
[131] Raine, *Depositions*, no. lxviii, p. 70.
[132] Raine, *Depositions*, no. lvii, pp. 62–3.
[133] CRO, QJF 84/1 1656, fo. 104r.

an hour-long disturbance in the churchyard, 'deteining many people about him as it had been a place of marketing', 'to the Great abuse of the Lords-day'.[134] However, while many Quaker interjections follow a set format in the nature and timing of the interruption, by no means were all reported disturbances caused by Quakers. An incident during a church service at Folkington in Sussex in June 1656, caused by Thomas Lashmer the younger, described as drunk and swearing, was presumably not.[135] Likewise with a riot in the church at Buckland Dinham in Somerset in April 1653 for which six men were presented to quarter sessions, although 'tumults' or 'mutinies' sometimes ensued after Quakers had their say.[136] Often the evidence is ambiguous. Tobyas Gullocke was presented on 26 December 1658 for coming into Midsomer Norton church in Somerset the previous day, the Lord's day, and calling out to the preacher Mr Thurlby during his sermon 'Come downe Rogue' and saying that 'Christ was a bastard'. Gullocke had denounced another man as 'a Lyer and the author of Lyes', the sort of remark commonly made by Quakers; but the fact that the service was conducted by a visiting preacher on Christmas Day, a festival officially banned, was perhaps the issue.[137]

Women were involved in around thirty per cent of incidents, sometimes boldly challenging ministers. In Yorkshire in July 1652, Mary Fisher reportedly called out to the preacher at Selby, 'Come downe, thou painted beast,' while in July 1656 Agnes Wilson apparently called Thomas Danby, the minister at Keighley, the Antichrist.[138] At Elsted in Sussex in April 1652, spinster Barbara Osborne was cited for disturbing the minister by quarrelling with Katherine Farrell.[139] Around half of disputes relating to church seating involved women, but officials soon became exasperated when the contesting parties were women. In October 1652, the Devonshire quarter sessions minuted a 'Controversie' over church seats at Ashprington between Alice Westcott and Mistress Susan Perrott involving the presence of counsel for both sides. The two women were ordered to 'sitt in the same seate together peaceablye' or else take their cases to law.[140] Similarly, on 13 July 1658 at Sidmouth, Sibilla Carter was ordered to sit where the church

[134] TNA, ASSI 45/5/1, nos. 30–31.

[135] ESRO, QI/EQ2, fos. 20r–v; QR/112, fo. 17r.

[136] SHC, Q/SO/5 fos, 357r, 380r.

[137] SHC, Q/SR/96/36.

[138] Raine, *Depositions*, no. xlix, p. 54; no. lxxvi, p. 78.

[139] WSRO, QR/W73, nos. 8, 11.

[140] DHC, QS/1/9, 5 Oct. 1652.

officers appointed and 'therein to demeane herselfe peaceably' or be bound over.[141]

Pew disputes were a perennial problem; during the interregnum they never became a huge part of the secular courts' business, a mere one or two cases a year in the late 1640s, becoming slightly more frequent in the 1650s. Usually they were dealt with at quarter sessions, only transferring to assizes where there was serious obstruction or evidence of political disaffection or where disputes had become protracted. Disagreements at Mottisfont church in Hampshire, sequestered from Dr Edward Stanley, headmaster of Winchester College, sometimes involving his son-in-law Giles Coles, rumbled on for several years. At Michaelmas quarter sessions 1651, two husbandmen, John Poore and Richard Canterton, were found guilty of trespass in disturbing the minister. At Michaelmas 1653, carpenter Edward Crowder and mason David Briant were presented for a trespass in pulling down the seat of widow Clemence Hutchins and John and Mary Poore. In 1654, differences regarding the 'pulling up of the seates' of Mr Richard Kent, once again involving Hutchins, Poore and Crowder, were referred to the assizes.[142]

For some reason, pew disputes were disproportionately reported in Devon, with just under half the cases. No similar problems were observed in nearby Somerset, where the existence of several surviving pew plans for the 1650s suggests matters were more in order.[143] At Bishopsteignton in 1657, the churchwardens were poorly rewarded for their efforts to erect, at their own cost, new seats 'in vacant places' for sixty parishioners coming from a distance. Parishioners had not suffered as a result, they argued, either keeping their old pew or gaining a more 'eminent' one and all were now 'fully now in sight and hearing of the Minister both in his Pew and Pulpitt'. Nevertheless, the 'plucking downe ... seats of new ereccion' was threatened 'by some few hasty persons'.[144] The motivations for the protests were unclear, although the loyalist from whom the parish had been sequestered, Henry Westlake, was still alive, and according to his daughter, sometimes 'by stealth' still preaching at the church, which may have prompted resistance to puritan efforts to refashion the church layout.[145]

---

[141] DHC, QS/1/9, 13 July 1658.

[142] HRO, Q1/3, pp. 220, 284, 296, 311; Q4/1, fos. 92r, 94r, 106r; WR, p. 190; TNA: SP 29/10, fo. 168; PROB 11/309/134, will of Edward Stanley, 1662.

[143] SHC, D/P/cur.n/4/1/2, North Curry, 1653; D/P/wel/4/1/4, Wellington, 1650–90; D/P/ashn/2/1/1, Ashington, 1654; D/P/b.hl/4/1/1, Bishops Hull, 1650; D/P/b.on.s/2/1/1, Burnham-on-Sea, 1657.

[144] DHC, QS/1/9 1652-1661, 20 April 1658, 13 July 1658, 5 Oct. 1658.

[145] WMS E12.151.

Interregnum pew disputes predominantly involved those of genteel pretensions. Yet they were not always conducted with civility; around half involved physical challenges, individuals taking someone else's seat or blocking other people's access. Assaults and affrays relating to seating were reported in January 1648 at Llandwrog in Caernarfonshire, in April 1648 at Witton Chapel in Cheshire and in July 1652 at Widecombe in Devon; a weapon was drawn during a dispute at Mary Tavy in Devon the same year.[146] At Rostherne in Cheshire in 1659, female parishioners attested to the rude behaviour of young Thomas Wilkinson, thrusting and pinching others with feet, shoulder and knees in order to claim a pew assigned to others for forty years.[147]

Verbal and physical abuse of clergy and clergy wives, as well as anti-clericalist comment, were reported to secular authorities throughout the interregnum. At Melling in Lancashire in July 1647, Mr Cuthbert Halsall rebuked Robert Woolfall for speaking 'some scandalous words against some ministers'; Woolfall replied that 'he would speake what hee pleased'.[148] People were now 'buried like dogs', commented Laurence Coxley from Malpas in Cheshire in 1647; Mr Mainwaring's preaching 'was base and naught', and 'not worth a turd'.[149] In 1652, Henry Penny of Charlton Horethorne was presented to Somerset quarter sessions for 'bidding the minister kisse his breech'.[150]

Quakers and other sectarians were responsible for much verbal anticlericalism, terming ministers 'Baal's priests', 'blasphemers', 'son of perdition', 'Caine', 'swine', a 'raveninge wolfe in sheepes cloathing' or murderers.[151] But abuse came from the opposite quarter as well. At Hartlebury in Worcestershire, the former seat of the bishop, at Midsummer 1656, Michael and Katherine Cooke were accused of abusing and cursing the minister Mr Wright, and vilifying his new 'laudable' practices of 'Catechizing and personal instruction' as 'rantizing'.[152] At Mobberley in Cheshire in April 1656, gentleman Richard Brutch was cited for loudly calling Robert Barlow, minister there, 'a drunken Rascall', 'a Cavalier Rascall and a Malignant' who 'came to putt out a Cavalier and are a worse

---

[146] GA, XQS 1648/4; CRO, QJF 76/2, fo. 11r; DHC, QS/1/9, 23 July 1652; QS/4/57, Michaelmas 1652.

[147] CRO, QJF 87/1, fo. 55.

[148] LA, QSB/1/292/13.

[149] CRO, QJF 75/4, fo. 88r.

[150] SHC, Q/SO/5, fo. 346v.

[151] TNA, ASSI 45/5/2, no. 25; Raine, *Depositions*, no. lxxvi, p. 78; WSRO, QR/W84, no. 38; ESRO, QR/108, fo. 108r; CRO, QJF 82/4, fo. 99v.

[152] WAAS, 1656, packet no. 93, nos. 22–3.

yourselfe'; 'you ... have cozened yor owne father, and the whole Parish'.[153]
The intruded incumbent at Modbury, William Collins, was detested by his
parishioners, according to a later account in the John Walker archive.[154] In
August 1655, one of them was cited to quarter sessions for claiming Collins
had a 'neck as big as a bull' and was 'fed like a hog'.[155] A similar bovine
nickname of 'Eaton Bull' was apparently used in 1657 against Samuel
Eaton, the third interregnum minister at Stockport since its sequestration
from Edmund Shalcrosse in 1644; parishioners called him a 'sacrilegious
thief', claiming he sent his congregation to the devil and had embezzled
money intended for the church's poor.[156]

Prosecutions for non-conformity

With all its potential as an arena for disputes and disquiet, opting out
of church altogether may have seemed like an attractive option. Non-
attendance, punishable since the Tudor period, was now relatively lightly
pursued, even before the statute requiring attendance at the local parish
church was repealed in 1650. Very few people at all were cited anywhere
for non-attendance between 1653 and 1655. Often complaints only arose
in association with other offences such as political disaffection, scolding,
haunting or running disorderly alehouses, or witchcraft. The statute required
attendance at some place of worship, so those failing to worship anywhere
could still be prosecuted for their failure to attend their parish church,
'privat plase of meeting for the worship of God' (Northamptonshire, 1657),
'other place for exercising holy devotion' (Cheshire, 1657) or to attend
'public ordinances' (Devon, 1656, 1658), leading to a late rise in prosecution
in an effort to reassert religious order in 1658.[157]

The campaign against non-attendance was linked to that against recusancy,
both most enthusiastically and regularly prosecuted in Cheshire, at quarter
sessions and assizes. In other counties, despite the intense anti-Catholicism
of the early 1640s, prosecution of recusants was sporadic before the 1650s,
with lists of recusants made in some years but not others, or only specific

---

[153] CRO, QJF 84/4, fo. 111r.

[154] WMS C2.411.

[155] DHC, QS/4/59.

[156] CRO, QJF 85/4, fos. 19r, 70–72.

[157] 'September 1650: Act for the repeal of several clauses in statutes imposing penalties for
not coming to church', in A&O, pp. 423–25. British History Online <http://www.british-
history.ac.uk/no-series/acts-ordinances-interregnum/pp423-425> [accessed 8 April 2020];
J. Wake, Quarter Sessions Records of the County of Northampton (Northamptonshire Record
Soc., Hereford, 1924), p. 167; TNA, CHES 21/4, fos. 366r, 386r.

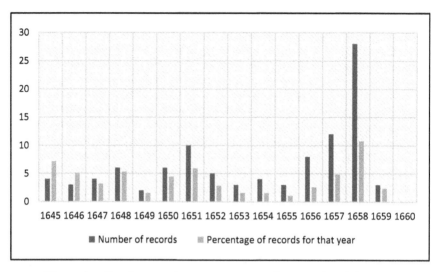

Figure 6.4. Legal cases relating to non-attendance at church by year.

individuals or families denounced. Yet of all types of divergent religious practice, recusancy was prosecuted the most during the interregnum. Systematic presentment stepped up a gear in Hampshire and Sussex and Northamptonshire, counties with known recusant populations, from 1655 onwards following central orders from the Council of State.[158] Enthusiasm for persecuting Catholics was less pronounced in Devon and Somerset.

Other types of religious non-conformity were not so systematically targeted at quarter sessions (see Figure 6.4). Despite the emergence of divergent religious beliefs and the 1650 statute against blasphemy, this charge appears infrequently, with only twenty-five cases, including accusations of blasphemous swearing, charges of blasphemy or quoted statements that could be interpreted as such. The sample includes sixty-eight recorded cases against Quakers, less than half the number involving Catholics.[159] Large Quaker gatherings in 1655 and 1657 clearly alarmed authorities, but it seems significant that there are very few records of the regime closing

[158] TNA, SP 25/76, fo. 265, 16 Aug. 1655; SP 25/76, fo. 265, 4 Sept. 1655; HRO, Q4/1, fos. 8r–17r, 118v–123v, 124v–128v, 150r–151v; WSRO, QR/W90, no. 63; QR/W91, no. 72; Wake, *Northampton*, pp. 125, 127–8, 161–5, 172–3, 175, 177–8, 229, 231, 235.

[159] Only recorded cases are discussed here; they cannot tell us how many non-conformists were summarily punished without appearing in quarter sessions or assize records. Additionally, some of the recorded but unspecified cases of church disorders may have involved Quakers.

down private meetings of any type not seen as posing a threat to public order.[160] Although use of the prayer book was not officially permitted, and was listed as an offence to be investigated by clerical ejectors, set up in 1654, prosecutions for ritual use of the prayer book at quarter sessions or assizes were fewer than those of Catholics or Quakers.[161] However, the prayer book had been officially 'abolished'; those found guilty could be treated severely, sometimes tried at assizes, as a warning to others, and if still beneficed, often lost their living as a result.[162] Such prosecutions most commonly related to prayer-book marriages. Beneficed clergy living dangerously, ejected loyalists and schoolmasters all dabbled in clandestine old-style marriages. Cheshire schoolmaster Thomas Wilson conducted prayer-book weddings at night to avoid detection. But in January 1655, he was arrested at the behest of Colonel Thomas Croxon and imprisoned. Eight months later, he petitioned for release to support his wife and five children, saying that what he did 'was for mere necessitye, and hee is very sorrye for his offence'.[163] Wedding couples were said be 'pretending' to be married, questioned about whether they had slept together, and treated as if they had fornicated.[164] On the other hand, there were some bizarre ideas about marriage circulating: a Somerset man persuaded a girl to sleep with him on Lammas Day 1649 by reading chapter 2 verse 15 of Malachi, and a seventy-six-year-old man from New Malton in Yorkshire, accused of incontinency in 1653 after marrying a fifteen-year-old using the 'words of the old marriage according to the former manner', conceived that as a 'papist' the marriage laws need not apply to him.[165] A rash of bigamy cases in Essex between 1647 and 1652 included a Colchester man who claimed scriptural justification from Timothy, saying that because it said a bishop should have only one wife, this implied laymen were permitted more.[166]

Prosecutions relating to burials or baptisms are rare in official records, suggesting either a reluctance to stir up unnecessary controversy at

[160] DHC, QS/4/59; SHC, Q/SR/95/182.

[161] C. Durston, 'By the book or with the spirit: the debate over liturgical prayer during the English Revolution', *Historical Research*, lxxix (2006), 50–73, at p. 64.

[162] C. Durston, 'Policing the Cromwellian Church', p. 191; see, for example, TNA, SP 18/123 fo. 166 and WSHC, A1/110: 1653 E 254; 1654 H 134, cases of Robert Mossom, 1650, and Thomas Earle, 1652.

[163] CRO, QJF 84/1, fos. 56–57; QJF 84/3.

[164] CRO, QJF 82/4, fos. 46–47.

[165] TNA, ASSI 45/4/3, no. 5; SHC, Q/SR/81/47–48; Malachi 2:15: 'let none deal treacherously against the wife of his youth'.

[166] ERO, T/A/465/2: 8 July 1647, 1 Nov. 1647, 18 Dec. 1647, 12 March 1651/2; Q/SR 341/97; 1 Timothy 3:2: 'A bishop then must be blameless, the husband of one wife.'

sensitive times, or an ambivalence towards traditional practice apparent in the legal records themselves, where witnesses regularly dated events to Christmas, Candlemas, 'our ladye daye', Easter, Whitsun, Michaelmas, Lammas, Alhollandtide or Saint James tide.[167] Others, more mindful of their phraseology, preferred 'Christide' instead, or the 'tyme Commonly called Christmas'. New habits of dropping the saint from church names were adopted by some.[168] In the Exeter quarter sessions order book, most refer to the cathedral as 'Saint Peter's' until 1654, when 'Peter's' begins to predominate.[169] Sometimes the very idea of church or cathedral was in question. A 1654 Exeter record refers to the Sabbath 'morning exercise' in 'publique meeting places', 'commonly called' churches; a 1655 Yorkshire assize deposition to the 'place Commonly Called the Parish Church of Barton'.[170] Choice of language was meaningful, its variability a token of a confused mental outlook. Opinions seemed more polarized in the final years of the interregnum, with authorities struggling to repress church revels in Devon and Cheshire and the 'unwarrantable custom' of the 'tyde or feast' day at Bingley in Yorkshire. Heated arguments occurred over a maypole at Rowton in May 1659; a bullbaiting during Cheadle Wakes in September 1658 was denounced as an unwelcome revival of a 'Currupt observacion' 'now almost forgotten', but a 'great concourse' of people reportedly attended.[171]

The legal records investigated here demonstrate much activity around the public performance of religion and Christian morality. Many categories of offences did not decline, indeed they were often prosecuted with increasing vigour under the Major-Generals and/or in the last years before Cromwell's death. Psychologically this might be interpreted as the fetishizing of a particular type of order to counter the social and economic effects of civil war and to spare those self-identifying as God's creatures from providential punishment. But employing a mechanism for implementing outward religious order was not the same thing as effecting true and widespread spiritual reformation, if this was indeed ever thought possible, and probably as counter-productive as the earlier Laudian approach to order

---

[167] SHC, Q/SR/82/87; Q/SR/87/11; ESRO, QR/89, fo. 47r.

[168] CRO, QJF 83/4, fo. 63r; QJF 79/1, fo. 63r; TNA, ASSI 45/5/2, 1655; SHC, Q/SR/81/47–48; Q/SR/95/201–202; Q/SR/91/100; DHC, ECA, fo. 325r; QS/4/60, 64, 66–7.

[169] DHC, ECA, fos, 198r, 202v, 214v, 215r, 232v, 257r, 302r, 336v, 355r, 357v, 368v, 414v–415r, 422v–423r, 429r, 431v, 448r.

[170] DHC, ECA, fo. 238v; TNA, ASSI 45/5/3, no. 13.

[171] CRO, QJF 87/2/2, fo. 111r; QJF 86/3, fo. 11r; DHC, QS/4/63; WYAS, Quarter Sessions Indictment Book, 7 August 1658, fos. 133v, 177v.

focused on church layout and ceremonial decorum. Although the pattern of prosecutions for swearing and Sabbath-day misbehaviour probably tell us more about the relative priorities of authorities than the scale of actual misbehaviour, their very frequency suggests they instead provoked widespread antipathy, often materializing in imaginative, humorous and indirect ways.

Writing in 1652, Thomas Cobbet had argued that though it was the duty of the civil magistrate to punish corruption, there was a clear distinction between the ecclesiastical and civil spheres. Civil sovereignty did not extend over religious belief: rooting out error had traditionally been the preserve of the Church.[172] But the Church and its clergy were both conceptually and practically weak, and divided. The secular courts could be effective against offences like assault which were actionable at common law, and to enforce parliamentary statutes. It is also notable that two frequently prosecuted offences, Sabbath breach and swearing, had considerable weight of moral consensus against them, as secular offences which pre-dated the Civil Wars, and were merely prosecuted with increased vigilance after them. The renewed prosecution of Catholics in the mid–late 1650s was likewise building on long-established prejudices and secular practices. The authorities' success in assuming the disciplinary functions of the disestablished Church, for example in acting against dilapidated churches or pew disputes, seems to have been more mixed. Secular prosecution was a blunt and ineffective tool at best for enforcing religious discipline and of little purpose against divergent religious ideas. Cases appearing in the official records of secular authorities were those where passions and factionalism had got too far out of hand to be contained by informal means, and were probably indicative of many more occasions of bad feeling that never got reported to secular courts not designed to deal with them, and also of lower-level summary reactions, by justices, constables or the military, which went unrecorded. The secular authorities, while often including among them individuals driven by a powerful sense that the prosecution of religious misbehaviour served both God and the state, found it difficult to organize themselves collectively to

---

[172] Secular authorities appropriated this power with the Blasphemy Ordinance of 1648 and the Blasphemy Act of 1650, but as has been shown, prosecutions were infrequent; C. Prior, 'Rethinking church and state during the English Interregnum', *Historical Research*, lxxxvii (2014), 458; 'May 1648: An ordinance for the punishing of blasphemies and heresies ....' & 'August 1650: An act against several atheistical, blasphemous and execrable Opinions ...', in *A&O*, pp. 409–12, 1133–6, *British History Online* <http://www.british-history.ac.uk/no-series/acts-ordinances-interregnum/pp409-412> [accessed 8 April 2020].

act against it. They busied themselves with relatively incontestable offences against public religious order. Divergence from the broad mainstream of godly puritan doctrine bothered them intensely, but they lacked corporate resolution in dealing with it, with the result that private beliefs and behaviour, if they did not offend against the appearance of outward order and conformity, were usually left to softer forms of persuasion, and often, in practice, alone.

7. Scandalous Ayr: parish-level continuities in 1650s Scotland

Alfred Johnson

'Scandal' as understood in most of sixteenth- and seventeenth-century Europe was a different social stigma from that more familiar to historians of the eighteenth century and later. In recent years, historians such as Karen Spierling have brought to light debates surrounding scandal during the sixteenth century, not just among theologians but also laypeople. John Calvin wrote of scandal as a religious category for behaviour which could be a 'stumbling block', a hindrance or distraction, to faith for others in a community. The same concept applied in Scotland during the mid seventeenth century, where 'scandalous' behaviour was an important concern at parliamentary as well as parish level. While some historians of early modern Scotland have written about 'scandal' and more particularly 'scandalous carriage' mainly in terms of sexual misdemeanours, clergymen and elders applied the term to sins such as drunkenness and verbal abuse. 'Scandalous carriage' was a prominent concern for Ayr's kirk session (church discipline) in the first half of the 1650s. These cases of 'scandalous carriage' reveal continuities in how the Ayr session viewed 'scandal' during the period, including similarities with Calvin's concerns about behaviour springing from and leading to unbelief, and laypeople disputing with the clergy and elders over what constituted scandal. The contestable nature of 'scandal', the importance of 'scandal' in Scottish society in the mid seventeenth century, and disagreements between laity and clergy over what constituted scandal during the 1650s, all indicate that scandal remained an unstable and contested religious category.

Early modern scandal

Scandal was an important if contestable matter for early modern Europeans. It was significant enough for John Calvin to write his treatise *Concerning Scandals* in 1550, dividing them into three categories. The first was 'intrinsic' scandal, which came from the gospel itself, 'in men's opinion at any rate', and consisted essentially of the gospel message as something that appeared foolish to the unbeliever. The third was 'fictitious calumnies', levelled at the gospel 'to cause people to have nothing further to do with it'. Calvin's second category, covering disturbances, quarrels and people living dissolute lives, is of most interest for historians of social discipline. It included a concern over atheistic thinking and the behaviour that followed from it. People who espoused 'atheistic views', Calvin wrote, 'play the role of the buffoon in order that they may have greater licence for belching out blasphemies'. Calvin mentioned their 'pleasant, jocular way' and use of 'slanted witticism' to 'obliterate all fear of God'.[1] His view of atheism thus followed from a common early modern concern over atheism as a mocking, profane or sceptical attitude towards doctrine.[2] Calling such behaviour 'scandalous' partly reflected the Calvinist call for godly and sober deportment. In addition, Calvin called atheistic thoughts a form of spiritual adultery. While the reformer also listed theft, dishonesty, marital infidelity and neglect of family life as examples of scandalous actions, one of the most notable features of the second category of scandal was the breadth of possible behaviour which could be what he called (in John Fraser's translation) a 'stumbling block'. These behaviours, Calvin noted, often emerge following 'the appearance of the Gospel' among a community. In historical context, the reformer meant this to refer to the arrival of Protestantism.[3] Previously hidden ungodliness became newly visible in the light of the gospel's behavioural expectations. Calvin thus defined scandal as a religious category in which the actions of an individual hindered belief among the broader community. This framework is of interest not only in studying Geneva, where Calvin had a personal influence, but also other places where Calvinism took hold.

In a recent important article, Karen Spierling highlighted the need for historians of early modern Europe to focus their attentions on the contested nature of scandal. Spierling wrote of scandal in the Geneva *consistoire* (consistory) during the sixteenth century, during which time both clergy and laity debated what constituted scandalous behaviour. Broadly, Spierling analysed scandal as a religious category in the manner Calvin outlined, in which bad behaviour could be an obstacle to faith or cause of confusion. In this context, people disagreed over who was scandalizing whom. Geneva's consistory record includes instances of people disputing the label given to

---

[1] J. Calvin, *Concerning Scandals*, trans. J. Fraser (Edinburgh, 1978), pp. 8, 12–14, 62, 64, 73.

[2] L. Dixon, 'William Perkins, "Atheisme", and the crises of England's long Reformation', *Journal of British Studies*, l (2011), 790–812, at pp. 791, 793.

[3] Calvin, *Concerning Scandals*, pp. 13, 118.

their behaviour. The main instance of the kind of dispute and negotiation Spierling cited was the consistory's lengthy investigation of a woman called L'Annonciade, on the grounds that her conduct towards a man called de Roviere had offended her neighbours. L'Annonciade disputed the charge, arguing that ministers had allowed her to spend time with de Roviere, and that her behaviour could therefore not be scandalous.[4] This and other examples underline the potential interest for historians of scandal as a concept discussed by the ordinary parishioner as well as the early modern intellectual.

One of Spierling's most important observations was the difference between the scandal which undermined the early modern community's faith and social cohesion and the scandal grounded in individual shame familiar from the eighteenth century onwards. Scandal mattered in sixteenth-century Geneva primarily because the actions of an individual damaged the community, at a time when religious observance and conduct was important in community identity. While the public circumstances which made a sin or crime a scandal would usually lead to a neighbour or church elder calling 'scandal', Spierling cited an example of the term being used among family members. Thus the wife of a tavern owner told the consistory that she considered her husband leaving the family and going out to gamble after dinner 'to be a scandalous thing'.[5] That she expressed such concern does not necessarily imply that her husband was hindering her beliefs but rather that she considered his activities a bad example for her children and the broader community. In either case his individual shame appeared not to have been the concern. Spierling opened up the question for other early modern historians, in that she recognized the difference between these two understandings of scandal without analysing when and how the transition occurred.

Spierling's work expanded significantly on previous histories of the Genevan *consistoire*, which have treated scandal as trivial. E. William Monter's otherwise thorough study of the *consistoire* during 1559–69 refers only passingly to the matter of scandal. Despite highlighting how prominent scandal was in the consistory's concerns, Monter wrote simply of 'scandal' as 'a miscellaneous group which literally covers a multitude of sins'.[6] More recently, Scott Manetsch observed that scandal prominently included 'kissing and flirting, dirty jokes, pornography, cross-dressing, use of love

---

[4] K. Spierling, ' "*Il faut éviter le scandale*": debating community standards in Reformation Geneva', *Reformation & Renaissance Review*, xx (2018), 51–69, at pp. 52–4, 56–9, 64.

[5] Spierling, '*Il faut éviter*', 54–5, 65.

[6] E. William Monter, *Calvin's Geneva* (London, 1967), p. 101; E. William Monter, 'The Consistory of Geneva, 1559–1569', *Bibliothèque d'Humanisme et Renaissance*, xxxviii (1976), 467–84, at p. 483.

potions, and suspicious frequentations'.[7] Both Monter and Manetsch played down the importance of scandal, referring to such offences as 'minor', in Manetsch's words, or 'trivial', in Monter's.[8] Nevertheless, the description of such apparently trivial behaviours as scandal offers the possibility that in analysing scandal, historians can shed light on matters such as civility and honesty, which concern smaller behavioural issues such as etiquette as well as broader issues of overall conduct.

Much of historians' interest in scandal as a religious category concerns the sixteenth century. Beat Hodler's work from the 1990s sketched the debate surrounding the significance of scandal as a sixteenth-century matter which 'soon passed away'. He highlighted the influence of New Testament passages on scandal as a stumbling block to other believers, and the work of Thomas Aquinas, in defining scandal as any 'inappropriate word or action which offers occasion for error or sin'. In contrast to Spierling's work, while Hodler wrote of scandal as a religious category, he emphasized the public nature of such offences. His work is significant in drawing attention to the need for historians to study scandal as a religious category in identity and 'everyday problems of the right behaviour'. Moreover, Hodler pointed out the increased prominence of a negative understanding of scandal within Protestant communities.[9] In more recent years, Emily Butterworth has described scandal as an obstacle to an individual's position within a social group and as a threat to community unity. Significantly, Butterworth observed that 'references to scandal in the sixteenth century retained a strong sense of its theological origins alongside vernacular meanings of outrage and dishonour'.[10]

Hodler, Butterworth and Spierling thus present three models of the relationship between the religious and secular understandings of scandal. Hodler's work described scandal as a religious category concerning public offences, with no apparent reference to a secular definition.[11] Butterworth

---

[7] S. Manetsch, *Calvin's Company of Pastors* (Oxford, 2013), p. 205; S. M. Manetsch, 'Pastoral care east of Eden: the Consistory of Geneva, 1568–82', *Church History*, lxxv (2006), 274–313, at p. 293.

[8] Manetsch, 'East of Eden', 293; Monter, 'Consistory', 483.

[9] B. Hodler, 'Protestant self-perception and the problem of *scandalum*: a sketch', in *Protestant History and Identity in Sixteenth Century Europe*, ed. B. Gordon (Aldershot, 1996), i. 23–30, at pp. 23, 27, 29–30.

[10] E. Butterworth, 'Scandal in Rabelais's *Tiers Livre*: divination, interpretation, and edification', *Renaissance and Reformation*, xxiv (2011), 23–43, at pp. 24, 26, 33; E. Butterworth, *The Unbridled Tongue: Babble and Gossip in Renaissance France* (Oxford, 2016), p. 150.

[11] Hodler, 'Protestant self-perception', pp. 23–4.

wrote of secular and religious understandings sitting alongside each other, and possibly merging, during the sixteenth century.[12] Spierling presented scandal as a corporate religious category during the sixteenth century and as an individual secular category from the eighteenth century.[13] The difference between Butterworth's and Spierling's views is worthy of further investigation. In this light, church discipline in seventeenth-century Scotland presents a case study of interest. The seventeenth century, in particular, presents the possibility of studying the shift implied in Spierling's work.

Scotland's kirk (church) provides a relevant comparison because the Scots experienced a Reformation modelled strongly on Calvin's Geneva. The Scottish reformers applied the *polis*-wide discipline of the Geneva *consistoire* in the kirk sessions of parishes across the lowlands during the sixteenth and seventeenth centuries. While the sessions could impose discipline for sins and offences ranging from drunkenness to Sabbath breach, verbal abuse to keeping inappropriate company, they were stereotyped as being obsessed with sexual offences such as fornication. This perception, apparent in works by historians such as Jenny Wormald or Christopher Whatley, has received statistical support in Michael Graham's book on Jacobean kirk sessions. But more recent work, most notably John McCallum's statistics on Fife parishes, has called into question this image of the sex-obsessed kirk session.[14]

The perception that kirk sessions were obsessed with sex has influenced how historians of Scotland's Reformation have discussed scandal. Analyses of scandalous carriage, a term which at face value could refer to all sorts of behaviour much as in the Genevan *consistoire*'s cases of scandal, are particularly indicative. When writing of the 1650s, Lesley Smith observed the connection between sex and scandalous carriage.[15] More tellingly, Rosalind Mitchison and Leah Leneman wrote about scandalous carriage in relation to sexuality and social control. Given their research focus on matters of sexuality and illegitimacy, Mitchison and Leneman's discussion

---

[12] Butterworth, 'Scandal in Rabelais', 26.

[13] Spierling, '*Il faut éviter*', 54–5.

[14] M. Graham, *The Uses of Reform: 'Godly Discipline' and Popular Behaviour in Scotland and Beyond 1560–1610* (Leiden, 1996), p. 281; J. McCallum, *Reforming the Scottish Parish: The Reformation in Fife 1560–1640* (Farnham, 2010), p. 229; C. Whatley, 'Order and disorder', in *A History of Everyday Life in Scotland, 1600–1800*, ed. E. Foyster and C. Whatley (Edinburgh, 2010), pp. 191–216, at pp. 195, 197, 205; J. Wormald, *Court, Kirk and Community: Scotland 1470–1625* (Edinburgh, 1991), p. 136.

[15] L. Smith, 'Sackcloth for the sinner or punishment for the crime? Church and secular courts in Cromwellian Scotland', in *New Perspectives on the Politics and Culture of Early Modern Scotland*, ed. J. Dwyer, R. Mason and A. Murdoch (Edinburgh, 1982), pp. 116–32, at p. 129.

of scandalous carriage as 'any show of physical intimacy between the sexes outwith marriage', but not demonstrably fornication, may perhaps have been a matter of emphasis rather than category definition. Mitchison and Leneman researched the Scotland of 1660–1780, a time which had less of the social, political and religious upheaval of the 1640s and 1650s. Apparently trivial actions, such as a couple taking a walk, could lead to a detailed investigation 'and even if nothing more could be proved, a reproof' on the basis of their connection to sexual offences.[16] In *The Culture of Protestantism in Early Modern Scotland*, Margo Todd mentioned family disharmony and children begging as also causes of scandal to the Reformed community. Despite this, she wrote of Perth youths' 'scandalous behaviour in violation of matrimonial chastity or pre-marital abstinence'.[17] In providing statistics for the Burntisland kirk session, John McCallum defined 'scandalous carriage' as 'all sexual misbehaviour short of fornication or adultery'.[18]

As with histories of Geneva, ecclesiastical histories of Scotland have often given little space to scandal. None of Smith, Mitchison and Leneman, Todd or McCallum centred their analyses on scandal, with the topic appearing briefly as a sub-point. The brevity of these references follows from an emphasis on continuities, especially in Todd's work. In each of these analyses, the scandal described at first resembles the scandal of individual embarrassment of the eighteenth century and afterwards. The examples of scandalous carriage in Mitchison and Leneman's and Todd's works could also or even instead make sense with the understanding of scandal present in Spierling's work. A couple taking a walk, for instance, were committing a public offence which could by example lead other people to sin and lead them away from faith, even if the session were unable to find anything more sinister. These brief analyses of scandal, seen in the light of works on scandal in Calvinist consistories on the continent, underline the possibilities present in using Scotland's kirk session records to explore scandal.

Scandal in mid-seventeenth-century Scotland

Scandal was an important matter in mid-seventeenth-century Scotland. The late 1630s and 1640s were a period of religious and political upheaval in Scotland, with the 'Constitutional Revolution' parliaments of the 1640s making laws independently of Charles I, and often reflecting the religious

---

[16] R. Mitchison and L. Leneman, *Girls in Trouble: Sexuality and Social Control in Rural Scotland 1660–1780* (Edinburgh, 1998), pp. 2, 91–2.

[17] M. Todd, *The Culture of Protestantism in Early Modern Scotland* (London, 2002), pp. 265, 267, 304.

[18] McCallum, *Reforming the Scottish Parish*, p. 193.

climate.[19] The parliament of January 1649 passed the Act of Classes, which determined who would be allowed to participate in parliamentary meetings. The act excluded those who had royalist sympathies, or had simply not voiced any opposition to Charles I. In addition, the Act of Classes banned for a year those who were 'given to uncleanliness, bribery, swearing, drunkenness or deceiving or are otherwise openly profane and grossly scandalous in their conversation, or who neglect the worship of God in their families'.[20] The parliament which passed this law was one dominated by radical Covenanters, who had Oliver Cromwell's support. This parliamentary interest in scandal had the potential to increase attention to it in the kirk sessions.

The Scottish parliament treated the definition of 'scandal' as something assumed to be common knowledge in other acts during the 1640s. Later in 1649, Scotland's parliament passed an Act against Scandalous Persons.[21] This act, like many from the 1640s which followed from the concerns of the National Covenant of 1638, placed the main work of enforcing the law on kirk sessions. Nominated persons would assist the kirk sessions, which no longer needed civil processes in addition to ecclesiastical discipline. The 1649 act began by citing 'the act made at Perth in the year 1645 … to exact the penalties and inflict corporal pains against scandalous offences that are not capital'. Here, as in the Act of Classes, the definition of scandal appears to have been assumed. While the records of the parliament at Perth in 1645 do not contain an act against 'scandalous persons' by that name, the 1649 act may have been referring to the 7 August 1645 Act Against Swearing, Drinking and Mocking of Piety.[22] This act, in turn, referred to an act of 1641, again unspecified by name, which called for all Scots 'to be good examples to others of all godliness, sobriety and of righteousness' in the light of 'the open abundance of all vices dishonourable to God', which the lawmakers believed had led to God inflicting recent 'heavy judgements'. The requirement that people 'be good examples' is the positive form of the concern in Geneva that people who acted scandalously were stumbling blocks to others.[23] The 1645 act thus emphasized swearing, drinking and the

---

[19] J. Miller, *The Stuarts* (London, 2006), pp. 119–20; D. Stevenson, *Revolution and Counter-Revolution in Scotland, 1644–1651* (London, 1977), p. 130; J. Young, 'The covenanters and the Scottish Parliament, 1639–51: the rule of the Godly and the "Second Scottish Reformation"', in *Enforcing Reformation in Ireland and Scotland 1550–1700*, ed. E. Boran and C. Green (Aldershot, 2006), pp. 131–58, at p. 134.

[20] *Records of the Parliaments of Scotland to 1707* [hereafter *RPS*], ed. G. MacIntosh et al., <https://www.rps.ac.uk> [accessed 21 Dec. 2016], 1649/1/43.

[21] *RPS*, 1649/1/128.

[22] *RPS*, 1645/7/24/54.

[23] *RPS*, 1645/7/24/54, 1649/1/128.

mocking of piety as setting bad examples, and the 1649 act in turn called such behaviour scandal in a way which resembled the use of scandal in Spierling and Hodler's work.

The graded fines imposed in the 1645 Act Against Swearing, Drinking and Mocking of Piety relate at least in part to the greater social and moral influence of people with higher social standing. Tellingly, however, ministers would be fined 'one fifth of their year's stipend'. The law thus placed a much higher expectation on ministers above all others to set a good example to everybody else. In private acts in 1633, parliament had awarded an annual stipend of 500 merks to the ministers at Burntisland and Pittenweem.[24] At 100 merks the fine would be markedly higher than for the barons, who faced fines of only 20 merks. When converted into pounds, the severity of the ministers' fine is even more apparent. Where the fine for noblemen was £20, 100 merks equated to £66 13s 4d. By contrast, servants would pay 20 shillings. The higher fine for the clergy reflected a bigger scandal if a minister swore, drank or acted impiously, and illustrates the importance of the religious dimension of scandal.

While some historians have researched and written about the kirk session during the interregnum, parish discipline in Scotland during the 1650s remains somewhat understudied. Lesley Smith's work in the 1980s highlighted the continuing presence of session discipline at a time when other kirk activities such as the General Assembly had been interrupted. A proclamation by English commissioners in Scotland in January 1652 announced a restructuring of Scotland's legal system which excluded the kirk sessions. The occupying government told judges not to regard any oaths previously sworn before ecclesiastical discipline. Commissions of the Peace would replace the kirk sessions in judging cases of blasphemy, slander and fornication. These changes would only take effect in 1655, however, along with the introduction of the Council of State presided over by Lord Broghill. None of the proposed changes, Smith noted, was followed up. The efficiency and effectiveness of the kirk sessions ensured their continuing presence during the interregnum, despite the desire of occupying soldiers and governors to create a comprehensive system to replace them.[25] Smith's work is highly valuable and illuminating, but in focusing on the continuation of kirk session activities under a new and foreign form of government and justice it overlooks the possible effects of the interregnum on session interests.

---

[24] *RPS*, 1633/6/169, 1633/6/172.
[25] Smith, 'Sackcloth for the sinner', pp. 118, 120–1, 125, 130.

In more recent years, Chris Langley's work has done much to explore how the Constitutional Revolution and interregnum played out at parish level. His recent work on Scotland's 'second Reformation' has focused on how communities worshipped during the mid seventeenth century. A significant theme in *Worship, Civil War and Community 1638–1660* is how the flexibility of worship, with variations from parish to parish, continued from the Jacobean period through the 1650s. This flexibility ensured the continuing centrality of the Church in the lives of ordinary people during the chaos of the mid seventeenth century. Yet despite these continuities at parish level, Church leaders during the 1640s 'became increasingly concerned with sins of political disaffection'. While the line between political rebellion and moral sin became blurred during the Constitutional Revolution, the presence of English troops in Scotland during the Cromwellian occupation necessitated the kirk sessions exercising moderation and avoiding overly divisive charges.[26] While Langley's work is illuminating, historians can do much more on the subject of ecclesiastical disciplinary interests during the mid seventeenth century. Scandal, as in this chapter's case study, is one such subject.

While it is not central to his analysis, Langley briefly referred to 'a concern with public scandal' as one of three 'interrelated concepts of decorum' along with 'an emphasis on personal, emotional decency and increasingly politicized notions of soldiers'. Langley applied the concept of scandal particularly to how parishioners and clergy handled customs relating to death. Parishioners could cause scandal by having too many people at a lykwake, watching over a recently deceased person, by encouraging superstition and perhaps provoking social disorder. Clergymen, on the other hand, worked to avoid public scandal by verifying deaths.[27] Discussing this custom, Langley hints at the sort of 'sexual offences' scandal familiar to historians of early modern Scotland, while also noting the sort of non-sexual behaviour that could be a hindrance to the community's legitimate religious practice. While brief, these examples highlight the possibilities of exploring scandal in interregnum Scotland.

Ayr's kirk session and scandal

Ayr's kirk session offers a valuable case study in the matter of scandal in consistorial records, and the interests and activities of kirk sessions during the interregnum, because it saw an increase in the number of people appearing

[26] C. Langley, *Worship, Civil War and Community, 1638–1660* (London, 2016), pp. 8, 53–4, 57.

[27] Langley, *Worship*, pp. 153, 156.

before it for 'scandalous carriage' during the early 1650s. As the session had been established during the Jacobean age, this increased focus on scandalous carriage showed a notable change from traditional priorities. By population size, early modern Ayr had none of the significance of Edinburgh, Glasgow or Aberdeen. Alexander Webster recorded Ayr's population as 2,964 in 1755, a century after the Cromwellian occupation. By contrast, Edinburgh including the parish of St Cuthbert's had a population of 43,315, and 23,546 people lived in Glasgow.[28] Webster's numbers provide a good indication of Ayr's population during the interregnum, which would have been affected by both the possible absence of many male inhabitants and the presence of English soldiers. Ayr was thus neither the most populous town, nor the most religiously or politically important. The session's interest in scandal, presented in the statistics in Table 7.1, may be exceptional.

The statistics presented in Table 7.1 place the Ayr session's interest in scandalous carriage in context. Presenting kirk session interests in aggregates over a long period of time tends to flatten out yearly fluctuations, which may be statistically significant. Such aggregates can lead to an assumption that session interests and activity remained steady and average from year to year. Even allowing for this flattening out, some longer-term trends and continuities become apparent. The session's activity increased significantly in the 1650s. However, dividing the 1650s into two halves demonstrates a significant drop in the session's recorded activity in 1656–61, compared to 1650–5. While fornication remained the primary concern during the first half of the 1650s, more people appeared for Sabbath breach in six years than in the previous eleven.

This peak in the Ayr session's activity in the later 1640s and early 1650s was part of the first of two surges in Scottish kirk session efforts mentioned in passing by Philip Benedict in his *Christ's Churches Purely Reformed*. The mid-seventeenth-century surge (the second occurred during the early eighteenth century) began during the 1640s.[29] The Ayr session's surge is notable in that it peaked during the interregnum. During the 1640s, the session saw relatively few people per year, ranging from fourteen in 1641 to sixty in 1648. The numbers for 1648 do not include the eighteen banns of marriage announcements that year. In contrast, the numbers for 1651–7 start at eighty-nine (or 126 with banns announcements) in 1651, trough in 1652 with fifty-two (or eighty with banns announcements), peak in 1653

---

[28] *Scottish Population Statistics*, ed. J. G. Kyd (Edinburgh, 1952), pp. 15–16, 26, 29, 51.

[29] P. Benedict, *Christ's Churches Purely Reformed: A Social History of Calvinism* (London, 2002), pp. 469–70.

Table 7.1. Numbers of people appearing before Ayr kirk session 1631–61[a]

	1631–8	1639–49	1650–5	1656–61
Fornication/adultery/filthiness	162	139	168	87
Sabbath breach	41	90	108	10
Banns of marriage (couples)	3	87	159	148
Verbal abuse	57	59	36	16
Drunkenness	1	30	14	6
Scandalous carriage	1	21	63	8
Inappropriate company	9	12	8	1
Family disputes/neglected worship	2	3		
General behaviour	5	2		1
Ale selling	4	2	4	
Assault	1	2		
Long disobedience	1			9
Excommunications	1			6
Fighting on Sabbath	19			
Church seating	1			
Baptism	1			
Nocturnal activities	6			
Opposition to England		30		
Religious orthodoxy/covenant		18	14	
Corporate repentance regarding pestilence		17		
Conduct in church		4	4	
Overlying infant		2		
Uncategorized		2	7	
Theft		1		
Testificats			37	94
Witchcraft			2	
Total	**315**	**521**	**624**	**386**

[a] CH2/751/2/308–CH2/751/3/2/566.

with 140 (or 178 with banns announcements) and end with seventy-one (108 with banns).[30]

The surge in Ayr's session activities occurred later than some sessions during the Constitutional Revolution and interregnum. South Leith's kirk session, notably, recorded more cases from 1643. This apparent increase in the session's activity may have been because of David Aldenstoune's work as the session's clerk at South Leith. Fornication, previously dominant in the South Leith session's record, became significantly less important as the session prioritized Sabbath breach and verbal abuse.[31] While historians can easily identify Aldenstoune's influence in South Leith's changing priorities after 1643, the religious climate of the Constitutional Revolution may have influenced the session's apparent desire to discipline comparatively minor offences.

The Ayr session statistics compare interestingly with work on continental consistory statistics in works by Monter and Manetsch. During the 1970s, Monter, writing on urban excommunications in Geneva for 1564–9, placed scandals and lying as the main reason for people to be excommunicated. The *consistoire* excommunicated 347 in that time, which was eighteen per cent of all excommunications. Of those, 213 were male and 134 female. Scandal and lying were significantly less prominent in Geneva's rural excommunications, at almost twelve per cent, and again with significantly more men than women charged.[32] Manetsch's work on Geneva presented a similar pattern. In two different sets of statistics, scandal was the third highest priority in city suspensions (over eight per cent for both 1568–82 and 1542–1609). In both statistics, quarrelling (over twenty-nine per cent for 1568–82 and nearly twenty-eight per cent for 1542–1609) was the main concern. In Manetsch's work too, scandal was a less common concern in rural suspensions.[33] While excommunications and suspensions are not directly comparable, the prominence of scandal in both sets of statistics of sixteenth-century Geneva is notable. Before the mid seventeenth century, the number of people appearing in Ayr kirk session for scandalous carriage, regardless of the disciplinary action taken, was a far less significant proportion of the session's concern compared to the excommunications and suspensions in sixteenth-century Geneva.

---

[30] CH2/751/2/345ff (1641); CH2/751/3/1/52ff (1648), 149ff (1651), 203ff (1652), 263ff (1653); CH2/751/3/2/503ff (1657). [All kirk session 'CH2' sources from National Records of Scotland].

[31] CH2/716/15–35. *South Leith Records*, ed. D. Robertson (Edinburgh, 1911), i. 43.

[32] Monter, 'Consistory of Geneva', 479–80.

[33] Manetsch, *Company of Pastors*, pp. 206, 209; Manetsch, 'East of Eden', 295.

Despite its earlier relative unimportance, 'scandalous carriage' became a significant concern in the early 1650s. As one of only seven interests to appear in all four periods surveyed above, scandalous carriage was a subject of considerable interest, particularly in 1651–3. In 1651 and 1652, it was the Ayr session's main disciplinary concern. Twenty-five people appeared before the session in 1651 and eighteen in 1652. In 1653, when forty-eight people appeared before the session for fornication, adultery or filthiness, and forty-two for Sabbath breach, fourteen people appeared before the session for scandalous carriage. And what these statistics fail to show is the Ayr session's remarkable zeal in pursuing such cases. In 1652, the session followed up scandalous carriage cases fifty-six times and heard fourteen witnesses. In contrast, they followed up Sabbath breach cases twenty-seven times, and filthiness cases twenty-four times with three witness reports.[34]

This interest in scandalous carriage is one of several examples in Ayr's mid-seventeenth-century kirk session of what Margo Todd once called a 'periodic crackdown on fashionable crimes'.[35] Todd's comment may best apply to the crackdowns within a year, such as when a session makes an announcement regarding Sabbath breach and in subsequent weeks focuses attention on bringing previously neglected offenders to repentance. Todd's words appear to apply to more sustained changes in session interests. Historians can seek to understand what circumstances may have led clergymen and elders to depart from their usual practices and priorities.

Margo Todd and Judith Pollman correctly advise that the manuscripts of consistory and kirk session records are not reliable sources for generating crime statistics. Aside from water damage and other forms of wear, kirk session manuscripts occasionally show evidence of pages having been removed. Moreover, what is recorded does not necessarily include what the Stirling Holy Rude kirk session called 'privie admonitiounis', the early modern equivalent of a twentieth-century policeman clipping a youth over the ears.[36] In studying consistorial records, historians encounter not only the failings of the people who appeared before the clergy and elders, but also the interests, and even failings, of the elders themselves. This in itself is interesting, especially in a period like the mid seventeenth century. The statistics nonetheless provide a more grounded general impression of the place scandal had in kirk session interests during this period than a

---

[34] CH2/751/3/1/149ff, 203ff, 263ff.

[35] Todd, *Culture of Protestantism*, p. 13.

[36] Todd, *Culture of Protestantism*, pp. 16–18; J. Pollmann, 'Off the record: problems in the quantification of Calvinist church discipline', *The Sixteenth Century Journal*, xxxiii (2002), 425–30, 438.

solely qualitative analysis could do. Yet the qualitative evidence is highly important too, and to that we now turn.

Scandal was more prominent in the Ayr kirk session's interests than the category 'scandalous carriage' might suggest. The statistics for Ayr presented earlier show cases of 'scandalous carriage' where the session provided no specific label for the offence. Kirk sessions referred to scandal more widely than in the 'scandalous carriage' cases alone, even before the 1640s. The Aberdeen session, for example, called Thomas Hogg's wife to public repentance before the pulpit and also put her in ward, in April 1638. She had committed 'scandalous behaviour in the kirk' and 'uttered imprecations'. That her 'scandalous behaviour' was in the church makes it likely that she had interrupted the service with physical violence or possibly attended while intoxicated.[37] Whatever her actions had been, their location lessens the likelihood that her scandalous behaviour had involved sexual misconduct.

Reflecting this broader use of scandal, the phrase 'scandalous carriage' covered both all kinds of unproven sexual conduct and many other forms of misconduct. In one typical case, on 8 January 1644, the Ayr session admonished a married couple for 'unchristian and scandalous carriage'. David Ferguson and Margaret Gardiner's scandalous carriage had been 'railing, scolding and flyting ane with ane uther and the said David for stryking of his said wife with futt [and] hands and chieflie in the tymes of thair drunkenes'.[38] While the divide between public and private spaces during the early modern period was not so clear-cut as in the twentieth century, the dispute between the couple appears to have started at home and become apparent outside.[39] Their disorderly marriage was scandalous in disrupting the community, where the clergy expected husbands and wives to behave well towards one another, and provide a good example to other couples. Conflict and drunkenness undermined the religious life of others in the community.

The Ayr session also used the term 'scandalous carriage' for non-sexual matters elsewhere in their records. On 28 August 1643, Ayr's clergy and elders expressed a concern that people 'in burgh and land of both sexes, old [and] young' were committing scandalous carriage by neglecting worship, keeping inappropriate company, drunkenness, idleness, marital disharmony, parents

---

[37] CH2/448/4/201. *Selections from the Records of the Kirk Session, Presbytery, and Synod of Aberdeen* (Aberdeen, 1846), p. 111.

[38] CH2/751/2/413.

[39] A. Cowan, 'Gossip and street culture in early modern Venice', *Journal of Early Modern History*, xii (2008), 313–33, at pp. 314–6.

failing to catechize and instruct their children, children disrespecting their parents, and neighbours verbally abusing each other.[40] The session responded by dividing the parish into areas for the session to patrol, a practice also recorded in session registers such as those of Stirling and Burntisland during the Jacobean period.[41] As well as underlining the significance of scandal in Constitutional Revolution discipline, the establishment of patrols in the 1640s shows the clergy intensifying their efforts to reform the population in a local setting.

More tellingly, the absence of specific reference to sexual offences in the Ayr session's act of 28 August demonstrates that Scottish historians have commonly defined scandal too narrowly and not necessarily in line with what kirk sessions themselves understood. Instead, the Ayr session's concern about scandal resembles Calvin's writing of atheistic thinking in scandal. Each of the behaviours the session listed stemmed from a lack of fear of God. Ayr's kirk session returned to the matter of scandal based in 'neglecting of Christiane duties' during 1646 and also 1648, which indicates the significance of scandal in the session's considerations during the period even in the absence of a statistically significant number of actual 'scandalous carriage' cases.[42]

The Ayr session's concern over scandal was also evident elsewhere in Scotland at this time. The Kirkcaldy presbytery passed an act on 7 August 1644 'considering the greate abounding of the scandalous sinnes of drunkenness, curseing and swearing, and profana[tio]ne of the lords day'. Continuing in such 'gross and scandalous sinnes' after a second or third offence would result in a parishioner being barred from the Lord's Supper. The act also mentioned flyting, railing and miscalling of neighbours, though the presbytery did not directly call those behaviours 'scandalous'.[43] Here, while the act makes a modicum of sense with a twentieth-century definition of scandal, the early modern religious understanding fits best. Drunkenness, cursing, swearing and breaking the Sabbath were scandalous actions not in that they caused private shame so much as that they acted as a stumbling block to the salvation of individuals in the wider community. In this light, by barring repeat offenders from the Lord's Supper the clergy and elders aimed temporarily to remove from communion anyone who could lead others astray.

[40] CH2/751/2/402-3.
[41] CH2/523/1/12; CH2/1026/1/2.
[42] CH2/751/2/459; CH2/751/3/1/80. Calvin, *Concerning Scandals*, pp. 62, 64.
[43] CH2/636/34/497.

Parish-level continuities

Ayr's kirk session records illustrate the continuities in how the session pursued cases of scandal, its concern over unbelief, and how the laity sometimes disputed accusations of scandal. The Ayr session's use of 'scandal' during the 1650s was not a significant departure from its recent practice. The session examined Jonet Kirk on 5 March 1649 for the 'scandalous cariage' of scolding on the streets. One witness reported that she had called someone a 'sland bluid beggar lown' and refused to co-operate when two session members tried to persuade her to go home. Another witness had seen 'hir clapping with hir hands [and] stamping with her feet in the open streits'.[44] Matthew Alexander appeared before Ayr's clergy and elders two months later for the 'scandalous behaviour' of drunkenness, wife beating and Sabbath breach.[45] The nature of Alexander's offence, recorded in a short summary, underlines how scandal could act as a broad term for several offences in Calvinist discipline.

The way these concerns continued during the 1650s demonstrates at parish level how the scandal of the interregnum followed from scandal as understood in previous years. William Mitchell, a town clerk, appeared before the Ayr session at the end of 1650 for the 'ordinar sin of drunkennes'. The session referred to 'the great paines' they had taken 'to reclaime him from his scandalous cariag'.[46] In August 1652, Elizabeth Houston, Isobel Kennedy and Margaret Ferguson also appeared before the session for drunkenness, which the clergy and elders called 'scandalous carriage'. Houston was 'so drunk that sho was caried to the court of gaird with in houres at night and th[ai]r stayed till the morning'. Houston, Kennedy and Ferguson had all been drinking with soldiers who had been billeted at their houses, which the session called 'very scandalous'. In Houston's case, the session noted that she had previously kept an 'honest' house.[47] The use of 'honest' as an antonym of 'scandalous' suggests, perhaps, the corrupting influence the session believed the soldiers were having on women previously living lives of Christian propriety.

While drunkenness and inappropriate company hinted at possible sexual offence without necessitating it, violence and verbal abuse also persisted as forms of scandal. Thomas Cawter appeared before the session in January 1651 for 'scandalous speaches' against James McDougall. While at church one Sunday, he had called McDougall a thief and struck him.[48] Cawter's

---

[44] CH2/751/3/1/96.

[45] CH2/751/3/1/103.

[46] CH2/751/3/1/149.

[47] CH2/751/3/1/241.

[48] CH2/751/3/1/159.

scandalous carriage recalls not only Jonet Kirk's verbal abuse, but also Thomas Hogg's wife before the Aberdeen session of 1638. The session summoned Jon and Jonet Boyd the following year for 'flyting and base cariag'. Jonet particularly had been living 'scandalouslie and not christianlie' in scolding her husband.[49] The session's investigation echoes its concern over Matthew Alexander's physical violence towards his wife, and over David Ferguson and Margaret Gardiner's scandalous carriage in 1644. The session's involvement in such marriage difficulties might seem invasive to today's readers, especially the concern over the 'scandal' of the couple's actions within the community. Since the divide between public and private was not so clear in the early modern period, however, the actions of a married couple could more easily affect the community. Moreover, in a positive sense the presence of such cases in kirk session records highlights the interest that clergymen and elders had in people behaving responsibly within marriage.

Several 'scandalous carriage' cases from 1651 arose from concern over what Calvin termed 'atheistic thoughts'. On 6 January, for example, the Ayr session saw William McKerrall for drunkenness. Since his accusation he had committed 'scandelous cariage such as suering and blasphemie'. The clergy and elders put him in the place of public repentance until he showed signs of actually having repented. Most kirk sessions did not list swearing and blasphemy as 'scandalous carriage'. The Ayr session did not go any further in describing McKerrall's words or the manner of his swearing and blasphemy: the behaviour perhaps fitted Calvin's description of people acting without fear of God, if not necessarily playing the buffoon.[50] Any public and deliberately offensive expression of religious dissent could be scandalous. This concern over scandal makes sense when considering the mid seventeenth century as a second Reformation in Scotland. Placing swearing and scandal in this context recalls Calvin's writing of previously hidden ungodliness coming to light after the new presence of the gospel in a community.[51]

Later in the same month, William Livingston and William Cunningham appeared before the session for actions which pointed to scandal through atheistic thoughts. Livingston had been laughing when people were leaving church. The location of his laughter, where clergymen expected a serious demeanour, suggested a mocking disposition towards religious matters regardless of the target of his laughter. The session deemed Livingston's misbehaviour 'scandelous to gods people', which highlights the corporate

[49] CH2/751/3/1/216, 218.
[50] CH2/751/3/1/150; Calvin, *Concerning Scandals*, p. 62.
[51] Calvin, *Concerning Scandals*, p. 13.

nature of scandal during the mid seventeenth century.[52] Livingston's actions would in all likelihood not have scandalized God's people by making them look bad in the eyes of unbelievers in land or burgh. 'Scandal' here describes Livingston's laughter as a potential threat to the faith of others. While the session does not use the phrase 'scandalous carriage', it points to the effect that one man's irreligious behaviour might have by making it easier for others to have no fear of God, undermining the religious life of the community. Whatever Livingston may have been laughing at, the session seems to have taken his mirth as an example of buffoonish, light carriage which suggested he had no fear of God. Cunningham's 'sinful and scandalous cariag' had been leaving church in the middle of a service without explaining why.[53] Here, again, scandal was a community matter. Leaving a service without explanation, if not punished, would give other members of the congregation with a less than firm faith an excuse to absent themselves without explanation.

Calvin's concern over buffoons and their irreverent behaviour 'at feasts and in discussions' may have been part of the reason the Ayr session also regarded penny bridals as scandalous carriage. Alexander Osburne and Marion McGrain appeared before the session on the February of 1651 for 'hir sinfull cariag' and 'his great sin and abuse ... of drinking, fiddling, [and] dancing' at their penny bridal, which lasted three days and nights. The session charged seven people who had been at that rather wild and prolonged penny bridal with 'sinfull miscarriage'. Scandal in this instance involved 'drinking and promiscuouse dancing for the most pairt of that first night and the nixt day following for som tym th[e]rof'.[54] The session's use of scandal as encompassing drinking and dancing, in the light of Calvin's treatment of scandal and the reformer's influence on Scotland, suggests that the session's concern was with the threat that riotous excess of every kind presented to the offenders' and others' salvation.

Penny bridals could, however, be scandalous not only in drinking and dancing. The kirk session of Humbie, a hamlet in East Lothian, made an act regarding penny bridals in 1645 which limited the number of attendees to twenty. In addition, the session required 'that there be no pyping or dancing at all befor or after dinner or supper', that people leave after eating, 'and

[52] CH2/751/3/1/153; R. Anselment, *Betwixt Jest and Earnest* (Toronto, 2016), pp. 9, 20; F. McCall, 'Continuing civil war by other means: loyalist mockery of the Interregnum Church', in *The Power of Laughter and Satire in Early Modern Britain*, ed. M. Knights and A. Morton (Suffolk, 2017), pp. 84–106, at p. 102; C. Shrank, 'Mocking or mirthful? Laughter in early modern dialogue', in Knights and Morton, *Power of Laughter*, pp. 48–66, at pp. 48–50, 65.

[53] CH2/751/3/1/154–5.

[54] CH2/751/3/1/157–9.

withal that there be no lowse speaches, filthie communication and singing of badie songs or prophane minstrelling'. While the Humbie session's concerns shared notable parallels with the Ayr session, Humbie's clergy and elders did not refer to such behaviour as 'scandal'. Despite this, Humbie's session act demonstrates clearer parallels with Calvin's discussion of scandal and buffoonish behaviour, particularly in its reference to 'lowse speaches' and 'filthie communication'.[55] The drinking and dancing highlighted by the Ayr session could distract others from salvation by providing an opportunity to live similarly dissolute lives. Loose speeches and filthy communication, on the other hand, fit more closely Calvin's description of 'pleasant, jocular' speech and 'slanted witticism'.[56] Regardless of how many other sessions used 'scandal' to refer to penny bridals, the Ayr session's description of drinking and dancing at penny bridals as 'scandalous carriage' emphasizes that kirk sessions were not 'narrowly obsessed with sex' and aimed to promote belief in word and action.

The corporate nature of scandal was a significant feature when laypeople negotiated or disputed the session's words. Sara Duncan appeared before the session on 5 December 1653 for the sort of behaviour that scandalous carriage cases usually denoted. She asked the Ayr session, however, to remove her scandal from her, with reference to her former association with one James Barrie. While the session register for that day did not detail what had occurred, Duncan 'profesed hir sorrow for hir sinfull [and] scandalous cariag' while at the same time denying 'any sinfull [and] carnall acting with the said James Barrie'. The session, being unable to find James Barrie and investigate further, ordered Sara Duncan to repent publicly on the next Sunday. While her case resembles many scandalous carriage incidents during the seventeenth century, a significant feature of her supplication to the clergy and elders was her claim that she had been 'scandaled' in addition to that 'she was scandalous to the Lordes peiple'.[57]

While William Livingston appeared to have accepted that his conduct had been 'scandelous to God's people', the session record hints here that Sara Duncan was disputing the nature of scandal. The nature of kirk session registers makes it difficult to determine Duncan's exact words, and thus whether she acknowledged that her behaviour had been 'scandalous carriage' or 'scandalous to the Lordes peiple'.[58] She may have recognized herself the hurt her actions could have given the believers in her community while at

---

[55] J. Bain et al (eds), *Miscellany of the Maitland Club* (Edinburgh, 1840), i. 435–6.

[56] Calvin, *Concerning Scandals*, p. 62.

[57] CH2/751/3/2/337.

[58] CH2/751/3/2/337.

the same time maintaining she had not done anything wrong beyond that. That she had been 'scandaled', in this case, could point to the situation being a hindrance or distraction for her or that she had experienced a level of shame. Her use of scandal in reference to herself, however, suggests instead that the 'sinfull [and] scandalous cariag' for which she had professed her sorrow was the kirk session's term rather than hers. In saying she had been 'scandaled', Duncan's words recall L'Annonciade disputing how the Geneva *consistoire* called her behaviour scandalous.[59] Sara Duncan, that is, may have believed her scandal to be scandal taken from external perceptions of her actions rather than given by anything inherently sinful. Duncan's dispute differs from L'Annonciade's in that she did not cite a clergyman allowing her to behave as she did. This may point to a layperson rejecting the concept of scandal as imposed by the clergy more generally.

In another suggestive case, Marie Hunter appeared before the session on 24 July 1654 for being with an Englishman 'scandalouslie among the corne' and had been 'kising others on the way coming home'.[60] Several Ayr women accused of scandalous carriage during the early 1650s were so accused because of their associations with occupying English troops.[61] The use of 'scandalous carriage' in this context may have been an example of the sort of caution highlighted in Langley's *Worship, Civil War and Community*. Such hesitance within this context, however, would suggest that the normally zealous session simply looked the other way instead of probing into a possible sexual misdemeanour. The session may have been insufficiently staffed for the purposes of such an investigation. With fifteen members listed on 24 July 1654, however, the Ayr session was not significantly smaller than the nineteen members present at the start of 1640.[62] It may simply have been that the women concerned did not go as far as fornication, or managed to keep anything further from surfacing.

Marie Hunter's case demonstrates more clearly than Sara Duncan's how laypeople and elders could disagree on what constituted scandal. Hunter confessed to being with Jon Wedrick, the English soldier, in the fields. Despite this, she 'effrontedlie [and] obstinatlie denied any scandalous cariag'. Her denial, in effect, was over what the session had called her actions rather than what she had done. The session referred to her mere presence in the field with Wedrick as scandal, without saying what they had been doing 'among the corne'. Wedrick reported that he intended to marry

---

[59] Spierling, '*Il faut éviter*', 64.

[60] CH2/751/3/2/407.

[61] CH2/751/3/1/225–6.

[62] CH2/751/3/2/407; CH2/751/2/324.

Marie Hunter and while in the fields 'did fall a sleip besyd her'. He also stated that 'he had don no wrong or miscariag' in kissing her on the way home.[63] Wedrick's words may, perhaps, indicate the cultural divide between English honest courtship and the Scottish cause for detailed inquiry.[64] More tellingly, Hunter's denial of scandal highlights a clash between two understandings of what constituted scandal. In a clearer manner than Sara Duncan's denial of scandal, Hunter and Wedrick understood scandal to be in actions which were inherently sinful. Ayr's kirk session by contrast saw scandal in a couple being in isolation, which hindered or distracted others from salvation by being an opportunity both for the couple and others, who may have used Hunter and Wedrick's example as a step towards sin.

Negotiating or disputing scandal was not limited to women, as seen in Spierling's work and this chapter thus far. The session saw William Logan in early December 1651 for persistent overfamiliarity with Margaret Murchie, a married woman. Logan initially attempted to counter the accusation of 'scandalous cariag' by claiming that 'some evill spirit, and presumption' had led him to frequent Murchie's company. Where Sara Duncan and Marie Hunter had denied any scandal had occurred, Logan denied that he and Murchie 'had ever com[m]ited any wickednes togither'.[65] Here, again, the layperson referred to the absence of any acts inherently sinful, rather than the potential of seemingly innocent actions to lead to sin and threaten one's faith.

Logan and Murchie's statement of repentance explicates the idea of scandal as behaviour which causes people to stumble. The 'hynous sin' they had committed 'by ane too much conversing togidder and familiaritie' was that they 'provoked our yok fellowes in mariag to jealousie, and suspri[c]es'.[66] The way they had been too familiar with each other, in other words, had caused other married couples to commit the sin of jealousy. The 'susprices' Logan and Murchie mentioned the other married couples committing could mean injury, wrong, outrage or oppression.[67] Their overfamiliarity, that is, may have soured relations among and between other married couples, possibly by suspicion or clashes based in different expectations of how much people could relate to others' spouses. Here, the 'scandal [and]

---

[63] CH2/751/3/2/407.

[64] Mitchison and Leneman, *Girls in Trouble*, p. 92.

[65] CH2/751/3/1/200–1.

[66] CH2/751/3/1/201.

[67] 'Supprise: n 3. Injury, wrong; outrage, oppression. Chiefly, to do or mak supprise.' (*Dictionary of the Scots Language*, 2004). <https://www.dsl.ac.uk/entry/dost/supprise_n> [accessed 10 Dec. 2020].

offence' was in directly causing the sin, rather than presenting the possibility that others would do likewise.

Conclusion

The interregnum, by its name, suggests a discontinuity or series of discontinuities, a break from the past or interval between two time periods which would have otherwise perhaps been smoothly linked. At parish level, the Ayr session's increased interest in 'scandalous carriage' was a break from their more usual priorities. This apparent discontinuity, however, disguises significant continuities in how kirk sessions handled scandal. While the presence of English soldiers, for instance, is particular to the 1650s, the session's interest in scandal is recognizable from the 1640s in Scottish kirk sessions as well as from sixteenth-century Geneva. The concern over scandal in mid-seventeenth-century Scotland, when seen in the light of Calvin's writing that scandal emerges after the appearance of the gospel among a community, indicates that while Scotland's lowlands were thoroughly reformed on paper, the clergy and elders who formed the kirk sessions had concerns over persistent unbelief and considered belief to be fragile and easily undermined.

The continuities within the Ayr session's interest in scandal hold an important development from the sixteenth century. Ayr's parishioners differ most significantly from the Genevans cited in Spierling's work in that individual laymen and women did not call others' actions scandalous, and sometimes disputed accusations of scandal, challenging whether an action was inherently sinful. Scandal in the Ayr session's records, if not in Ayr's society more generally, was still a corporate and religious category in the mid seventeenth century, much as it had been in Geneva a century before. Despite this, the laity's understanding of scandal provides an intriguing link to the scandal of individual shame familiar from more recent history. In considering only inherently sinful actions as scandal, the parishioners who disputed accusations of scandal shifted the emphasis away from the stumbling block principle and its focus on the potential of apparently innocent acts to hinder or distract others from faith. This understanding of scandal as arising from particular acts connects more readily to the scandal of individual shame in both its stronger focus on an individual's actions, and in how clearly a line could be drawn between what was and was not sinful and scandalous. While scandal remained a religious category during the mid seventeenth century, the disputes between Ayr's parishioners and clergy suggest that the category was still unstable and debatable.

Traditionalist religion: patterns of persistence and resistance

8. Malignant parties: loyalist religion in southern England

Rosalind Johnson

Throughout the 1640s and 1650s, the commitment to change by the godly met with significant resentment, obstruction and defiance. Dissatisfaction with godly reforms found expression in continued adherence to old patterns of public worship, and, outside the church, in persistent disregard of attempts to enforce moral behaviours. This discontent with parliament's attempts at religious reform found its expression in parish churches, which continued to use the Book of Common Prayer and to celebrate the sacrament of holy communion at Christmas, Easter, Whitsun and other major festivals, in defiance of parliament.

This chapter examines the evidence for loyalist religion at a parish level, with a focus on the churchwardens' accounts of selected parishes in southern England as case studies. The chapter comprises all parishes within Hampshire and the Isle of Wight, the Bristol city parishes, the Somerset hundreds of Taunton Deane and Wells Forum, the Wiltshire towns of Devizes, Marlborough, Salisbury and Wilton, and two rural Wiltshire parishes.[1] This allows for a comparison between both urban and rural areas. It includes the major urban centre and port of Bristol, as well as smaller market towns. Of the urban settlements, four had cathedrals: Bristol, Salisbury, Wells and Winchester. Most churchwardens' accounts are to be found in local record offices, though two printed volumes of Wiltshire churchwardens' accounts were examined for this chapter: a volume of accounts for the Salisbury parishes of St Edmund's and St Thomas's, and a volume for the Devizes parish of St Mary's.[2] Further evidence for loyalist

---

[1] For Hampshire and the Isle of Wight, see R. N. Johnson, 'Protestant dissenters in Hampshire, c.1640–c.1740' (unpublished University of Winchester PhD thesis, 2013), pp. 46–65, 222. The two rural Wiltshire parishes were Stratford sub Castle and Winterslow, both near Salisbury.

[2] *Churchwardens' Accounts of S. Edmund & S. Thomas, Sarum 1443–1702*, ed. H. J. F. Swayne (Salisbury, 1896); *The Churchwardens' Accounts of St Mary's, Devizes 1633–1689*, ed. A. Craven (Wiltshire Record Soc., 69, Chippenham, 2016).

R. Johnson, 'Malignant parties: loyalist religion in southern England', in *Church and people in interregnum Britain*, ed. F. McCall (London, 2021), pp. 195–215. License: CC BY-NC-ND.

religion is found in vestry minutes and other parish records, minutes of parliamentary and local committees, quarter session and assize records, and contemporary printed accounts.

Despite the evidence for non-co-operation with parliament's attempts to reform parish worship, less attention has been paid by scholars to loyalist religion in the parishes than to the parliamentary reforms, or the impact of radical sects. As Fiona McCall has commented, there has been little attention paid to royalist support below gentry level, a remark which is equally applicable to loyalist religion.[3] Nevertheless, there have been a number of studies on the topic, including those by McCall, Bernard Capp, Judith Maltby and John Morrill.[4] A. G. Matthews's *Walker Revised*, on loyalist clergy ejected from their livings, though published over seventy years ago, is still widely cited.[5] Some local studies have been made of loyalist congregations and conformist clergy for the localities surveyed for this chapter. Hampshire has been examined by Andrew Coleby in the context of a study of local government, by Andrew Thomson in his work on the clergy of the diocese of Winchester, and in this author's own doctoral thesis.[6] John Reeks has studied Somerset in a thesis based on substantial research into churchwardens' accounts, while religious disruption in Bristol is discussed in Harlow's volume on seventeenth-century Bristol ministers.[7]

Fincham and Tyacke state that the changes introduced by Archbishop Laud in the 1630s were largely abolished during the religious revolution of the 1640s; these included railed altars, decorated interiors and a formal ritualism.[8]

[3] F. McCall, *Baal's Priests: The Loyalist Clergy and the English Revolution* (Farnham, 2013), p. 4.

[4] McCall, *Baal's Priests*; B. Capp, *England's Culture Wars* (Oxford, 2012); J. Maltby, '"The Good Old Way": prayer book Protestantism in the 1640s and 1650s', in *The Church and the Book*, ed. R. N. Swanson (SCH, 38, Woodbridge, 2004), pp. 233–56; J. Maltby, '"Extravagencies and impertinencies": set forms, conceived and extempore prayer in revolutionary England', in *Worship and the Parish Church in Early Modern Britain*, ed. N. Mears and A. Ryrie (Farnham, 2013), pp. 221–43; J. Morrill, 'The Church in England 1642–1649', in *The Nature of the English Revolution*, ed. J. Morrill (London, 1993), pp. 148–75.

[5] *WR*.

[6] A. M. Coleby, *Central Government and the Localities: Hampshire 1649–1689* (Cambridge, 1987); A. Thomson, *The Clergy of Winchester, England, 1615–1698: A Diocesan Ministry in Crisis* (Lampeter, 2011); Johnson, 'Protestant dissenters in Hampshire', pp. 46–65.

[7] J. Reeks, 'Parish religion in Somerset, 1625–1662: with particular reference to the churchwardens' accounts' (unpublished University of Bristol PhD thesis, 2014); J. Harlow, assist. J. Barry, *Religious Ministry in Bristol 1603–1689: Uniformity to Dissent* (Bristol Record Soc., 69, Bristol, 2017).

[8] K. Fincham and N. Tyacke, *Altars Restored: The Changing Face of English Religious Worship, 1547–c.1700* (Oxford, 2007), p. 274.

By the late 1640s there were few signs of Laud's reforms remaining.[9] Parliament had set out to purify churches of 'popish' ornamentations and practice even before the start of the Civil Wars, and these efforts continued throughout the 1640s.[10] Episcopacy was abolished in October 1646.[11] Yet this did not mean that parishioners wished to abolish the practices of the Elizabethan and early Stuart Church which had preceded the Laudian reforms, or that they whole-heartedly embraced the reforms imposed on them by parliament. There remained a strong attachment to the Book of Common Prayer, despite its replacement in 1645 with the *Directory for Publique Worship*,[12] and an evident desire to continue the sacramental cycle of communion at major festivals in many parishes.

The religious reforms desired by the parliamentarians were held up by the fighting of the Civil Wars, and a fully functioning, country-wide Presbyterian system of Church government was never established.[13] Nevertheless, large numbers of clergy found themselves condemned as malignants and deprived of their livings for failure to conform to these reforms; one figure suggests 2,425 English benefices were deprived of a clergyman (not necessarily the incumbent) between 1643 and 1660.[14] The number of ejections varied from county to county. In Hampshire, seventy-two benefices had been sequestered between 1643 and 1660, though the majority of Hampshire sequestrations were in the years 1645 and 1646.[15] Out of a total of 253 parishes, this represents sequestrations of around twenty-eight per cent.[16] The neighbouring counties of Berkshire, Dorset and Wiltshire all saw slightly more sequestrations, between thirty-one and thirty-three per cent, while neighbouring Sussex saw twenty-six per cent of its livings sequestered.[17] In Somerset, 104 benefices were sequestered.[18] Bristol had seen several ejections in the 1640s, but after 1655, despite action against scandalous ministers being part of the remit of the Major-Generals from that year, no Bristol minister was ejected, possibly

[9]   Fincham and Tyacke, *Altars Restored*, p. 274.

[10]   Morrill, 'The Church in England', p. 154.

[11]   Morrill, 'The Church in England', p. 152.

[12]   *The Directory for the Publique Worship of God* (London, 1645).

[13]   J. Spurr, *English Puritanism 1603–1689* (Basingstoke, 1998), pp. 11–12; Coleby, *Central Government*, pp. 56–7.

[14]   *WR*, p. xv.

[15]   *WR*, pp. xiv, 17, 179–91; Coleby, *Central Government*, p. 10.

[16]   Coleby, *Central Government*, p. 10.

[17]   McCall, *Baal's Priests*, p. 130.

[18]   *WR*, p. xiv.

because the town was poorly supplied by parish minsters and could ill afford to lose those men remaining.[19]

In the 1650s, the new regime resolved that further action was needed if a truly godly Church was to be established. An ordinance of 1654 established a body of central commissioners or 'Triers' to examine candidates to the ministry, and a further ordinance was passed for ejecting scandalous and insufficient ministers.[20] But the ejectors appear to have managed to remove only around 200 men between 1654 and 1659, though the number of ejected ministers varied from county to county: Wiltshire was one of the counties that suffered most, with around twenty ministers ejected.[21]

Churchwardens' accounts, as used in this chapter, have been used by several scholars to research evidence of prayer-book loyalism in the parishes.[22] They are, as Valerie Hitchman commented, a rich source for historians.[23] Andrew Foster commended churchwardens' accounts for the fascinating insights they provided into social and religious life during the early modern period.[24]

But it is acknowledged that there are methodological problems with using churchwardens' accounts, particularly in the survival rate of the records. According to Hitchman, of some 12,000 parishes in early modern England and Wales, around 3,350 have surviving churchwardens' accounts.[25] Yet, as Hitchman noted, few of these records are complete, and, as Foster commented, it can be difficult to compare sets of accounts as not all itemize individual expenses.[26] In the period covered by this chapter some records survive for only part of this time, others survive for intermittent years. Some survive only as isolated single sheets of accounts. Not all are kept as itemized

---

[19] Harlow, *Religious Ministry*, p. 6.

[20] C. Durston, 'Policing the Cromwellian Church: the activities of the county ejection committees', in *The Cromwellian Protectorate*, ed. P. Little (Woodbridge, 2007), pp. 188–205, at p. 189.

[21] Durston, 'Policing', p. 195.

[22] For example: Morrill, 'The Church in England'; Reeks, 'Parish religion in Somerset'; R. Hutton, *The Rise and Fall of Merry England* (Oxford, 1994).

[23] V. Hitchman, 'Balancing the parish accounts', in *Views from the Parish: Churchwardens' Accounts c.1500–c.1800*, ed. V. Hitchman and A. Foster (Newcastle-upon-Tyne, 2015), pp. 15–45, at p. 15.

[24] A. Foster, 'Churchwardens' accounts of early modern England and Wales: some problems to note, but much to be gained', in *The Parish in English Life 1400–1600*, ed. K. L. French, G. G. Gibbs and B. A. Kümin (Manchester, 1997), pp. 74–93, at p. 85.

[25] Hitchman, 'Balancing the parish accounts', p. 15.

[26] Hitchman, 'Balancing the parish accounts', p. 15; Foster, 'Churchwardens' accounts', p. 85.

accounts of expenditure; some are summary accounts and records of parish officials only. Even where churchwardens' accounts survive, their fragile state of preservation may mean they are unable to be used by researchers.[27]

Survival rates vary from county to county. Hitchman's study of eight counties in south-east England found 397 parishes with surviving seventeenth-century accounts, representing some twenty-one per cent of the total parishes within the area of her study. This she acknowledged as a high survival rate, due to several factors including a higher population density and economic prosperity than elsewhere in the country.[28] Morrill's study of churchwardens' accounts found a total of 150 records, but this covered all then-extant records in nine county record offices, with some records from elsewhere.[29] In Somerset, Reeks found forty-two usable churchwardens' accounts, which represented around ten per cent of all parishes.[30] These records are not evenly distributed over the county; a study of the records for Wells Forum found churchwardens' accounts for the period under examination in this chapter in only one parish, that of Wells St Cuthbert.[31] The surviving accounts for the parishes of Taunton Deane do not include any for the parishes of Taunton itself.

Of 253 livings in the county of Hampshire and the Isle of Wight, itemized churchwardens' accounts for the period 1645–60 survive for only twenty-three parishes, and even these accounts are not necessarily complete in every year.[32] Only a single sheet of itemized accounts survives for Hambledon (1647) and for Breamore (1654–5).[33] Many of the churchwardens' accounts for the Hampshire market town of Fordingbridge are undated.[34] The accounts for Stoke Charity in Hampshire survive from 1657, but no itemized disbursements are recorded until 1665.[35]

---

[27] Hutton, *Rise and Fall of Merry England*, p. 263.

[28] Hitchman, 'Balancing the parish accounts', pp. 16–18. The counties studied were Bedfordshire, Berkshire, Buckinghamshire, Essex, Hertfordshire, Kent, Middlesex (excluding the Cities of London and Westminster) and Surrey.

[29] Morrill, 'The Church in England', p. 164. The record offices used were Cambridgeshire, Cheshire, Dorset, Gloucestershire, Herefordshire, Norfolk, Suffolk, Wiltshire and Worcestershire, together with some records still held by individual parishes in Cheshire and Norfolk, and notes and transcripts from Bristol and Shropshire.

[30] Reeks, 'Parish religion in Somerset', p. 8.

[31] SHC, D/P/w.st.c/4/1/1.

[32] Coleby, *Central Government*, p. 10; Johnson, 'Protestant dissenters in Hampshire', pp. 53, 62, 222.

[33] HRO, 46M69/PW10; 47M48/7; SHC, D/P/tru/4/1/a.

[34] HRO, 24M82/PW2.

[35] HRO, 77M84/PW1.

In Wiltshire, churchwardens' accounts survive for the period 1645–60 for the Salisbury parishes of St Edmund's, St Thomas's and St Martin's, but not for the now-demolished church of St Clement's just outside the city boundaries in Fisherton Anger.[36] The full set of churchwardens' accounts surviving for St Mary's Devizes is not matched by any accounts from St John's, the other parish church in Devizes. Of the two parishes in Marlborough, accounts survive from St Peter's church, but not from St Mary's.[37] A fully itemized set of accounts survives for Winterslow during the 1640s, but from 1653 onwards the churchwardens recorded only summary accounts and names of parish officials, a situation which continued well beyond the Restoration.[38] The survival of accounts may reflect the disruptions of war in the 1640s and the availability of suitable churchwardens. In March 1647, the Wiltshire assizes held at Salisbury heard that in many parishes in the county there were no churchwardens, and that in other parishes those elected to the office had refused to serve.[39] Throughout the period the varying abilities of churchwardens in the parishes may be reflected in the depth of information in the surviving accounts.

Churchwardens' accounts are more likely to survive for urban than rural areas, according to Foster's findings for the period 1558–1660.[40] There may be a number of reasons for this, including the likelihood of churchwardens in towns being more business-like than rural churchwardens and thus taking better care of the parish records.[41] It was noted in this chapter that churchwardens' accounts from market towns (including those with cathedrals) tended to be more detailed than those from rural areas, some exceptionally so; those of Wells St Cuthbert included details of payments from parishioners for seats in the church, and for each funeral knell sounded by the bell-ringers.[42]

Nevertheless, the importance of churchwardens' accounts is that they may record the purchase of bread and wine to celebrate the sacrament of

---

[36] *Accounts of S. Edmund & S. Thomas*; WSHC, 1899/65, 1899/66. St Clement's was demolished in 1852, see T. Wright, 'The last days of St Clement's Church, Fisherton Anger', *Sarum Chronicle*, vii (2007), 2–12.

[37] WSHC, 1197/21. It is possible accounts were lost in Marlborough's devastating fire of 1653.

[38] WSHC, 3353/33; 3353/34.

[39] *Western Circuit Assize Orders 1629–1648*, ed. J. S. Cockburn (Camden Fourth Series, 17, London, 1976), p. 249.

[40] Foster, 'Churchwardens' accounts', p. 83.

[41] Foster, 'Churchwardens' accounts', p. 83.

[42] SHC, D/p/w.st.c/4/1/1.

holy communion at feast days, a practice banned by parliament in 1647.[43] The accounts may also record the purchase of the 1645 *Directory for Publique Worship*, which replaced the Book of Common Prayer. Churchwardens' inventories may record existing copies of the prayer book after this date.

Evidence for the Directory *and the Book of Common Prayer*

Those dissatisfied with the Book of Common Prayer had long sought reform. The *Directory for Publique Worship* was published in 1645, approved by an ordinance of parliament to replace the prayer book. Unlike the prayer book it was not a series of fixed liturgies, but rather a set of directions for worship.[44] Although use of the prayer book was banned, use of the *Directory* was optional, and perhaps less than a quarter of parishes in the country acquired a copy.[45] Parliament endeavoured to distribute copies of the *Directory* to the parishes, but it is doubtful how efficiently it was distributed, and even six months after its publication only ten per cent of parishes had a copy.[46] This may suggest that it was unpopular, but Judith Maltby noted that it was an inexpensive volume that might have been purchased by clergy themselves, rather than by churchwardens. Furthermore, it appears to have gone through over fifteen editions, which suggests it was not that deeply unpopular.[47]

Churchwardens' accounts and inventories may be assumed to mention the *Directory*, yet few of the surviving records from parishes studied in this chapter actually do mention it. Of the Hampshire parishes, only two sets of accounts from 1645–6 explicitly mention a directory, at South Warnborough and at Headbourne Worthy.[48] In Wiltshire, the Winterslow churchwardens purchased a directory, though apparently not until 1646–7.[49] These are all rural parishes. There are references in other accounts which hint at the purchase of the *Directory*. The accounts for the Hampshire parish of North Waltham record a payment for a new book, which may refer to the *Directory*.[50] Other references are uncertain. In the Hampshire parish of East Worldham, the water-damaged churchwardens' accounts may refer to an untitled book

[43] Hutton, *Rise and Fall of Merry England*, p. 212.

[44] Maltby, 'Extravagencies and impertinencies', p. 225.

[45] Spurr, *English Puritanism*, p. 117.

[46] Morrill, 'The Church in England', p. 153.

[47] Maltby, 'Extravagencies and impertinencies', p. 229.

[48] HRO, 70M76/PW1, fo. 31v; 21M62/PW2/1.

[49] WSHC, 3353/33, fo. 122v.

[50] HRO, 41M64/PW1, fo. 51.

bought in 1645–6.[51] A reference to untitled books was made in the 1644–5 accounts for two Bristol parishes.[52] Bristol was under royalist control from July 1643 to September 1645, so it seems unlikely that these were copies of the *Directory* (unless clandestinely acquired) but this does not explain why no directories appear to have been recorded in the churchwardens' accounts after the city fell to the parliamentarian forces.[53]

The evidence for purchase of the *Directory* is, therefore, inconclusive, and many churches may never have acquired a copy. Inventories of Church property for the period 1645–60 similarly show a lack of copies of the *Directory*. Several Bristol churches listed books in their inventories, but none mentioned a directory. The church of St Michael on the Mount Within inventoried a Bible and the *Paraphrases* of Erasmus in 1645 and 1654.[54] All Saints' church held two Bibles and the *Paraphrases*, according to an inventory of 1652.[55] St Mary Redcliffe had a Bible in an inventory taken in 1650–1.[56] A Bible could be the only book recorded in a parish inventory; the 1647 inventory of Winchester St Peter Chesil also recorded only one Bible.[57]

If churchwardens were not buying the *Directory*, some were disposing of their prayer books and the *Book of Homilies*, another banned volume.[58] In the Hampshire parish of Ellingham, the inventory of April 1639 included a Bible, two communion books and the *Book of Homilies*. By April 1650 only the Bible remained.[59] The churchwardens of Winchester St John parish included a Bible and two prayer books in their inventory of 1643, but by 1646 the Bible was the only book listed.[60] In Wiltshire, the inventory for Devizes St Mary's church of 1646 listed two prayer books, among other books held by the church. The prayer books were no longer listed by the time the next inventory was taken in 1650–1, though the church kept its

---

[51] HRO, 28M79/PW1, p. 19.

[52] BA, P.Xch/ChW/1/b; P.StW/ChW/3/b, p. 116.

[53] J. Lynch, *For King & Parliament: Bristol and the Civil War* (Stroud, 1999), pp. 2, 160.

[54] BA, P.St M/V/1/a, fos. 28, 38v.

[55] BA, P.AS/ChW/3/a, inventory of 1652.

[56] BA, P.St MR/ChW/1/d, p. 464.

[57] HRO, 3M82W/PZ3, fo. 7v.

[58] The *Book of Homilies* was banned, although not Jewel's *Apology* nor the *Paraphrases* of Erasmus. Churchwardens were required to surrender copies of the Book of Common Prayer to the county committees. Morrill, 'The Church in England', p. 164.

[59] HRO, 113M82/PW1, fos. 34v, 39v; 113M82/PZ2, pp. 19, 23.

[60] HRO, 88M81/PW2, fos. 58v, 59.

copy of the *Paraphrases* of Erasmus and its *Book of Martyrs*, and had acquired two psalm books.[61]

Other parishes held on to their prayer books, despite an order to surrender them.[62] Southampton St Lawrence recorded four prayer books in 1637, which were still there in an inventory made *c*.1648, and in subsequent inventories made in 1651 and 1655. The four books were recorded after the Restoration, which suggests the parish was holding on to its pre-1645 prayer books.[63] In Wells St Cuthbert parish, an inventory of 1649 recorded four old prayer books, which remained in the church's hands at least until 1663, despite the purchase of the new prayer book in September 1662.[64] In Wiltshire, the churchwardens of St Edmund's in Salisbury recorded two prayer books in 1634, which they still held in 1649.[65] By *c*.1647 the churchwardens of Marlborough St Peter's no longer held the prayer book they had rebound in 1643–4, though they still kept the *Book of Homilies*.[66] In Bristol, St Philip's had a Bible and three other printed books in its inventory taken in 1653; the other three books were not described, and it is possible the churchwardens were being discreet about copies of the prayer book.[67]

Parish inventories may not be a wholly authoritative guide to the possessions of the church. Not all inventories listed books, but this did not mean the church possessed none. At North Waltham, none of the inventories made by the churchwardens from 1640 to 1660 listed any books, not even a Bible. Yet as noted above, the churchwardens purchased a new book, possibly the *Directory*, in 1645–6, and there was a further entry in the accounts of 1657 for a payment made to binding the church Bible.[68]

If the *Directory* is conspicuous by its absence in the inventories and accounts, then so is the prayer book. This raises the question of what service book the minister was using. Some ministers may have used the *Directory* with remembered parts of the prayer-book services. Both Maltby and McCall have found evidence of ministers memorizing prayer-book services, while Spurr considered the possibility that ministers creatively employed

[61] *Accounts of St Mary's, Devizes*, pp. 45, 61.

[62] Morrill, 'The Church in England', p. 164.

[63] Southampton Archives, PR4/2/1, fos. 126, 151v, 154v, 161–175v.

[64] SHC, D/P/w.st.c/4/1/1, accounts Oct. 1649, entry Sept. 1662, accounts 23 Dec. 1662 to 31 Dec. 1663.

[65] *Accounts of S. Edmund & S. Thomas*, p. 375.

[66] WSHC, 1197/21 fos. 94, 100r.

[67] BA, P.St P and J/V/1, p. 11.

[68] HRO, 41M64/PW1, fos. 48–56v.

their own forms of worship.[69] There is no evidence for either practice in the parishes examined for this chapter, but that is not to say that it did not occur. That some parishes held on to their old prayer books suggests that the prayer book continued to be used. Morrill's study of churchwardens' accounts suggests that it was not a minority of parishes that did this, but rather that it was commonly used in the parishes.[70]

Evidence for the celebration of major festivals

The practice of celebrating major festivals was condemned in the *Directory for Publique Worship*. Festival or holy days, having no scriptural warrant, were no longer to be continued.[71] In 1647, the Long parliament reiterated this with an ordinance confirming the abolition of the celebration of Christmas, Easter and Whitsun, and the restrictions continued to be enforced with further parliamentary legislation during the 1650s.[72] The *Directory* did permit the celebration of communion at other times, though how often was to be decided by individual ministers and congregations.[73] There were also issues concerning who should be admitted to take communion, though the debate over 'open' or 'closed' communion is beyond the scope of this chapter.[74]

John Morrill's study of 150 parishes in East Anglia and western England found that, despite the introduction of the *Directory*, eighty-five per cent of those parishes were holding festal communions in 1646, and forty-three per cent held communion at Easter 1650. While this represents a decline, Morrill then found that the proportion of parishes celebrating the sacrament at major festivals actually rose during the 1650s, until by Easter 1660 the sacrament was celebrated in just over half the parishes in Morrill's study.[75] Ronald Hutton's research came to a somewhat different conclusion. His study of 367 churchwardens' accounts found that instances of festal communions did decline during the 1640s but that the decline continued during the 1650s. Only thirty-four of Hutton's parishes regularly recorded

---

[69] Maltby, 'Good Old Way', pp. 241–2; Maltby, 'Extravagencies and impertinences', p. 240; McCall, *Baal's Priests*, p. 238; Spurr, *English Puritanism*, p. 117.

[70] Morrill, 'The Church in England', pp. 164–5.

[71] *The Directory for the Publique Worship of God* (London, 1645), p. 40.

[72] Hutton, *Rise and Fall of Merry England*, p. 212; Capp, *England's Culture Wars*, pp. 23–33.

[73] *Directory*, p. 23.

[74] On open and closed communion in the parishes, see Capp, *England's Culture Wars*, pp. 123–7.

[75] Morrill, 'The Church in England', p. 174; Hutton, *Rise and Fall of Merry England*, pp. 213–14.

communion services at major festivals during the 1650s, while another sixteen held them at Easter only.[76]

If the studies by Morrill and Hutton demonstrate a decline in festal communions for at least part of the period, they do not indicate a total eradication of the practice. The sacramental cycle continued to be celebrated, as confirmed by David Underdown's study of the West Country.[77] Such observances were not without risk. At Christmas 1657, John Evelyn and his wife were among those in the congregation threatened by parliamentary troopers as they went up to take communion during a service held at a London private house.[78]

Although Morrill found forty-three per cent of the parishes in his study celebrating Easter in 1650, these findings were not replicated in the parishes studied for this chapter. None of the Hampshire or Bristol parishes recorded buying bread and wine at Easter 1650, nor did any of the Somerset parishes studied in the hundreds of Wells Forum and Taunton Deane. Not all parishes with surviving accounts necessarily have accounts covering Easter 1650, which means that unrecorded celebrations may have taken place, and undated entries in existing accounts may disguise a festal communion. The Hampshire parish of Chawton celebrated communion on holy days regularly throughout the 1640s and 1650s and may well have celebrated at Easter 1650, but there is a gap in the records for the period 1649–51.[79] Another Hampshire parish, North Waltham, celebrated communion on several occasions in the period, including festivals, and undated references to the purchase of bread and wine for Easter may hide a celebration of 1650.[80] Neither parish appears to have suffered the ejection of its minister during this period, which implies an accommodation between incumbent and parishioners over the practice.[81]

If the evidence for Easter 1650 is uncertain, parishes in southern England were still celebrating communion at major festivals during the last half of the 1640s and during the 1650s. Of the total of twenty-three parishes studied in Hampshire and the Isle of Wight with surviving accounts itemized for one or more years between the introduction of the *Directory* in 1645 and the Restoration in 1660, fifteen accounts contained references to the purchase of bread and wine for communion, and ten of these contained at least one

---

[76] Hutton, *Rise and Fall of Merry England*, pp. 213–14.

[77] D. Underdown, *Revel, Riot and Rebellion* (Oxford, 1987), pp. 257–63, 267.

[78] Maltby, 'Good Old Way', p. 241.

[79] HRO, 1M70/PW1.

[80] HRO, 41M64/PW1, fos. 51v–52v.

[81] *WR*, pp. 179–91.

reference to the purchase of bread and wine for communion at a major festival during the period 1645 to 1660. Nine of these parishes were rural; only one, Fordingbridge, was a market town.[82] In some Hampshire parishes the sacramental cycle was celebrated frequently. The churchwardens of Chawton made explicit reference on seven occasions in the 1650s to bread and wine purchased at Christmas, and on eight occasions to bread and wine purchased for Palm Sunday and Easter. In 1655, communion was apparently celebrated on the Sunday after Christmas, not on the day itself.[83] Upham churchwardens' accounts record payments for bread and wine at Easter on five occasions between 1647 and 1659, as well as on two occasions in the same period for Whitsuntide, and, in the accounts drawn up for 1654, for Christmas and Low Sunday as well.[84] At Easton, surviving accounts from 1655 record celebration of the sacramental cycle in the period up to the Restoration on two occasions each for Easter, Christmas and Whitsun.[85] The parish of Soberton recorded an Easter communion and one other communion in the accounts for 1658 and 1659.[86] Although the surviving evidence is limited, this does indicate some measure of support for the old prayer book, and consequently, a lack of support for the forms of worship outlined in the *Directory*. Furthermore, while some parishes, such as Upham, focused on Easter as the occasion when communion would be celebrated, it is noticeable that those parishes which continued to celebrate the sacramental cycle tended to celebrate at least the three major festivals of Christmas, Easter and Whitsun, even though Christmas, a festival associated with secular merry-making, might have been expected to be abandoned even if Easter continued to be celebrated.

In Wiltshire, the Salisbury parish of St Edmund's purchased bread and wine throughout the 1640s and 1650s, so holy communion was celebrated, but the churchwardens made no reference to it being purchased for festivals.[87] This may be a reflection of the practices of the rector of St Edmund's, John Strickland, who was ejected from the living in 1662 for non-conformity, and later ministered to dissenting congregations.[88] The accounts for St Thomas's Salisbury include payments for bread and wine made throughout the 1640s and 1650s, but there is no record of the sacrament on major feast

[82] Johnson, 'Protestant dissenters in Hampshire', p. 222.

[83] HRO, 1M70/PW1, fos. 35v–45.

[84] HRO, 74M78/PW1, fos. 4v–15.

[85] HRO, 72M70/PW1, fos. 1v, 3v, 4v.

[86] HRO, 50M73/PW1, fo. 2v.

[87] *Accounts of S. Edmund & S. Thomas*, pp. 216–33.

[88] *CR*, pp. 467–8.

days, though in 1651 holy communion was celebrated on 21 December, the Sunday before Christmas Day.[89] Yet Christmas was celebrated at least once at St Thomas's in the period, as a payment of one shilling is recorded for dressing and cleaning the church for Christmas 1655.[90]

The churchwardens' accounts for St Mary's Devizes record payments for bread and wine for Easter and Low Sunday in 1645.[91] Further entries in the accounts for the last half of the 1640s record communions at Easter (including Palm Sunday and Low Sunday), though only on one occasion at Christmas.[92] Bread and wine continued to be purchased throughout the 1650s, and though these entries are without explicit mention of dates or festivals, communion may still have been celebrated at Easter and at other major festivals.[93] Elsewhere in Wiltshire, festival communions were celebrated in Wilton (where the church was also cleaned for Christmas 1646), and similarly in the village of Stratford sub Castle; in both churches there are entries for festal bread and wine up to the Restoration.[94]

The accounts of several Bristol churches record the purchase of bread and wine for communion during the period, but almost invariably do not record the occasions at which the sacrament was administered. Of the few occasions when it was, communion is recorded as being celebrated at St Michael on the Mount Within on Palm Sunday on one occasion in the early 1650s, while Easter was celebrated at St Mary Redcliffe in 1646 and 1648.[95] St Mary's also rang its bells at Whitsuntide on at least three occasions between 1649 and the Restoration.[96] Festive occasions could be celebrated by other means than communion; the rosemary, bay and holly purchased by the churchwardens of St John the Baptist in the 1650s may have decorated the church at Christmas.[97]

In the Somerset hundreds of Taunton Deane and Wells Forum, the evidence is handicapped by the survival of the records. At Trull, in Taunton Deane, a single surviving sheet of accounts drawn up by a churchwarden in 1655 records a payment of 3s for bread and wine at Whitsuntide, though

[89] *Accounts of S. Edmund & S. Thomas*, p. 328.

[90] *Accounts of S. Edmund & S. Thomas*, p. 331.

[91] *Accounts of St Mary's, Devizes*, pp. xix, 40.

[92] *Accounts of St Mary's, Devizes*, pp. xix, 47, 48–9, 51, 53.

[93] *Accounts of St Mary's, Devizes*, pp. xx, 54–93.

[94] WSHC, 1241/15; 1241/16; 1076/19, fos. 42v–53.

[95] BA, P.St M/V/1/a, fo. 35v; P.St MR/ChW/1/d, pp. 377, 407.

[96] BA, P.St MR/ChW/1/d, pp. 422, 437, 516.

[97] BA, P.St JB/ChW/3/b. On the use of rosemary, bay and holly to decorate churches at Christmas, see Morrill, 'The Church in England', p. 166.

no other payments for bread and wine at any other time.[98] In the parish of Wells St Cuthbert, where accounts survive from 1649, there are regular references to bread and wine for communion, though the occasions are not usually specified. In 1654, communion was celebrated on Christmas Eve, but the following communion was celebrated on 9 April 1655, which was not Easter Day, which that year fell on 15 April. A celebration of communions recorded for 28 October 1654 and 2 November 1655 suggest a celebration of Allhallowtide.[99]

What is noticeable is that in the Hampshire parishes of South Warnborough and Headbourne Worthy, and the Wiltshire parish of Winterslow, all parishes where a *Directory* was purchased, there are also references in the accounts to the purchase of bread and wine for communion on a holy day. Similarly, in the parish of North Waltham, where the purchase of the new book may indicate a *Directory*, bread and wine were purchased for festal communions. In South Warnborough there are several references to the purchase of bread and wine, at least one of which, at Easter 1648, was for a festival.[100] Headbourne Worthy's accounts of May 1648 record the purchase of bread and wine for Christmas, Easter and Whitsun.[101] The Winterslow churchwardens recorded payments for bread and wine at eight separate communions in their accounts to Easter 1645, including at Whitsuntide, Palm Sunday and Easter Day.[102] In the year to Easter 1647, communion was celebrated on four occasions, including Easter Day, and the following year the accounts record bread and wine purchased for Palm Sunday and Easter Day.[103] At North Waltham there are references in the accounts drawn up in September 1654, some eight or nine years later, to bread and wine purchased for Christmas, Palm Sunday, Easter Day and Midsummer, and a further set of accounts, for the year 1659, includes payments made for bread and wine at Christmas, Palm Sunday and Easter.[104]

Clearly, even those parishes which purchased the *Directory* cannot be assumed to be free of prayer-book loyalists, although it may be that the festal communions were being celebrated using the *Directory*. It is not possible to make authoritative statements on the evidence of only three or four parishes, especially as the evidence for purchase of a *Directory* at North

---

[98] SHC, D/P/tru/4/1/a.

[99] SHC, D/P/w.st.c/4/1/1; see fo. 69v for communions in 1654–5.

[100] HRO, 70M76/PW1, fos. 31v, 33v.

[101] HRO, 21M62/PW2/1.

[102] WSHC, 3353/33, fo. 121.

[103] WSHC, 3353/33, fos. 122v, 124.

[104] HRO, 41M64/PW1, fos. 50v–58v.

Waltham is open to debate, but a possible explanation could be that an outward compliance did not reflect the actual beliefs of the parishioners. It may also indicate divisions of opinion among the congregation, but it could equally indicate a compromise between different factions within a congregation, or between the congregation and the minister.

If the surviving evidence of the Hampshire churchwardens' accounts is representative of the county as a whole, then over two-fifths of the parishes in the county would, at some time, have celebrated communion at the major festivals. The evidence of the Wiltshire accounts also indicates a significant minority of parishes that were celebrating the major festivals. This implies a definite grassroots reaction against the religious orders of parliament, and of willing disobedience of those orders by ministers. Why churchwardens willingly recorded evidence of this resistance in the accounts is unclear. Kevin Sharpe's theory was that the fullest records were kept by the most diligent churchwardens, who were most inclined to order.[105] If this was the case, then this inclination to order was reflected in a clear loyalty to the old prayer-book ways, even to the extent of recording evidence of that loyalty in the accounts. The recording of the purchase of bread and wine for festivals, and the listing of banned prayer books in inventories, may also indicate a need by the churchwardens, and the congregation more generally, for control in an uncertain political, social and religious period. The act of writing down the evidence for the continued observance of banned practices further suggests a deliberate act of non-compliance. More practically, churchwardens may have recorded expenditure to prove to fellow parishioners and the minister that they had honestly and conscientiously discharged their duties during their time in office. The accounts were unlikely to be scrutinized by those outside the parish. Occasionally, however, records might be examined by local magistrates; there is some evidence of this in Hampshire in the 1650s.[106]

The loyalty to the old ways on the part of the churchwardens may or may not have been shared by the minister. Durston and Maltby noted that a number of ministers loyal to the prayer book's form of worship managed to keep their cures and clandestinely provide services based upon it. But some, when challenged by the authorities, claimed to have been under pressure from their parishioners to do so. As an act of 1650 removed the legal requirement to attend one's parish church, it may have been that some parish ministers were providing prayer-book services not under coercion, but through the need to keep their parishioners and prevent them transferring

[105] K. Sharpe, *The Personal Rule of Charles I* (London, 1992), p. 390.

[106] HRO, 29M79/PW1, fo. 21; 29M84/PW1, fos. 27v, 33; 47M81/PW1, fo. 46.

their allegiance to another church.[107] The threat of parishioners deserting their parish church for radical sects such as the Baptists and Quakers was all too real for some ministers. Robert Abbot moved to rural Hampshire after large numbers of his Kent parishioners left to join sectarian groups.[108]

A more positive interpretation can be put on the evidence of the churchwardens' accounts. Alexandra Walsham suggested that belief in a Christian duty of charity and neighbourliness had led to a tolerance that over-rode the demands made by the authorities.[109] Although she was referring to the period of Restoration persecutions, the comment is as relevant during the period of the English Revolution. There is no reason to suppose that all parishes were seething cauldrons of discontent, and the churchwardens' accounts and inventories may well indicate harmony between a minister and his parishioners. Compromise between loyalists and puritans enabled a degree of peace and unity, which is reflected in those parishes which continued to celebrate Easter and Christmas communions.[110] Yet historians invariably write about cases of conflict, rather than instances of toleration, and published studies have tended to focus on minsters who were ejected, not on those who remained.[111] There is no equivalent to *Walker Revised* for those ministers who were *not* ejected. This reflects the records available: court cases, records of county committees, published accounts of ejected clergy. In contrast, positive relationships between clergy and laity have left little trace in the historical record.

Other evidence for loyalist religion

The evidence of the churchwardens' accounts for the celebration of communion at major festivals is suggestive of continued use of the prayer book in at least some parishes. There is other evidence for the use of the prayer book in contemporary sources. In 1647, the Hampshire minister Philip Oldfield was accused of using the prayer book, among other offences.[112] In the same year Robert Clarke, ejected from Andover, had, with the support of several parishioners, attempted to continue to officiate there,

---

[107] Durston and Maltby, *Religion*, p. 8.

[108] Capp, *England's Culture Wars*, p. 130.

[109] A. Walsham, *Charitable Hatred* (Manchester, 2006), p. 272.

[110] C. Boswell, *Disaffection and Everyday Life in Interregnum England* (Woodbridge, 2017), pp. 213–14.

[111] For example, McCall, *Baal's Priests*; I. Green, 'The persecution of "scandalous" and "malignant" parish clergy during the English Civil War', *EHR*, xciv (1979), 507–31.

[112] BL Add. MS. 15671, fo. 158v; *WR*, p. 188.

and obstructed the efforts of others to do so.[113] In or around 1655, some Winchester clergy petitioned Oliver Cromwell, by then Lord Protector, about the activities of Mr Preston, sequestered minister of Droxford and former prebendary of Winchester cathedral, who had for several years been holding prayer-book services in the abandoned church of St Michael's, Kingsgate Street and receiving financial support from his congregation. Other former Winchester cathedral clergy were alleged to be conducting private communion services around the city.[114]

Parliament's attempt at religious reformation also met with opposition from Hampshire congregations as well as from the clergy. In March 1651, the Hampshire quarter sessions heard a petition from Andover that some inhabitants of neighbouring villages had been ignoring the laws regarding travel on the Lord's day.[115] But enforcing Sabbath observance remained a problem. In 1656, the quarter sessions felt it necessary to issue an order banning church ales, since such festivals were frequently held on a Saturday evening, leaving the participants totally unfit to attend to their Sabbath duties.[116] That such an order was issued suggests that festivities were still being held.

In Wiltshire, a loyalist service in Fisherton Anger church was disrupted by parliamentarian soldiers in 1647, the godly minister having been ousted by royalists.[117] In the same year, the Wiltshire Assizes heard that the national day of fasting and humiliation held on the last Wednesday of each month was being ignored by many people, and that the Lord's day was not being observed in many places.[118] Nathaniel Forster, an ejected Wiltshire minister, is said to have read the prayer book to congregations at his home in Salisbury, and to a condemned woman on the night before her execution in 1655.[119]

Throughout Wiltshire there was evidence of clergy demonstrating obstinate loyalty to the old prayer book practices. In October 1645, Thomas Hickman, parson of Upton Lovell, obliged his parishioners to come up to the altar rails if they wished to receive communion.[120] In 1646, several clergymen were accused of using the prayer book, among other offences.

---

[113] BL Add. MS. 15671, fos. 110–110v.

[114] BL Add. MS. 24861, fos. 113–114r. The manuscript is undated. Coleby, *Central Government*, p. 59, assigns it a date of November 1655.

[115] HRO, Q1/3, p. 73.

[116] HRO, Q1/3, pp. 292–3.

[117] *True Intelligence from the West* (London, 1647); McCall, *Baal's Priests*, p. 202.

[118] Cockburn, *Western Circuit*, p. 249.

[119] *WR*, p. 372; Capp, *England's Culture Wars*, p. 120.

[120] BL Add. MS. 22084, fo. IV [reverse]; *WR*, pp. 373–4.

Christopher Ryly, rector of Newton Tony, was accused of bowing at the name of Jesus and bowing to the altar; not surprisingly, he also extolled the prayer book. His devotion to ceremonial was not the only charge against him; among a long list of alleged misdemeanours was the accusation that he had said women ought not to read the scriptures.[121] Thomas Lawrence, rector of Fugglestone with Bemerton, was accused of having railed the communion table and turned it altar-wise.[122] In Chilmark, the rector Robert Walker was accused of using the prayer book despite having been given a copy of the *Directory*.[123] A similar accusation to that against Walker was levied against James White, rector of Rollestone, who stated that he would rather lose his living than part with the prayer book.[124] Not all loyalist clergy were on the receiving end of accusations; some received support from their one-time congregations. Leonard Alexander, sequestered vicar of Collingbourne Kingston, continued to receive the tithes of his former parishioners who preferred to pay their tithes to him, rather than to John Norris, the intruded minister.[125]

Rogationtide perambulations of the parish boundaries, though abolished by ordinance in 1644, continued to take place.[126] As Hutton has commented, they had the obvious function of teaching the youth of the parish where its boundaries lay.[127] Sixty-eight per cent of Hutton's London parishes with surviving records observed the practice during the interregnum.[128] The practice was also observed at Winchester and in Bristol, though no evidence was found by this study in the churchwardens' accounts for its observance in rural Hampshire.[129] It is likely that in towns and cities with several small parishes, a knowledge of the boundaries had importance for practical reasons such as poor relief, and turning the event into a festive occasion was more likely to encourage parishioners to attend.

It is worth considering if there was any difference in the practice of loyalist religion between urban and rural parishes, and if there were any unique characteristics in the cathedral cities of Bristol, Salisbury, Wells

---

[121] BL Add. MS. 22084, fo. 4 [reverse]; *WR*, pp. 379–80.

[122] BL Add. MS. 22084, fos. 8r–8v, 9, 11 [reverse]; *WR*, p. 376.

[123] BL Add. MS. 22084, fo. 9 [reverse]; *WR*, p. 381.

[124] BL Add. MS. 22084, fo. 50r [reverse]; *WR*, p. 382.

[125] BL Add. MS. 15671, fo. 115; *WR*, p. 369.

[126] Morrill, 'The Church in England', p. 166.

[127] Hutton, *Rise and Fall of Merry England*, p. 217.

[128] Hutton, *Rise and Fall of Merry England*, p. 217.

[129] Hutton, *Rise and Fall of Merry England*, p. 217; BA, P.StM/V/1/a, fos. 36v, 37v; P.StJB/ChW/3/b; P.StMR/ChW/1/d; P.StJ/V/1/2, p. 69; P.Tem/Ca/20/1.

and Winchester. With the abolition of episcopacy in 1646, Richardson has observed that cathedrals became preaching houses, if they had any function at all. Many were damaged during the Civil Wars, and in 1651 the Commons even debated their demolition.[130] Cathedrals suffered disproportionately; at least fifteen of twenty-six cathedrals were seriously vandalized.[131] While some did became preaching houses, others were turned over to secular use.[132] Winchester cathedral was badly damaged by parliamentarian troops.[133] In 1649, the traveller John Taylor gave a poor report of the state of the cathedral churches at both Wells and Salisbury, implying that services were no longer held in the latter.[134] But cathedral cities were not only identified by their cathedrals; they were also important market towns and centres of trade and commerce. With the removal of bishops, deans and chapters, their importance as official ecclesiastical centres had substantially diminished. But as urban areas they would be more likely than rural areas to have a population of enough loyalist religionists to support an official or unofficial minister, and loyalists from the rural hinterland may also have attended services.

Loyalist ministers may have found it more practical to establish themselves in towns, but prayer book loyalism functioned in both rural and urban parishes. For example, in Wiltshire holy communion was celebrated at festivals in the market towns of Devizes and Wilton, but also in the rural parishes of Stratford sub Castle and Winterslow. Each parish no doubt had its own unique set of characteristics, such as the existing religious persuasions of both minister and congregation, the state of relationships between them, and influences outside the parish community.

The Restoration and after

Both Morrill and Hutton found evidence in churchwardens' accounts that at the Restoration many parishes returned to the prayer-book sacramental cycle.[135] This was, as Morrill noted, an outbreak of enthusiasm

---

[130] R. C. Richardson, 'Humphrey Ellis and the antichrists', Friends of Winchester Cathedral, *Record Extra Archive* <https://www.wincathrecord.org> [accessed 9 Dec. 2020]; *Journal of the House of Commons*, vol. 6, 1648–1651 (London, 1802), p. 535.

[131] Morrill, 'The Church in England', p. 154.

[132] Morrill, 'The Church in England', pp. 154–5.

[133] HRO, W/K1/13/1, fo. 96; W/K1/13/2.

[134] J. Taylor, *John Taylor's Wandering, to see the Wonders of the West* (s.l., 1649), pp. 4, 20–1.

[135] Morrill, 'The Church in England', p. 174; Hutton, *Rise and Fall of Merry England*, p. 214.

at the restoration of the old forms of worship, in complete contrast to the sometimes lukewarm reception given to the Church order imposed by parliament.[136]

This enthusiasm was reflected in many of the parishes studied for this chapter. Several recorded painting the king's arms in the church: at Marlborough St Peter's in Wiltshire and at Upham in Hampshire, among other churches.[137] Surplices, previously proscribed, were purchased, as were copies of the prayer book. In Somerset, Wells St Cuthbert purchased the new prayer book in September 1662, but still kept their four old prayer books.[138] Many Hampshire parishes bought copies of the prayer book, on occasion buying the old prayer book before the new one was issued in 1662, and some bought a new surplice.[139] At least two parishes, North Waltham and Soberton, bought copies of the *Book of Homilies*.[140]

In Wiltshire, Marlborough St Peter's, an apparently 'godly' church in the 1640s which had frequently hosted visiting preachers, had by April 1663 conformed in its purchase of a prayer book and a surplice.[141] Devizes St Mary's churchwardens hastily paid 14s for prayer books shortly after the Restoration.[142] Having paid for these prayer books, the churchwardens then purchased a copy of the new prayer book in 1662–3, along with a new surplice.[143] The church of St Edmund's in Salisbury was ordered to move its communion table back to the east end of the church (the position of the altar) and ensure that it was railed.[144] This suggests some reluctance, but the church did buy six prayer books in the year to 1662.[145] Elsewhere in the city, St Thomas's churchwardens bought a prayer book in the year 1660–1, and recorded a payment for holly, rosemary and bay, probably to decorate the church at Christmas; by 1663 the churchwardens had also bought a copy of the new prayer book and a surplice.[146]

---

[136] Morrill, 'The Church in England', p. 174.

[137] WSHC, 1197/21, fo. 114v; HRO, 74M78/PW1, fo. 16.

[138] SHC, D/P/w.st.c/4/1/1, Sept. 1662, accounts 23 Dec. 1662 to 31 Dec. 1663.

[139] HRO, 1M70/PW1, fos. 47–48v; 41M64/PW1, fo. 60v; 88M81W/PW2, fo. 86v; 70M76/PW1, fo. 39v; 28M79/PW1, p. 50; 47M81/PW1, fo. 62v.

[140] HRO, 41M64/PW1, fo. 60v; 50M73/PW1, fo. 6.

[141] WSHC, 1197/21, fos. 95v, 96, 98, 99, 116v.

[142] *Accounts of St Mary's, Devizes*, pp. 96–7.

[143] *Accounts of St Mary's, Devizes*, p. 104.

[144] *Accounts of S. Edmund & S. Thomas*, p. 238.

[145] *Accounts of S. Edmund & S. Thomas*, p. 237.

[146] *Accounts of S. Edmund & S. Thomas*, pp. 333, 336.

In conclusion, larger-scale studies such as those by Morrill, Hutton and Hitchman are invaluable for an overview of the extent of loyalist religion at a national or regional level. At a local or county level, however, the picture begins to fragment. Broad trends are less observable, and statistical analysis less viable. Unquestionably, in some parishes the major festivals of Christmas, Easter and Whitsun continued to be celebrated with the service of holy communion. In other areas, notably in the Bristol parishes, old ritual practices continued but these did not necessarily extend to festal communion. But to what extent the sacramental cycle continued in any locality is difficult to quantify, given the survival rate of the records, and the detail with which they were maintained by the churchwardens. A single surviving sheet of accounts is evidence for the sacramental cycle being celebrated, but not of the extent to which festivals were celebrated throughout the period. Churchwardens' accounts and other records have survived in sufficient numbers to enable historians to ascertain that loyalist religion existed, and indeed flourished, in many parishes during the Civil Wars and interregnum, but the lost and incomplete accounts mean that the full extent of the practice can never be truly known. What can be deduced from this chapter, as from other studies, is that there was something of a failure to totally eradicate the practices familiar to many from before 1640. Despite the efforts of central government, the attempts of the godly in the localities, and the ejection of unreformed ministers, loyalty to the prayer book and to sacramental observance at major religious festivals seems to have remained in a significant minority of parishes for which records survive. Attempts at moral reformation were also only partially successful, as the justices sought to impose these changes on what appears to have been an uninvolved citizenry. The efforts of the godly to reform religious worship in the parishes could not undo the religious practices of many years previous to these attempted reforms. This failure to reform the public worship and personal piety of the populace would explain the relative ease with which Anglicanism was re-established in England, after the Restoration.

9. 'God's vigilant watchmen': the words of episcopalian clergy in Wales, 1646–60

Sarah Ward Clavier

Introduction

The upheavals of the Civil Wars and interregnum were cataclysmic for lay people whose lives and fortunes were laid on the line for either the king or parliament. Many otherwise obscure clergy also found their lives, Church and ministry turned upside down, as did the bishops whose offices were abolished. Although a number of scholarly works have done much to illuminate the lives of the non-elite and non-radical laity from 1642 to 1660, there is still much to discover about the response of the moderate and episcopalian clergy to the changes they faced.[1] And face them they did: the Civil Wars had profound consequences for Church organization, doctrine, liturgy and the exercise of a pastoral ministry. While the numbers and patterns of sequestered clergy are still under discussion, the activities of a large body of educated and locally influential episcopalian clergymen who were fundamentally opposed to the post-1646 regimes have been largely overlooked.[2] These activities were a real concern for the regimes of the Commonwealth and Protectorate, and efforts to control or limit the influence of oppositional clergy were fruitless.

The sufferings of the episcopalian clergy have been variously represented in existing historiography. Some have underplayed the physical deprivations of ejected clergy. Others have highlighted the violence and poverty that

---

[1] For example, C. Boswell, *Disaffection and Everyday Life in Interregnum England* (Woodbridge, 2017); B. Capp, *England's Culture Wars* (Oxford, 2012); D. Underdown, *Revel, Riot and Rebellion* (Oxford, 1985).

[2] This includes conformist episcopalians as well as ejected clergy. It is hard on the available evidence to disagree with John Spurr that conformists maintained an 'Anglican' identity and that the relationship between conformity and opposition was more complex than previously assumed. There is not space here to discuss the opposition of Presbyterians, or to explore in any depth the difference between conformists and ejected clergy, but these should prove fruitful in further studies. J. Spurr, *The Restoration Church of England, 1646–1689* (London, 1991), p. 6.

---

ordinary clerics (and their families) faced if they did not conform.[3] The picture is clearly varied. On the other hand, the spiritual deprivations of ejected or even reluctantly conformist clergy have been greatly neglected. Despite contemporary descriptions of fears concerning loss of vocation, the state of their parishioners' souls and the potential for a wrathful divine response to religious changes, this aspect has gone comparatively unnoticed. The almost entirely secular modern Western world finds spiritual deprivation more alien than other forms of suffering, and the interdisciplinary nature of such research more challenging. To ignore it entirely, however, neglects a key aspect of episcopalian clerical determination to resist the religious mores of the 1650s. This chapter will explore spiritual suffering and resistance, examining in particular the experience of clergy in Wales. Studies of royalism, though they in no way rival the amount of research on radicalism and parliamentarianism, have now uncovered significant aspects of the political ideas and experience of the king's supporters from 1642.[4] Research on royalist and episcopalian clergy is less well developed but engages with key themes such as sequestration, identity, conformity and exile.[5] Wales has often taken a back seat in such studies. The work of Philip Jenkins in the 1980s and 1990s demonstrated what could be done

[3] F. McCall, *Baal's Priests* (Farnham, 2013), esp. pp. 150–76; M. Wolfe, *'There Very Children Were Soe Very Full of Hatred': Royalist Clerical Families and the Politics of Everyday Conflict in Civil War and Interregnum England* (SCH, 40, Woodbridge, 2004), pp. 194–204; A. Laurence, *'This Sad and Deplorable Condition': an Attempt Towards Recovering an Account of Northern Clergy Families in the 1640s and 1650s* (SCH, 12, Woodbridge, 1999), pp. 465–88.

[4] Some recent examples among the burgeoning literature include: S. Ward Clavier, ' "Round-head Knaves": the ballad of Wrexham and the subversive political culture of Interregnum north-east Wales', *Historical Research*, xci (2018), 39–60; A. Hopper, ' "The Great Blow" and the politics of popular royalism in Civil War Norwich', *EHR*, cxxxiii (2018), 32–64; F. McCall, 'Continuing civil war by other means: loyalist mockery of the interregnum Church', in *The Power of Laughter and Satire in Early Modern Britain*, ed. M. Knights and A. Morton (Martlesham, 2017), pp. 84–106; A. Milton, 'Anglicanism and royalism in the 1640s', in *The English Civil War: Conflict and Contexts, 1640–49*, ed. J. Adamson (Basingstoke, 2009), pp. 61–81; B. Robertson, *Royalists at War in Scotland and Ireland, 1638–50* (Farnham, 2014).

[5] Examples include S. Ward Clavier, 'The Restoration episcopacy and the Interregnum: autobiography, suffering, and professions of faith', in *Church Polity in the British Atlantic World, c.1636–1688*, ed. E. Vernon (Manchester, 2020), pp. 242–59; K. Fincham and S. Taylor, 'Episcopalian identity 1640–62', in *Anglicanism*, i (2017) 457–82; I. M. Green, 'The persecution of "Scandalous" and "Malignant" parish clergy during the English Civil War', *EHR*, xciv (1979), 507–31; J. Maltby, 'Suffering and surviving: the Civil Wars, the Commonwealth and the formation of "Anglicanism", 1642–60', in Durston and Maltby, *Religion*, pp. 158–80; S. Mortimer, 'Exile, apostasy, and Anglicanism in the English Revolution', in *Literatures of Exile in the English Revolution and its Aftermath, 1640–1690*, ed. P. Major (Farnham, 2010), pp. 91–103; R. Warren, ' "A knowing ministry": the reform of the Church under Oliver Cromwell' (unpublished University of Kent PhD thesis, 2017).

with the fertile records of royalism and episcopalianism in South Wales.[6] Lloyd Bowen has uncovered fascinating insights into religion immediately prior to 1642, as well as the role of the clergy in royalist print and sedition.[7] Yet as both Jenkins and Bowen have commented, Wales was home to an intricately connected and deep-rooted royalist and episcopalian community in the mid seventeenth century. It was a refuge for exiled English clergy, and saw a remarkable flourishing of anti-regime and anti-puritan writings. This makes Wales an important regional case study for the examination of opposition in the 1640s and 1650s. Clearly there were parliamentarian supporters, radical sects and a huge amount of conformity with interregnum regimes. But behind this the oppositional milieu is extremely easy to find in diaries, notebooks, sermons, manuscript ballads and printed pamphlets; in English and Welsh; in North and South Wales. Welsh episcopalian clergy comforted themselves and each other, opposed 'innovations' in Church and state, maintained the moral and practices of the Church of England, and encouraged opposition. They did this in oral and written forms. Their words form the basis of this chapter.

Recent scholarship has discussed seditious, oppositional or controversial words during the 1640s and 1650s. Lay and ecclesiastical writers worried about the changing meanings of words and their shifting nature. They saw linguistic instability as a way to explain a deeply unstable political and religious climate, while using rhetorical devices to express binary oppositions and encode their enemy as unnatural or monstrous.[8] References to instability, fear and the consequences of improper or unusual

---

[6] P. Jenkins, ' "The sufferings of the clergy": the Church in Glamorgan during the Interregnum. Part one: an introduction', *Journal of Welsh Ecclesiastical History*, iii (1986), 1–17; 'Welsh Anglicans and the Interregnum', *Journal of the Historical Society of the Church in Wales*, xxvii (1990), 51–9; 'The Anglican Church and the unity of Britain: the Welsh experience, 1560–1714', in *Conquest and Union: Fashioning a British State, 1485–1725*, ed. S. G. Ellis and S. Barber (London, 1995), pp. 115–38.

[7] L. Bowen, 'Seditious speech and popular royalism', in *Royalists and Royalism during the Interregnum* (Manchester, 2010), pp. 44–66; 'Royalism, print, and the clergy in Britain, 1639–40 and 1642', *Historical Journal*, lvi (2013), 297–319.

[8] S. Achinstein, 'The politics of Babel in the English Revolution', in *Pamphlet Wars: Prose in the English Revolution*, ed. J. Holstun (London, 1992), pp. 14–44; Bowen, 'Seditious speech', pp. 56–7; T. Cooper, *Fear and Polemic in Seventeenth-Century England: Richard Baxter and Antinomianism* (Aldershot, 2001), pp. 4–5, 7; S. Covington, ' "Realms so barbarous and cruell": writing violence in early modern Ireland and England', *History*, xcix (2014), 487–504; D. Cressy, 'Lamentable, strange, and wonderful: headless monsters in the English Revolution', in *Monstrous Bodies/Political Monstrosities in Early Modern Europe*, ed. L. Lunger Knoppers and J. Landes (London, 2004), pp. 40–63, at pp. 47–8; G. Tapsell, ' "Parliament", "liberty", "taxation", and "property": the civil war of words in the 1640s', in *Revolutionary England, c.1630–1660: Essays for Clive Holmes*, ed. G. Southcombe and G. Tapsell (London, 2017), pp. 73–91, at 75–7.

sexual or political behaviour litter the works and reported words of many different groups in the interregnum.[9] The lay religious writer and erstwhile parliamentarian John Lewis of Llanbadarn Fawr, for example, wrote in 1658 of how the spirit of discord 'chiefly lurks in *meer words*'.[10] He suggested that preachers prescribe for the common people 'sober Rules for reading the Scriptures' as otherwise they tended to 'prefer their own fancy before the soundest Interpretations, hence, and the like, the strange opinions, and crased extravagancies of many in these times (as those we call Quakers, and others deluded, but happly well-meaning souls)'.[11]

Welsh clergymen contributed to these discussions publicly, in sermons, pamphlets and comments in parish registers, and more privately in their own notebooks, written accounts and testaments. These texts had a variety of purposes.[12] Some appear to have been written to vent private frustration or to note strange events, others to engage in contemporary politico-religious controversies. The latter argued against both Roman Catholics and sectaries, and aimed to sustain the morale and loyalty of royalists and episcopalians. Disaffected clergymen, whether conformist or ejected episcopalians, certainly remained a distinct source of worry for the Commonwealth and Protectorate regimes. Bowen labelled them 'important disseminators of anti-Republican speech', and pointed to the bills of June 1649 and March 1650 intended to further control ministers' seditious speech as evidence of the regimes' concerns.[13] There is not room in this chapter to cover in depth all elements of episcopalian writings, so the discussion here will focus on four principal themes: a wicked and unnatural political and religious situation; a distinct sense of divine providence operating in a fallen world; a community of righteous sufferers; and the need to defend the Church, its doctrines and its validity.

Civil War context, 1641–7

Episcopalianism has been described as the 'ideological cement' of royalism, and if for some royalists that was the case, the clergy were the skilled

---

[9] J. de Groot, *Royalist Identities* (Basingstoke, 2004), especially ch. 4.

[10] J. Lewis, *Eyaggeloigrapha* (London, 1659), p. 4.

[11] Lewis, *Eyaggeloigrapha*, pp. 10–11.

[12] They come from a huge range of forms and genres, all with different rhetorical and literary conventions. The imaginative and rhetorical frameworks of these texts are key to their formation, and all efforts have been made to take this into consideration in this chapter. Covington, 'Writing violence', pp. 487–8.

[13] Bowen, 'Seditious speech', pp. 49–50.

craftsmen who employed it.[14] From the beginning of the Long parliament and the first trumpets of 'paper war' between king and parliament, the episcopalian clergy acted as intermediaries between the king and his people. Clergymen were at the heart of the intensive circulation and promotion of conservative pro-episcopacy petitions in 1641 in what Ronald Hutton termed 'the most efficient mass-media system of the age'.[15] John Walter has described the way that such petitions were 'published' from the pulpit as well as the quarter sessions and assizes in England, while David Zaret has discussed the support of petitions with sermons and hectoring by clergy of all stripes.[16] The correspondence of Dr David Lloyd, warden of Ruthin, and the North-East Welsh royalist commander Sir Thomas Salusbury demonstrates the organizational involvement of the clergy. Lloyd wrote that he had sent Salusbury:

> the subscription of Ruthen and llanrydd; you shall receive likewise that from Nantvayr I think best to returne that for more hands, which are very ready there ... I know not how things pass in Clocaynog, Evenechlyd and llanvoorog,

[14] Milton, 'Anglicanism and royalism', p. 61.

[15] *The humble petition of ... the six Shires of Northwales, ... March the 15th 1641* (London, 1642); *To the honourable court the House of Commons ... the humble petition of many hundred thousands, inhabiting within the thirteen shires of Wales, ... 12 of February, 1641* (London, 1642); *The humble petition of ... the County of Flint, presented to his Majesty at York, the fourth of August, 1642* (London, 1642); *Two Petitions presented to the Kings most Excellent Majestie at York, the first of August, 1642. The first from the Gentery, Ministers, Freeholders, and other Inhabitants of the Counties of Denbeigh, Anglesey, Glamorgan, and the whole Principality of Wales ...* (York and London, 1642); *Three Petitions presented, to ... Parliament ... III. The Humble petition of the ... the six shires of Northwales. ... March the 5* (London, 1642); Bowen, 'Royalism, print', 299, 301; R. Hutton, *The Royalist War Effort 1642–1646* (Harlow, 1982), p. 13.

[16] Unfortunately, no evidence remains as to the authorship of the North Welsh petitions, which only exist in draft, copy or printed form with no original signatures surviving. Judging from his correspondence, the organizer in Flintshire appears to have been Sir Thomas Salusbury of Lleweni, but there is nothing to confirm his involvement in authoring the petitions. Unlike Cheshire, Rutland and Essex, therefore, it is very difficult to comment on the confessional politics at play locally in Flintshire or Denbighshire. J. Walter, 'Confessional politics in pre-Civil War Essex: prayer books, profanations, and petitions', *The Historical Journal*, xc (2001), 677–701, at p. 677; R. Cust, 'The defence of episcopacy on the eve of Civil War: Jeremy Taylor and the Rutland petition of 1641', *Journal of Ecclesiastical History*, lxxxi (2017), 59–80; P. Lake, 'Puritans, popularity and petitions: local petitions in national context, Cheshire, 1641', in *Politics, Religion and Popularity: Early Stuart Essays in Honour of Conrad Russell*, ed. T. Cogswell, R. Cust and P. Lake (Cambridge, 2002), pp. 259–89; D. Zaret, 'Petitioning places and the credibility of opinion in the public sphere in seventeenth-century England', in *Political Space in Pre-Industrial Europe*, ed. B. Kümin (Farnham, 2009), pp. 175–96, at p. 186.

if you wilbe pleasd to write one line to Jack Wynne, he may easily oversee the work in those three parishes.[17]

It is not unreasonable to speculate that Lloyd had 'published' the petition in the parish churches mentioned, confirming that practice in Wales operated similarly to that in England. Clergymen read the King's Declaration of June 1642 in their parish churches, and aided in the circulation of official royalist print in what Lloyd Bowen has called a 'ready-made state information system'.[18] Parish churches were also the venue for the administration of the royalist 'Protestation and Oath', initially administered in July and August 1642, probably as a rival to the parliamentarian 'Protestation' of 1641 and 1642.[19] The royalist oath, locally tailored to include the names of prominent parliamentarians, was especially effective in north-east Wales, and prevented Sir Thomas Myddelton from raising a parliamentarian regiment (even from his own tenants) within Wales itself.[20] One anonymous field report stated that 'I knowe none, nether have hard of any that have nott taken a solemne vowe and oath against all that shall stand up for the parliament', describing the 'common sort' as instinctively royalist and episcopalian 'as for there Religion; they cry God and [the] king; and will nott heere of any other way of salvation'.[21] Myddelton's declaration against the oath described a 'Councell of War' held at Shrewsbury, in which it was agreed that Commissioners of Array would distribute the royalist protestation to be printed and 'to be by them sent to the clergy, and by them taken, and by them to be tendered to all

[17] Lloyd was deprived of his benefices during the interregnum, and according to his Restoration petition was sequestered, imprisoned and plundered 'to his utter impoverishment, ruyne of his estate, and undoing of himselfe, his wife and children'. During the Civil War itself, he apparently entertained 'Prince Rupert and Prince Maurice, and other chief Commanders and Officers of the Royall Army, and once your Royall Father himselfe', NLW Llewenni 194: Dr David Lloyd to Sir Thomas Salusbury, Ruthin, 21 July 1642; TNA, SP 29/12 fo. 6, petition of Dr David Lloyd of Ruthin, Aug.? 1660.

[18] Bowen, 'Royalism, print', 299.

[19] *The Private Journals of the Long Parliament*, ed. V. F. Snow and A. S. Young (3 vols, New Haven, 1992), iii. 251, 299.

[20] Myddelton's printed plea for the Welsh to ignore the oath as illegal was unsuccessful and he was forced to recruit from London, Essex and East Anglia. The text of the oath is printed in Myddelton's 'Declaration' and survives in manuscript form in a collection of royalist documents. The two documents agree on the wording of the oath. BL Add. MS. 46399A, fos. 78–9: A Protestation and oath to be taken by the Inhabitants of the Sixe Counties of Northwales; Sir Thomas Myddelton, *A declaration published by Sir Thomas Middleton ... Setting forth the Illegality and Incongruity of a pernicious oath and protestation, imposed upon many peaceable subjects within the said counties ...* (London, 1644). TNA, SP 28/346, accounts of Sir Thomas Middleton, 1643; SP 28/139: accounts of Capt. Roger Sontley on behalf of Sir Thomas Myddelton.

[21] NLW, Chirk F 13646: anonymous field report.

Parishioners of the age of sixteen yeares and upwards, and to take the names of all who shall take the same, and of them who refuse, to be severally and distinctly returned' to the local authorities.[22]

If this is an accurate recounting of the procedure of the royalist oath, the parish clergy played a vital role in preventing the parliamentarian cause from gaining a foothold in North Wales. They were, as Lloyd Bowen has observed, 'voices of religious and social order' at a time when the social and political order was threatened.[23] They were trusted intermediaries who formed, for the illiterate, a bridge between the printed word of the king and his people. From 1641 a system, perhaps initially informally established, spreading the king's proclamations via parish churches and their clergy, became a vital aspect of the royalists' communications. Subsequent warrants, proclamations and orders were distributed via local officers but also the clergy.[24] This included one commanding the inhabitants of parishes in Flintshire to arm themselves and muster against 'rebellious Assemblies and other open acts of hostility' near Chester, which commanded 'everie Minister in each parish Church to publishe the whole cause aforesaid and Contents of this our warrant in the vulgar languadge gieving their best exhortations to their parishioners of their forward obedience hereunto'.[25] Sir Thomas Myddelton's officers, petitioning parliament for his exemption from the Self-Denying Ordinance of 1645, argued that the people of North Wales were 'seduced by the universal dissension of the ministers, there being not (that we can learn) in all the six counties two beneficed ministers that have shewed any affection to the present church reformation or readiness to enter into the National Covenant'.[26] As bilingual intermediaries between the king and the monoglot Welsh people, resident in their parishes and familiar with their region, the clergy were ideally placed to exhort their parishioners to support the royalist cause.[27]

[22] Myddelton, *Declaration*, p. 2.

[23] Bowen, 'Royalism, print', 310.

[24] Bowen, 'Royalism, print', 314.

[25] WCRO, CR 2017/TP646, warrant to the high constables of the hundred of Counsillt, 8 Dec. 1642.

[26] Sir Thomas himself complained of the same problem. *The Letter Books of Sir William Brereton*, ed. R. N. Dore (2 vols, Gloucester, 1984), i. 335; Bod, MS. Tanner 60, fo. 41: Sir Thomas Myddelton to Speaker Lenthall, Red Castle, 31 March 1645.

[27] Indeed, parliamentarian commentators claimed that due to their bilingual skills and effective role as interpreters for their people, the Welsh clergy had an unhealthy influence over their parishioners. They ascribed Welsh royalism at least partly to the royalism of the clergy and their control of the information flow. This seems to take little account of other forms of information gathering, via commercial travellers, Welsh-speaking inhabitants of England and other 'bilingual agents'. Bowen, 'Royalism, print', p. 314.

Given the wrathful printed response to this oath by Myddelton and in parliament, and its success in terms of royalist recruitment, it is perhaps no wonder that 'delinquent' clergymen throughout Wales were ejected and sequestered after the end of the First Civil War partly on the basis of their tendering of the oath and other royalist proclamations. Eubule Lewis, rector of Newtown in Montgomeryshire, for example, was charged in 1647 with having published 'Capells oath, urdgeing the necessity of engaging therein, for the defence of the Kinge and parishioners owne right, and requiring the parishioners presence at the alter to effect the same'.[28] Chaplains within royalist garrisons, clerics who fought for the king and those preaching in his favour were similarly ejected and reviled. Walter Harris of Wolves Newton in Monmouthshire was ejected for 'setting forth a soldier in the late tyrants war against the Parliament', Thomas Vaughan of Llansantffraid (brother of the poet Henry Vaughan) for being 'in armes personally against the Parliament', and Jacob Wood of Crickadarn for 'assisting the King in the late Warrs, praying for his successe in publick'. Many others were accused of enmity towards parliament, malignancy and assisting the king in more general ways.[29] There were certainly sufficient clergymen in the king's garrisons at the end of the First Civil War to make them a suspect group. Surviving articles of surrender, such as those of Denbigh and Harlech from 1647, demonstrate that there were enough clergymen in garrisons for them to be discussed as a category in their own right. The Denbigh Articles, for example, stipulated that 'the clergymen now in the garrison who shall not uppon composition or otherwise be restored to the Church livinges, shall have liberty and passes to go to London to obtayne some fitting allowance, for the livelihoode of themselves and families'.[30] Though detailed records of royalist chaplains are extremely sparse, and no attempt has yet been made to reconstruct the chaplaincy in any detail, it is clear from lists of prisoners and petitions for relief that Welsh clergy were among their number.[31]

[28] Lewis was also accused of having 'sett furth scandalous versis of the Parliament', preaching that 'that the Parliament did pretend the takeing downe of Bushopps, and alsoe replied in these words ... beloued, their ayme is at the crowne' and 'in his sermon published that true it was, the puritans had one good Condicon, that is, they would not sweare in a yere nor speake one true word in seaven yeres'. Flintshire Record Office, D/E/1424: sequestration charges against Eubule Lewis, rector of Newtown, 6 Aug. 1647.

[29] WMS E7.

[30] WCRO, CR2017/C179/1: articles of surrender for Denbigh, 1647.

[31] The parliamentarian account of the surrender of Caernarfon described 'some Prelates, and prelaticall Clergy in Carnerven very malignant' present there, and made a plea for 'honest and godly painfull Ministers' to educate the 'most ignorant, and brutish people; who know very little of God'. HL/PO/JO/10/1/195, list of prisoners taken at Denbigh

Despite the ejections of 1646 and early 1647, this kind of assistance apparently persisted through the Second Civil War. An army 'charge' of 6 July 1647 accused two Welsh Presbyterian MPs (among other, more politically significant charges) of having spared Welsh episcopalian clergy from their deserved fate:

> all disaffected and scandalous ministers though in their sermons they usually reviled and scandalized the parliament and their proceedinges calling them revvels and Traitors and not only incensing the people against the parliament but usually takeing upp armes and leading their parishoners in armes uppon any alarm against the parliament, and many other desperate delinquentes have bin and still are taken off and freed from sequestration.[32]

The episcopalian clergy were at the heart of the rebellion, and at the sides of the royalist gentry and people of the region. Their words, whether spoken or written, persuaded and encouraged royalists of different social and economic groupings. With this context in mind, and the image of the episcopalian clergy as politically subversive enemies to the government, it is no wonder that they were viewed with suspicion throughout the interregnum. They were seen as 'persuading the people for the King', and their potential to carry on doing that was clear.[33]

Political words

The Welsh clergy did indeed carry on 'persuading the people'. Rowan Williams has written of Henry Vaughan that he attempted in the 1650s to create a 'Church of words' to substitute for the destroyed or subverted Church of England.[34] The episcopalian clergy built their own 'Church of words' to sustain and embolden the orthodox. From the outbreak of civil war in 1642 there was on all sides, and in most places, a sense of incredulity and bewilderment at the unnatural situation of division, disorder and conflict. William Roberts, bishop of Bangor, expressed the enormity of the

---

fight, 4 Nov. 1645; Anon, *A letter from His Excellencies quarters ... Also, a full Relation of all the whole Proceedings at Ragland Castle* (London, 1646); Anon, *The taking of Carnarven* (London, 1646); M. Griffin, 'The foundation of the Chaplaincy Corps', *Journal of the Society for Army Historical Research*, lxxx (2002), 287–95, at p. 287.

[32] BL, Egerton MS. 1048, fos. 51–82: a particular charge of impeachment in the names of his Excellencie Sir Thomas ffarefax and the Army under his Comaund ... July 6 1647.

[33] The political actions and exile of the Welsh clergy will be explored in a forthcoming book chapter by this author. *Calendar, Committee for Compounding: Part 3*, ed. M. A. E. Green (London, 1891), p. 1826.

[34] R. Williams, 'Reflections on the Vaughan brothers: poetry meets metaphysics', *Scintilla*, xxi (2018), 11–21, at p. 18.

events when he wrote to his clergy on 31 August 1642. He asked that the clergy contribute to a financial donation to the king's cause and argued that in doing so they were contributing to the 'preservation of the universe'.[35] This rhetoric was to become common. A newly monstrous world, called into existence by wickedness, a universe and stable order at risk – this is an impression repeated throughout episcopalian clerical writings from 1647 to 1660. The trope of monstrosity can be seen in a diverse range of contexts. A 1647 manuscript ballad, interleafed within a volume of Chirk parish records, described the social inversion, hypocrisy and treachery of those then in authority across North Wales, a many-headed monster now in control of local government and religious policy.[36] Rowland Watkyns's poem 'Strange Monsters' speaks of all parliamentarians as monsters:

> Of diverse monsters I have sometimes read
> Some without feet, and some without a head.
> No fouler monsters can hot Africk bring,
> Than rebels are without their head the King.[37]

An entry by the rector Gabriel Hughes in the parish records of Cerrigydrudion, Denbighshire, described a comet that presaged 'Great calamities to husbandmen detriment of cattel putrefaction of corn ... Hott feavers and agues severall heresies and new scismes, varieties of lawes, toleration of unlawfull things, religious men not regarded, death of great comanders, new inventions, tempest, coruscations'.[38] The compiler of the *Cwtta Cyfarwydd* noted in 1644 under the heading of 'Rebellion etc.' the coincidence of 'the enemies vizt Sir Thomas Myddleton kt his armie tooke Ruthin and imprisonned such male persons as they tooke hold, and a great raine and fowle weather happened and fell upon Friday and Saturday before'.[39] The incumbent of Northop, Flintshire, wrote in the early 1650s

---

[35] The clergy were an important source of funds as well as support for the royalist cause. *Two letters, the one being sent to the Lord Bishop of Peterborough, the other sent from the Bishop of Bangor, to the Ministers of his Diocese. Wherein is discovered the readines of the ill affected Clergy, toward the furnishing of his Majesty with moneys for the mayntaining of Warre against his Parliament* (London, 1642), p. 3; Hutton, *Royalist War Effort*, p. 137.

[36] DRO, PD/19/1/212: a new ballad of the plagues wherewith Wrexham in denbighshire is sorely tormented this yeare 1647.

[37] For the wider discourse on monstrosity and headlessness at the time, see R. Watkyns, *Flamma Sine Fumo* (London, 1662), p. 15; C. Hawes, 'Acephalous authority: satire in Butler, Marvell, and Dryden', in *The Oxford Handbook of Literature and the English Revolution*, ed. L. Lunger Knoppers (Oxford, 2012), pp. 639–55.

[38] DRO, PD18/1/1: Cerrigydrudion Parish Registers 1590–1735.

[39] This also has providential connotations. BL Add. MS. 33373, fo. 144: Y Cwtta Cyfarwydd.

that the late times now seemed to him a 'ridled wonder', and mused on its cause. He considered whether the world had grown childish, or the devil victorious, before querying whether it was because:

> the modellers and cantoners of Commonwealth and Church cannot endure to tread in beaten paths but will be antipodes to all those whose feet stand streight? If so (untill I can see them walking on their own heads as they have alreadie troden upon the heads of the people) I will proceed in my journey on the plains and not onely feed the sheep that they may be glorious Saints in heaven, but also suckle the lambs that they may be gracious sheep on earth.[40]

An anonymous 'Ejected Priest' was said to have 'preached publiquely that the spirit in the preachers approved by parliament was a hobgobling spirit, and that the present powers were traytors and rebells that had shed innocent bloud'.[41] All of these clergymen associated the monstrous, unusual or 'unnatural' with the events of the times, and especially with the upending of society and the destabilization of the natural order. It was a rhetoric that episcopalians and royalists could exploit successfully, especially when society and religion lacked the settled nature of the pre-1640 years.[42] The phenomena identified above were signs of wickedness and instability, and, by association, of providential judgement.

Providence, God's judgement against the people of England and Wales for their wickedness and sinfulness, was attributed as the cause of all the people's woes. Providential causes were ascribed to events big and small by almost all early modern Christian groupings, including those of all sides from 1641 onwards.[43] As Alexandra Walsham has argued, it was an 'ingrained parochial response to chaos and crisis, a practical source of consolation in a hazardous and inhospitable environment, and an idea which exercised practical, emotional, and imaginative influence upon those who subscribed

[40] NLW, MS. 12463B, notebook of the Reverend Archibald Sparke.

[41] Though from a hostile source, these sentiments mirror those found in private recollections, the correspondence of royalist laity, and notebooks or diaries of individuals such as Sparke. Anon., *A relation of a disputation between Dr Griffith and Mr Vavasor Powell* (London, 1653), p. 3.

[42] Boswell, *Disaffection*, pp. 206–7; A. D. Cromartie, 'The persistence of Royalism', in *The Oxford Handbook of the English Revolution*, ed. M. J. Braddick (Oxford, 2015), pp. 397–413, at p. 404.

[43] For example, Catholics, Quakers, godly Protestants and interregnum episcopalians. G. Browell, 'The politics of providentialism in England, c.1640–1660' (unpublished University of Kent PhD thesis, 2000), p. 9; N. Pullin, 'Providence, punishment and identity formation in the late-Stuart Quaker community, c.1650–1700', *Seventeenth Century*, xxi (2016), 471–94; P. Lake and M. Questier, *The Antichrist's Lewd Hat* (London, 2002), pp. 322–4.

to it'. It had 'near universal acceptance' and helped Protestants of all stripes to understand the events of their own lives and that of the nation more broadly.[44] According to the sermons of episcopalian and royalist clergy, God was judging his people by withdrawing his love and favour, 'whereby darknesse followeth; and so all miseries and mischiefes, fire and brimstone, storme and tempest, warres, famines, plagues, and all evills'.[45] While the parliament's actions of rebellion were sinful, it would not do to blame parliament for all the miseries, as other sins have 'provoked God to stirre up these Rebels to punish us'.[46] God had sent 'the sword and speceallie (as here) by such intestine and civill war into a land noe doubt, the cause thereof, is not for the mantaynance of the laws of the land, but for the mantaynance of the law of the Lord God'. Pride, vanity, luxury and division had stirred up God's wrath.[47] The kingdom, through the long peace granted by God from enemies abroad, had become complacent, profane and sinful.

> Soe that we may complayne that our peace was a very storme, a storme of syn that brought on this Kingdome a storme of *woe*. Though Gods heavie hand hath long forborne us, and expecting our penitency and amendment hath binn full of patience and longsuffering, yett he hath att last redoubled his stroakes uppon us; Wherein forraigne enimies could not annoy us, he hath made our selfes to ruine one another.[48]

As in Jacobean Paul's Cross sermons, the 'Israelite paradigm' was invoked frequently from 1642 to 1660 by episcopalian clergy, across a spectrum spanning moderate Calvinists to Laudian ultra-royalists. Comparisons between the two nations, who both sinned against God and were punished, were threaded throughout printed and manuscript sermons of the 1640s and 1650s.[49] Israel's example, as well as that of other biblical examples like Nineveh and Egypt, was used to demonstrate what had happened, but also what would happen further should the kingdom not change its ways. Such

[44] A. Walsham, *Providence in Early Modern England* (Oxford, 2001), pp. 2–3.

[45] G. Williams, *A Sermon Preached at the Publique Fast the Eighth of March, in St Maries Oxford* (Oxford, 1644), pp. 5–7.

[46] Williams, *Sermon*, p. 29.

[47] Providentialism was not confined to the ministry. Clarendon also identified 'long plenty, pride, and excess' as a cause of providential judgement in his *History of the Rebellion*. FSL, V.a. 616, sermon book of Alexander Griffith, sermons dated 4 April 1643 and 19 May 1643; Cromartie, 'Persistence', p. 398.

[48] FSL, V.a.616: sermon book of Alexander Griffith, sermon dated 6 June 1644.

[49] M. Morrissey, 'Elect nations and prophetic preaching: types and examples in the Paul's Cross Jeremiad', in *The English Sermon Revised*, ed. L. A. Ferrell and P. McCullough (Manchester, 2001), p. 52.

comparisons were a long-established convention in English sermons, yet in a period of armed conflict, governmental instability and severe and burgeoning religious division, they had significantly extra weight.[50] Only prayers, peace, a healing of divisions and ultimately God's mercy would bring calm once again. Indeed, division was both a cause and effect of divine wrath. The Welsh petitions of 1642 described how the mere report of attacks on the Church had led to 'insolence and contempt' in the minds of the ill-affected, leading to 'scruples and jealousies'.[51] While the test of faith inherent in these providential punishments was severe and hard to bear, it could be seen positively overall. Providential suffering within Protestantism had long been seen as beneficial, a test of commitment to Christ and a way to purify or refine the Christian community.[52] Although the tests in the 1640s and 1650s were for some significantly more severe than the daily troubles of earlier times, there was also a sense that this should be a chance for the healing of divisions and the reformation of sinful behaviour. If Protestantism was 'born in crisis and conflict', if that was where Protestants found their identity as opposed to the slow slog of everyday life, the interregnum was in many ways a rhetorical and emotional gift.[53] It was also a source of division in itself, however, as Geoffrey Browell has persuasively argued. By providing the various factions with divine and biblical support for their claims, providentialism radicalized politics and made reconciliation harder – preaching in favour of peace and unity was all very well, but the different shifting factions generally only envisaged peace and unity on their own terms.[54] The idea that the righteous would endure suffering nobly, that they would see it as evidence of divine displeasure and a motivator for personal and national reformation, is evident in the rapid creation of an episcopalian community of suffering.

From the earliest ejections to the Restoration in 1660, the episcopalian clergy quickly articulated the idea of a community of suffering. This was divided into two parts. First, there was the suffering of the parishes and

---

[50] Morrissey, 'Elect nations', p. 53.

[51] *Three Petitions.*

[52] This is more prominent within godly writings but is clearly evident in interregnum episcopalian texts as well. A. Walsham, 'The happiness of suffering: adversity, providence and agency in early-modern England', in *Suffering and Happiness in England 1550–1850*, ed. M. Braddick and J. Innes (Oxford, 2017), pp. 45–64, at pp. 51–6.

[53] It is clear that the sense of mission galvanized interregnum episcopalians and fired them in 1660 to restore (or create?) a Church of England that would meet the challenges of the previous twenty years. A. Ryrie, *Being Protestant in Reformation England* (Oxford, 2013), pp. 417–19.

[54] Browell, 'Providentialism', p. 17.

believers that were left without ministers to attend to their spiritual needs. They were abandoned, left in a spiritual wilderness, to drift into irreligion. In parishes supplied with intruded clergy they were, in the view of those who preceded them, teaching errors which were prejudicial to the salvation of the people. The concern of the ejected clergy, therefore, was not only pique at their replacement but fear for the parishioners that they were forced to leave behind. As William Nicholson pointed out, the itinerants were not 'ubiquitaries', and so were as non-resident as their ejected episcopalian predecessors.[55] Second, there was the suffering of the clergy themselves, both spiritual and physical. For ejected clergymen who did not have access to wealthy patrons to whom they could act as chaplains, the 1650s were hard. Not all were awarded the 'fifths' for their financial maintenance, and even those who were struggled to keep large families on a small sum of money. Some were forced to take up other professions and others to beg for charity. Furthermore, all ejected clergymen (and arguably many clerical conformists) were united in spiritual suffering. It is a generally neglected aspect of the ejections that the episcopalian clergy were exiled from the legal execution of their ministry, of the rites of the Church and the Propagation of the Gospel as they had taught it for generations. Physical and financial discomfort was, no doubt, extremely pressing, but spiritual deprivation was also real and a source of suffering. This united the deprived bishops with the most obscure curates, chaplains or rectors.

Fear for their own fates was accompanied in clergy writings by a fear for the spiritual lives and destinies of their congregations. These concerns included both what *was* being taught, performed and preached by intruded ministers, itinerants or radical sects, and the question of whether anything was being taught or provided at all (if a living was empty due to ejection). This connected to wider anxieties about providential judgement – if the kingdom was not being fed with the right spiritual food, how could it regain its health, or the approval of God? Godfrey Goodman justified his tract against the Socinians by outlining how:

> I finde that the fonts where we are baptized, and make profession of the Trinity, and the Incarnation, they are generally pulled down. I finde that the solemnity and joy at Christs Nativity, was forbidden ... I found that in very many parishes the church-doors were locked up, and there was not so much as any publick meeting, the churches generally decaying, and never repaired; that many men would not have their children baptized.[56]

[55] W. Nicholson, *A plain, but full exposition of the catechisme of the Church of England* (London, 1655), sig. A3.

[56] G. Goodman, *The Two Great Mysteries* (London, 1653), dedicatory epistle to Oliver Cromwell, sig. A3.

The absence of religious instruction or service of any kind stirred the consciences of those who supported the regime as well as those who opposed it. John Lewis wrote at length of the well-intentioned but ultimately negative impact of the changes since the Propagation of the Gospel in Wales. In his gentle but ultimately damning account of the Propagation, he explained how 'they put out most of the old ministers, and for ought of them I know, *most* of them well deserving it, but the defect and complaint is, that their vacant places are not yet sufficiently supplyed'.[57] Lewis recommended that preaching should not be the only priority of those ministers that remained, that traditional festivals (for example, Christmas celebrations) should be tolerated, and that the common people should not be discouraged from going to church, as to do that was to 'perswade them to have no account or esteem to such places, but to value them as every other ordinary place'.[58] Citing his own experiences as a parishioner in Llanbadarn Fawr, with no settled minister and too poor a stipend after impropriations to attract one, he suggested that those episcopalian ministers who could be persuaded to conform 'should be restored (at least) to some incouragements to exercise their gifts and talents in, and because the *harvest is great, and labourers few*, and that for want of supply *Gods worship* and service is in hazard to suffer among us'.[59] This attitude corresponds with that of another layman, with very different political opinions – the royalist poet, translator and jurist Rowland Vaughan of Caergai, who also spoke of the silencing of 'sound doctrine and its professors', and of the loss felt by those who had lost their ministers.[60] Given that between 1643 and 1654 perhaps no more than five per cent of the English population attended religious assemblies other than at the parish church, they were probably right to worry.[61] John Spurr has argued that the liberty of the 1650s harmed parish-based religion more by allowing absence from church than because of the spread of sectarianism.[62]

In the words of ejected minister Thomas Powell of Cantref, Breconshire, the congregations of ejected ministers were 'wandering, like sheep without a shepherd, journeying here and there seeking God's Word, which is nowhere

[57] Lewis, *Eyaggeloigrapha*, p. 3.

[58] Lewis, *Eyaggeloigrapha*, pp. 12, 15.

[59] Lewis, *Eyaggeloigrapha*, p. 26.

[60] Epistle dedicatory to Jasper Mayne, *Pregeth yn erbyn schism: neu, Wahaniadau yr Amseroedd hyn*, trans. into Welsh by R. Vaughan (London, 1658); D. Densil Morgan, *Theologia Cambrensis: Protestant Religion and Theology in Wales* (2 vols, Cardiff, 2018), i. 151–2.

[61] Spurr, *Restoration Church*, p. 5.

[62] Spurr, *Restoration Church*, p. 5.

to be found'.[63] His neighbour and fellow ejectee Rowland Watkyns of Llanfrynach wrote of how the 'false coyn' of schismatic preaching would lead to an 'itch of disputation' and a 'scab of errour' that would soon run through the whole flock. He, unlike the various tinkers and tailors, would shut his own shop, but pray 'Lord let thy tender vine no longer bleed/ Call home thy shepheards which thy lambs must feed'.[64] The poet Henry Vaughan, in his 'Prayer in time of persecution and heresy', wrote that for the laymen, 'Thy service, and Thy Sabbaths, Thy own sacred Institutions and the pledges of Thy love, are denied unto us: Thy ministers are trodden down, and the basest of people are set up in Thy holy place.'[65] William Nicholson of Llandeilo Fawr used the landscape of Wales within his metaphorical discussion of the travails of Welsh parishioners, writing that the 'people are scattered upon these mountains without a Shepherd'. They are, he argued,

> become like the prophets lodge in a garden of cucumbers, deserted ruin'd: No cottage on a hill more desolate, more defaced, the people having no encouragement to resort to that place, where they have neither minister to pray with, or for them, or to sing praises to God with them, nor any at all in many places, no not so much, as a gifted man (as they use to glosse it) to instruct them.[66]

Alexander Griffith wrote to Cromwell of how 'in a short space, the Ancient Clergy were (for the most part) indiscriminately ejected, the Tithes Sequestred, the Parishes left unsupplied, the blessed Ordinance of Christ taken away from

[63] These lines are contained within 'A prayer composed on entry to a ruined church where no sermon has been heard nor service held for many a year', which ends Powell's *Cerbyd Jechydwriaeth* (The Chariot of Salvation) (1657), translated and quoted within Morgan, *Theologia Cambrensis*, i. 150.

[64] Breconshire, where Powell, Watkyns and other members of the poet Henry Vaughan's circle lived, suffered particularly under the Propagation. From 'The new illiterate lay-teachers' in Watkyns, *Flamma*, pp. 43–4; *Oxford Dictionary of National Biography*, Rowland Watkyns, <https://doi.org/10.1093/ref:odnb/70939>.

[65] H. Vaughan, *The Mount of Olives ...* (London, 1652), pp. 66–8. There is extensive scholarship on Henry Vaughan's royalism, circle and politico-religious opinions. Just two recent examples: A. Rudrum, 'Resistance, collaboration, and silence: Henry Vaughan and Breconshire royalism', in *The English Civil Wars in Literary Imagination*, ed. C. Summers and T-L. Pebworth (Columbia, Mo., 1999), pp. 102–18; N. Smith, 'Henry Vaughan and Thomas Vaughan: Welsh Anglicanism, "chymick", and the English Revolution', in Knoppers, *Oxford Handbook of Literature and the English Revolution*, pp. 409–24.

[66] From Nicholson's epistle dedicatory to his parishioners at Llandeilo Fawr, Carmarthenshire. Nicholson, *A plain, but full exposition*, sig. A3. The reference to a 'lodge in a garden of cucumbers' is taken from Isaiah 1:8, where the prophet refers to Zion as being abandoned by God.

the Inhabitants, and they wholy debarred from any spiritual comfort to their pretious soules, by any power or *dispensation* of gospell-ministry'.[67] There is no doubt that all of these individuals had, to a greater or lesser extent, a measure of self-interest in the supply of clergymen to the poor parishioners of Wales. It seems unnecessarily cynical, however, to view their concerns for those 'lambs' as mere selfishness or rancour. Powell and Nicholson were only two of the ejected clergyman in Wales who wrote catechisms, instructional books or spiritual guides (in English or Welsh) that were intended to substitute as far as possible for the loss of clerical instruction. Many people and parishes in Wales were clearly unprovided for spiritually. The charge of abandonment was in many places, therefore, a fair one. Some ejected Welsh clergy tried to offer their parishioners a level of orthodox religious guidance in print, to provide for their flock in the place of a shepherd.

The sufferings of the Welsh clergy themselves were described in their own contemporary accounts and alluded to in many others. John Gauden described how destructive had been the 'storms and distresses of times (which wett many others to the skin, but it stripped of the cloathes and flayed of the very skins of many clergymen and all bishops especially)'.[68] Even James Berry, the Major-General responsible for Wales from autumn 1655 to January 1657, commented on the 'sad condition' of the ejected and sequestered clergymen and schoolmasters in 1655, and the extent of charity given by only one gentleman, Sir Thomas Myddelton of Chirk, in the 1640s and 1650s indicates the level of need.[69] Many suffered financial need. Those without private incomes or unsequestered landholdings were forced to rely on their relatives, or farming their remaining land. Nathan Jones of Merthyr Tydfil described the 'extortion and cruelty' of those who forced him to attend a committee in London in 1649, depleting his financial means and leaving him and his family impoverished, not paying him his allowance as awarded, and driving him into debt despite his not being ejected or sequestered at that point.[70] Edward Evans was installed curate of Llanllwchaiarn in 1645

[67] A. Griffith, *A true and perfect relation of the whole transactions concerning the petition of the six counties of South-Wales ... for a supply of Godly ministers, and an account of ecclesiasticall revenues therein* (London, 1654), sig. A2.

[68] J. Gauden, *Hiera Dakrya, Ecclesiae Anglicanae Suspiria, The tears, Sighs, Complaints, and Prayers of the Church of England* (London, 1659), p. 637.

[69] Myddelton, a former parliamentarian Major-General, moved gradually to a royalist and episcopalian oppositional stance from the late 1640s onwards, playing a prominent part in Booth's rebellion in 1659. Thurloe, iv. 334: James Berry to Thurloe, Wrexham, 21 Dec. 1655; NLW: Chirk F 12550, 13 Apr. 1657; Chirk F 12551, 13 Oct. 1655.

[70] Jones was later ejected, and the radical Jenkin Jones apparently intruded. Jones's account of his treatment before his ejection is transcribed in C. Wilkins, *The History of Merthyr Tydfil* (Merthyr Tydfil, 1867), pp. 93–7.

but was unable to get to his living because of 'danger of lieff and for feare of the enemies' in that area.[71] Others suffered physical violence, imprisonment and the seizure of their possessions. David Lloyd of Ruthin, for example, was imprisoned and plundered 'to his utter impoverishment', while Thomas Price was imprisoned, then on his release wounded, and lost his 'whole estate'.[72] Griffith Williams, preaching as early as 1644, compared the treatment of the orthodox clergy with that of the Christians of the Primitive Church – traduced and described as the causes of wars and sedition. Now, he argued, they were described by their enemies as 'Papists, and idolatrous, and the causes of all these calamities that are fallen upon this land; and therefore let them be deprived, degraded, and destroyed'.[73]

Godfrey Goodman, bishop of Gloucester and scion of an old Denbighshire family, left behind many testaments to his experiences from 1642 until his death in 1656. In one account, he described being shot at, attempts to seize him by lawyers, the plunder of his houses, searches of his belongings, theft of moneys intended for charitable purposes, the destruction of his property in Gloucester, his flight to a 'poor mountaine cottage', and the loss of his historical and theological writings. He seemed bewildered at the abuse directed at him – for example, 'Mr Prinne a gentleman I neither knew nor ever offended is more invective and bitter against me', – had no success in law or in gaining an allowance, and felt his office and person disrespected by his inferiors.[74] His petitions to parliament were unsuccessful, whether for restitution of his belongings, his tithes or the one parsonage that he held *in commendam*.[75] In his final printed work Goodman pled

> in behalf of my brethren the clergy, that what hath been violently taken from them, their cause never heard, or what a Committee hath done, being no Court of Record, being not upon oath, and their power lasting onely during the parliament, that men upon slight pretences might not lose their freeholds, to the great prejudice of the laws and liberties of this nation; and sequestrations, which are but for a time, might not be continued for ever.[76]

---

[71] BL Add. MS. 33373: Y Cwytta Cyfarwydd, fo. 145v.

[72] TNA, SP 29/12, fo 6: petition of Dr David Lloyd of Ruthin, Aug.? 1660; SP 29/7, fo. 124, petition of Thomas Price, July 1660.

[73] Williams, *Sermon*, p. 11.

[74] Prynne attacked Goodman (among others) in W. Prynne, *The Looking Glasse for all Lordly Prelates* (1636), pp. 43–4; BL, Egerton MS. 2182, fos. 2–9v: Bishop Goodman's prayer and account of his sufferings, 1650.

[75] PA, HL PO/JO/10/1/265, the humble petition of Godfry Goodmen once Bushopp of Glocester, 27 July 1648; *ODNB*, Godfrey Goodman.

[76] Goodman, *The Two Great Mysteries*.

Goodman himself died having converted to Catholicism and been much criticized for it. John Gauden, among others, defended Goodman's decision as prompted by the treatment of the Church. Goodman, he said, had been:

> provoaked beyond all measure and merit ... by those who professed Reformation (and yet so much in his sense and experience did deforme and destroy the Church of England) it is no wonder if dying and dejected he chose rather to depart in communion with the Church of Rome, then to adhere to the Church of England which (as Eliah) he though now decayed and dissolved (at least to its visible order and polity) ... Not that he owned (I hope) a communion with the Roman Church as Popish, but as far as it was Christian; not as erroneous in some things, but as orthodox in others.[77]

Another example is provided by the ejected Christ Church chaplain and royalist poet Thomas Weaver, who described the fate of the Maurices of Llanbedr, a clergyman and his wife who were attacked by parliamentarian soldiers. He was imprisoned, and she wounded:

> That lo! a curs't rebellious crew, whoose shame
> Was lost wth theyr Allegeance, rudely came
> And rob'd the fayre Mauricia, & her Mate
> Who doth upon the Sacred Altar waite.
> Slaves! did you not Divinitie espy
> In his high ffunction, & in her bright eye?[78]

Such physical violence ran contrary to the ideal in terms of treating opponents. Royalist armies in the First Civil War were asked to treat clergy as non-combatants (although no doubt this was neither always the case, nor always respected).[79] Such reports were, therefore, meant to shock, and to demonstrate the unnatural, hypocritical and monstrous behaviour of the times. As Fiona McCall has demonstrated in relation to England, it was the violent conduct towards the clergy that was most frequently remembered in accounts of their suffering. The interregnum was a time when violent assaults became 'ubiquitous', legitimized by warfare and often propagated by soldiers.[80] The contrast to previous eras makes its recording unsurprising, and yet does not diminish its impact upon the clergy and their families.

---

[77] Richard Smith quotes Gauden and Heylin on Goodman in his defence of episcopacy and catalogue of the episcopate, FSL, V.a.510 (unfoliated): a collection of all the archbishopps and bishops of the realm of England; Gauden, *Hiera Dakrya*, p. 637.

[78] Bod, MS. Rawlinson poet 211, fo. 18: on Mrs Maurice of Llanbeder's wound which she receau'd by a round-head.

[79] Griffin, 'Foundation of the Chaplaincy Corps', 295.

[80] McCall, *Baal's Priests*, p. 160.

The loss of their ministerial calling, or vocation, was another lament of the ejected clergy. The Church historian Thomas Fuller wrote in 1646 of his longing to 'bee restored to the open exercise of my profession, on termes consisting with my Conscience, (which welcome Minute, I doe heartily wish, and humbly wait for; and will greedily listen to the least whisper sounding thereunto)'.[81] This was not the preserve of prominent English ejected clergy. Welsh clerical petitioners in 1660 frequently referred to the removal from the exercise of their 'ministeriall duty'.[82] It is tempting to see this as mere convention, part of the form of petitioning for the Restoration, and yet the loss of their vocation formed an important aspect of their suffering.[83] Aside from petitions and personal narratives, episcopalian clergy wrote about their loss most frequently in prefaces to printed works, demonstrating (as Fuller did) their yearning to minister to their congregations once more. William Nicholson, for example, wrote to his parishioners that:

> I with griefe write, I have not been suffered, but peremptorily to make use of my talent to your benefit, or any other: being ejected and silenc'd, not for any crime then alledg'd, or for ought I can understand to be alleag'd against me, except it were that I could not be perswaded to subscribe the engagement. For that I suffer, and I would to God, that in it, I suffered only.[84]

Another common theme was a fear for the Church of England and a desire to defend it against those who claimed it was illegitimate, popish or tyrannical. This defence manifested itself in a variety of ways. From 1642,

---

[81] T. Fuller, *Andronicus* (London, 1646), sig. A3, quoted in W. B. Patterson, 'Thomas Fuller as royalist country parson during the Interregnum', in *The Church in Town and Countryside*, ed. D. Baker (SCH, 16, Oxford, 1979), pp. 301–14, at p. 303.

[82] PA, HL PO/JO/10/1/289, petition of Richard Evans, clerk, vicar of Llanasa, Flintshire, 27 July 1660; HL PO/JP/10/1/290, petitions of David Lloyd, clerk, doctor of the laws, vicar of Llanfair Dyffryn Clwyd, 23 June 1660, Hugh Lloyd, clerk, vicar of Denbigh, 21 July 1660, William Mostyn, clerk, rector of Christleton, Cheshire, 19 June 1660.

[83] The vocation, or 'calling', to the ministry of the 17th-century Church of England has barely been explored by historians or theologians. There are a few works on discernment or calling to the non-conformist ministry. The topic will be the subject of further work by this author. M. Birkel, 'Leadings and discernment', in *The Oxford Handbook of Quaker Studies*, ed. S. Angell and B. Pink Dandelion (Oxford, 2013), pp. 245–59; D. Hall, 'A description of the qualifications necessary to a gospel minister – Quaker ministry in the eighteenth century', in *The Ministry: Clerical and Lay*, ed. W. J. Sheils and D. Wood (SCH, 26, Oxford and Cambridge, Mass., 1989), pp. 329–41; G. Hayes, 'Ordination ritual and practice in the Welsh-English frontier, circa 1540–1640', *Journal of British Studies*, xliv (2005), 713–27; D. Wykes, '"The Minister's calling": the preparation and qualification of candidates for the Presbyterian ministry in England, 1660–89', *Nederlands Archief voor Kerkgeschiedenis*, lxxxiii (2004), 271–80.

[84] Nicholson, *A plain, but full exposition*, sig. A3v.

defence of 'the publique liturgie therof in the ancient liberties and form of government as they do now stand established by law' against 'innovation' was central to Welsh support for Charles I. Episcopacy was especially mentioned, as 'that form which came into this *island* with the first plantation of religion here … near or in the time of the Apostles themselves'. Its antiquity was a sign of God's approval and protection, and to alter it was to risk disaster.[85] The subsequent defence of the Church throughout the 1640s and 1650s was to stray very little from these basic foundations – the Church was legally established, was beloved of the people, historically valid and protected by God, and its government was sound. Such matters were, for example, at the heart of the Anglesey Rising of 1648. It was two clergymen, Michael Evans and Robert Morgan, who drafted the declaration of the rising, stating that 'out of conscience towards God, and loyalty to his anointed … [we] with all humbleness prostrate ourselves, our lives and fortunes, at his majesty's feet'. Those making the Declaration professed that they would 'maintain the true Protestant religion by law established, his Majesty's royal prerogative, the known laws of the land, just privileges of parliament, together with our own and fellow subjects' legal properties and liberties'. They declared the Commonwealth government in London to be enemies and traitors, and swore to proceed against them. This declaration was read in English and Welsh to all those who had flocked from across North Wales to rise on Anglesey.[86]

Defence of the Church of England's liturgy and practices also happened in disputations.[87] Dr George Griffith, future bishop of St Asaph, debated with the millenarian Vavasor Powell both in person and in print. In this debate, Griffith was allegedly supported by 'carnall cavaliers and outed clergie-men', 'thirty or forty of the scum of two or three counties' and a lawyer ('one of the long robe'). One of the clergymen was identified as Mr Jones, chaplain to Lord Herbert, and another 'Mr Kyffin', probably John Kyffin who had been variously vicar of Llansilin, vicar choral of

---

[85] *Three Petitions.*

[86] Evans was chaplain to Lord Bulkeley of Baron Hill, and later chaplain to the important loyalist family Mostyn of Flintshire. Morgan was former chaplain to Dr William Roberts, bishop of Bangor, and was himself bishop of Bangor from 1666 to 1673. The bishop of Ossory, Dr Griffith Williams, claimed involvement in the Declaration, but the only evidence of this is within his own work, and Williams's testimony on other issues has been seen as suspect or self-serving. R. Llwyd, *The Poetical Works of Richard Llwyd* (London, 1837), pp. 59–60; G. Williams, *The persecution and oppression … of John Bale … and of Gruffith Williams* (London, 1664), p. 10.

[87] See B. Capp, 'The religious marketplace: public disputations in Civil War and Interregnum England', *EHR*, cxxix (2014), 47–78.

St Asaph, prebend of Meliden, vicar of Oswestry and rector of Manafon in Montgomeryshire. He was ejected by sequestrators.[88] During the debate, Griffith defended the validity of the calling of episcopalian clergy. He argued against the Church harbouring popery, instead accusing the radicals of being 'good agents for the Papists' as numbers had increased since the Propagation had removed ministers. Griffith defended set forms of prayer, attacked by Powell as used in the place of God-given gifts of prayer, as described in scripture and most convenient for the people.[89] He also defended episcopal ordination, the singing of psalms as a Protestant practice, and the conduct of his parishioners in demanding traditional services.[90] During the debate and in the printed dispute that followed, George Griffith was connected ideologically and politically by Powell and his allies with another controversialist and determined foe of Powell – Alexander Griffith of Glasbury.[91] Alexander Griffith was described as George Griffith's 'Master-Minter' in one hostile pamphlet, which outlines a sermon preached by Alexander Griffith at Kinton in Herefordshire on 30 September 1652 and a resulting disputation, in which he argued that there was no separation between saints and sinners until the end of the world. It seems from the summary that both Griffiths argued for mixed congregations, a concept that was anathema to the Fifth Monarchist radicals of Powell's group.[92]

Another consistent defender of the Church along the Welsh border was John Cragge of Llantilio Pertholey, Monmouthshire. Although Cragge

[88] A Mr J. Kyffin, clearly a clergyman, is addressed by Edward Lloyd of Llanforda as one who did 'officiate heare and tooke the sole Care of our soules, you principld me for heauen'. It seems from the royalist translator and poet Rowland Vaughan's preface to a sermon attacking schism that he was also present at the disputation. Anon., *A Relation of a Disputation between Dr Griffith and Mr Vavasor Powell* (London, 1653), pp. 2, 4, 7, 10; Bod, MS. Ashmole 1825, fo. 105: Edward Lloyd to Mr. J. Kyffin, Llanforda, 1647; D. R. Thomas, *A History of the Diocese of St Asaph*, pp. 250, 339, 657; *Alumni Oxonienses, 1500–1714*, ed. Joseph Foster (4 vols, Oxford, 1891), ii. 866; Vaughan (trans.), *Pregeth yn erbyn schism*, sig. A2.

[89] For radical disdain of set forms of prayer, see Judith Maltby, ' "Extravagencies and impertinencies": set forms, conceived and extempore prayer in Interregnum England', in *Worship and the Parish Church in Early Modern Britain*, ed. A. Ryrie and N. Mears (Farnham, 2013), pp. 221–43, especially pp. 234–6.

[90] G. Griffith, *A Welsh Narrative, Corrected, and Taught to Speak True English, and Some Latine* (London, 1652), pp. 5–6, 13–14.

[91] Anon., *A Relation of a Disputation*, p. 5.

[92] The description of this sermon seems very detailed to be an outright fabrication, though Griffith had been ejected by this point and so was apparently preaching illegally. The disputation at the heart of this pamphlet exchange was possibly an early volley in the fight against Powell and the propagators, central to Alexander Griffith's later pamphlets. Anon., *A Relation of a Disputation*, p. 5; Capp, *England's Culture Wars*, p. 112; Spurr, *Restoration Church*, p. 18.

published a number of sermons and is mentioned in passing in scholarly articles, his involvement in a typically rancorous disputation and pamphlet exchange has gone comparatively unremarked. Following a sermon given by the anti-paedobaptist John Tombes in Abergavenny on 5 September 1653, Henry Vaughan, Anthony Bonner, a neighbouring minister, and Cragge undertook a dispute in St Mary's Church, followed the next week by a sermon on the same text by Cragge.[93] This five-hour dispute focused on the admissibility of infant baptism, but Cragge's later printed texts also argued about church marriage, the legality and advisability of tithes and the advisability of Church discipline. Cragge was certainly not one to mince his words, describing the consequences of the sin thus: 'All places have become *Aceldamaes*, houses of blood, fields of blood, ditches of blood, towns of blood, Churches of blood, in this land, that was once *Insula pacis*, an Island of peace.'[94] At the 1656 funeral sermon of James Parry, uncle to Rowland Watkyn and former vicar of Tedstone, Cragge lambasted the state of the Church and the state, describing how 'God hath not restrained violence against us, so as he did against those of our profession in the daies of old,' although he acknowledged that the sins of the clergy had played their part.[95] On infant baptism, Cragge took a similarly firm line. Comparing the events in Germany with Britain's current state, he rooted them in anabaptism, arguing that magistracy and ministry, going hand in hand, were both discarded by those who rebelled in favour of heresy and faction. Casting the orthodox clergy as the watchmen, and heretics as the 'starved snake', he described the effect of heterodoxy in religion:

> it dissolves the bond of obedience, unrivets the sacred tye of love amongst subjects, breeds exacerbation of mind, and exulceration of affections, lays secret trains, and privie mines, for tumults, uproars, seditions, massacres, and civil wars, as in Germany, where the Anabaptist grew so populous, that (as Sleiden records) they could not be vanquished, till almost a hundred thousand of them were slain by the united forces of the Empire.[96]

---

[93] Cragge wrotes that he substituted for Bonner because of Bonner's age; Bonner's will indicates that he was eighty-two when he died in 1663. Bonner was vicar of Llanwenarth, a village near Abergavenny. Henry Vaughan was 'Schoolmaster of the Town, formerly a Fellow of Jesus College in Oxford', an able disputant and described by Tombes himself as 'modest and intelligent', NLW, LL/1663/75; Anon., *A Publick Dispute Betwixt John Tombs, B. D. Respondent, John Cragge M. A., and Henry Vaughan Opponents, Touching Infant-Baptism ...* (London, 1654); J. Tombs, *A Plea for Anti-paedobaptists* (London, 1654), p. 5.

[94] J. Cragge, *A Cabinett of Spirituall Iewells ...* (London, 1657), p. 121.

[95] Cragge, *Cabinett*, p. 136; Watkyns, *Flamma*, p. 73.

[96] J. Cragge, *The Arraignment, and Conviction of Anabaptism* (London, 1656), sigs A3–4.

The rhetorical style of episcopalian disputants is striking but such strident language was far from confined to one side or faction. The defence of the established Church as a guarantor of stability, discipline and peace was a potent one, however, as was the argument that it confused and unsettled the ordinary people. To return to language and words briefly, for Cragge, 'Libertie in religion is like free conversing without restraint'. An interjector in the Abergavenny dispute, an apothecary, was silenced by a 'gentleman of authoritie … that it was not fit for a man of his place, and calling, to speak'.[97] Towards the end of the 1650s, it seemed clear to many that lack of restraint had been disastrous, and that order, peace and unity should have been preserved. Disputations were a double-edged sword. On the one hand, they were fractious and divisive, seemingly further indicative of sinful behaviour and strife. On the other, they were powerful opportunities for episcopalian clergy to prove their worth in learning and wisdom, to silence radicals and to rally their communities.

Conclusion

The clergy were God's 'vigilant watch-men', 'his souldiers, stewards, angells'.[98] They guarded their people and, on a wider stage, the state and the Church.[99] In doing so, whichever ecclesiastical position they represented, they saw themselves as protecting true Christian religion. In a world in which religion and politics were indivisible even as coalitions and positions shifted, this was a potent role. As Tim Cooper has argued, a community labels as deviant those practices or beliefs that seem to attack its most cherished values. Opposition to groups as diverse as the anti-paedobaptists, Socinians and Catholics, therefore, was rooted in inner fears, and the interregnum was a time of 'collective fear', 'moral panic' and anxiety about moral and doctrinal disorder and excess.[100] Dolly McKinnon has written of how the spring tides by the North Sea were 'the object of early modern individual and community fear … interpreted as God's anger'.[101] According

---

[97] Cragge, *Arraignment*, p. 19.

[98] FSL, V.a. 616, sermon Book of Alexander Griffith: sermon dated 4 April 1643 and 1646; Cragge, *Cabinett*, p. 151.

[99] Cooper, *Fear and Polemic*, p. 4.

[100] Davis argues that such overwhelming fear even led to the invention of groups like the Ranters. Cooper, *Fear and Polemic*, p. 95; J. C. Davis, *Fear, Myth and History: The Ranters and Historians* (Cambridge, 1986), pp. 94–5, 99.

[101] D. Mackinnon, '"Jangled the belles, and with fearful outcry, raysed the secure inhabitants": emotion memory and storm surges in the early modern East Anglian landscape', in *Disaster, Death and the Emotions in the Shadow of the Apocalypse, 1400–1700*, ed. J. Spinks and C. Zika (Basingstoke, 2016), pp. 155–64, at p. 156.

to McKinnon, community responses to disasters reflected different calibrations of fear, ones that could forge bonds, and consolidate a sense of individual and collective identity and emotional memory in order to generate emotional resilience'.[102] For episcopalians after 1646, the religious and political situation was analogous to a monstrous environmental disaster. The world as they knew it was largely swept away, and there was the potential to lose the liturgy and identity of the Church.

Clergy words, therefore, were central to the continuance of the traditions, practices and identities of the Church of England. The clergy were praised for 'bottoming' royalists, and it was acknowledged by the parliamentarian regimes that hostile clergy made life very difficult for the authorities: 'like priest, like people, and like magistrates, like people'.[103] In articulating defences of the Church they appealed at different points in the period to those who felt destabilized and lost among the new developments. Descriptions of sufferings were another way to motivate the faithful, with plentiful biblical material on the deprivations of God's chosen people, the fate of the wicked and the traducers of true religion on hand to vindicate both episcopalian clergy and laity. Sermons (particularly at royalist funerals), disputations and pamphlet wars provided a religious corollary to a royalist social community, using the arts of rhetoric and learning to bolster the self-image and morale of the Church. God's watchmen guarded their traditions, gave voice to opposition and provided a beacon for individuals and communities who found themselves in unaccustomed opposition in the period 1646 to 1660.

[102] Mackinnon, ' "Jangled" ', p. 157.

[103] Bod, MS. Ashmole 1025, fo. 105: Edward Lloyd to Mr J. Kyffin, Llanforda, 1647; Capp, *England's Culture Wars*, p. 41.

Remembering godly rule

10. 'A crack'd mirror': reflections on 'godly rule' in Warwickshire in 1662

Maureen Harris

In 1657, loyalist Church of England clergyman Thomas Aylesbury, born and educated in Warwickshire but serving in Wiltshire, published *A Treatise of the Confession of Sinne*.[1] Although the treatise had been completed by 1639, Aylesbury added an epilogue nineteen years later recalling the soldiers in 1645 who had violently disturbed his church service, slashed the Book of Common Prayer in pieces with their swords and deprived him of his livings.[2] He reflected on his experience of 'godly rule' as a time when the clergy were 'disesteemed' and when

> Monstrous-shapen heresies [were] open proofs [of Lying Spirits]; in whose conceits Religion seems like a crack'd Mirror, broken in pieces by their vain imaginations, and reflecting multiplied images of their conceited Divinity.[3]

With this powerful simile, Aylesbury expressed what the political and religious changes of the 1640s and 1650s meant to him. The 'crack'd mirror', smashed like stained glass by puritan zealots, described the state of reformed Protestantism, 'splintered into a plethora of rival groups, frequently locked in acrimonious competition'.[4]

This chapter examines how puritan and loyalist Warwickshire clergy around 1662 experienced, responded to and remembered the effects of 'godly rule' in the 1640s and 1650s and how they reacted to its overturning in the 1660s. Fiona McCall has explored the struggle of loyalist clergy and their families to suppress painful memories of harassment and ejection under 'godly rule', while David Appleby has examined the 'Farewell' sermons of 'godly' ministers removed in August 1662, noting their 'sense

---

[1] T. Ailesbury, *A Treatise of the Confession of Sinne* (London, 1657).

[2] C. Alsbury, 'Aylesbury, Thomas (bap. 1597, d. 1660/61)', in *Oxford Dictionary of National Biography*, <https://doi.org/10.1093/ref:odnb/930> Aylesbury was attacked while celebrating divine service at Hornisham, WMS C4.62.

[3] Ailesbury, *Treatise*, pp. 338–41.

[4] B. Capp, *England's Culture Wars* (Oxford, 2012), p. 112.

M. Harris, '"A crack'd mirror": reflections on 'godly rule' in Warwickshire in 1662', in *Church and people in interregnum Britain*, ed. F. McCall (London, 2021), pp. 245–271. License: CC BY-NC-ND.

of injured innocence' and the emotional dislocation seen, for instance, in Richard Alleine's stunned comment: 'This Morning I had a Flock, and you had a Pastour: but now behold a Pastour without a Flock, a Flock without a Shepheard.'[5] These reactions illustrate the first stage of Elisabeth Kübler-Ross's well-known 'five stages of grief' (denial and isolation, anger, bargaining, depression and finally acceptance), which she sees as an 'intense emotional response to the pain of a loss … the reflection of a connection that has been broken'. While she focused on grief after bereavement, others extended her five stages to the 'invisible grief' of loss suffered in often-overlooked circumstances: retirement, redundancy, physical or mental disability, marginalization and oppression, exactly the sort of grief experienced by the displaced clergy under 'godly rule' and in the early 1660s. It was grief resulting from loss of role, status and position in the community, financial security, home and often precious possessions.[6]

Here we explore examples of the Warwickshire clergy who exhibited not denial but Kübler-Ross's second stage of grief, when denial turns to anger as part of the process of remembering, recollecting and reorganizing, culminating in healing and acceptance.[7] Their memories, sometimes distorted by the 'cracked mirror' of religio-political belief, add much to our understanding of the influence of the 1640s and 1650s on both the loyalist and 'puritan' clergy during the 'regime change' of the early 1660s.

Warwickshire's 192 parishes, thirty-one curacies and fifteen chapelries saw continuous military activity in the Civil Wars and were largely under parliamentarian control thereafter.[8] It was a religiously diverse county. Eighteen of its 288 gentry families, mainly in the south and west, had Catholic heads, but it also had a strong puritan heritage. From the 1630s, inspirational puritan ministers preached and lectured weekly in the largest towns, Coventry, Warwick, Birmingham and Stratford, but puritanism, and later separatism, were also found in smaller towns and rural parishes, particularly in the north and east of the county: Richard Vines at Nuneaton,

---

[5] F. McCall, 'Children of Baal: clergy families and their memories of sequestration during the English Civil War', *Huntington Library Quarterly*, lxxvi (2013), 617–38, at p. 618; F. McCall, *Baal's Priests: The Loyalist Clergy and the English Revolution* (Farnham, 2013), p. 56; D. J. Appleby, *Black Bartholomew's Day: Preaching, Polemic and Restoration Nonconformity* (Manchester, 2007), pp. 82, 38.

[6] E. Kübler-Ross, *On Death and Dying* (London, 1970); E. Kübler-Ross and D. Kessler, *On Grief and Grieving* (London, 2014), p. 227; L. Machlin, *Working with Loss and Grief* (London, 2009), pp. 29–30; R. Bright, *Grief and Powerlessness* (London, 1996), pp. 46–9.

[7] Kübler-Ross and Kessler, *On Grief*, p. 25.

[8] Based on J. L. Salter, 'Warwickshire clergy, 1660–1714', 2 vols (unpublished University of Birmingham PhD thesis, 1975), i, pp. 290–1.

James Nalton at Rugby and Anthony Burgess at Sutton Coldfield all attracted large audiences.[9]

The clergy, as parish leaders, played a vital role after 1642 in interpreting events, inevitably revealing their own religious, political and cultural beliefs, sometimes with dangerous consequences. Scholarly consideration of the clergy between 1640 and the Restoration has focused on loyalist and puritan ejectees, concluding that 'the majority of parish clergy were not disturbed', but this is as untrue of Warwickshire as Pruett found it to be of Leicestershire.[10] By late 1662, five-sixths of Warwickshire's parishes and curacies had changed hands (see Figures 10.1 and 10.2) and the clergymen occupying the livings included a mixed group: ejected loyalists who had returned in 1660, intruded 'godly' ministers who had conformed, new loyalists who had replaced departed puritans and those who had remained throughout.

Flight and ejection, 1642–57

Ejected loyalists were not the only clergy to leave their parishes in the 1640s and 1650s. In Warwickshire, fourteen parishes were abandoned in the early war years by puritans and loyalists: the 'godly' Francis Roberts of Birmingham fled for his life to London, and was soon joined there by Samuel Clarke of Alcester and Anthony Burgess of Sutton Coldfield, while Simon Moore of Frankton fled to Coventry. Royalists Henry Twitchet of Stratford and Robert Kenrick of Burton Dassett and puritans James Nalton and Benjamin Lovell of Preston Bagot joined their armies. Thirty Warwickshire ministers were formally ejected from parishes scattered across the county, with some clustering around the parliamentarian garrisons of Coventry and Kenilworth where more intense scrutiny was likely.[11]

Where a cause was specified, loyalist Warwickshire ejections were usually for 'scandal in life and doctrine', but 'doctrine' covered a variety of offences, some from years before. Thomas Lever, minister of Leamington Hastings from 1619 and Stockton from 1628, was charged in 1636 with assaulting a parishioner in church, one of several similar assaults by ministers at that time, possibly over clerical pluralism and 'Laudian' ceremonies in

---

[9] A. Hughes, *Politics, Society and Civil War in Warwickshire, 1620–1660*, revised ed. (Cambridge, 2002), pp. 62–3, 75, 79–81.

[10] J. Spurr, *The Restoration Church of England, 1646–1689* (New Haven, Conn., 1991), p. 6; J. H. Pruett, *The Parish Clergy under the Later Stuarts: the Leicestershire Experience* (Urbana, Ill., 1978), pp. 11–15.

[11] McCall, *Baal's Priests*, pp. 130–1; I. M. Green, 'The persecution of "scandalous" and "malignant" parish clergy during the English Civil War', *HER*, xciv (1979), 507–31, at p. 523.

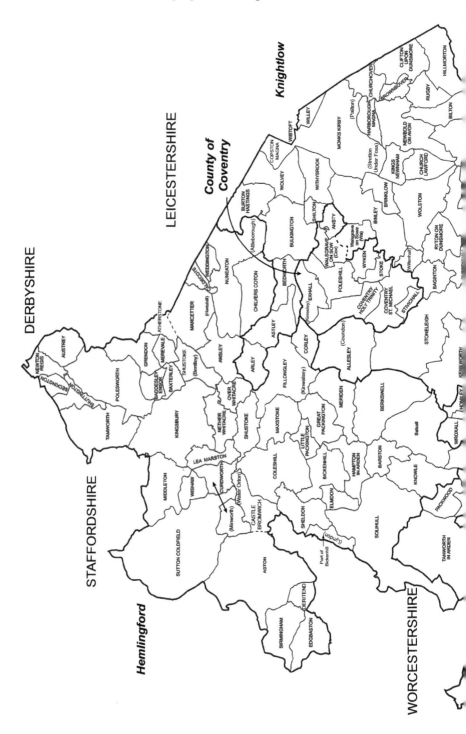

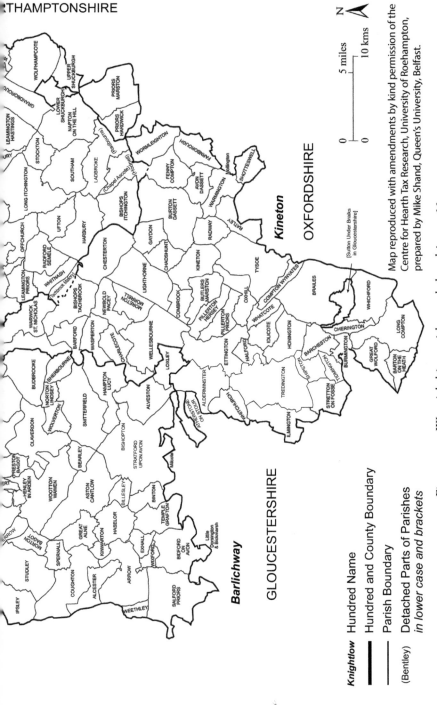

Figure 10.1. Warwickshire parishes and chapelries, c.1660.

an area of growing religious radicalism in east Warwickshire.[12] In 1640, Lever 'obstinately refused' to sign the 'Protestation Oath' and, following further brawls with parishioners in Napton church, by 1645 his living was sequestered for his 'malignancy against the Parliament'.[13] His removal was probably due to non-puritan beliefs, pluralism and persistent anti-parliamentarian allegiance but Leamington Hastings was a rich living for Warwickshire, worth £150 to £300, and McCall has suggested that while religio-political allegiance was relevant, reformers might target higher-value livings where puritan clergy would have greatest influence.[14]

Moral offences, termed 'scandal in life', also led to sequestration. George Wilcockson was removed from Wolvey for drunkenness, and John Williams of Halford for drunkenness, swearing, neglect of his cure and promoting Sabbath sports.[15] In 1655 Robert Beake, puritan mayor of Coventry, ordered 'the outing of [Michael] Walford, minister of Wishaw, for scandal in life', probably for drunkenness or swearing since Beake zealously punished both.[16] As Bernard Capp has suggested, such moral 'crimes' were characteristic of defiant 'Cavalier' culture, provoking fierce punishment by godly parliamentarians, although exaggerated accusations of drunkenness were easily made by zealous puritans condemning moderate social drinking in the alehouse by loyalist clergy.[17] Thus, there was a political element to removal for moral offences, just as there was for royalism or the seldom-mentioned rejection of puritan doctrine.

Robert Jones of Long Compton's ejection for drunkenness masked a more significant reason for his removal: he served the parish of wealthy Catholic landowner Sir William Sheldon.[18] Six more ejectees ministered in parishes where influential Catholics or notorious royalists lived. Edward Mansell, incumbent of Stoneleigh and chaplain to Lord Leigh, who hosted the king when Coventry's gates were shut against him in 1642, was inevitably ousted when Leigh's estates were sequestered.[19] John Doughtie, pluralist minister of Lapworth, was removed in 1646 after parishioners accused

[12] *Warwick County Records, Quarter Sessions*, ed. S. C. Ratcliff and H. C. Johnson (6 vols, Warwick, 1935–41) [hereafter 'QS' plus volume number] vi, eg pp. 7, 44, 53.

[13] BL Add. MS. 15669, fo. 78v.

[14] McCall, *Baal's Priests*, pp. 101, 130–1.

[15] WR, p. 367.

[16] *Diary of Robert Beake, Mayor of Coventry, 1655–1656*, ed. L. Fox (Dugdale Soc., 31, Oxford, 1977), p. 114.

[17] Capp, *Culture Wars*, pp. 99, 162.

[18] Bod, MS. Bodl 324, Minute Books, Committee for Plundered Ministers [CPM], fos. 101–101v.

[19] Walker, *Attempt*, p. 312.

him of consorting with papists, among other anti-puritan offences, despite his earlier sympathy for Calvinism.[20] A successful parish minister had to cultivate relationships with patrons, landowners and 'chief inhabitants' whatever their religio-political beliefs, and this might harm them as parliamentarian control increased in the 1640s.

In some cases, the primary cause of sequestration was personal animosity towards the clergyman, often masked by spurious allegations. George Teonge, ejected from Kimcote in Leicestershire, returned to his Wolverton rectory in Warwickshire, acquired in 1619.[21] He was one of thirty-eight Leicestershire clergymen questioned in 1646 by the puritan county committee on accusations of 'delinquency and scandall'. McCall has discussed Teonge's detailed answers to sixteen accusations of 'Laudian' practices and royalist support initiated through the enmity of his main accuser, but Teonge was further undermined by several court cases for loan repayments, which created hostility with local puritan gentry.[22] Teonge's responses reveal the frustration of the many accused clergy who complied with Laudian directives for worship but were later forced to adopt contradictory parliamentary ones and were outmanoeuvred by hostile parishioners manipulating critical timescales.

Daniel Whitby, ejected from an Essex parish and serving in Warwickshire from 1650, published an account of his frustrated efforts to answer accusations during an interrogation following his sermon defending the Church of England liturgy.[23] The mind-games used in such interrogations were part of the sequestration process. Ejections themselves were sometimes violent and involved threat, fear and humiliation. Thomas Baker of Baxterley was absent when his wife was evicted at pistol-point and, together with the children and household goods, thrown out by local parliamentary captain and magistrate Waldive Willington, after Baker had refused for some months to leave the parsonage.[24] As McCall suggested, ejected ministers, as former authority figures in the parish, felt this loss of dignity, status and identity deeply. Some, like the eighty-year-old royalist Francis Holyoake, rector of Southam, met this loss with anger rather than denial,

---

[20] *WR*, p. 363; *History of the University of Oxford*, ed. N. Tyacke (Oxford, 1997), iv. 584; J. Morgan, 'Doughtie, John (1598?–1672), *ODNB*, <https://doi.org/10.1093/ref:odnb/7854>.

[21] George and his son Henry usually signed as 'Teonge' but were referred to as 'Tongue', 'Tonge' and other variants.

[22] WMS C11.5; F. McCall, 'Scandalous and malignant? Settling scores against the Leicestershire Clergy after the First Civil War', *Midland History*, xl (2015), 220–42; Green, 'Persecution', p. 514; TNA, C 6/153/144, C 8/145/114.

[23] D. Whitby, *The Vindication of a True Protestant* (Oxford, 1644).

[24] WMS C3.11, C11.2 & 3; BL Add. MS. 15671, fos. 80, 142v, 164.

hindering sequestrators for months. So did Roger Jones of Long Compton and George Wilcockson of Wolvey until threatened with custody and loss of 'fifths', respectively.[25] This was very different from the ejections of puritan ministers on a specific date in 1662, which were tragic but predictable, and seldom life-threatening.

Contemporary clerical narratives often reveal the anger and bitterness of loss through ejection. At Exhall, John Riland recorded how soldiers 'with Swords ... brake in upon me, threw me out of my Living' and took books and precious papers from his Oxford lodgings; George Teonge lost sermons and 'writings' and Baker's wife had her first husband's valuable library seized at pistol-point. Daniel Whitby remembered the abuse: 'I have lived these three yeares in the ayre of Reproaches; a Popish Priest, Malignant, false-Doctrine-Preacher.'[26] John Allington, post-Restoration vicar of Leamington Hastings, after sequestration from a Rutland living in 1646 published an open letter justifying his loyalist beliefs to the 'godly' minister, Stephen Marshall, who remained, as Allington bitterly remarked, 'a light in that very House in which I stand eclips'd'.[27] Such vivid memories of ejection reflect the anger, pain and the need to repeat and re-evaluate remembered events typical of the early stages of grief following a painful loss.

A network of Warwickshire gentry sheltered ejected clergymen, probably in return for spiritual guidance rooted in the Church of England liturgy, just as a Rutland gentleman supported John Allington's Anglican services in the 1650s.[28] Thomas Whelpdale 'retired' to live with his Warwickshire relative, Sir Thomas Burdett of Bulkington. Despite Burdett's co-operation with the godly regime as a Warwickshire JP, he appointed Whelpdale to serve Newton Regis where he was plundered and ejected for loyalty to king and Church.[29] Burdett's son, Sir Francis, while Derbyshire sheriff, sheltered both Whelpdale and Thomas Baker of Baxterley, the latter also supported by royalists George Chetwynd of Grendon Hall and Mr Corbin of Polesworth.

The royalist Dilkes of Maxstoke Castle probably maintained prayer-book services, although their manor house was a parliamentary garrison until 1645. By 1648 their loyalist parson, Valentine Jackson, had moved south to Leamington Priors and was charged with using the Book of

[25] Bod, MS. Bodl 324, fo. 138; BL Add. MS. 15671, fos. 9v, 54, 181, 191, 203v.

[26] J. Riland, *Elias the Second his Coming* (Oxford, 1662), 'Epistle to the Reader'; WMS C11.4, C2.458; Whitby, *Vindication*, p. 1.

[27] J. Allington, *A Briefe Apologie for the Sequestred Clergie* (London, 1649), p. 1.

[28] WMS C4.62, information from F. McCall.

[29] WMS C7.124; P. Tennant, *Edgehill and Beyond: the People's War in the South Midlands, 1642–1645* (Stroud, 1992), p. 272; Hughes, *Politics*, pp. 347–64.

Common Prayer.[30] Bishop William Juxon 'retired' to Little Compton on the Warwickshire/Gloucestershire border but celebrated Anglican services around conservative south Warwickshire unmolested.[31] This undercover gentry network allowed loyalist clergy to maintain Church of England worship under 'godly rule', just as Catholic gentry had supported priests in the early seventeenth century.

Puritan intruders in the 1640s and 1650s

'Godly rule' was intended to promote moral and doctrinal reform, but there is little evidence of a vigorous policy in Warwickshire despite some action against swearing and disorderly Sabbath drinking in the early 1650s. Its effectiveness is hard to assess since reforms were pursued piecemeal by ministers, patrons and army officers and, as Ann Hughes has noted, by individual justices working largely out of sessions, creating problems of implementation.[32] Intruded puritan minister Simon Dingley, with parish support, suppressed six of Brinklow's seven alehouses for causing neglect and quarrels among children and servants but the 'godly' intruder at Whitchurch was presented in 1654 for selling ale without a licence. Jarvis Bryan was removed from Aston after trouble with parishioners; puritan pluralist Daniel Eyre's church service at Bishop's Tachbrook was disturbed in 1650 and Henry Cooper, vicar of Stoneleigh from 1646, was in continuous dispute with parishioners who supported sequestered royalist Sir Edward Leigh.[33] 'Godly rule' was also unlikely to succeed in polarized parishes like Henley-in-Arden, where radical pastors such as shoemaker John Fawkes were prevented from preaching in 1653 by a 'riotous assembly' of innkeepers, and where in 1655 the JPs had to suppress maypoles 'and other heathenish' customs threatening law and order.[34] Other 'profane and popish' parishes like Wixford and Coughton attracted 'godly' reformers with a 'missionary zeal' to convert ungodly souls, provoking resistance from Catholic parishioners, while in 1656 puritan William Perkins established a grammar school at 'Catholic' Salford Priors 'as a counterweight to anti-Puritan forces'.[35]

---

[30] QS VI, p. 87. An indictment of 1653 accused John Allington of reading the Book of Common Prayer, bowing to the altar and delivering the sacrament in his Rutland parish, Walker, C4.62, information from F. McCall.

[31] B. Quintrell, 'Juxon, William (bap. 1582, d. 1663)', ODNB, <https://doi.org/10.1093/ref:odnb/15179>.

[32] Hughes, Politics, pp. 284–6; QS III, p. 4, QS VI, p. 111.

[33] CR, p. 82; QS VI, p. 91; QS III, pp. 128–9, 151–2, 246; QS VI, pp. 103, 110.

[34] Hughes, Politics, pp. 321, 324; QS VI, p. 107; QS III, pp. 195–6.

[35] S. K. Roberts, 'William Perkins of Salford Priors and his educational charity, 1656–2004' (Dugdale Soc. Occasional Papers, 45, Bristol, 2005), pp. 1–30, p. 13.

Constant changes of minister thwarted attempts to promote moral reform, and encouraged parishioners' spiritual self-reliance and dependence on more radical preachers. The high turnover of five incumbents at Leamington Hastings between 1643 and 1661 was unusual but not unique.[36] In 1646, the manorial lord Sir Thomas Trevor was thanked by the churchwardens for appointing John Lee as a vicar who would uphold the 'sanctity and dignity of the ministeriall office' after Thomas Lever's death but Trevor was politically suspect.[37] Impeached in 1641 and sentenced to imprisonment in 1643 for supporting 'ship money', he cooperated with the parliamentary regime as principal exchequer judge but retired to his Warwickshire estate following the king's execution.[38] Lee, as Trevor's protégé, was therefore under the same parliamentary scrutiny and was ejected in 1649 for 'malignancy', swearing and drunkenness, cultural markers separating 'godly' from loyalist clergy. Lee resisted the intruder, Gilbert Walden, described by Walker as an 'eminent independent'.[39] Walden was therefore forced to petition Oliver Cromwell in 1655 to confirm his position, claiming that Lee constantly challenged his right to be minister. Supported by 'severall dissaffected Lawyers', Lee initiated suits at Warwick assizes for arbitration against Walden, but these were ignored by Coventry's mayor, Robert Beake.[40]

Lee's challenge brought the legal weakness of the Cromwellian regime into focus. About a sixth of Warwickshire's parish clergy had been ejected under 'godly rule' by the mid-1650s and dozens of puritan ministers had been intruded, like Walden at Leamington Hastings. 'Usurped' authority had ousted Lee from a parish to which he had been legally appointed, so how could an intruded puritan minister exert his clerical authority or pursue godly reform when it rested on such shaky legal foundations?

The Warwickshire clergy of 1660–2

The Church of England was largely re-established by late 1662, when four distinct groups of clergy occupied Warwickshire livings: returning loyalists, conforming puritans, new loyalist recruits and those who had remained. Figure 10.2 attempts to locate these individuals in their parishes at the risk of over-simplifying complicated changes occurring over two decades. Some clergy, for example Francis Folliatt of Berkswell and Nicholas Greenhill of

---

[36] Tennant, *Edgehill*, p. 233.

[37] WCRO, CR 1319/101.

[38] E. I. Carlyle, revised W. H. Bryson, 'Trevor, Sir Thomas (c.1573–1656)', *ODNB*, <https://doi.org/10.1093/ref:odnb/27735>.

[39] WMS C3.13, 608.

[40] TNA, SP 18/97, fo. 139, 23 May 1650.

Whitnash, died before they could be ejected. 'Intruders' could be loyalist as well as puritan: Daniel Whitby, who served at Arrow on ejection from Essex, resigned and returned to Essex in 1661, while William Morris of Kenilworth and Thomas Fawcett of Aston-juxta-Birmingham were ejected from other counties and served briefly in Warwickshire before being ejected again. 'Returners' were loyalists who successfully re-established themselves in former parishes but some, like John Doughtie at Lapworth, were refused re-entry. Others, like Francis Holyoake of Southam, died before they could seek readmission. Sometimes rectors remained, such as Francis Bacon at Astley, while the vicar or curate departed.

'New incumbents' were usually, but not necessarily, loyalist: Gilbert Walden, the puritan intruder ejected for radical religious practices at Leamington Hastings, conformed at Baginton, home parish of the royalist Sir William Bromley, while William Smith, 'intruder' at Baddesley Clinton, moved to Marton in 1660. Conversely, 'conforming intruders' were usually, but not always, 'puritans': William Stevenage took over the vicarage of Tysoe from his father, John, who served from 1605 till his death in 1654 and had 'articles' brought against him in 1646.[41] 'Remainers' were a varied group and included the 'godly' Thomas Pilkington of Claverdon and the fervent royalist Walwyn Clarke of Oxhill. The kaleidoscope of religious practice in 1662 indicated in Figure 10.1 was therefore even more complex than it appears, though with a general preponderance of conforming puritans in the southern and eastern hundreds of Kineton and Knightlow as opposed to the northern and western hundreds of Barlichway and Hemlingford.

More striking still is the fact that although the implementation of 'godly rule' and its overturning over two decades had affected the Restoration clergy in different ways, there were many similarities in their experiences and how they recorded them. Three major issues affected them all: titles to livings, clerical remuneration and, after 1662, religious separatism.

Disputed titles

The architects of the religious settlement from 1660 had to agree whether episcopally instituted clergy who had resigned, fled or been ejected should be allowed to return and replace sometimes well-established and respected intruded ministers and, where no returnee was available, whether un-episcopally ordained intruders should be allowed to stay.[42] This affected ministers like Samuel Beresford of Aston-juxta-Birmingham, ordained by

---

[41] Bod, MS. Bodl 324, fo. 25.

[42] I. M. Green, *The Re-establishment of the Church of England, 1660–1663* (Oxford, 1978), pp. 8–9.

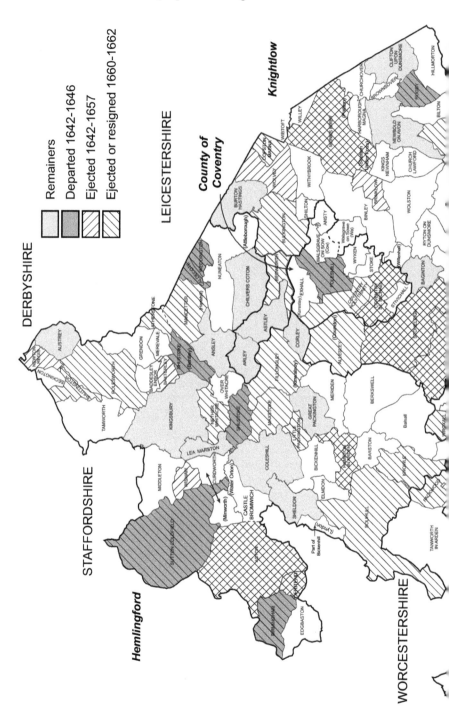

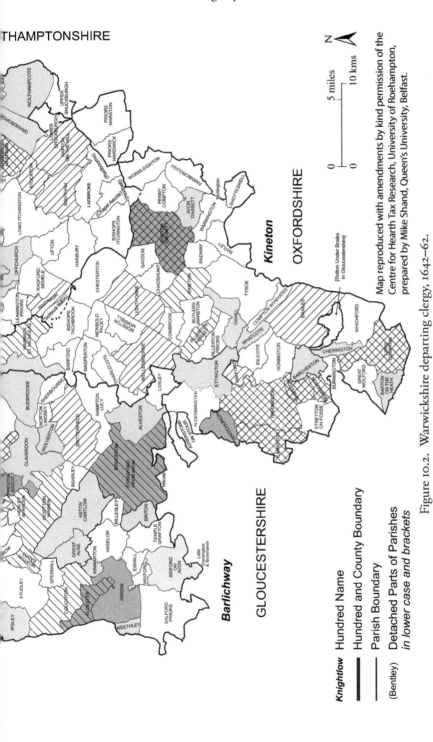

Figure 10.2. Warwickshire departing clergy, 1642–62.

the Wirksworth *classis*, William Swaine of Withybrook, ordained by John Bryan and Obadiah Grew in Coventry during the wars, and many men appointed by the Committee for Plundered Ministers (CPM) or the 'Triers'.

Two examples illustrate how Warwickshire's intruded ministers in the early 1660s had to work hard to retain their livings, as memories of 'godly rule' were used against them, just as loyalists Christopher Harvey and Walwyn Clarke, as we shall see below, struggled to stay in their parishes in the 1640s and 1650s. Puritan Richard Pyke had been appointed by Cromwell in 1656 to the rich Nuneaton vicarage from which four loyalist ministers tried to unseat him in 1660. Three of them petitioned for the king's presentation stating Pyke was dead but Thomas Holyoake, who knew Pyke was alive, instead used loaded images of loyalist suffering to further his cause: his father (Francis of Southam) forcefully ejected from the parsonage, his mother 'barborously beaten and wounded' so she died, a servant killed and a valuable living lost. Holyoake secured the title but complained that Pyke refused to let him enter. He had ten witnesses swear that Pyke had 'in the pulpit several times justified the horrid Murther of his late Majestie' and prayed against Charles II, yet Pyke held on.[43] Ability to retain a living depended on local support and whether the minister's doctrinal 'brand' fitted. The 'godly' Nuneaton 'chief inhabitants' did not want a loyalist parson and supported Pyke, as well as welcoming several displaced Presbyterian ministers into town following the ejections of 1662.

In Tanworth-in-Arden another intruded puritan minister, Ralph Hodges, had been approved by patron and parishioners in 1646 but was summoned before the bishop in 1663 about his 'sins', and in 1667 had to make excuses for using the wrong prayer book.[44] When a parishioner challenged Hodges' title to the living he claimed his ordination papers had been lost when the bishop's palace was 'taken by the enemy', an explanation that may have been true and must have been accepted since he remained till his death in 1675, though his weakened authority led to numerous tithe disputes.[45] As Ian Green has argued, it was several years before post-Restoration ecclesiastical officials, unfamiliar with men intruded by the parliamentary regime, knew from ecclesiastical visitations which ministers were true conformists and

---

[43] TNA, SP 29/20, fo. 174 (Bacon), 175 (Holyoake); SP 29/12, fo. 160 (Holyoake); SP 29/21, fos. 151, 274–5 (Bunning, Ridgeway). Holyoake (also 'Holyoke', 'Hollioke' et al.) had tried previously to secure the living of Tattenhill, Staffordshire (information from F. McCall).

[44] PA, HL/PO/JO/10/1/208, 209; WAAS, 795.02/BA2302/7/1548, 13/3142.

[45] WAAS, b795.02/BA2237/1. Eccleshall Castle was indeed besieged and raided by parliamentarian forces in 1643.

which puritan-leaning clergy, like Hodges, favoured unorthodox modes of worship and pastoral care.[46]

Clerical remuneration

The second major issue facing the clergy from 1660 was income, following disruption of ecclesiastical systems under 'godly rule', and with damaged churches needing repair. Under the parliamentary regime, clerical income sequestered from 'scandalous and malignant' clergy and 'delinquent' lay impropriators had been used to augment poor stipends, and the end of augmentation in 1660 seriously depleted some clerical incomes. Poor rate and tax assessment was also confused. The parliamentarian regime adopted a 'pound rent' system, to the clergy's disadvantage, but in 1660 this was identified with 'godly rule' and the justices returned to 'yardland' assessments, provoking many disputes between clergy and parishioners.[47] Under 'godly rule', the clergy had paid taxes and levies like other parishioners, but from 1660 they sought to re-establish their separation, resulting in disputes over their liability for constables' levies and similar lay taxation.

Enclosure, changes in farming practices and land deals during the period of 'godly rule' had also disadvantaged the clergy. In 1661, Alderminster vicar Nathaniel Swanne complained that his predecessor 'never took any care to defend the Rights' of the vicarage and had allowed some compositions to be lost.[48] The Barcheston churchwardens noted 'There was an enclosure made in the late war, to the great detriment of the church,' and enclosures at Allesley in 1652 created disturbances.[49] A Kenilworth vicar described in 1717 how ecclesiastical income for the living had gradually diminished. The pre-Civil War manor had been largely 'woods, parks and Chace', but in the 1640s Cromwell's officers had seized it, felled the woods, enclosed the land and created individual farms for profitable corn-growing, while reduced tithe-acreage left less income for successive clergymen. In 1660, one of the lessees to the impropriate tithes was a 'Rigid Dissenter from the Church' in what was by now a strongly non-conformist town. 'Godly rule' had thus ensured that tithe income remained low and control had passed to the non-conformist laity.[50]

---

[46] Green, *Re-establishment*, pp. 173–4.

[47] QS VI, 'Introduction', pp. xxix, xxxv–xxxvi. 'Yardland' assessments were based on acreage held while 'pound rent' was calculated on actual yearly value.

[48] WAAS, b795.02/BA2237/1.

[49] VCH, *Warwickshire*, vi. p. 4.

[50] WCRO, CR 311/55, pp. 45–6, 52.

Tithes and dues were re-established as the main source of clerical income, reviving disputes which had long been a source of friction between clergy and laity. In addition, religiously radicalized parishioners such as Quakers now refused to pay, leaving hard-pressed clergy to finance expensive suits against them in the ecclesiastical courts. Cases were also fought elsewhere. John Cudworth, Kinwarton rector from 1661, initiated a chancery suit on discovering that a yardland of the rectory glebe had been lost on the death of a sequestered Catholic landowner who had taken it from Cudworth's predecessor in return for a composition.[51]

Post-Restoration court cases sometimes revived memories of experiences under 'godly rule'. In 1666, John Goodwin, rector of Morton Bagot, was accused of simony by two 'chief inhabitants' during several disputes over advowson rights and tithes which employed competing memories of the 1650s. Goodwin was accused of acquiring the presentation by paying for the release of the former patron from imprisonment for a debt incurred through supporting the royalist military, and he was remembered as 'a royalist' while his opponents were said to have appropriated the advowson and presented a 'puritan' to keep Goodwin out.[52] Hostilities under the 'godly regime' could hardly be forgotten when post-Restoration witnesses recalled old allegiances, suitably refashioned to fit the new political order.

Religious separatism

The growth of radical religion under 'godly rule' and the religious separatism resulting from enforcement of the Act of Uniformity presented loyalist and puritan clergy of 1662 with their greatest challenge. Flight, ejection and changes of clergy under 'godly rule' had left parishes without consistent spiritual leaders. The ensuing vacuum had allowed religious extremism and clerical disrespect to flourish. Samuel Clarke, who fled from Alcester in 1643, was shocked when he returned in 1647 to learn that parishioners had moved to Warwick for safety where

> falling into the company of Anabaptists, and other Sectaries, they were levened with their Errors; and being now returned home, they had set up private meetings ... and many young Men ... as Children begotten by [Clarke's] Ministry to God, were turned Preachers.[53]

---

[51] M. Harris, '"Schismatical people": conflict between clergy and laity in Warwickshire, 1660–1720' (unpublished University of Leicester PhD thesis, 2015), Appendix 2D; TNA, C6/178/8.

[52] WAAS, b795.02/BA2237/1 & 3; 794.052/BA2102/Vol.11(ii), pp. 36–40, 96, 104.

[53] S. Clarke, *Lives of Sundry Eminent Persons* (London, 1683), p. 9.

Growing religious extremism affected half of Warwickshire's ejected returners, especially those in the east and south-east where radical Protestantism had always been strong, while religious diversity and monetary disputes influenced all four groups of post-Restoration Warwickshire clergy. By tracing each of the clergy groups of 1662, puritan and royalist, we can see how they reacted in surprisingly similar ways to the effects of 'godly rule' as part of the healing process after a traumatic event.

Returners

Loyalist ministers ejected in the 1640s and 1650s experienced the same loss of income, role and status as their puritan fellow ejectees in 1662 but with the additional fear of interrogation, violence, imprisonment or worse at a time of military rule. Eleven of them returned triumphant but as McCall has noted, they were 'out of touch, out of practice, old-fashioned'.[54] Bartholomew Dobson of Wellesbourne chose to remain in his second living but he was among ten Warwickshire ministers who petitioned the House of Lords for restitution of the tithes and profits from their sequestered parishes. The petitions are brief and formulaic but while emphasizing consistent loyalty to the restored monarchy, some reveal the anger of loss suppressed for some fifteen years.

Thomas Stringfield of Ashow and Edward Nicholls of Snitterfield simply recorded for how long they had been by the 'Userped powers most illegally ejected and thrust out'. John Doughtie's petition is more revealing.[55] His wife was repeatedly denied payment of her 'fifths' by the clerical intruder, the parliamentary captain Benjamin Lovell.[56] Doughtie's angry petition demanded that his dues, with arrears, were repaid to him personally rather than to local officials named in the order. It was refused and the intruded minister, William Caudwell, remained, possibly because Doughtie had been removed on accusations of supporting 'papists' and denying the authority of scripture. In an area of strong Catholic and non-conformist sympathy, Restoration officials and Merton College patrons may not have been willing to risk Doughtie fomenting religious unrest.

By contrast, Joseph Crowther of Tredington's petition unusually reflected on how his ejection affected parishioners to their 'great discomfort ... who have not had the benefitt of the Sacraments for ten years last past'. Royalist

---

[54] McCall, *Baal's Priests*, pp. 255–6.

[55] PA, HL/PO/JO/10/1/289, 290, 291.

[56] BL Add. MS. 15669, fo. 220; *The Cromwell Association Online Directory of Parliamentarian Army Officers*, ed. S. K. Roberts (2017), *British History Online* <http://www.british-history.ac.uk/no-series/cromwell-army-officers> [accessed 21 Dec. 2018].

William Clerke of Brinklow recorded the precise date of his ejection in 1643 for supporting 'his sacred Majestie' and for supposedly exchanging intelligence with royalists, 'to the utter undoing of himselfe, and his whole family'.[57] The focus on details and angry expressions of injustice in these brief petitions indicates the level of suppressed grief that regime change had finally allowed to surface.

However, the return of these loyalist ministers was not without difficulties. After fifteen years of puritan ministry in Brinklow, William Clerke's return in 1660 was not universally welcomed. His churchwardens were uncooperative and in 1663 Clerke presented to the church courts the township's leading non-conformists, who were associated with a larger meeting at Stretton-under-Fosse in Monks Kirby.[58] There the loyalist returner, William Stapleton, had been sequestered for 'malignancy' in 1645, his 'godly' replacement quickly departing and leaving an empty pulpit that was eventually occupied in 1651 by the puritan Richard Martin. The spiritual vacuum, as Clarke found at Alcester, allowed religious radicals to emerge. Local Baptists 'violently [broke] open' the church doors during Martin's service while John Onely, a local radical preacher, claimed that infant baptism and Anglican ministers were unlawful and 'that Himselfe was as much an Apostle as Paul'.[59] On Richard Martin's ejection in 1660, William Stapleton was restored to Monks Kirby but Baptist disturbance, church non-attendance and parental refusal of child baptism continued, with Onely's Long Lawford house becoming the local meeting place. Meanwhile, Richard Martin and two of his fellow clerical ejectees, Richard Loseby from Copston Magna and William Swaine from Withybrook, set up a Presbyterian meeting at Stretton-under-Fosse.[60]

Similar non-conformist conventicles in north-east Warwickshire troubled Thomas Baker of Baxterley and Thomas Johnson, Whelpdale's replacement at Newton Regis. Johnson's parishioners, among whom may have been some local sectarians, presented him for being a 'contentious and litigious person that hath very much molested [them] with continual suits' and for not repairing the chancel.[61] From the 1650s, Quaker groups

[57] PA, HL/PO/JO/10/1/288, 289.

[58] SRO, B/V/1/69, B/V/1/72; J. H. Hodson, 'Supplement to the introduction: Warwickshire nonconformist and Quaker meetings and meeting houses, 1660–1750', in *Warwick County Records*, ed. H.C. Johnson (Warwick, 1953), QS VIII, pp. lxix-cxxxviii, at p. xcvii; Hughes, *Politics*, p. 67.

[59] WCRO, CR 2017/C10/52, cited in Hughes, *Politics*, p. 319.

[60] SRO, B/V/1/69; Hodson, 'Supplement', pp. lxxxiii–lxxxiv.

[61] SRO, B/V/1/69. The roofing lead had allegedly been stripped by the puritan intruder, Walker, C7.124.

emerged following George Fox's visits to Polesworth relatives: 'near a 100' participants were meeting at Baddesley Ensor in 1655.[62] Baker and Johnson repeatedly presented church non-attenders and private conventicles in the early 1660s, while in 1663 William Wragge, vicar of Polesworth, presented several parishioners, including the two churchwardens, for keeping their hats on in church during prayer time.[63]

Another unhappy 'returner' was John Philpot, appointed rector of Lighthorne in 1643 by the later-sequestered royalist Sir Thomas Pope. Philpot was reportedly taken prisoner in 1644 when the royalist Compton House garrison fell to the parliamentarians. Whether he had taken refuge or was fighting for the king is unclear but surprisingly he claimed to have been 'very serviceable to parliament'. In the 1650s, Philpot was ousted and a godly minister was admitted by the 'Triers' in 1658 but removed when Philpot returned in 1660.[64]

Philpot had been a divisive figure under 'godly rule' and his return to Lighthorne resulted in a petition in 1661 to remove him. Twelve parishioners listed crimes that would appeal to the restored ecclesiastical hierarchy: induction 'by a troope of souldiers', parliamentary allegiance, war crimes including rape and scandalous living, and harassment of parishioners with continuous suits and ruin, quarrelling, drunkenness and allowing the chancel 'to lye like a Pidgeon house'.[65] Philpot retaliated by presenting six parishioners in the church courts between 1662 and 1664 for tithe-refusal.[66] The churchwarden, a tithe-refuser, and his wife were accused by Philpot of church non-attendance and attending religious meetings elsewhere. In defence they said Philpot was 'contentious' and not 'a fit person to administer the sacrament unto them'. They admitted they had heard preaching by 'Mr [Richard] Mansall', a former parliamentary officer and last in a succession of intruded puritan ministers at nearby Burton Dassett, who joined other post-Restoration ejectees to lead a meeting attracting eighty to 100 separatist followers.[67]

---

[62] G. Lyon Turner, *Original Records of Early Nonconformity*, (3 vols, London, 1911–14), ii. 788–9, 800; Hodson, *Supplement*, p. cv; N. Penney (ed.), *The Journal of George Fox* (2 vols, Cambridge, 1911), ii. 352–3.

[63] SRO, B/C/5/1663, B/V/1/73, B/V/1/69.

[64] *WR*, p. 365; Thomason Tracts E51/10: *Kingdom's Weekly Intelligencer*, 11–18 June 1644; Tennant, *Edgehill*, p. 234; TNA, SP 28/182/1.

[65] WAAS, 778.7324/BA2442/686A; Tennant, *Edgehill*, p. 234.

[66] WAAS, 795.02/BA2302/4/1065, 5/1330, 6/1467.

[67] WAAS, b795.02/BA2237/1, 807/BA2289/12(ix); *CR*, p. 342; Turner, *Original Records*, i. p. 60.

Ejections of puritan clergy between 1660 and August 1662 and attempts to suppress reformed Protestant worship through the Act of Uniformity simply created a body of displaced ministers available to serve parishioners who preferred the religious practices of the 1650s. Just as ejected loyalist clergy like Baker and Whelpdale had been sheltered by gentry sympathizers in the 1640s, now ejected non-conformist ministers were supported by the Stanhopes, Newdigates and Nethersoles in north Warwickshire, the Temples in the south-east, and the 'chief inhabitants' of Coventry, Birmingham and Nuneaton, creating new problems for loyalist clergy returning to a spiritual world distorted by the 'crack'd mirror' of religious orthodoxy.

Remainers

Thirty-seven loyalist and puritan clergy remained in their parishes between 1642 and the early 1660s, all experiencing anger and disappointment: for loyalists, at the suppression of the Church of England, and for puritans at the Restoration, because of their dashed hopes for a reformed Protestant Church. Historians have tended to view 'remainers' as untouched by 'godly rule'; indeed, the puritan Thomas Pilkington of Claverdon was said to have led 'the uneventful life of the country parson'.[68] This was impossible since in war-torn Warwickshire 'remainers' often suffered as much as loyalist ejectees. 'Articles' were brought against them entailing detailed interrogation, while parliamentary officers plundered and targeted them for free quarter. One clerical wife was 'glad to see the sequestration' with its award of 'fifths', after her husband had been twice imprisoned leaving her with only £10 a year to maintain her family.[69]

Sometimes loyalist clergymen surprisingly retained their livings. Christopher Harvey, vicar of Clifton-on-Dunsmore, and Walwyn Clarke of Oxhill both escaped ejection. In the 1640s, Harvey had published devotional poems, expressed 'sundry doubts' about signing the Protestation Oath and written a treatise against rebellion. His loyalist views must have been known, resulting in articles against him, crippling taxation and heavy plundering by parliamentarians during the war.[70] He responded by publishing new poems defending church festivals and utensils, but remained at Clifton until his

---

[68] P. Styles, 'A seventeenth century Warwickshire clergyman, Thomas Pilkington, vicar of Claverdon', in P. Styles, *Studies in Seventeenth Century West Midlands History* (Kineton, 1978), pp. 71–89, at p. 71.

[69] WMS C2.352, Thomas Fawcett, briefly a loyalist intruder at Aston-juxta-Birmingham.

[70] PA, HL/PO/JO/10/1/118; Hughes, *Politics*, p. 325n; BL Add 15670; WCRO, CR 4292, Clifton-on-Dunsmore 'Loss Account'. Harvey claimed for disproportionately heavy taxation and losses including over 560 wool fleeces (part of his tithe dues) which, with some weapons, were valued at £65.

death in 1663 through a combination of a 'godly' upbringing, royalist and puritan gentry protection and the sheer disinclination of the parliamentary regime to remove what Judith Maltby calls disgruntled but diligent ministers who were 'not quite dangerous enough'.[71]

Walwyn Clarke, rector of Oxhill, an 'outspoken royalist … harassed by parliamentary soldiers for his frequent insults', was a more surprising survivor. He had articles brought against him in 1646 and was heavily taxed and plundered, but again remained through powerful local support from the initially neutral Underhills.[72] Puritan 'remainers' were probably largely unmolested, but loyalists often experienced great pressure, surviving through local circumstances particularly where lower-value livings were less attractive to puritan intruders.[73]

Puritan intruders who conformed

Considerable attention has been paid to the hundreds of clergy nationally who lost their livings through ejection or resignation by August 1662, but far less to the puritan intruders who to some extent conformed, as some of their loyalist counterparts had done with the 'godly regime'. In Warwickshire, over fifty-five 'puritans' supposedly conformed, though sometimes with difficulty.[74] Richard Pyke at Nuneaton was vulnerable due to his appointment by Cromwell. He was in bitter conflict with royalist schoolmaster William Trevis, who was ejected from his Cambridge fellowship and arrived in Nuneaton, like Pyke, in 1656. In 1662 and 1665, Trevis was accused of drunkenness and brutal treatment of his pupils, causing riots and sit-ins at the school, while townsfolk attacked him and his house with firearms.[75] Pyke publicly declared his hatred of Trevis, probably for exaggerating Pyke's parliamentarian past, but Trevis survived because local JPs and the bishop needed some royalist balance in 'puritan' Nuneaton to preserve order.

Moderate puritan conformists like Pyke were vilified by victorious royalists for responsibility for civil war and regicide. By contrast, William

[71] R. Wilcher, 'Harvey, Christopher (1597–1663)', *ODNB*, <https://doi.org/10.1093/ref:odnb/12511>; J. Maltby, 'From *Temple* to *Synagogue*: 'Old' conformity in the 1640s–1650s and the case of Christopher Harvey', in P. Lake and M. Questier (eds), *Conformity and Orthodoxy in the English Church c.1560–1660* (Woodbridge, 2000), pp. 88–120.

[72] Tennant, *Edgehill*, p. 57; Bod, MS. Bodl 324, fo. 28v; TNA, SP 28/182/2.

[73] Clifton was valued at about £40 to £50 and Oxhill about £80 per year, Salter, 'Warwickshire clergy', i. 222; D. M. Barratt, *Eccleslasticial Terriers of Warwickshire Parishes* (2 vols, Dugdale Soc., 22, Oxford, 1971), ii. p. 201.

[74] The figure excludes about 12 puritan 'remainers'.

[75] D. L. Paterson, *Leeke's Legacy: a History of King Edward VI School Nuneaton* (Kibworth Beauchamp, 2011), pp. 60–72.

Caudwell, the intruder at Lapworth, was accused by 'godly' parishioners of not being puritan enough. In 1664/5 Caudwell was summoned for 'correction' at the church court, accused of adultery by Alexander Lilly and two young Lapworth wives.[76] One witness, John Price, claimed Caudwell frequented alehouses, held unseemly meetings and caused 'much discord and Dissenssion' between marital partners. Another, a tithe-refuser, added that Caudwell frequented cockfights, and hinted at his bribery of witnesses. Nevertheless, some parishioners supported Caudwell as sober, honest and chaste. In 1665 Caudwell accused Price as a drunkard, swearer and blasphemer who had paid the two women to lie in order to discredit him. He described Lilly as 'an hater of Episcopal government', who had not received the sacrament for seven years, 'and is at enmity and hateth the sd Mr Caudwell … because he conformeth to the government of the Church … and [wants] to be revenged of him for that and for his sueing him for his just debts'.[77] These depositions reveal Caudwell's guilt at betraying the 'godly' cause by conforming and his understanding of how his 'godly' parishioners blamed him for co-operating with the restored but unreformed Church.

Puritan ministers intruded into 'Catholic' parishes faced different problems. Timothy Kirke had arrived in the parishes of Exhall and Wixford in the late 1650s from Leicestershire where he had been curate to the 'notable puritan' Richard Clayton, an associate of James Nalton of Rugby. In late 1660 an attempt was made to oust him, accusing Kirke of fighting for parliament against the king. Local JPs investigated but disproved the allegations, praising Kirke for his 'godly' ministry and preaching. By October 1661, Kirke had subscribed to the Articles and promised obedience to the Church of England but rather than accommodating his largely Catholic Wixford parishioners, by the mid-1660s Kirke was accusing them of 'popish' behaviour in church, recusancy, not paying church fees and unproven marriages. This culminated in serious accusations and violence against Kirke as his relationship with his parishioners broke down entirely.[78] He probably remained because he was useful to local officials in suppressing

[76] F. McCall, 'Continuing civil war by other means: loyalist mockery of the interregnum Church', in *The Power of Laughter and Satire in Early Modern Britain: Political and Religious Culture, 1500–1820*, ed. M. Knights and A. Morton (Woodbridge, 2017), pp. 84–106 discusses royalist accusations of scandal against interregnum puritan ministers.

[77] WAAS, b795.02/BA2237/3; 794.052/BA2102, pp. 8–23, 34–41; M. Harris, '"Weapons of the strong": reinforcing complaints against the clergy in post-Restoration Warwickshire, 1660–1720', *Midland History*, xliii (2018), 190–207.

[78] M. Harris, 'The "Captain of Oliver's Army" and the Wixford Catholics: clerical/lay conflict in South Warwickshire, 1640–1674', *Warwickshire History*, xvi (2015/16), 170–86.

Catholic hopes of religious freedom amid fears they might provoke nationwide disorder. Thus conforming puritans, like returning loyalists, faced many difficulties at the Restoration arising from memories of the 1640s and 1650s. Past allegiances and distortions of the 'crack'd mirror' of religion created social and spiritual fragmentation in communities which continued to be deeply divided by successive changes of regime.

Ejected puritans and 'new loyalists', 1660–2

Ann Hughes calculated that thirty-three Warwickshire clergy and three lecturers and schoolmasters lost their places under the Act of Uniformity in 1662.[79] The removal of Gilbert Walden of Leamington Hastings and John Humphrey of Coughton illustrates how loyalists used the distortions of the 'crack'd mirror' to attack puritan intruders. As we have seen, John Lee disputed Walden's right to the Leamington Hastings vicarage but died in 1659. Walden expected to remain as vicar, but Sir Thomas Trevor's son, who succeeded on his father's death in 1656, instead presented Tristram Sugge to the living, while in July 1660 twenty-three Leamington inhabitants petitioned for Walden's removal. They listed fourteen grievances in a reversal of the religio-political accusations made against loyalist clergymen like Daniel Whitby and George Teonge in the 1640s.[80]

Walden was accused of bringing parliamentary troops to terrorize loyalists into providing free quarter and paying exorbitant taxes, reviving wartime memories even though Walden had not arrived until 1650. He was also accused of persuading some parishioners, 'moste woemen & servants to become Members of a particular congregacion', and refusing others communion, child baptism, visiting the sick and burial. Leamington's petitioners, like Teonge's Kimcote parishioners in the 1640s, distorted historical time and selected anti-puritan experiences to create a shared 'social memory' of their past under 'godly rule' representing Gilbert Walden, instead of the ejected Thomas Lever, as the 'malignant' minister.[81]

John Humphrey arrived in the Throckmortons' 'Catholic' parish of Coughton in 1659 or 1660, claiming to have been ordained by the bishop.[82] However, in May 1661 he appeared for 'correction' before the newly revived church court, accused by the two churchwardens of a curious mix of 'Laudian' and 'puritan' offences against the restored Church. These

[79] Hughes, *Politics*, pp. 326–7.

[80] PA, HL/PO/JO/10/1/294; Walker, C3.13.

[81] J. Fentress and C. Wickham, *Social Memory* (Oxford, 1992), p. x.

[82] Presumably George Morley, consecrated bishop of Worcester in October 1660.

included defaming 'the Liturgie and government' of the Church, vilifying holy scripture, encouraging work, dancing and sports on the Sabbath, sex and drinking offences and calling his Coughton parishioners 'a companie of illiterate Ideotts, Atheists and ungodly persons'.[83] The allegations against Humphrey, like those against Teonge and Walden, manipulated timeframes during a period of regime change. Humphrey allegedly said, presumably early in 1660, that the Church of England had been 'torne in peices by heresys and scismes, & was but in a halting and lame condition haveing neither head, nor eyes, neither King, nor Bishops to defend & direct it', which was true, as he maintained, 'at that time'. When he was accused a year later, the Church of England was being reinstated and he could legitimately be challenged for defaming it, despite describing himself as an 'orthodox Divine'. As Ian Green suggests, until the Act of Uniformity was passed in May 1662, there was no clear definition of what orthodoxy actually was.[84] Humphrey was in the unenviable position of arriving in Coughton when the Church of England was in a state of flux, leaving him unable to establish his authority and vulnerable to attack from several quarters because of uncertainty as the religious settlement unfolded.

As the non-conforming clergy left their parishes in 1662, new loyalists were appointed to replace them but often experienced great difficulty where puritanism had flourished under 'godly rule'. In 1665, the Kenilworth churchwardens undermined the new minister James Chapman's authority by employing William Maddocks, the ejected pastor, as a preacher.[85] At Burton Dassett, the former parish 'register' who supported the ejected non-conformist Richard Mansell, refused to relinquish the parish register to the new incumbent until December 1665.[86] At Alcester, Henry Teonge, son of George of Wolverton and Kimcote, replaced the ejected puritan pastor Samuel Ticknor in 1662, yet Ticknor remained in Alcester as 'godly' pastor of a large Presbyterian congregation, many of them affluent tradesmen. Teonge, like his father, had initially been a faithful puritan, but as an intruded loyalist in a town with a strong puritan heritage, comparisons with Ticknor were inevitable and allegations were made of Teonge's pastoral neglect, ungodly drinking and oath-swearing. One witness had not been to church since Teonge arrived, claiming that 'if there were a man of a good

---

[83] WAAS, 795.02/BA2302/4/985; b795.02/BA2237/1.

[84] Green, *Re-establishment*, p. 136.

[85] SRO, B/V/1/72.

[86] E. C. Westacott, 'Some account of the parish of Burton Dassett, Warwickshire, from Nov. 1660 to Jan. 1665', *Transactions of the Birmingham Archaeological Society*, lx (1940), 96–111; WCRO, DR 292/1.

life and conversation and a laborious man' as minister [meaning Ticknor] he would attend constantly.[87] The strength of local puritanism ensured that Ticknor was the suffering minister while Teonge was forced into the role of scandalous 'Cavalier', suggesting obvious similarities with loyalist ejections under 'godly rule'.

The mirrors of memory

The 'Act of Free and General Pardon, Indemnity and Oblivion' of August 1660 was intended to 'bury all Seeds of future Discords and remembrance' nationally, but for many clergy (and indeed laity) this was neither possible nor desirable. At the local level, it offered a chance for the cathartic release of emotions and the re-evaluation of the memories of 'godly rule'. By examining the written forms in which loyalist and puritan clergy recorded their painful memories we can see how widely emotions of suffering and loss impinged on post-Restoration politico-religious concerns.

An early opportunity to record painful events was in the 'Accounts' demanded for each parish in 1646/7 by the victorious parliamentary regime, anxious to acknowledge losses incurred through its military activity in the First Civil War.[88] Royalist Francis Holyoake recorded angrily in the Southam account: 'noe notice taken of the number of soldiers and their horses which have bin quartered with me at severall tymes. And I never received a penny for any quarter ... besides divers other things plundered at severall times by souldiers'. Walwyn Clarke, ultra-loyalist rector of Oxhill from 1643, was also heavily penalized, recording over £56 in 'Contribution', the quartering of thirty-five Warwick soldiers one night and the fact that he sent his carts and labourers to work on parliamentary fortifications for a regime he fiercely opposed.[89]

The clergy also used parish registers, the repositories of communal memory, to create permanent memorials of personal experiences and emotions under the 'godly regime'. In the Southam register, Holyoake recorded the burial of a soldier on 23 August 1642 after a 'Battle fought Betweene the Lord Brooke & the Earle of Northampton', while the allegiance of the Warmington scribe is evident from his record of 'Edgehill fight' between 'our Sovereigne Lord King Charles and Thearle of Essex' and the subsequent burial of soldiers in the churchyard and fields.[90] After the death of the Avon Dassett

[87] PA, HL/PO/JO/10/1/277; WAAS, 795.61/BA2638.

[88] A. Hughes, '"The Accounts of the Kingdom": memory, community and the English Civil War', *Past & Present*, ccxxx, suppl. (2016), 311–29.

[89] TNA, SP 28/183/28, 182/2.

[90] WCRO, DR 50/1, DR 281/1.

rector, Francis Staunton, in 1669, his son recorded his father's sufferings 'per multas tribulationes et perturbationes' since his arrival in 1629. They were unspecified, but other records reveal Staunton's losses through military activity and poor-levy disputes with parishioners in the 1660s.[91]

Moderate puritan Thomas Pilkington of Claverdon used his register like a personal notebook, writing Latin epitaphs on deceased parishioners. One man moved to the next village during the war and was 'infected with heresies', never attending church services thereafter. Pilkington copied out a 1653 Warwickshire petition to parliament concerning 'poisonous defamacions' against faithful ministers. He recorded Charles II's Restoration after Monck's success in '[breaking] in peices the fanatic Army and powers then ruling ... unjustly', and carefully recorded confirmation of his title to the living in 1664.[92] Ejected loyalist John Wiseman, minister of Rowington, recorded angrily in the register that he was 'By usurped Authority these many years wrested wrongfully out of my Living'.[93] Thus, registers could be used by the clergy to record facts and events under parliamentary rule and to express inner feelings in a semi-public format as a historical memorial for themselves and their communities.

Similar narratives and emotions surface occasionally in clerical wills. Puritan minister Josiah Slader senior, lecturer at Birmingham from 1623 to 1636, and subsequently minister at Broughton, Oxfordshire, from where he fled in 1642, used his will to record his removal from nine successive parishes from which 'the Bishops drove me (except the last) which the Cavaliers did'.[94] The will of John Batty minister of Warmington recalled his wartime experiences in a parish that saw much military activity when 'god of his mercy reserved me from the violence of souldiers'.[95] He also complained of a debt owed by 'Mr Richard Wootton', described by the CPM as a 'plundered minister driven from Warmington', but by Hughes as a parliamentary officer and 'unsavoury cleric' denounced by parishioners in 1647.[96]

While wills rarely recorded experiences of war and 'godly rule', church court records frequently did so, even years after the event, as we saw in John Goodwin's dispute at Morton Bagot. In Alderminster, churchwarden Nicholas Milward's complaints in the Court of Arches in 1666 against

---

[91] WCRO, DR 66/1; TNA, SP 28/186; QS IV, p. 248, QS V, p. 17.

[92] WCRO, DR 1/1; Styles, 'Pilkington', p. 86.

[93] WCRO Rowington register, N5/1.

[94] TNA, PROB 11/288/58, Josiah Slader, Buntingford Westmill, Hertfordshire, 1656.

[95] TNA, PROB 11/197/285, John Batts (Batty), clerk of Warmington, 20 Aug. 1646.

[96] Hughes, *Politics*, p. 205; BL Add. MS. 15669, fo. 80v.

the vicar were a curious mixture of Nathaniel Swanne's alleged 'Cavalier' behaviour (drinking, playing sports, pastoral neglect) and puritan disrespect for church utensils and the altar, plus his military activity for parliament as 'a Captaine against the Kinge under the pretended government'.[97] Milward emphasized Swanne's disloyalty in order to discredit him in an example of what Matthew Neufeld suggested were 'war stories ... not so much about re-fighting the Civil Wars as engaging with the political framework constructed by the Restoration regime'.[98]

The secular courts, and particularly Chancery court cases, of the 1650s and 1660s are another rich source of clerical accounts of experiences under 'godly rule', since the clergy suffered heavy financial losses but often had the means to litigate. Narratives might be presented in great detail, suggesting the constant retelling that Kübler-Ross has shown is part of healing after trauma.[99] When George Teonge of Kimcote was threatened with violence in a suit for outlawry in the 1650s, he recorded that he was 'out of favour of the tymes', 'driven away' by violence for loyalty to the king, 'plundered of his goods', and his wife and children 'thrust out'. It is a detailed narrative full of anger and indignation as he relived his suffering at the time of loss.[100]

Numerous published accounts of painful experiences under the parliamentary regime were produced by Warwickshire clergy. Some appeared soon after the event, like John Doughtie's *The King's Cause* of 1644, with its angry complaint about 'a Warre continued, a cruell bloody Warre ... against ... a good and peaceful King'. Daniel Whitby's *Vindication* and John Allington's *Brief Apologie* were passionate defences of their religious positions. Allington's painful memories of 'godly rule' still festered thirty years later when he delivered a Coventry visitation sermon, bitterly critical of those 'who make an huge scruple of *any Recreation* upon the Lord's day, who ... made none at all of *Rebellion, Schism, Sedition, Heresy*' and who 'boggle at a *Surplice*, who made nothing of *Plundering, Killing, and Cutting of Throats!*'[101]

Appleby has shown how the sermons of puritan clergy ejected in 1662, as 'godly rule' was finally overturned, were published for political ends and often employed military metaphors to recall civil-war memories. However,

[97] LPL, Court of Arches, D1413. This was a court of appeal for cases from local ecclesiastical courts.

[98] M. Neufeld, *The Civil Wars after 1660: Public Remembering in Late Stuart England* (Woodbridge, 2013), p. 86.

[99] Kübler-Ross, *On Grief*, p. 62.

[100] TNA, C 8/145/114.

[101] J. Allington, *The Reform'd Samaritan* (London, 1678), p. 2.

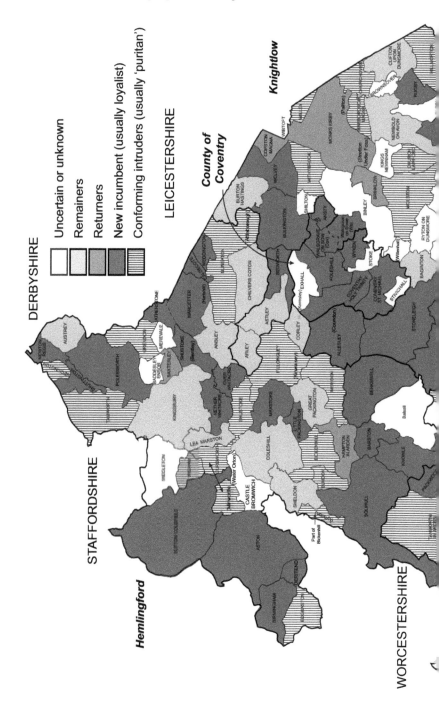

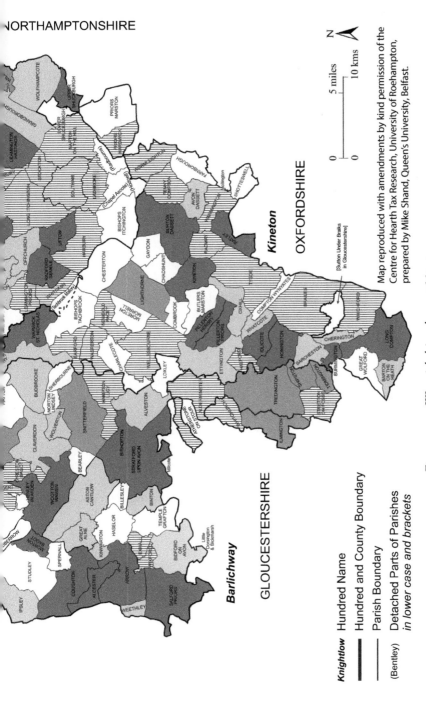

Figure 10.3. Warwickshire clergy, 1660–2.

similar military metaphors had been used to recall puritan clerical suffering in publications since the 1640s.[102] James Nalton of Rugby wrote of faith as 'a Fort or Castle', besieged and 'assaulted with batteries and onsets', reflecting his parliamentary army service in 1643. Puritan minister Francis Roberts fled battle-torn Birmingham in 1643 and wrote in 1648 of 'these crazy times' when 'Lives, Liberties, Health ... are in such extremity of extraordinary uncertainties', while Samuel Clarke's 1654 sermon at the Feast for Warwickshire gentlemen recalled the 'many Widdowes, and Orphans of godly Ministers ... whose husbands, and Parents have been ruined, and undone in the late plundering times', particularly in Warwickshire.[103]

Conclusion

This chapter has shown that Thomas Aylesbury's 'mirror of religion', cracked by civil war and 'godly rule', both reflected and distorted the suffering of puritan and loyalist clergy in Warwickshire. Their experiences were surprisingly similar: puritans who attempted to bring 'godly rule' to a sinful nation were abused at Wixford, Stoneleigh and Leamington Hastings, while Aylesbury's 'multiplied images' of heresy described the radical groups disturbing 'godly' ministers at Monks Kirby and Bishop's Tachbrook. The legacy of 'godly rule' perpetuated this disruption beyond 1662, after hopes of 'godly reformation' under a unified national Church were shattered, undermining the ministry of loyalist clergy in parishes like Brinklow and Alcester for decades to come. While some ministers exhibited what McCall has called the 'conventions of reticence' in their suffering under 'godly rule', this chapter has shown that, by contrast, other clergymen experienced Kübler-Ross's 'second stage' of grief, recalling their loss of role, status and livelihood with emotions of anger, bitterness and a sense of injustice as religion's mirror, cracked and distorted by twenty years of political upheaval, now reflected 'multiplied images' of spiritual orthodoxy in a changed religious world.[104]

---

[102] Appleby, *Black Bartholomew's Day*, p. 220.

[103] J. Nalton, *The Cross Crowned ...* (London, 1661), p. 16; F. Roberts, *Believers Evidences for Eternal Life* (London, 1648), 'Epistle Dedicatory', pp. 8–9; S. Clarke, *Christian Good-Fellowship* (London, 1653), p. 10.

[104] McCall, *Baal's Priests*, p. 1.

Index

Abbot, John, 113
Aberdeen, 52, 180, 184, 187
Abergavenny, 239–40
adultery. *See* sexual offences: adultery
advowsons, 41, 66–7, 95–6, 260
Alcester, Warwickshire, 247, 260, 262, 268, 274
Alcock, Lewis, 160
aldermen, 12, 63
Alderminster, Warwickshire, 259, 270
alehouses, 9, 38, 128, 141, 143–7, 153, 165, 250, 253, 266
Allington, John, 252–3, 271
Anabaptists. *See* Baptists
Anglicanism
    High Church, 134
    traditionalist, 138, 168, 193–217, 238, 253
Anne of Denmark, Queen, 116
Antichrist, the, 162, 213, 227
anticlericalism, 143, 164, 245
antipuritanism, 13, 219, 250–1, 253
Apostles, the, 77, 237, 262
Aquinas, Thomas, 174
archbishops, 1, 15, 73, 80, 93, 115, 196, 253
archdeacons, 19–20, 25, 36–7
Ardingly, Sussex, 113, 128, 132
Arminianism, 15, 77, 123
army, the, 139, 169, 270
    in Scotland, 178–80, 190
    parliamentarian, 78, 124, 127–8, 151, 222, 226
    royalist, 7, 124, 127–8, 151, 224, 235
army officers, 9–10, 24, 26, 36, 52, 63, 128, 130, 142, 145, 152, 154, 160, 167–8, 197, 218, 233, 253

parliamentarian, 251, 261, 263–4, 270–1
    royalist, 127, 221–2
Array, Commissioners of, 222
Arrow, Warwickshire, 255
artisans, 12, 114, 118, 132, 147, 156, 161, 163, 253, 268
Arundel, Sussex, 23, 117, 127–8
Ashburnham family, 124
atheism, 172, 185, 187, 268
augmentations, 11, 15, 26, 41, 46–7, 49, 56–7, 60–1, 63, 69, 76, 78, 91, 259
Aylesbury, Thomas, 274
    A Treatise of the Confession of Sinne, 245

Bacon, Francis, of Astley, Warwickshire, 255
Baker, Thomas, 251–2, 262–4
ballads, 218–19, 226
baptism, 7, 23, 28–9, 32–3, 123, 155, 167, 181, 230, 239, 262, 267
Baptists, 1, 5, 9–10, 12, 15, 77, 79, 118, 138, 210, 239–40, 260, 262
Barking, Essex, 156, 159
Barton, William, 12–13, 15
Bastard, Thomas, 97–8
Baxter, Richard, 5, 14–15, 37, 74, 76, 79, 219
Baxterley, Warwickshire, 251–2, 262
Beake, Robert, 250, 254
Becket, William, 81
Bedfordshire, 42, 48, 199
bells, church, 7, 146, 159, 200, 207
Benn, William, 106
Bere Regis, Dorset, 97–8

ecclesiastical discipline, 177–8
ecclesiastical hierarchy, 2, 19, 25, 36,
46, 139, 213
ecclesiastical jurisdictions, 27
economic crises, 31
Edinburgh, 172, 175–6, 180,
182, 189
Edsaw, John, 112
Edwards, Thomas, 14
Gangraena, 14
Ejectors, the, 15, 27, 36, 72, 129,
167, 198
elders, church, 171, 173, 183–7,
189–90, 192
emotions
anger, 246, 251–2, 261–2, 270–1
grief, 246
enclosures, 93, 259
England, regions of,
eastern, 72
north-eastern, 72
northern, 42
north-western, 72
south-eastern, 72, 199
southern, 42, 159, 193–217
south-western, 72–3, 159
western, 42, 204–5
episcopacy, 1, 3, 19, 34, 36, 38, 41,
73, 79, 197, 213, 218, 221, 235,
238, 266
abolition of, 30
episcopalianism, 16, 20, 36 81, 220
and episcopalians, 16, 20, 36
Erasmus
Paraphrases, 202–3
Erastianism, 139
Essex, 5–6, 23, 28, 42, 48, 70, 72–3,
77–8, 82, 124, 140, 143, 147, 167,
199, 221–2, 251, 255, 269
Essex, Earl of, 124, 127, 247
eucharist, the. *See* communion
Europe, 171

Evans, Edward, curate of
Llanllwchaiarn, 233
Evans, Richard, vicar of
Llanasa, 236
excommunication, 181–2
executions, 3, 114, 151,
154–5, 211
Exeter, 14, 63, 96, 127, 137, 147, 155,
168

family conflict, 181
family history, 33
family networks, 96, 98, 128
farming, 87–9, 92, 94–5, 98, 100–1,
109, 122,147, 233, 259
fasts, 10, 54, 143, 211
feasts, 25, 32, 189, 201
Fife, Scotland, 175–6
Fifth Monarchy, 1, 74, 238
fines, 10, 14, 28, 146, 150–1, 153–4,
178
Flintshire, 147, 221, 223–4, 226,
236–7
flooding, 58, 90–1
food, 147–8
Fox, George, 12, 263
Frampton, Robert, Bishop of
Gloucester, 68
freehold property, 234
Frewen family, the, 115
Accepted, Bishop of York, 115
funerals. *See* burials

Gage family, the, 134
gaming, 38, 144, 173
garrisons, parliamentarian, 58, 103,
106, 109, 127, 224, 247
garrisons, royalist, 127, 151, 224, 263
Garston, Lancashire, 58
Gatford, Lionel, 7
Gauden, John, Bishop of Worcestor,
233, 235

non-residency. *See* clergy,
non-residency
Norfolk, 7, 24, 31, 41–2, 44,
48, 55–6, 59, 61–3, 72, 78,
96, 199
North Waltham, Hampshire, 201,
203, 205, 208–9, 214
Northamptonshire, 10, 48, 78, 140,
165–6
Norwich, 11, 13–15, 22, 42–3, 63,
80, 218
Nottinghamshire, 48, 140
Nuneaton, Warwickshire, 247, 258,
264–5

oaths, 151–4, 178, 234, 268
Engagement, the, 3, 11,
13, 54
Oath of Uniformity, 1662,
105–7
Protestation, the royalist, 222,
250, 264
oral communication, 29, 150
order, 129, 168, 170, 223
ordination. *See* clergy, ordination
Oxford, 113, 127, 252
Oxfordshire, 48

pamphlets, 12, 219–21, 238
parishes, 37, 42, 44, 55–6, 42–3, 50,
55–9, 61, 91, 104, 143, 156–61,
212, 247
clerks, 128, 156–7
division of, 15, 41, 43, 45–6,
58–62, 64
factions within, 52, 74
inventories, 202–3
large, 42, 44, 54, 60, 91
neighbouring, 52, 54, 56, 59–61,
115–16, 134
poor and/or populous, 56–7, 60,
62, 99
records, 25–7, 226

registers, 1, 19, 21–4, 26, 29, 31,
33, 100–1, 113, 128, 131–2,
220, 226, 268, 270
registrars, 23, 31, 132, 268
Scottish, 179
secular functions of, 36
suburban, 55, 57, 60
traditions, 36
uniting of, 11, 15, 26, 41, 43–4,
50, 58–63, 91
urban, 15, 57, 60, 63
vacant, 57, 60
parishioners, 1–2, 5–6, 10–12,
14–15, 32, 38–9, 52–4, 56–7,
59–60, 64, 73– 4, 77–8, 81, 83,
90– 2, 99–101, 106–7, 109, 119,
128–34, 146, 155, 157–9, 163–5,
179, 192, 197, 200, 205, 209–12,
218, 223–4, 230, 232,–3, 236,
238, 250–1, 253–4, 258–64, 266,
267–8, 270
Parker, John, 150
parliament, 28, 30, 34, 146, 171,
234, 237
bills in, 46, 63, 220
clerical representation in, 36
House of Commons, 62, 128, 160
House of Lords, 36, 261
Long, the, 41, 45, 60, 66, 70, 204,
221–2
members of, 12, 46, 49, 51, 77, 82,
96, 108, 139, 225
petitions to, 30, 63
Rump, the, 2, 46, 50, 60, 62, 69
parliament, acts of, 44, 49–50, 63, 70,
131, 139, 149–50, 154–5, 157,
165, 169, 204
1649 Act for the Maintenance of
Preaching Ministers, 47
1653 Marriage Act, the, 8, 22–3,
33, 132–3
1662 Act of Uniformity, 83, 260,
264, 267–9